DATE DUE

D1061547

A VIEW OF
PROGRAMMING LANGUAGES

ernard

B. A. GALLER
University of Michigan

A. J. PERLIS
Carnegie-Mellon University

ADDISON-WESLEY PUBLISHING COMPANY

Reading, Massachusetts

Menlo Park, California · London · Don Mills, Ontario

This book is in the
ADDISON-WESLEY SERIES IN
COMPUTER SCIENCE AND INFORMATION PROCESSING

Consulting Editors

Michael A. Harrison
Richard S. Varga

Second printing, June 1973

Copyright © 1970 by Addison-Wesley Publishing Company, Inc. Philippines copyright 1970 by Addison-Wesley Publishing Company, Inc.

All rights reserved. No part of this publication may be reproduced, stored in a retrieval system, or transmitted, in any form or by any means, electronic, mechanical, photocopying, recording, or otherwise, without the prior written permission of the publisher. Printed in the United States of America. Published simultaneously in Canada. Library of Congress Catalog Card No. 72-100860.

ISBN 0-201-02324-5
ABCDEFGHIJ-MA-7876543

JOINT UNIVERSITY LIBRARIES
SCIENCE
LIBRARY
NASHVILLE, TENNESSEE

PREFACE

This book about the programming of digital computers is not a detailed study of a single language or a set of techniques. It is an attempt to identify and study the interactions between some of the primitive elements of programming.

Originally we intended to write an introductory text but during the early stages decided it would be too restrictive to hold back on any programming ideas. We strove for readable style, assuming whatever mathematics was necessary and a fair background in programming. Actually, our use of formal mathematics was quite limited, and lack of background in that area should be no problem.

What level of programming background is assumed? A reasonable first course in computer science, in which the reader has written and successfully executed several programs. The language of his programs is immaterial, since we are concerned with ideas, not details. Although exercises at the end of each section make it useful as a text, we hope the book will be read also by experienced programmers. We have tried to clarify many programming concepts already in common use, as well as to introduce some ideas for the future. We hope and expect that any programmer who spends most of his life communicating in FORTRAN, COBOL, PL/I, or ALGOL will find new and challenging ways to think about his programs.

Chapter 1 begins with one of the most primitive and unstructured of all computers, the Markov Algorithm, which has no loops, subroutines, conditional statements, or labels. In short, it looks quite different from any current programming environment, but it does provide a stark background against which one can introduce those concepts slowly enough to appreciate the problems of their introduction and the implications of their availability. By the time the Algorithm Machine is reached, we have added conditional statements, loops, labels, subroutines, and addressable storage. The Algorithm Machine puts ideas of interpretation and translation into interesting perspective. There follow some ideas on the creation of algorithms from observations on transformations one wishes to make on data. The discussion of addressable storage and the sections that follow are not needed for the remaining chapters, except in relation to some motivational references at the beginning of Chapter 3.

Chapter 2 introduces a somewhat modified version of ALGOL 60 as an extension of the flowchart representation of algorithms. Some reasons for particular constructions are explored, as well as some problems of internal representation. By the end of the chapter, we have introduced a quite complete ALGOL language, on which the remaining discussions are based. We strongly emphasize, however, that the ideas presented apply to all higher-level languages. ALGOL is merely a convenient carrier, and previous knowledge of the language is not essential.

In Chapter 3 we take the point of view that data structures should be described in a natural way within the programming language. We discuss a wide variety of data structures in current use and extend the ALGOL of Chapter 2 with statements that embed data structures into the language so that their use and specification is natural to the programmer for his application. This approach to data structures is only beginning in some languages, certainly not those in major use. Although Chapter 4 can be understood without a thorough grasp of Chapter 3, much of its motivation stems from the language extensions needed to accommodate data structures.

Chapter 4 develops in detail one approach to modifying and extending a higher-level language such as ALGOL. We review the specification of a language in such a way that it can be extended. The internal treatment of extensions is also considered at some length, together with an algorithm for producing efficient code based on language extensions so introduced. We explore in detail several examples of areas where such "extension by definition" is very useful.

One of our goals is to point out the feasibility and desirability of including such definitional facilities in languages in common use. *We certainly hope that programmers involved in the design and implementation of programming languages will take up this challenge.*

In many parts of this book we have not attempted complete development; our goal has been to explore and to extend. For our light treatment or complete omissions of some popular areas in programming research we do not apologize; complete coverage of all programming was not our goal. If we succeed in stimulating others in certain directions, we shall be satisfied.

We wish to express our appreciation to the many people who contributed to this book. In particular, we are grateful to Professor A. van Wijngaarden and his colleagues at the Mathematisch Centrum in Amsterdam for providing the physical environment in which most of the book was written, and to those who read early versions of the manuscript and contributed valuable comments, such as Gary Pirkola, Elliott Organick, Thomas E. Cheatham, Jr., Jim Gray, Neil Barta, and Michael Harrison. Our appreciation goes as well to Mrs. Diane Hill, who typed the entire manuscript. To the many others who encouraged us with comments and suggestions we are also grateful.

Ann Arbor, Michigan   B. A. G.
Pittsburgh, Pennsylvania   A. J. P.
May 1970

CONTENTS

CHAPTER ONE

ALGORITHMS

1.1 INTRODUCTION

An *algorithmic activity* is a procedure for carrying out a task. The real and abstract worlds are constantly setting forth tasks to be done; their variety appears endless. Similarly, the procedures for carrying them out appear to be in very large supply; in fact, these procedures appear to encompass all human activity, discouraging systematic study. Fortunately, we may focus our attention on a subset of these tasks, namely, transformations of sequences of symbols. Examples of such tasks are (1) reversal of the order of the symbols in a sequence, (2) combination of two sequences of digits into a third sequence (according to the procedures of arithmetic), and (3) rearrangement and interrogation of information organized into lists, files, arrays, and so on. Many believe that this subset of tasks is really a "basis"; i.e., in terms of these transformations on symbols, all real and abstract tasks can be specified. The word "believe" is appropriate, since no mathematical proof of such an assertion has been given. We may take this statement as being akin to a *theory* for which evidence continues to accumulate.

Actually, all tasks are given symbolic representation in terms of a language if any external communication is required for or during their performance. Many tasks are so complex they require a high degree of spatial and temporal interaction of many devices, as well as sophisticated coordination and communication (again by means of language) among them. This mixture of devices, communication, and control we may call an *organization*. As we shall see, an important property of any task—and therefore of any algorithmic activity for carrying out that task—is the relationship it has to a larger organization containing it. It is only in its relationship to larger tasks—and larger, more general algorithmic activities—that its purpose and function can be fully understood and appreciated.

The very intent of the specification of an algorithmic activity is that some agency or device besides the originator shall perform it. Of course, as soon as an activity is described so as to be executable by a device, it becomes a meaningful command to that and every other device capable of understanding the description. For these devices it is no longer a mere *activity*; it is an *algorithm*. Each device will therefore require that an activity be specified in some way appropriate to it (i.e., as an algorithm for it), before it can perform the activity. Activities for one device may be algorithms for another, and vice versa. One activity that machines are often called upon to do, in fact, is the transformation of an algorithm for machine *A* into the language appropriate for algorithms for machine *B*. In other words, while it is an algorithm for *A*, it is only an activity for

B, because *B* cannot interpret the particular description of the activity which was appropriate for *A*. The transformation (often called a *translation*) makes it interpretable by *B*—and probably no longer by *A*. When this translation process can be described precisely as an algorithmic activity and cast in appropriate form for interpretation by some machine *C*, it becomes an algorithm for *C*. Other terms are often used for the pair (algorithmic activity, algorithm). Examples are (algorithm, program), (program, code), and (source program, object program). In each case, the second term is associated with a device which can execute it.

It should also be intended, in specifying an algorithmic activity, that it be applicable to more than one instance of the initial (input) data; i.e., its domain of applicability must be a *collection* of initial values of the data. An activity for computing a particular man's paycheck on a particular date is nowhere near as useful as one that can compute his check on any required date; and still more useful is the activity for computing the entire payroll at any required time. Furthermore, unless variability, such as dependence on the date of execution, is specifically included, activities are expected to produce the same results (i.e., output) when allowed to operate on the same input at different times.

Once we agree on the form in which activities may be specified as algorithms for some device, we may ask certain questions about any algorithmic activity we may encounter. First, is it an algorithm; i.e., does it have the required form? Second, since most tasks have states of completion, does this algorithm arrive at a state of completion; i.e., does it terminate after a finite number of steps? Third, if it does terminate, does it produce the desired result; i.e., is it a correct algorithm for the task in hand? These properties do not necessarily follow from the form in which algorithmic activites are specified, and their determination usually requires some analysis.

Some implications of the preceding remarks are: (1) Activities should be expressed as sequences of unambiguous steps, or *commands*. (2) The order of execution of these commands will usually be critical, since each transforms the data which resulted from the action of its predecessors. (3) These commands are to be capable of interpretation and execution by a device familiar with the form of the specification. (4) The activity should be applicable to more than one example of the initial data.

1.2 MARKOV ALGORITHMS

A. A. Markov [1] has provided a way of specifying a large class of activities which he calls *normal algorithms*. (We shall frequently use the abbreviation MA for a Markov normal algorithm.) In this form of specification, the basic task out of which all others are constructed is a rule for replacement of characters from a linear sequence, or *string*, by other characters. For example, the rule $\alpha\gamma \rightarrow \alpha$ (read: "$\alpha\gamma$ is replaced by α") assumes that a string of characters—for example, $\gamma\alpha\beta\beta\alpha\gamma\alpha\gamma$—is being considered, and represents the replacement of the leftmost occurrence of the pair $\alpha\gamma$ by α, that is, the deletion of γ the first time it occurs (if at all) with α at its left. In the example, we would produce the string $\gamma\alpha\beta\beta\alpha\alpha\gamma$. To make complex replacements from simple ones, a sequence of such replacement rules may be constructed and a particularly simple control regime imposed to determine the order in which the rules are applied to a character string provided as input. We shall develop these ideas further in what follows.

It was Markov's thesis that any algorithmic activity involving the manipulation of characters—not necessarily displayed in a one-dimensional pattern—could be specified as a normal algorithm. In its verifiability, this thesis is akin to a physical law which is substantiated by all attempted experiments, but which can never be tested in all generality, since no independent finite means exist for characterizing all algorithmic activities. Several other (independent) means of specifying algorithmic activities have been developed, e.g., Turing machines [2], general recursive functions [3], and Post systems [4], and each has acquired its badge of generality from the others. All such systems have been shown to be equivalent; i.e., an activity which can be specified as an algorithm in one can be so specified in the others.

The rules appearing in MA's involve characters, which inevitably come from a set of characters called an *alphabet*. The finite collection of individually identifiable marks making up the domain of the data of the algorithm will be called the *data alphabet*. For example, we shall sometimes use as an alphabet or as a data alphabet the lower-case letters a, b, $c, \ldots, x, y, z$. The choice of marks to identify characters in an alphabet is dominated by convenience and understood by context. Thus the one mark 123 represents the integer one-hundred-twenty-three in decimal notation. However, 123 may also be three marks in the alphabet: 0, 1, 2, 3, 4, 5, 6, 7, 8, 9. For these three marks to correspond to the integer one-hundred-twenty-three requires additional context, e.g., a declaration of convention. Whenever conventions not generally accepted in ordinary speech or in standard mathematics are introduced in this book, there will be a clear signal to the reader.

One fundamental algorithmic activity is the representation of the marks of a large alphabet—and hence, strings of characters in that alphabet—in terms of collections of marks of a smaller alphabet. Thus, in the English language, the many words one can use, which can be regarded as forming an alphabet for constructing sentences, are represented as strings of characters from a small alphabet of individual letters. A necessary property of such a representation is unique decomposability; i.e., a string of marks can be uniquely decomposed into a string of recognizable marks called *substrings*. Naturally, not all substrings require the same number of marks. The correspondence chosen generally depends on the larger algorithmic activity in which the given activity is embedded (see "Representation of characters by numeric codes" in Chapter 2). For example, the alphabet consisting of two distinguishable marks—one obviously will not suffice—one for enumeration (say "1") and one for punctuation (say "α") can be used to represent any alphabet required in the description of an activity. Thus we could let $\alpha 1$, $\alpha 11$, $\alpha 111, \ldots$, represent a, b, $c, \ldots$, respectively. The string *abaca* would then appear as $\alpha 1 \alpha 11 \alpha 1 \alpha 111 \alpha 1$, which can clearly be transformed back to the English alphabet whenever necessary.

The script letter $\mathscr{A}$ will denote the set of alphabets to be used. The capital letters A, B, C, ... will denote particular alphabets, i.e., elements of $\mathscr{A}$. Now when we write a rule such as

$$\beta\xi \to \beta$$

where ξ is one of many characters which should be deleted, we shall want to be assured that *any* of these characters that occurs immediately after β will be so handled. In other words, we want ξ to play the role of a *variable* whose values come from some set of characters (i.e., from some particular alphabet). This set is called the *domain* of the variable. On the other hand, we still wish β to represent only β. We shall say that, in general, each character in a rule is a variable over some domain. For some, such as β, the domain may consist of only one character, whereas for others it may be a large collection of characters. In all cases, however, each character in a rule must have its associated domain.

In a Markov algorithm, each rule specifies a replacement to be made, under appropriate circumstances, on a string found in a particular place called the *register* and denoted by R. The register is assumed to have a recognizable left end—that is, we can always pick out the first character of the string which it contains—but its right end can be extended indefinitely. The *contents of R*—that is, the string of characters it contains—will always have a finite length at any given moment, and this length could be calculated by an algorithmic activity. Though it will seldom be an appropriate activity for the tasks we shall undertake, a brief description of this activity would be as follows: Enlarge the data alphabet A to include a new character, say β. Insert a punctuation character α at the left end of the register R. Then move α past each character of the original string in R, each time inserting another β into the string. When no characters remain to the right of α, move each β to the left end of the register, and then delete α. The string of β's at the left end represents a count of the original characters. In the notation for MA's which we shall develop, this activity can be written

algorithm Characters (A, β); **A** ξ;	*Comments*
0: $\alpha\xi \rightarrow \beta\xi\alpha$;	Move α right, introduce β.
1: $\xi\beta \rightarrow \beta\xi$;	Move β to left end of orig- inal string.
2: $\alpha \rightarrow$. ;	Delete α and stop.
3: $\rightarrow \alpha$ **end**	Introduce α initially.

Its interpretation will become clear as we proceed.

Each Markov algorithm will be given a name, such as $\tilde{H}$† or Copy, and it will begin with a *heading*, for example,

$$\text{algorithm } \tilde{H}(A1, A2); \text{ A1 } \xi_1, \xi_2, \xi_3; \text{ A2 } \eta_1, \eta_2;$$

where $A1$ and $A2$ in the parentheses are thus declared to be the disjoint alphabets that $\tilde{H}$ works on (i.e., the union of $A1$ and $A2$ is the data alphabet for $\tilde{H}$); ξ_1, ξ_2, and ξ_3 are declared to be variables with domain $A1$; and η_1 and η_2 are variables with domain $A2$. Variables so declared are called *generic variables* for their respective alphabets. Any characters used in rules within the algorithm and not declared in the heading are assumed to act like punctuation and are called *local variables*; they have domains which contain only themselves and which carry their names. In particular, they are not in the data alphabet for the algorithm unless specifically declared to be so in the heading. Later, in Section 1.4, we shall see an example of the use of a local variable. There an algorithm $\widetilde{K1}$ is defined whose job is to delete α and everything to its left if there is anything there, but otherwise to do nothing. In $\widetilde{K1}$, ξ is a generic variable for A, and μ is a local variable:

$$\text{algorithm } \widetilde{K1}(A, \alpha); \text{ A } \xi;$$
$$0: \xi\alpha \rightarrow \mu;$$
$$1: \xi\mu \rightarrow \mu;$$
$$2: \mu \rightarrow . ;$$
$$3: \rightarrow . \text{ end}$$

As with the algorithm Characters, the interpretation of $\widetilde{K1}$ will become clear shortly.

---

† Names bearing a tilde, such as $\tilde{H}$ or $\tilde{H}2$, will be assumed to be local to the current discussion, and these names may be used again in a different context and with different meanings.

We note that *by convention* such characters as the colon, comma, semicolon, arrow, and period, and the symbol **end** are not included as either generic or local variables. Though they are characters to the printer and to the reader of this text, they are outside the alphabets on which our Markov algorithms work. They are called *metaconstants*. Interestingly enough, when we wish later to create a Markov algorithm which works on other Markov algorithms as data, these punctuation characters will have to be encoded as part of the data! They will need to play the same role then as they do now for us, i.e., allow the representation of a Markov algorithm to be parsed correctly into its constituent parts. We note in passing that sometimes it will also be convenient to have a generic variable whose domain is a union of several alphabets. Thus we may have a heading like

$$\textbf{algorithm } \tilde{H}(A1, A2, \alpha); \textbf{A1 } \lambda; \textbf{A1} \cup \alpha\, \xi; \textbf{A1} \cup \textbf{A2}\, \eta;$$

In the algorithm Characters, shown earlier, the heading is

$$\textbf{algorithm } \text{Characters}(A, \beta); \textbf{A } \xi;$$

Here ξ is a generic variable whose domain is the original data alphabet A. The data alphabet for Characters is $A \cup \beta$. There is one local variable, α, in this MA.

After the heading, we find the sequence of *rules* of the algorithm, numbered consecutively from 0 and separated by semicolons. The last rule appearing in the sequence is terminated by the symbol **end** instead of a semicolon. A typical rule has the form

$$i: \delta_1 \delta_2 \ldots \delta_k \rightarrow \mu_1 \mu_2 \ldots \mu_m;$$

where i is the number of the rule, also called a *label*, and the δ's and μ's are from the *alphabet in which the algorithm is written*. This alphabet consists of the local variables used in the rules of the algorithm; constants (i.e., explicit symbols) from the data alphabet; and generic variables. Thus the alphabet in which the algorithm Characters is written is $\alpha \cup \beta \cup \xi$. The strings $\delta_1 \delta_2 \ldots \delta_k$ and $\mu_1 \mu_2 \ldots \mu_m$ are called the left-hand side (LHS) and right-hand side (RHS) of the rule, respectively. We require that any generic variables occurring among the μ's also occur among the δ's.

The intent of the rule is as follows: Starting from the first (leftmost) character, the contents of R are examined for the first occurrence of a string of consecutive characters $c_1 c_2 \ldots c_k$ such that c_j is in the domain of δ_j, for $j = 1, \ldots, k$, and such that if $\delta_p = \delta_q$ for some p, q, then $c_p = c_q$. (The last condition implies that all occurrences of a generic variable in the LHS will be associated with the same character in the string.) If such a string is found, the characters $\delta_1, \delta_2, \ldots, \delta_k$ are assigned to $c_1, \ldots, c_k$, respectively, and the rule is said to be *applicable*. Otherwise, the rule is said to be *inapplicable*. If the rule is applicable, a string is formed from the correspondents of the generic variables among the μ's and the remaining characters, in the order of occurrence in the RHS, and the result, possibly empty, is substituted in R for the string $c_1 \ldots c_k$. The contents of R are not affected by inapplicable rules. For example, suppose i is a rule of the form

$$i: \alpha_1 \xi_2 \alpha_3 \xi_4 \;\rightarrow\; \beta_1 \xi_4 \beta_3 \xi_2;$$

where ξ_2 is a generic variable with domain $\{c_1, c_2, c_3\}$ and ξ_4 is a generic variable with domain $\{c_4, c_5, c_6\}$. If in R we have $\gamma_0 \gamma_1 \alpha_1 c_3 \alpha_3 c_4 \gamma_3 \gamma_4$, then rule i is applicable, and after rule i has been applied, R contains $\gamma_0 \gamma_1 \beta_1 c_4 \beta_3 c_3 \gamma_3 \gamma_4$.

The register, R, is assumed to have the empty, or null, symbol † at its left end, so if the LHS of rule i is empty,

$$i: \;\rightarrow\; \mu_1 \mu_2 \ldots \mu_m;$$

then rule i is always applicable. In this case, the μ's cannot be generic variables, since we would not know which values of their domains to use.

It was with this interpretation of a rule in mind that we remarked earlier that $\beta \xi \rightarrow \beta$ had the effect of deleting any character in the domain of ξ which immediately followed an occurrence of β. If β is itself a generic variable over some alphabet, then any character of the domain of ξ will be deleted if it follows any character from the domain of β. The reader should verify that this interpretation follows from the preceding discussion of the intent of a rule.

An MA is then a finite sequence of such rules upon which an order of testing for applicability is imposed, hereafter called the *order of execution*, as follows: (1) Execution begins with rule 0. (2) After the transformation of an applicable rule is performed, as described above, the next rule tested is rule 0. (3) If for some i, rule i is found to be inapplicable, then the next rule tested is $i + 1$. (4) If it ever happens that no rule is applicable, the algorithm terminates in a state called a *stalemate*. An algorithm is applied to a string (called a "word" by Markov) initially assumed to be in R. When the algorithm terminates, the *result* is the string in R at that time. If $\tilde{H}$ is the name of the algorithm, then the result of applying $\tilde{H}$ to an initial string P will be denoted $\tilde{H}(P)$.

As an example of a complete MA, we consider the task of replacing all occurrences of the character α in a string P by β, and all other charac-

---

† We shall denote the null symbol by Λ when it is necessary to make it explicit.

ters of an alphabet A (not containing β) by γ. The algorithm may be written

algorithm $\tilde{H}(A, \beta, \gamma)$; A ξ;
0: $\alpha \rightarrow \beta$;
1: $\xi \rightarrow \gamma$ **end**

Under the application of this algorithm, $\tilde{H}$, the string $\alpha\beta\gamma\delta\alpha\beta\gamma\delta$ would become $\beta\beta\gamma\gamma\beta\beta\gamma\gamma$. Note that if $\tilde{H}$ were applied to this string in turn, it would remain the same.

The property of $\tilde{H}$ which we have just seen is important; for example, $\tilde{H}(\tilde{H}(P)) = \tilde{H}(P)$. It appears that the result of applying an MA is bound to be such that the MA cannot change it again. This is an immediate consequence of always going back to rule 0 after applying a rule, and of terminating only when no rules are applicable. If the algorithm terminates at all, applying the MA again can produce no further change. While this is fine for some algorithms, such as the one we have just seen, it is clearly undesirable for all algorithms to behave in this way. An algorithm for reversing the order of the characters in a string, for example, should not be expected to give the same result when applied a second time to the result of the first application. Rather than change the sequencing rule, let us introduce another way to terminate an algorithm. To the previous listing of the order of execution we add another step: (5) If there is a period to the right of the RHS of an applicable rule, then the algorithm terminates after that rule is applied. Markov calls algorithms *closed* if they terminate in this way. The reader may now verify that the MA Characters, shown earlier, is indeed a closed algorithm, and that it performs the computation claimed for it.

Now we may write the algorithm for reversing the order of a string of characters from an alphabet A.

algorithm Reverse(A); A ξ, η;
0: $\alpha\alpha \rightarrow \beta$;
1: $\beta\alpha \rightarrow \beta$;
2: $\beta\xi \rightarrow \xi\beta$;
3: $\beta \rightarrow .$;
4: $\alpha\xi\eta \rightarrow \eta\alpha\xi$;
5: $\rightarrow \alpha$ **end**

Here A can be any alphabet not containing α and β. To see the successive stages of the transformation on a data word, let $A = (a, b, c)$, and let P be the string abc. Then, writing $\xrightarrow{i}$ for the application of rule i, we have

$abc \xrightarrow{5} \alpha abc \xrightarrow{4} b\alpha ac \xrightarrow{4} bc\alpha a \xrightarrow{5} \alpha bc\alpha a \xrightarrow{4} c\alpha b\alpha a \xrightarrow{5} \alpha c\alpha b\alpha a \xrightarrow{5} \alpha\alpha c\alpha b\alpha a$
$\xrightarrow{0} \beta c\alpha b\alpha a \xrightarrow{2} c\beta\alpha b\alpha a \xrightarrow{1} c\beta b\alpha a \xrightarrow{2} cb\beta\alpha a \xrightarrow{1} cb\beta a \xrightarrow{2} cba\beta \xrightarrow{3} cba.$

Note the use of the auxiliary character α to move the current head character to the right to become the head of the transformed part of the string, and the use of β to erase the α's. [Exercise 1.2.1 shows why β is needed, instead of $\alpha \rightarrow$, when all α's are in. Exercise 1.2.2 questions whether $\beta\xi\alpha \rightarrow \xi\beta$ would work.] Note also that Reverse works correctly even if R is initially empty.

This example shows that the order of the rules is critical. Rule 5 has to be applied before any other but cannot be above any other, because it is always applicable. Since two orderings—listing and time—are involved, we hereby make the declaration of convention for this book that the word pairs "above" and "below," and, within a single line, "left" and "right," refer to order of listing; and the pairs "before" and "after," and "preceding" and "following" refer to ordering in time.

It is easy to see that any MA which stalemates can be converted into one which is closed. This is done by appending the trivial algorithm

> **algorithm** End;
> $0: \rightarrow$. **end**

to it in an obvious way. Hereafter we shall assume that all algorithms are closed, if necessary, by this construction.

Since the algorithmic activity of appending one algorithm to another, as shown in the last paragraph, will often prove useful, we shall give here its explicit description. Suppose that $\widetilde{H2}$ is to be appended to $\widetilde{H1}$. The resulting MA will be denoted $\widetilde{H1}; \widetilde{H2}$. We assume that any variable generic in one is either not present in the other or is generic there for the same alphabet. Then the heading for $\widetilde{H1}; \widetilde{H2}$ is constructed by listing all disjoint alphabets (partitioning first any that are not already disjoint) and all generic variable declarations appearing in either $\widetilde{H1}$ or $\widetilde{H2}$. After the heading, we list the rules of $\widetilde{H1}$, replacing **end** with a semicolon, and then the rules of $\widetilde{H2}$. On the assumption that there are n_1 rules in $\widetilde{H1}$ and n_2 rules in $\widetilde{H2}$, the rules of $\widetilde{H2}$ are renumbered to $n_1, n_1 + 1, \ldots,$ $n_1 + n_2 - 1$.

As an example, we construct the closed MA

$$\widetilde{H3} = \widetilde{H}; \text{End}$$

from the stalemating algorithm $\widetilde{H}$,

> **algorithm** $\widetilde{H}(A, \beta, \gamma)$; A ξ;
> $0: \alpha \rightarrow \beta$;
> $1: \xi \rightarrow \gamma$ **end**

and the trivial terminating algorithm End, as follows:

> **algorithm** $\tilde{H}3(A, \beta, \gamma)$; **A** ξ;
> $0: \alpha \rightarrow \beta$;
> $1: \xi \rightarrow \gamma$;
> $2: \quad \rightarrow .$ **end**

As will be seen in Exercise 1.4.1, it is not necessarily or even often true that $(\tilde{H}1; \tilde{H}2)(P) = \tilde{H}2(\tilde{H}1(P))$. In other words, *appending* two algorithms is quite different from *composing* them as functions, i.e., applying one and then applying the other. It should be quite clear that the appending of End to an algorithm does not really change its effect. The algorithms $\tilde{H}$ and $\tilde{H}3$ are *equivalent*, according to the following definition. Two algorithms $\tilde{K}$ and $\tilde{L}$ are equivalent when they are equal as functions, that is (a) their domains and ranges are the same, and (b) if P is in the domain of $\tilde{K}$ (and hence of $\tilde{L}$), then $\tilde{K}(P) = \tilde{L}(P)$.

EXERCISES 1.2

1. What is wrong with the following algorithms to reverse the characters in a string?

> **algorithm** $\tilde{H}1(A)$; **A** ξ, η;
> $0: \alpha\xi\eta \rightarrow \eta\alpha\xi$;
> $1: \alpha \quad \rightarrow . \quad$;
> $2: \quad\quad \rightarrow \alpha \quad$ **end**

Example: $ab \overset{2}{\rightarrow} \alpha ab \overset{0}{\rightarrow} b\alpha a \overset{1}{\rightarrow} ba$

> **algorithm** $\tilde{H}2(A)$; **A** ξ, η;
> $0: \alpha\xi\eta \rightarrow \eta\alpha\xi$;
> $1: \quad \rightarrow \alpha \quad$;
> $2: \alpha \quad \rightarrow . \quad$ **end**

Example: $abc \overset{1}{\rightarrow} \alpha abc \overset{0}{\rightarrow} b\alpha ac \overset{0}{\rightarrow} bc\alpha a \overset{1}{\rightarrow} abc\alpha a \overset{0}{\rightarrow} c\alpha b\alpha a \overset{2}{\rightarrow} cb\alpha a \overset{2}{\rightarrow} cba$

(This exercise shows the need for β in algorithm Reverse.)

2. Can we combine rules 1 and 2 in Reverse into the one rule $\beta\xi\alpha \rightarrow \xi\beta$? What would the sequence of transformations on the string *abc* look like now?

1.3 COMPOSITION OF ALGORITHMS

Let us consider another example. Suppose we wish to determine whether P_1 and P_2 (strings over a data alphabet A) are identical. An algorithmic activity which will do this is:

1. Given P_1 and P_2 in R, say as $P = P_1*P_2$, where $*$ is a character not in A, reverse the characters of P_2. (We have already seen an algorithm, Reverse, which does this, but it will have to be modified to work on a substring only.) For example, if the two strings are both *abcd*, we should now have *abcd*dcba*.
2. Delete the pair of characters on either side of the $*$ so long as they are the same.
3. If R ever contains only the $*$, delete it. When the activity terminates, $P_1 = P_2$ if R contains only the empty string Λ, otherwise not.

To be able to carry out the second part of this activity, i.e., the elimination of pairs of equal characters, we recall that if the LHS of a rule contains a generic variable ξ more than once, the character in the alphabet corresponding to the leftmost occurrence establishes the correspondence for ξ, and all additional occurrences of ξ must match a character identical to that established by the first match; otherwise, the rule is not applicable. We may therefore write the second half, $\widetilde{H2}$, of the desired algorithm as follows:

$$\textbf{algorithm } \widetilde{H2}(A, *); \textbf{A } \xi;$$
$$0: \xi*\xi \rightarrow * \;;$$
$$1: * \quad\rightarrow . \;;$$
$$2: \quad\quad \rightarrow . \;\textbf{ end}$$

Writing $\widetilde{H1}$ for the reversal algorithm already discussed (i.e., Reverse modified to work only on a specified substring), we may now write the overall algorithm $\widetilde{H3}$ in functional notation as

$$\widetilde{H3}(P) = \widetilde{H2}(P_1*\widetilde{H1}(P_2))$$

There are still two fundamental problems in the use of algorithms which we must face before we are in a position to exhibit $\widetilde{H3}$ explicitly.

1. Given an algorithm which works on R, modify it to work on a specified substring of the contents of R.
2. Given two algorithms $\widetilde{H1}$ and $\widetilde{H2}$, construct an algorithm $\widetilde{H3}$ which is (equivalent to) $\widetilde{H2}$ applied to the result of $\widetilde{H1}$. We shall say that $\widetilde{H3}$ is the *composition of $\widetilde{H2}$ with $\widetilde{H1}$*, and we shall write this as $\widetilde{H3} = \widetilde{H2} \circ \widetilde{H1}$. Thus $(\widetilde{H2} \circ \widetilde{H1})(P) = \widetilde{H2}(\widetilde{H1}(P))$.

In handling these two problems, we shall use a common strategy. The principle is to transform the algorithms under consideration—and possibly some small auxiliary algorithms—so that (a) their order of execution, when combined, is correct, and (b) the result produced in R by each algorithm is an acceptable input word for the next algorithm to be applied.

We shall develop this strategy in the next section, but first we postulate a property to be possessed by all alphabets: If A is an alphabet, there exists a denumerably infinite family of disjoint "alias alphabets" $A^0, A^1, A^2, \ldots$, with $A^0 = A$, having the property that the characters of each A^i are in one-to-one correspondence with the characters of A, and hence with each other. The family $A^0, A^1, \ldots$ will be denoted $\{A\}$. It is clear that A plays no special role in $\{A\}$.

The correspondents in $A^1, A^2, \ldots$ of a character δ in A^0 form an equivalence class under the correspondence, and we shall exploit this by assuming that declarations in an algorithm heading which involve A and generic variables over A implicitly represent corresponding declarations for all of the aliases for A and for the variables equivalent to the generic variables appearing in the declarations. Thus, if the declaration $\mathbf{A}\ \xi$ appears, we may automatically use ξ^2 in rules in the algorithm as generic over A^2, subject to the correspondence with ξ. In other words, if ξ and ξ^2 happen to appear in the same applicable rule, and if ξ matches the character a in A in the data, then ξ^2 matches a^2 in A^2. As an example,

$$\textbf{algorithm } \tilde{H}(A);\ \mathbf{A}\ \xi;$$
$$0\colon \xi\ \rightarrow\ \xi^1\ \textbf{end}$$

replaces every character of A in P (the initial contents of the register R) by its correspondent in A^1.

If $\tilde{H}$ is an algorithm over an alphabet A, we write $\tilde{H}^1$ to mean the corresponding algorithm over A^1. More precisely, since various changes may be desired in the rules and declarations at the same time as the invocation of the alias alphabet A^1, we shall use a special notation to spell out a correspondence of two algorithms. A typical correspondence may be written

$$\tilde{H}^k\ \equiv\ \frac{\tilde{H}(A \cup \alpha, A, \text{`}\rightarrow\text{'}\ Q\ \text{`.'})}{\tilde{H}^k(A^k \cup \alpha \cup \beta, A^k, \text{`}\rightarrow\beta\text{'}\ Q)}$$

The first element of each of the parenthesized lists is the data alphabet for the algorithm named. Any subsequent entries in the lower list are considered to be replacements for their corresponding entries in the upper list. Replacement of one alphabet by another implies corresponding replacement of generic variables. Entries which are not names of alphabets are taken as explicit character strings, and replacement is made wherever possible throughout the original algorithms. Thus, with single quotation marks used around explicit characters, the last list entries in the example above imply the action of a Markov rule:

$$\text{`}\to\text{'} \; Q \; \text{`.'} \; \to \; \text{`}\to\beta\text{'} \; Q$$

in which Q is an arbitrary substring not containing any metaconstants (such as the period or semicolon), since it is not delimited by quotation marks. Less formally, the intention of the transformation above is to produce from an algorithm $\tilde{H}$ another algorithm $\tilde{H}^k$ by replacing the characters in the alphabet A by their aliases in A^k, by adjoining β to the data alphabet, and by specifying that anywhere one finds in $\tilde{H}$ a terminal rule (i.e., ending with a period), the period is to be dropped and the RHS is to be prefixed by β. Since the LHS is not specified, it may be anything. The RHS Q was mentioned because it was involved in the transformation.

As an example of the transformation specified above, let $\tilde{H}$ be

> **algorithm** $\tilde{H}(A, \alpha)$; **A** ξ, η;
> $0: \alpha\xi\eta \; \to \; \eta\xi$. **end**

Then $\tilde{H}^k$ is

> **algorithm** $\tilde{H}^k(A^k, \alpha, \beta)$; **A**^{k} ξ^k, η^k;
> $0: \alpha\xi^k\eta^k \; \to \; \beta\eta^k\xi^k$ **end**

(Now $\tilde{H}^k$ is no longer closed, but presumably it will be combined with other algorithms into a larger closed algorithm.) An interesting and useful property of algorithms which arises from such correspondences as

$$\tilde{H}^1 \equiv \frac{\tilde{H}(A)}{\tilde{H}^1(A^1)}$$

is that $(\tilde{H}(P))^1 = \tilde{H}^1(P^1)$, where for any string Q, we mean by Q^1 the string obtained from Q by replacing every character in A by its alias in A^1.

It is perhaps not yet apparent why we have discussed alias alphabets as part of the treatment of composition of algorithms. In an example earlier (the reversal algorithm), we remarked that the rule $\to \alpha$ must occur below all the others because it was always applicable. Yet it turned out to be the only rule applicable at the start of the execution of the algorithm. All the rules above it were inapplicable because they involved α or β, which were not in the data alphabet. In other words, because of the different alphabets involved in the rules, it was possible to control the order in which the rules were applied—always within the basic sequencing control of the MA. This same device of using different alphabets will enable us to combine algorithms effectively. It is now clear that combination of algorithms will require modification of (1) alphabets; (2) terminal rules, i.e., rules of the form $P \to Q.$; and (3) rules which have empty LHS's,

since a substring on which we wish to focus attention—to the exclusion of
any characters to the left and right of it—may not be at the left end of R.

1.4 SOME ALGORITHMIC CONSTRUCTIONS

The preceding section raised two basic problems: (1) the composition of
two (and hence, by induction, of several) algorithms; and (2) the restriction of an algorithm to a substring of the contents of R. In this section
we shall study these constructions and others which occur so often that
their explicit form should be exhibited and understood as early as possible.

The difficulty in constructing an algorithm $\widetilde{H3}$ which is the composi-
tion of $\widetilde{H1}$ and $\widetilde{H2}$ is that $\widetilde{H1}; \widetilde{H2}$, obtained by appending $\widetilde{H2}$ to $\widetilde{H1}$,
does not necessarily cause $\widetilde{H2}$ to be applied after $\widetilde{H1}$ is concluded. The
rules of $\widetilde{H1}$ are always tested for applicability before those of $\widetilde{H2}$, and
they may again become applicable at some inopportune time. We must
use some auxiliary rules to follow $\widetilde{H1}$, which, once they are applied, block
both $\widetilde{H1}$ and themselves from being applicable again. After our discussion
in the preceding section, it is clear that this blocking should be accomplished by the use of alias alphabets.

In the following discussion we shall denote by α and β two distinct
characters not in A (or in any alias of A). We define:

algorithm $\widetilde{H0}(A, \alpha)$; $\mathbf{A}\ \xi, \eta$;	*Comments*
$0: \xi\alpha \;\rightarrow\; \alpha\xi\ $;	Shift α left as far as possible.
$1: \alpha\xi \;\rightarrow\; \alpha\xi^1\ $;	Change first character to alias alphabet.
$2: \xi^1\eta \;\rightarrow\; \xi^1\eta^1$;	Use it to change remaining char- acters to alias alphabet.
$3: \alpha \;\rightarrow\; \alpha\ .\ \mathbf{end}$	Dummy statement to terminate.

The auxiliary rules, represented by $\widetilde{H0}$, will be placed above $\widetilde{H1}$. Note,
however, that none of the rules of $\widetilde{H0}$ is applicable until α or a character
of A^1 is present. Thus $\widetilde{H0}$ will not precede $\widetilde{H1}$ in execution.

Now let $\widetilde{K1}$ and $\widetilde{J1}$ be defined by the transformations

$$\widetilde{K1} \equiv \frac{\widetilde{H1}(A, \text{`}\rightarrow\text{'}\ Q\ \text{`.'})}{\widetilde{K1}(A \cup \alpha, \text{`}\rightarrow\alpha\text{'}\ Q)}$$

$$\widetilde{J1} = \widetilde{H0}; \widetilde{K1}$$

so that $\widetilde{K1}$ is equivalent to $\widetilde{H1}$ except that each previously terminating
rule now inserts an α somewhere into R. This α will trigger $\widetilde{H0}$ into action
within $\widetilde{J1}$, and it may easily be verified that $\widetilde{J1}(P) = \alpha(\widetilde{H1}(P))^1$. In other

words, we have arranged it so that no action is caused by $\widetilde{H0}$ until $\widetilde{H1}$ (now $\widetilde{K1}$) is finished. Then, because $\widetilde{H1}$ ends by prefixing an α to the contents of R, $\widetilde{H0}$ is activated to convert the characters of A in R over to their aliases in A^1. When this is done, $\widetilde{H1}$ will not be activated again. The reader is urged to try out this construction using Reverse or Characters in place of $\widetilde{H1}$ before proceeding.

Now suppose we wish to apply $\widetilde{H2}$ to the result of $\widetilde{H1}$. Let us assume that $\widetilde{H2}$ uses alphabet A^1 (since, as we have seen, we can always arrange this), and $\widetilde{H2}$ does not involve α as a local variable. (The latter condition can always be arranged by simply choosing different local variables, if necessary.) Thinking of $\widetilde{H2}$ as the set of rules to be carried out instead of the terminal rule 3 of $\widetilde{J1}$ (originally rule 3 of $\widetilde{H0}$), we insert $\widetilde{H2}$ at that point, as follows:†

$$\widetilde{K0} \equiv \frac{\widetilde{H0}(A \cup \alpha, \text{`}\alpha \rightarrow \alpha \text{ .'})}{\widetilde{K0}(A \cup \alpha, \Lambda)}$$

$$\widetilde{K3} = \widetilde{K0}; \widetilde{H2}; \widetilde{K1}$$

Then we have $\widetilde{K3}(P) = \alpha\widetilde{H2}(\widetilde{H1}(P))^1$, except that if $\widetilde{H2}$ happens to contain any rules of the form $\Lambda \rightarrow Q$ (for example, $\rightarrow \gamma$), they will be applicable even before the rules of $\widetilde{H1}$, since such rules are not blocked by alias alphabets. We could have avoided this by appending $\widetilde{H2}$ after $\widetilde{H1}$, but then similar rules in $\widetilde{H1}$ would prevent $\widetilde{H2}$ from being executed. We should have had to modify these particular rules in $\widetilde{H2}$ anyway, since they must be applied immediately to the right of α, and not at the very left end. (Why do we not need to modify rules of the form $Q1 \rightarrow Q2$ in $\widetilde{H2}$ to account for the α?) We therefore form $\widetilde{K2}$

$$\widetilde{K2} \equiv \frac{\widetilde{H2}(A^1, \Lambda \text{ `}\rightarrow\text{' } Q)}{\widetilde{K2}(A^1 \cup \alpha, \text{`}\alpha \rightarrow \alpha\text{' } Q)}$$

and redefine $\widetilde{K3}$

$$\widetilde{K3} = \widetilde{K0}; \widetilde{K2}; \widetilde{K1}$$

and now we do have the property $\widetilde{K3}(P) = \alpha\widetilde{H2}(\widetilde{H1}(P))^1$.

To finish the construction of the composition, all we need now is to convert all aliases back to characters in A, and then eliminate α. Derive $\widetilde{K4}$ from $\widetilde{K2}$ in much the same way as $\widetilde{K1}$ was derived from $\widetilde{H1}$ (i.e., let

---

† It is assumed here that whenever the bottommost rule of an algorithm is totally eliminated, the symbol **end** is moved to the preceding rule automatically.

terminal rules instead introduce a punctuation character which triggers another auxiliary algorithm):

$$\widetilde{K4} \equiv \frac{\widetilde{K2}(A^1 \cup \alpha, \text{'}\rightarrow\text{'} \ Q \ \text{'.'})}{\widetilde{K4}(A^1 \cup \alpha \cup \beta, \text{'}\rightarrow\beta\text{'} \ Q)}$$

We introduce an auxiliary algorithm $\widetilde{K5}$ very much like $\widetilde{H0}$.

algorithm $\widetilde{K5}(A, \alpha, \beta)$; **A** ξ, η;	*Comments*
0: $\xi^1\beta \ \rightarrow \ \beta\xi^1$;	Shift β left as far as possible.
1: $\beta\xi^1 \ \rightarrow \ \beta\xi$;	Change first character to alphabet A.
2: $\xi\eta^1 \ \rightarrow \ \xi\eta$;	Change remaining characters back to A.
3: $\alpha\beta \ \rightarrow \ $. **end**	Delete α, β and terminate.

We are now able to exhibit the desired $\widetilde{H3}$.

$$\widetilde{H3} = \widetilde{H2} \circ \widetilde{H1} = \widetilde{K5}; \widetilde{K0}; \widetilde{K4}; \widetilde{K1}$$

where it should be noted that the order of appending is very important. [Exercise 1.4.1 asks explicitly for $\widetilde{H3}$, given $\widetilde{H2}$ and $\widetilde{H1}$.] Note that α and β are completely local to this composite algorithm, so we may consider $\widetilde{H3}$ to be an algorithm over A, the alphabet (together with its alias A^1) over which $\widetilde{H1}$ and $\widetilde{H2}$ were defined. In actual practice, it must be possible for $\widetilde{H3}$ to have created for it local variables α and β not in A, whenever an alphabet A is presented to it. We observe that $\widetilde{H3}$ is an algorithm in its own right, so it may be composed with other algorithms in turn. [Exercise 1.4.3 now asks for the explicit algorithm for the problem: Is $P_1 = P_2$?] It should always be implicitly understood that in any process, such as multiple compositions, in which more than one alias alphabet is to be introduced, each successive alias is chosen from among those not yet used. [Exercise 1.4.2 asks for a double composition.]

Let us now consider the second construction proposed earlier for focusing of attention on a particular substring: Given σ and τ not in the alphabet A, and P in R of the form $Q_1\sigma Q_2\tau Q_3$, how can we arrange it so that an algorithm $\widetilde{H1}$ acts only on Q_2? Put another way, we wish to construct an algorithm $\widetilde{H2}$, to be denoted $\sigma| \ \widetilde{H1} \ |\tau$, such that $\widetilde{H2}(P) = Q_1\sigma\widetilde{H1}(Q_2)\tau Q_3$. (The special case based on $Q_1\sigma Q_2$, denoted $\sigma| \ \widetilde{H1} \ |\Lambda$, will be automatically included. The other special case $Q_2\tau Q_3$, denoted $\Lambda| \ \widetilde{H1} \ |\tau$, is obtained by replacing σ by Λ everywhere in the rest of this paragraph. A careful examination of this development will also reveal that if, in the case $Q_2\tau Q_3$, it happens that τ and Q_3 are not actually present, we will have $\Lambda\rfloor \widetilde{H1} \lfloor \tau = \widetilde{H1}$ on Q_2.) The algorithm $\widetilde{K0}$ is introduced to change the alphabet of Q_2 to be A^1.

> **algorithm** $\widetilde{K0}(A, \sigma)$; **A** ξ, η;
> 0: $\sigma\xi \rightarrow \sigma\xi^1$;
> 1: $\xi^1\eta \rightarrow \xi^1\eta^1$;
> 2: $\rightarrow$. **end**

Notice that rule 1 in $\widetilde{K0}$ no longer applies when τ is reached, since τ is not in the domain of η. We derive $\widetilde{K1}$ from $\widetilde{H1}$ so that $\widetilde{K1}$ works over A^1 and only to the right of σ:

$$\widetilde{K1} \equiv \frac{\widetilde{H1}(A \cup \sigma \cup \tau, A, \Lambda \ '\rightarrow' \ Q)}{\widetilde{K1}(A^1 \cup \sigma \cup \tau, A^1, '\sigma \rightarrow \sigma' \ Q)}$$

Then $\widetilde{K2} = \widetilde{K1} \circ \widetilde{K0}$ has the property that $\widetilde{K2}(P) = Q_1\sigma(\widetilde{H1}(Q_2))^1\tau Q_3$, and we need only remove aliases. Let $\widetilde{K3}$ be the following auxiliary algorithm:

> **algorithm** $\widetilde{K3}(A, \sigma, \tau)$; **A** ξ;
> 0: $\xi^1 \rightarrow \xi$;
> 1: $\rightarrow$. **end**

Then clearly $\widetilde{H2} = \sigma\rfloor \widetilde{H1} \lfloor \tau = \widetilde{K3} \circ \widetilde{K1} \circ \widetilde{K0}$. [Exercise 1.4.4 asks for a modification of $\widetilde{H2}$ so that applying $\widetilde{H2}$ to $Q_1\sigma Q_2\sigma\ldots\sigma Q_k\tau Q_{k+1}$ gives $Q_1\sigma\widetilde{H2}(Q_2)\sigma\ldots\sigma\widetilde{H2}(Q_k)\tau Q_{k+1}$.] Now we can see how it is possible to develop basic constructions such as composition and, without getting enmeshed in the detail involved, use these constructions as part of the available equipment in building additional ones.

Another important construction is that of the *control algorithm*. At the beginning of the preceding section, we saw an example of an algorithm which asks a question about the data; i.e., are P_1 and P_2 equal? On the basis of the answer to such a question, one may designate one or another of two algorithms to be applied next. The most complex decisions can then be generated from this two-alternative decision process. Three algorithms may be identified here: $\widetilde{H0}$ determines which one of $\widetilde{H1}$ and $\widetilde{H2}$ is to be next applied to the data P in R. $\widetilde{H0}$ is called the *control algorithm*, and $\widetilde{H1}$ and $\widetilde{H2}$ are called the *branches*. We now wish to construct a single algorithm $\widetilde{H3}$, called a *branching algorithm*, which may be denoted $\widetilde{H0}(\widetilde{H1}, \widetilde{H2})$, such that:

$$\widetilde{H3}(P) = \begin{cases} \widetilde{H1}(P) & \text{if} \quad \widetilde{H0}(P) = \Lambda \\ \widetilde{H2}(P) & \text{if} \quad \widetilde{H0}(P) \neq \Lambda \end{cases}$$

Our strategy will be to create a second copy of P (the initial data) on which to apply $\widetilde{H0}$, so that we do not destroy it in the process. In particular, we shall produce in R the following strings in succession, starting with P,

$$P, P\alpha P, \widetilde{H0}(P)\alpha P, \qquad \text{followed by} \qquad \begin{cases} \alpha P & \text{if} \quad \widetilde{H0}(P) = \Lambda \\ P & \text{if} \quad \widetilde{H0}(P) \neq \Lambda \end{cases}$$

and finally,

$$\widetilde{H1}(P) \quad \text{if } \alpha \text{ is present}$$
$$\widetilde{H2}(P) \quad \text{if } \alpha \text{ is not present}$$

Note that we can arrange to apply $\widetilde{H0}$ only to the left-hand copy of P by using the focusing notation $\Lambda\rfloor \widetilde{H0} \lfloor \alpha$. We first define Copy to produce $P\alpha P$:

algorithm Copy(A, α); **A** ξ, η;   *Comments*
0: $\xi\eta\beta \;\rightarrow\; \eta\beta\xi$;   *Move β left and interchange.*
1: $\alpha\xi \;\rightarrow\; \xi\beta\xi\alpha$;   *Duplicate character and mark with β.*
2: $\alpha \;\rightarrow\; \gamma$;   *Change to γ to allow move left.*
3: $\beta\gamma \;\rightarrow\; \rho$;   *Mark center position.*
4: $\xi\gamma \;\rightarrow\; \gamma\xi$;   *Move γ left to center.*
5: $\beta \;\rightarrow\; \delta$;   *Delete β's.*
6: $\delta \;\rightarrow\;$;
7: $\rho \;\rightarrow\; \alpha$.   ;   *Restore α.*
8: $\gamma \;\rightarrow\; \alpha$.   ;   *Handle case where $P = \Lambda$.*
9:    $\rightarrow \alpha$ **end**   *Insert initial α.*

The reader should verify before continuing that in fact Copy$(abc) = abc\alpha abc$, and that Copy$(\Lambda) = \alpha$. Let $\widetilde{K1}$ be another auxiliary algorithm which deletes α and everything to its left if there is anything there, but otherwise does nothing.

algorithm $\widetilde{K1}(A, \alpha)$; **A** ξ;
0: $\xi\alpha \;\rightarrow\; \mu$;
1: $\xi\mu \;\rightarrow\; \mu$;
2: $\mu \;\rightarrow\; .$;
3:    $\rightarrow\; .$ **end**

So far, we can construct $\widetilde{K2} = \widetilde{K1} \circ \Lambda\rfloor \widetilde{H0} \lfloor \alpha \circ$ Copy, which has the property that

$$\widetilde{K2}(P) = \begin{cases} \alpha P & \text{if} \quad \widetilde{H0}(P) = \Lambda \\ P & \text{if} \quad \widetilde{H0}(P) \neq \Lambda \end{cases}$$

Now we let $\widetilde{K3}$ be defined to convert αP to $P^1\alpha$, or to do nothing if no α is present.

> **algorithm** $\widetilde{K3}(A, \alpha)$; **A** ξ;
> 0: $\alpha\xi \rightarrow \xi^1\alpha$;
> 1: $\rightarrow$.   **end**

Since we now have either $P^1\alpha$ or P in R, depending on the decision implied by the control algorithm $\widetilde{H0}$, we shall now use the alphabet to decide between $\widetilde{H1}$ and $\widetilde{H2}$. Let $\widetilde{K4}$ be defined as

$$\widetilde{K4} \equiv \frac{\widetilde{H1}(A)}{\widetilde{K4}(A^1)}$$

and let $\widetilde{K5} = \underset{\alpha}{\Lambda\rfloor} \widetilde{K4} \lfloor \alpha \circ \widetilde{H2} \circ \widetilde{K3} \circ \widetilde{K2}$. Then

$$\widetilde{K5}(P) = \begin{cases} (\widetilde{H1}(P))^1\alpha & \text{if } \widetilde{H0}(P) = \Lambda \\ \widetilde{H2}(P) & \text{if } \widetilde{H0}(P) \neq \Lambda \end{cases}$$

and all that remains is to remove α and the aliases, if any. Let $\widetilde{K6}$ be defined as

> **algorithm** $\widetilde{K6}(A)$; **A** ξ;
> 0: $\xi^1 \rightarrow \xi$;
> 1: $\alpha \rightarrow$;
> 2: $\rightarrow$. **end**

and then $\widetilde{H3} = \widetilde{H0}(\widetilde{H1}, \widetilde{H2}) = \widetilde{K6} \circ \widetilde{K5}$. [Exercise 1.4.5 asks that $\widetilde{H3}$ be exhibited for a simple example of $\widetilde{H0}$, $\widetilde{H1}$, $\widetilde{H2}$.]

There are several possible generalizations of the two-way branching operation which we have discussed. Their construction is most easily seen by using trees with two branches leading from each node.

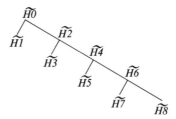

Figure 1.1

In Fig. 1.1, $\widetilde{H0}$, $\widetilde{H2}$, $\widetilde{H4}$, and $\widetilde{H6}$ are control algorithms, and it is intended that exactly one of $\widetilde{H1}$, $\widetilde{H3}$, $\widetilde{H5}$, $\widetilde{H7}$, and $\widetilde{H8}$ will be applied. By using the construction of the two-way branch repeatedly, with the second branch in each case again a branching algorithm, we may represent the entire tree of Fig. 1.1 as algorithm $\widetilde{H9}$.

$$\widetilde{H9} = \widetilde{H0}(\widetilde{H1}, \widetilde{H2}(\widetilde{H3}, \widetilde{H4}(\widetilde{H5}, \widetilde{H6}(\widetilde{H7}, \widetilde{H8}))))$$

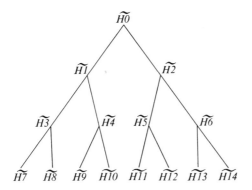

Figure 1.2

In Fig. 1.2, a long series of decisions is made before determining which of $\widetilde{H7}, \widetilde{H8}, \ldots, \widetilde{H14}$ is to be applied to the data. The total branching algorithm may be represented as

$$\widetilde{H15} = \widetilde{H0}(\widetilde{H1}(\widetilde{H3}(\widetilde{H7}, \widetilde{H8}), \widetilde{H4}(\widetilde{H9}, \widetilde{H10})), \widetilde{H2}(\widetilde{H5}(\widetilde{H11}, \widetilde{H12}),$$
$$\widetilde{H6}(\widetilde{H13}, \widetilde{H14})))$$

[Exercise 1.4.6 considers another possible tree, and Exercise 1.4.7 discusses binary labeling of trees.]

Another common construction, arising directly out of the branching operation, is the *iteration algorithm*. Here one is concerned with repeating some algorithm a number of times, each time changing the contents of R, until some condition is satisfied. An example of this would be to start with an algorithm Double, which has as its input data a string of n 1's, and which produces a string of 1's twice as long, that is, $2n$. Applying Double again yields $4n$, that is, 2^2n. After applying Double r times, one would have $2^r n$ 1's in R. Of course, if $n = 1$, we would have a way of generating 2^r. In this process we see the need for an overall control algorithm which applies Double the appropriate number of times. This control algorithm is quite independent of the choice of Double as the algorithm to be applied each time.

In general, one starts with a data word P in R, and the algorithm proceeds with the following repetitive process, where Q is initially P.

"If the control algorithm $\widetilde{H0}$, when applied to the contents Q of R, produces the null string Λ, the algorithm terminates with Q in R. If $\widetilde{H0}(Q) \neq \Lambda$, an algorithm $\widetilde{H2}$, called the *body of the iteration*, is applied to Q, and upon its termination the control process specified by this paragraph is to be invoked."

The preceding paragraph could also have been written as follows:

"Let the contents of R be called Q. If the control algorithm $\widetilde{H0}$, when applied to Q, produces the null string Λ, the algorithm terminates, leaving Q in R. If the null word is not produced by $\widetilde{H0}$, an algorithm $\widetilde{H2}$ is to be applied to Q, and upon its termination a copy of this paragraph is to replace the next sentence. This sentence is a dummy placeholder, to be replaced by a copy of this paragraph."

Obviously it would not be possible to make these copies before knowing the algorithms $\widetilde{H0}$ and $\widetilde{H2}$ and the datum P, since we would not know how many copies are needed. Thus, while it is tempting to write

$$\widetilde{H3} = \widetilde{H0}(\widetilde{H1}, \widetilde{H3} \circ \widetilde{H2})$$

where $\widetilde{H1}$ is a trivial terminal algorithm, we cannot do this unless we arrange to construct copies of $\widetilde{H3}$ during execution as needed.† We shall therefore use the first form of the description of the iteration algorithm, and we shall build it out of existing constructions, such as appending, composition, and branching.

An iteration algorithm produces in R a succession of words P_0, $P_1, \ldots, P_n$, such that

$$P_0 = P$$

and either

$$\widetilde{H0}(P_0) = \Lambda \qquad \text{and} \qquad n = 0$$

or

$$P_i = \widetilde{H2}(P_{i-1}), \qquad 0 \le i < n$$

and

$$\widetilde{H0}(P_i) \neq \Lambda, \qquad 0 \le i \le n - 1$$

and

$$\widetilde{H0}(P_n) = \Lambda$$

---

† This is indeed sometimes done, but we will consider it out of bounds here.

The value of n is of course a function of the datum P, for each choice of $\tilde{H}0$ and $\tilde{H}2$.

The construction of a single algorithm $\tilde{H}3$, denoted $\tilde{H}0(\tilde{H}2)$, which will represent the iteration of $\tilde{H}2$ under control of $\tilde{H}0$, is similar to that of the ordinary two-way branch algorithm. We first introduce an algorithm $\tilde{H}1$:

$$\textbf{algorithm } \tilde{H}1(A, \gamma);$$
$$0: \ \to \gamma \,.\ \textbf{end}$$

and then construct

$$\tilde{L}1 = \tilde{H}0(\tilde{H}1, \tilde{H}2) = \tilde{K}6 \circ \tilde{K}4 \circ \tilde{H}2 \circ \tilde{K}3 \circ \tilde{K}1 \circ \Lambda\rfloor \tilde{H}0 \lfloor \alpha \circ \text{Copy}$$

as before. We then eliminate the termination state of $\tilde{L}1$:

$$\tilde{L}2 \equiv \frac{\tilde{L}1(A \cup \gamma, \ \text{‘}\to\text{’} \ Q \ \text{‘.’})}{\tilde{L}2(A \cup \gamma \cup \delta, \ \text{‘}\to\text{’} \ \delta \ Q)}$$

so that $\tilde{L}2$ no longer terminates, but we can tell by the presence of γ that $\tilde{H}1$ was executed. Because of the way a two-way branch algorithm is constructed, there is still work to be done on R, such as removal of aliases, after $\tilde{H}1$ is finished. We can then tell by the presence of δ when the entire job of the branch algorithm is finished. Thus the character δ will prevent the terminating action implied by γ from occurring before the two-way branch algorithm is completely done. We now need $\tilde{L}3$ to take over when the branching algorithm finishes, i.e., when δ is generated. The job of $\tilde{L}3$ is to recognize γ, remove it, and terminate, or else start $\tilde{H}0$ again.

algorithm $\tilde{L}3(A, \gamma, \delta); A \cup \gamma \, \xi;$	*Comments*
$0: \xi\delta \ \to \ \delta\xi;$	Move δ to left end.
$1: \delta\gamma \ \to \ .\ \ ;$	If γ is present, delete it and δ and terminate.
$2: \ \delta \ \to \quad \textbf{end}$	Otherwise, delete δ and drop through to the branching algorithm again.

The desired algorithm $\tilde{H}3 = \tilde{H}0(\tilde{H}2)$ can now be given.

$$\tilde{H}3 = \tilde{L}3; \tilde{L}2$$

[Exercise 1.4.8 asks for an application of $\tilde{H}3$ to an iteration problem.]

EXERCISES 1.4

1. Let $\widetilde{H1}$ and $\widetilde{H2}$ be defined as follows:

> **algorithm** $\widetilde{H1}(A, \beta)$; $A \cup \beta \; \xi$;
> 0: $\rho\xi \rightarrow \xi\rho$;
> 1: $\rho \;\;\rightarrow\;\;$. ;
> 2: $\;\;\;\rightarrow \alpha\rho$ **end**

> **algorithm** $\widetilde{H2}(A, \alpha)$; $A \cup \alpha \; \eta$;
> 0: $\nu\eta \rightarrow \eta\nu$;
> 1: $\;\nu \rightarrow\;$. ;
> 2: $\;\;\;\rightarrow \beta\nu$ **end**

a) Give the explicit algorithms for $\widetilde{H2} \circ \widetilde{H1}$ and $\widetilde{H1} \circ \widetilde{H2}$, and show by simple application that $\widetilde{H2} \circ \widetilde{H1} \neq \widetilde{H1} \circ \widetilde{H2}$.

b) Give the explicit algorithms for $\widetilde{H1}$; $\widetilde{H2}$ and $\widetilde{H2}$; $\widetilde{H1}$, and show by simple application that they have the same effect as $\widetilde{H1}$ and $\widetilde{H2}$ respectively; thus $\widetilde{H1}$; $\widetilde{H2} \neq \widetilde{H2}$; $\widetilde{H1}$.

c) Show by simple applications that:

1) $\widetilde{H1}$; $\widetilde{H2} \neq \widetilde{H1} \circ \widetilde{H2}$
2) $\widetilde{H1}$; $\widetilde{H2} \neq \widetilde{H2} \circ \widetilde{H1}$
3) $\widetilde{H2}$; $\widetilde{H1} \neq \widetilde{H1} \circ \widetilde{H2}$
4) $\widetilde{H2}$; $\widetilde{H1} \neq \widetilde{H2} \circ \widetilde{H1}$

2. Define $\widetilde{H3}$ as follows:

> **algorithm** $\widetilde{H3}(A, \gamma)$; $A \cup \gamma \; \zeta$;
> 0: $\epsilon\zeta \rightarrow \zeta\epsilon$;
> 1: $\epsilon \;\;\rightarrow\;\;$. ;
> 2: $\;\;\;\rightarrow \gamma\epsilon$ **end**

Give the explicit algorithm for $\widetilde{H3} \circ \widetilde{H2} \circ \widetilde{H1}$ where $\widetilde{H2}$ and $\widetilde{H1}$ are as defined in Exercise 1.4.1.

3. Write the explicit algorithm for determining whether $P1 = P2$ as character strings. Assume $P1*P2$ is initially in R and that $P1 = P2$ if $R = \Lambda$ at the end.

4. Modify $\widetilde{H2} = \sigma\rvert \widetilde{H1} \lfloor \tau$ so that applying $\widetilde{H2}$ to $Q_1 \sigma Q_2 \sigma \ldots \sigma Q_k \tau Q_{k+1}$ gives

$$Q_1 \sigma \widetilde{H2}(Q_2)\sigma \ldots \sigma \widetilde{H2}(Q_k)\tau Q_{k+1}$$

5. Let a decision problem be: (1) examine a register R for β; (2) if there is a β in R, then (3) delete it; (4) if not, insert a β at the left end. Define a

control algorithm $\widetilde{H0}$ as follows:

$$\widetilde{H0}(P) = \Lambda \quad \text{if} \quad \beta \in R$$
$$\widetilde{H0}(P) \neq \Lambda \quad \text{if} \quad \beta \notin R$$

Then define two algorithms $\widetilde{H1}$ and $\widetilde{H2}$ so that $\widetilde{H1}$ deletes β and $\widetilde{H2}$ inserts β. Now apply the sequence

$$\widetilde{H3} = \widetilde{H0}(\widetilde{H1}, \widetilde{H2})$$
$$= \widetilde{K6} \circ {}_\Delta\lfloor \widetilde{K4} \lfloor_\alpha \circ \widetilde{H2} \circ \widetilde{K3} \circ \widetilde{K1} \circ {}_\Delta\lfloor \widetilde{H0} \lfloor_\alpha \circ \text{Copy}$$

to the two register configurations abc and βabc, where Copy, $\widetilde{K1}$, etc., are defined as in the derivation of the branching algorithm. Use the notation that

$$\widetilde{K6} \circ \cdots \circ \text{Copy}(abc) = \widetilde{K6} \circ \cdots \circ {}_\Delta\lfloor \widetilde{H0} \lfloor_\alpha (abc\alpha abc), \quad \text{etc.}$$

6. Instead of labeling algorithms in decimal (that is, $\widetilde{H6}$), we could just as easily label them in binary (that is, $\widetilde{H110}$). Furthermore, concerning a tree structure of two-way branching algorithms, we could label the algorithms in such a manner as to allow the label to indicate what decisions were made to get to the executed one. For example,

a) Start with $\widetilde{H1}$ as the label of the first control algorithm.

b) Label the algorithm on the next left branch $\widetilde{H10}$, and the algorithm on the next right branch $\widetilde{H11}$.

c) Continue as in (b), affixing 0 or 1 to the previous label for the left and right branch algorithms, respectively, until all algorithms have labels.

As an exercise, label in binary the two-way branching algorithms $\widetilde{H9}$ and $\widetilde{H15}$ shown in Figs. 1.1 and 1.2, respectively.

7. Express the branching algorithm represented by the following tree, in terms of the two-way branching algorithm notation.

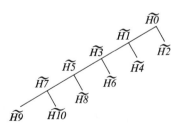

8. Let a simple iteration problem be to check R for occurrences of β, to eliminate β's one at a time until all β's are deleted, and then to terminate.

Define an algorithm $\widetilde{H0}$ such that

$$\widetilde{H0}(P) \neq \Lambda \quad \text{if} \quad \beta \in R$$
$$\widetilde{H0}(P) = \Lambda \quad \text{if} \quad \beta \notin R$$

and define an algorithm $\widetilde{H2}$ to delete one occurrence of β. Now apply the sequence

$$\widetilde{H0}(\widetilde{H2}) = \widetilde{L3}; \widetilde{L2} = \widetilde{L3}; \widetilde{K6'} \circ \Lambda| \ \widetilde{K4} \ |\alpha \circ \widetilde{K2} \circ \widetilde{K3} \circ \widetilde{K1} \circ \Lambda| \ \widetilde{H0} \ |\alpha \circ \text{Copy}$$

to the string $a\beta bc$ to see how the iteration algorithm works. Note that $\widetilde{K6'}$ is the $\widetilde{K6}$ defined for control algorithms (modified by the definition of $\widetilde{L2}$), and all other algorithms are as defined in the definitions of the branching algorithm and control algorithm, except, of course, $\widetilde{K4}$ (since $\widetilde{H1}$ is different this time) and $\widetilde{L3}$, which is new. Note also that when using the notation $\widetilde{L3}; \widetilde{K6'} \circ \cdots \circ \text{Copy}(a\beta bc)$, we must in effect apply one rule of Copy and then check if $\widetilde{L3}$ is applicable, apply another rule of Copy and check if $\widetilde{L3}$ is applicable, and so on, because of the way appending is defined.

1.5 ARITHMETIC ALGORITHMS

A natural collection of algorithmic activities to consider is the set of processes of ordinary arithmetic, as applied to nonnegative integers. To represent the nonnegative integers a variety of alphabets is available, such as decimal integers, binary integers, octal integers, and so on. A very simple alphabet, and the one which we shall adopt, is the alphabet G, consisting of the single character 1. We shall represent the integer n by the string $1\ 1\ 1 \ldots 1$ (with n characters). This string will also be denoted by 1^n on occasion. We shall use the lower case letters i, j, k, m, and n to specify arbitrary integers, other lower case letters (such as a, b, c, s, t and v) as local variables, and notations like "$n * m$ is in R" to mean that the contents of R is the string

$$\overbrace{1\ 1 \ldots 1}^{n} * \overbrace{1\ 1 \ldots 1}^{m} \quad \text{or} \quad 1^n * 1^m$$

1. The algorithm Plus for the addition of two numbers entered into R as $n * m$ is particularly simple:

$$\textbf{algorithm } \text{Plus}(G, *)$$
$$0: * \rightarrow . \textbf{ end}$$

2. The algorithm Diff for computing $|n - m|$ from $n * m$ in R is

$$\textbf{algorithm } \text{Diff}(G, *);$$
$$0: 1 * 1 \rightarrow *;$$
$$1: \quad * \quad \rightarrow . \textbf{ end}$$

3. The control algorithm Less, which starts with $n * m$ and leaves R empty if $n < m$, and nonempty otherwise, is

> **algorithm** Less$(G, *)$;
> 0: $1 * 1 \rightarrow *$;
> 1: $\quad * 1 \rightarrow \alpha$;
> 2: $\quad \alpha\, 1 \rightarrow \alpha$;
> 3: $\quad\quad \alpha \rightarrow .$;
> 4: $\quad\quad\quad \rightarrow .$ **end**

[Exercise 1.5.1 asks for Greater.]

4. The algorithm Mult for the product $n \times m$, given $n * m$ in R is:

> **algorithm** Mult$(G, *)$;
> 0: $b\, 1 \rightarrow 1\, b$;
> 1: $a\, 1 \rightarrow 1\, b\, a$;
> 2: $a \quad\rightarrow$;
> 3: $1 * \rightarrow * a$;
> 4: $* 1 \rightarrow *$;
> 5: $b \quad\rightarrow 1$;
> 6: $* \quad\rightarrow .$ **end**

The reader should try an example (say, $1\,1 * 1\,1\,1$) to see how the algorithm works in detail.

5. The algorithm Quot$_k$, for transforming any integer n in R into the integer (truncated) quotient of n divided by a fixed integer k, that is, $[n/k]$, is

> **algorithm** Quot$_k(G)$;
> 0: $* 1^k \rightarrow 1 *$;
> 1: $* 1 \quad\rightarrow *$;
> 2: $* \quad\rightarrow .$;
> 3: $\quad\rightarrow *$ **end**

Note that the asterisk is a local variable here, so it doesn't appear in the heading of the algorithm.

6. The control algorithm Odd for producing the character α if the integer n in R is odd, and Λ otherwise, is

> **algorithm** Odd(G, α);
> 0: $\alpha\, 1\, 1 \rightarrow \alpha$;
> 1: $\alpha\, 1 \quad\rightarrow \alpha$.;
> 2: $\alpha \quad\rightarrow$.;
> 3: $\quad\rightarrow \alpha$ **end**

7. The algorithm GCD for the greatest common divisor (gcd) of two positive integers m and n is easily derived from the property:

$$\gcd(m, n) = \begin{cases} \gcd(m - n, n), & \text{if } m \geq n \\ \gcd(m, n - m), & \text{if } m < n \end{cases}$$

[Exercise 1.5.2 asks for the proof of this assertion.] If we start with $m * n$ in R, reduce the larger by the smaller, and let the process continue until one of them is zero, the remaining integer is the desired gcd of m and n, since $\gcd(0, n) = n$.

$$\begin{array}{ll} \textbf{algorithm } \text{GCD}(G, *); \\ 0: 1\,a & \rightarrow a\,1; \\ 1: 1 * 1 & \rightarrow a\,*; \\ 2: 1\,* & \rightarrow *\,b; \\ 3: b & \rightarrow 1\ \ ; \\ 4: a & \rightarrow c\ \ ; \\ 5: c & \rightarrow 1\ \ ; \\ 6: * & \rightarrow .\ \ \ \textbf{end} \end{array}$$

The reader should try an example or two (say, $1\,1\,1\,1 * 1\,1$ and $1\,1 * 1\,1\,1\,1$) to see how the algorithm works. It is also interesting to wonder why it was necessary to introduce b and c.

8. The algorithm Div for division of n by m (where $m \neq 0$) is obtained as follows: Assume that $n * m$ is in R. We shall produce the result $q * r$, where $n = q \times m + r$, and $0 \leq r < m$.

algorithm Div$(G, *)$		*Comments*
0: $1\,c$	$\rightarrow c\,1$;	Move c's left to build q.
1: $b\,1$	$\rightarrow 1\,b$;	Move b's right to build r.
2: $1 * 1$	$\rightarrow *\,b$;	Carry out subtraction of m from n.
3: $c * b$	$\rightarrow c * d$;	The zero remainder case.
4: $* b$	$\rightarrow c * vb$;	Record one subtraction (v lets 9 work without invoking 2).
5: $* 1$	$\rightarrow * t$;	Nonzero remainder case.
6: db	$\rightarrow d$;	Delete apparent remainder in zero case.
7: $t\,1$	$\rightarrow t$;	Delete 1's. The b's remember r.
8: t	$\rightarrow s$;	
9: b	$\rightarrow 1$;	Let the b's change, to leave r.
10: v	$\rightarrow$;	
11: c	$\rightarrow 1$;	Let the c's change, to leave q.
12: $* d$	$\rightarrow 1 * .$;	Increase q by 1 to reflect zero remainder.
13: s	$\rightarrow$. ;	
14: $*$	$\rightarrow 1 *$ **end**	Division by zero case.

The reader should try an example (say, 1 1 1 ∗ 1 1) to see how the algorithm works. The algorithm Div has the property that $\text{Div}(n * m) = q * r$, provided that $m \neq 0$. Rule 14 of Div provides an infinite process of generating 1's in R if $m = 0$. The local variables, such as s, t, and v, play an important role in preventing earlier rules from being invoked at the wrong times. It is very difficult to organize—and to read—an algorithm like Div. As we have seen, certain programming devices can be invoked, such as composition and focusing, to make such complicated algorithms (and even more complicated ones) more manageable. An example is the algorithm which follows.

9. Since every positive integer n either is a prime (i.e., its only divisors are itself and 1) or can be expressed in a unique way as a product of prime factors (that is, $n = P_1^{n_1} \times P_2^{n_2} \times \cdots \times P_r^{n_r}$ where P_i are primes), suppose we now wish to find the prime factors of a positive integer n in R. This is a much more complex algorithm than Div, and it can best be handled by the techniques developed in the preceding section for constructing complex algorithms from simple ones. We begin with an analysis of the data to which the algorithm is to be applied. Since the algorithm is to find all prime factors of an arbitrary positive integer, it is reasonable that it have an iterative form. At each stage of application of the body of the iteration, then, the data should have the same general form as the input to the preceding stage of application. It is clear that we must define a "stage" quite precisely: Each stage must start with a number j (initially $j = 2$). We divide the current "value" n_k by j (initially $n_k = n$) as many times as possible, each time leaving a "value" for the next stage, and record j as one of the prime factors m_k each time the division was possible.

[Exercise 1.5.3 asks about a somewhat related algorithm which produces, from $n * m$ in R (assuming that m, n are not both zero):

Λ	if $m \mid n$	(Read "m divides n")
α	if $m \nmid n$	(Read "m does not divide n")
∞		(no termination, with an unbounded generation of 1's)
	if $m = 0$ and $n \neq 0$.]	

Using α, β, and γ as punctuation characters, we may visualize the contents of R as having a general form, at each intermediate stage, as follows:

$$n_k \, \gamma \, q * r \, \alpha j \, \beta \, m_k \, \beta \, m_{k-1} \, \ldots \, \beta \, m_1 \qquad \text{(a)}$$

where j is the current trial divisor, n_k the current data value, q and r are such that $n_k = q \times j + r$ (so that we are about to see if $j \mid n_k$ by testing for $r = 0$), and the integers $m_1, \ldots, m_k$ to the right of the β's are the prime factors (not necessarily distinct) already found. Thus, $n = n_k \times$

$m_1 \times \cdots \times m_k$ at each intermediate stage. Two cases arise, of course. (1) If $r = 0$, then we need to generate βj, recording a successful division, and in (a) replace n_k by q and r by j, to get ready for another division (since we will use Div, which destroys both dividend and divisor). (2) If $r \neq 0$, then increase j by 1, and in (a) replace r by the new j and replace q by n_k. In either of these cases, at this point (when Div is about to be applied again) the contents of R will be

$$n_k \, \gamma \, n_k * j \, \alpha \, j \, \beta \, m_k \, \beta \, m_{k-1} \ldots \beta \, m_1 \tag{b}$$

(The reader should try this process for $n = 12$ to believe it!)

Since our initial content of R is just n, we are lacking only the termination condition. It is clearly unnecessary to test as a factor of an integer s any integer t such that $t > \sqrt{s}$, since if $t > \sqrt{s}$ and divides s, then $w = s/t$ is a divisor of s such that $w \leq \sqrt{s}$. (Otherwise, if $w > \sqrt{s}$, we would have $wt > \sqrt{s}\sqrt{s} = s$, contradicting the definition of w.) If we thus restrict ourselves to divisors up to $\sqrt{s}$, we would catch w in this case instead of t. In other words, if we have not found a divisor of s below $\sqrt{s}$, there will not be one greater than $\sqrt{s}$. Therefore, as soon as $j > \sqrt{n_k}$, or equivalently $j^2 > n_k$, the process may be terminated, remembering that the final n_k is to be retained as a factor. The control algorithm $\widetilde{H0}$ which governs the entire iteration must leave a nonempty result if $j^2 \leq n_k$, and an empty result otherwise. To generate $\widetilde{H0}$, we will first focus, after obtaining (b) above, on the substring between γ and α: Let $\widetilde{K0}, \widetilde{K1}$ be the algorithms

> **algorithm** $\widetilde{K0}(G, \alpha, \beta, \gamma, \delta, *)$;
> 0: $* \rightarrow \delta$. **end**

> **algorithm** $\widetilde{K1}(G, \alpha, \beta, \gamma, \delta, *)$;
> 0: $\delta \rightarrow *$. **end**

Let $\widetilde{K2}$ be the algorithm Copy of the preceding section that generated $P \alpha P$ from P, except modified to generate $P * P$ instead. Then the control algorithm $\widetilde{H0}$, whose input is (b) above, may be written

$$\widetilde{H0} = \underline{\gamma}| \, (\text{Less} \circ \widetilde{K1} \circ \underline{\delta}| \, \text{Mult} \, \lfloor \Lambda \circ \underline{\delta}| \, \widetilde{K2} \, \lfloor \Lambda \circ \widetilde{K0}) \, \lfloor \alpha$$

remembering that the control algorithm Less applied to $n_k * j^2$ leaves R empty if $n_k < j^2$, nonempty otherwise. Looking just at the part on which $\widetilde{H0}$ focuses, we find that the following strings will be produced in succession, assuming that $j^2 > n_k$:

$$n_k * j, \quad n_k \delta j, \quad n_k \delta j \alpha j, \quad n_k \delta j^2, \quad n_k * j^2, \quad \Lambda.$$

We may now ask what the body $\widetilde{H2}$ of the iteration looks like, remembering that it is to be applied to (b). When $\widetilde{H0}$ determines that $n_k \geq j^2$, we must divide n_k by j to produce $q * r$, which is in the form of (a), and then ask whether $r = 0$ or $r \neq 0$. We have then that

$$\widetilde{H2} = \widetilde{H3}\,(\widetilde{L1}, \widetilde{L2}) \circ \underline{\gamma|}\,\mathrm{Div}\,\underline{|\alpha}$$

where $\widetilde{L1}$ and $\widetilde{L2}$ carry out the manipulation of cases (1) and (2) above, and $\widetilde{H3}$ is the trivial control algorithm $\widetilde{L0}$ focused onto r:

> **algorithm $\widetilde{L0}(G)$;**
> $0: \rightarrow .$ **end**

[The explicit forms of $\widetilde{L1}$ and $\widetilde{L2}$ are asked for in Exercise 1.5.4.]

We must now make sure that we can get from the initial input datum (which is just n), to the generral form (b) that the iteration expects as the contents of R. Since there are not expected to be any β's yet, and initially $j = 2$, we need an algorithm $\widetilde{H4}$ which generates the initial form

$$n\,\gamma\,n * 2\,\alpha\,2$$

which is

$$n_k\,\gamma\,n_k * j\,\alpha\,j$$

for $n_k = n$ and $j = 2$. [$\widetilde{H4}$ is asked for in Exercise 1.5.5.] The final form of the total algorithm, then, is

$$\widetilde{H6} = \widetilde{H0}\,(\underline{*|}\,\widetilde{L0}\,\underline{|\alpha}\,(\widetilde{L1}, \widetilde{L2}) \circ \underline{\gamma|}\,\mathrm{Div}\,\underline{|\alpha}) \circ \widetilde{H4}$$

except for cleaning up the result after it has been determined that $j^2 > n_k$, and no further divisions are possible. At this point R contains a string in form (b) above, and we need to delete the substring

$$\gamma\,n_k * j\,\alpha\,j$$

Let $\widetilde{H7}$ be

> **algorithm $\widetilde{H7}(G, *, \alpha, \beta, \gamma)$; $\mathbf{G} \cup \boldsymbol{\alpha} \cup * \xi$;**
> $0: \gamma\xi \rightarrow \gamma$;
> $1: \gamma \rightarrow \quad$;
> $2: \beta \rightarrow *$;
> $3: \quad \rightarrow .$ **end**

Then $\widetilde{H8} = \widetilde{H7} \circ \widetilde{H6}$ leaves the desired prime factors in R, separated by $*$'s.

A good deal of the complicated description and notation in the preceding discussion is due to the weakness of our language when it comes to specifying just what it is we wish to have happen to the data. If we could have stated in simple terms the successive transformations needed on the data, the entire activity would seem quite simple. Since the transformations on the data are generally chosen before the detailed steps of a specific algorithm are determined, a useful tactic would be to state precisely what transformations are desired and then deduce the algorithm from them. The creation of algorithms by such an algorithmic activity is the essence of programming. A treatment of string transformations which makes this activity quite automatic will be given in Section 1.10.† In that section the prime number algorithm just discussed will be deduced in this way from a description of string transformations.

EXERCISES 1.5

1. Give the control algorithm Greater which starts with $n * m$ and leaves R empty if $n > m$, and nonempty otherwise.

2. Prove: $\gcd(m, n) = \gcd(m - n, n)$ if $m \geq n$
$$= \gcd(m, n - m) \quad \text{if} \quad m < n$$

3. The algorithm $\widetilde{H0}$, which produces, from $n * m$ in R,

$$\begin{array}{ll} \Lambda & \text{if} \quad m \mid n \\ \alpha & \text{if} \quad m \nmid n \\ \infty & \text{if} \quad m = 0, n \neq 0 \end{array}$$

is as shown at the top of p. 33.

Apply $\widetilde{H0}$ to

1) $1111 * 11$

2) $11 * 1111$

3) $111 * 11$

4) $* 11$

5) $11 *$

6) What happens when $\widetilde{H0}$ is applied to $*$ (that is, $0 \div 0$)? Is this the conventional interpretation?

---

† As will be seen, the treatment there uses a representation for the data which is not appropriate for a "Markov machine," so the result is an algorithm for a "machine" other than the one we have been considering. For us, therefore, it remains an algorithmic activity.

algorithm $\widetilde{H0}(G, *)$

0:	$bc \rightarrow cb$;
1:	$xc \rightarrow cx$;
2:	$y1 \rightarrow cby$;
3:	$y \rightarrow$;
4:	$1*c \rightarrow *$;
5:	$b \rightarrow 1$;
6:	$x \rightarrow$;
7:	$1*1 \rightarrow 1*xy1$;
8:	$1* \rightarrow 11*$;
9:	$*c \rightarrow \alpha$;
10:	$\alpha c \rightarrow \alpha$;
11:	$\alpha 1 \rightarrow \alpha$;
12:	$\alpha \rightarrow \alpha$. ;
13:	$*1 \rightarrow *$;
14:	$* \rightarrow$. **end**

Algorithm for Exercise 3

7) Modify $\widetilde{H0}$ so that $0 \div 0 = \beta$ (i.e., indeterminate). Hint: All that need be done is to alter rules 13 and 14 and add 3 more rules.

4. Give the explicit forms of $\widetilde{L1}$ and $\widetilde{L2}$. Hint: Let $\widetilde{L1} = \widetilde{L13} \circ \widetilde{L12} \circ \widetilde{L11}$ and $\widetilde{L2} = \widetilde{L24} \circ \widetilde{L23} \circ \widetilde{L22} \circ \widetilde{L21}$, where $\widetilde{L21}$ deletes q and r, and the others accomplish the tasks indicated in the text.

5. Give the explicit form of $\widetilde{H4}$, the initializing algorithm.

1.6 MARKOV ALGORITHMS WITH LABELS

In the construction of Markov algorithms it has probably become clear that it is difficult to organize the ordering of initial, intermediate, and terminal conditions of the algorithm, since the control rule is so rigid. A more flexible control regime would really be desirable; i.e., a modification of Markov algorithms is needed which has more flexibility in the sequencing rule. On the other hand, since a wealth of theoretical results have been obtained for Markov's very general theory of algorithms, any modification of the nature of these algorithms should carry with it a proof that (1) each "modified" algorithm is equivalent to some Markov algorithm, and (2) every Markov algorithm has an equivalent "modified" algorithm.

We first describe the "modification" and then give the general construction by which any "modified" algorithm may be corresponded to an equivalent Markov algorithm, and any Markov algorithm corresponded to an equivalent "modified" algorithm. A "modified" algorithm hereafter shall be called a "labeled Markov algorithm " or LMA.

A labeled Markov algorithm has the same form and interpretation as an MA, except that between the RHS of a rule numbered k and the semicolon or **end** symbol there may appear either (1) a period, (2) a comma followed by an integer j_k, or (3) nothing. Examples of these three cases are

$$1)\quad 3:\beta \to . \ ;$$
$$2)\quad 3:\beta \to , 6;$$
$$3)\quad 3:\beta \to \ ;$$

In (1) and (3) the sequencing is as before. In (2) the scan for the next applicable rule continues from rule j_k if rule k was applicable, otherwise from rule $k + 1$. (j_k is called the *successor label* of rule k.) The successor of a rule of type (3), which has no explicit successor label j_k, is thus seen to be rule 0.

It follows immediately that an ordinary MA is already an LMA, and we therefore need not use a special designation for LMA's. Let us consider some examples of LMA's. (In each case the reader should try an example to see how the algorithm really works.)

1. The algorithm Reverse for reversing the characters in a string P:

> **algorithm** Reverse(A); **A** ξ, η;
> 0: $\to \alpha$, 1;
> 1: $\alpha\xi\eta \to \eta\alpha\xi$, 1;
> 2: $\xi\eta \to \alpha\xi\eta$, 1;
> 3: $\alpha \to$, 3;
> 4: $\to$. **end**

This may be compared with the original MA given earlier:

> **algorithm** Reverse(A); **A** ξ, η;
> 0: $\alpha\alpha \to \beta$;
> 1: $\beta\alpha \to \beta$;
> 2: $\beta\xi \to \xi\beta$;
> 3: $\beta \to$. ;
> 4: $\alpha\xi\eta \to \eta\alpha\xi$;
> 5: $\to \alpha$ **end**

2. The algorithm Copy for producing $P\alpha P$ from P:

> **algorithm** Copy(A, α); **A** ξ, η;
> 0: $\to \alpha\nu$, 3;
> 1: $\eta\xi\beta \to \xi\beta\eta$, 1;
> 2: $\alpha\xi\beta \to \xi\alpha$, 3;
> 3: $\nu\xi \to \xi\beta\xi\nu$, 1;
> 4: $\nu \to$. **end**

3. The algorithm for forming the product of two integers represented in R as $n * m$:

> **algorithm** Mult$(G, *)$;
> 0: $1 * \;\to\; * a$, 4;
> 1: $* 1 \;\to\; *$, 1;
> 2: $b \;\to\; 1$, 2;
> 3: $* \;\to\;$. ;
> 4: $b 1 \;\to\; 1 b$, 4;
> 5: $a 1 \;\to\; 1 b a$, 4;
> 6: $a \;\to\;$, 0 **end**

Note that this LMA is shorter by one rule than the earlier MA version, and its control flow is much more obvious.

4. The algorithm Div for producing $q * r$, representing the quotient q and remainder r of two integers $n * m$, so that $n = q \times m + r$:

> **algorithm** Div$(G, *)$;
> 0: $1 c \;\;\to\; c 1$, 0;
> 1: $c * b \to c *$, 1;
> 2: $b \;\;\;\to\; 1$, 2;
> 3: $b 1 \;\;\to\; 1 b$, 3;
> 4: $1 * 1 \to * b$, 3;
> 5: $* b \;\;\to\; c * b$, 0;
> 6: $* 1 \;\;\to\; *$, 6;
> 7: $1 * \;\;\to\; 1 1 *$, 7;
> 8: $b \;\;\;\to\; 1$, 8;
> 9: $c \;\;\;\to\; 1$, 9;
> 10: $\;\to\;$. **end**

[Exercise 1.6.1 asks for the rest of the arithmetic MA's in Section 1.5.]

We have already seen that every MA is already an LMA. Suppose now that one has an LMA $\tilde{H}$. An equivalent MA can be constructed as follows: Let the alphabet of $\tilde{H}$ be A and the highest rule number $n - 1$, so that $\tilde{H}$ has n rules. We shall make use of a new alias alphabet, A^{-1}, as well as $A = A^0, A^1, A^2, \ldots, A^n$, and the $2n + 2$ characters $\alpha = \alpha^0$, $\alpha^1, \ldots, \alpha^n, \beta = \beta^0, \beta^1, \ldots, \beta^n$, none of which are in

$$\bigcup_{i=-1}^{n} A^i$$

Let $B^i = A^i \cup \alpha^i \cup \beta^i$, $i = 0, 1, \ldots, n$, so that the B^i form a set of aliases as well, with $B = B^0 = A \cup \alpha \cup \beta$. (We shall not need B^{-1}.) We now begin to modify the LMA $\tilde{H}$. It will be clear that at each step we obtain an equivalent algorithm. The reader will probably find it useful to carry out the construction which follows for a simple algorithm, such as Copy in example 2 above, while reading this development.

For each terminal rule, delete the period and designate its successor as the rule labeled n. Any rule without an explicit successor is then given the successor 0. Now define a set S of integer pairs, $S = \{(r, s)\}$, whose members are determined as follows:

a) For all k such that $-1 \leq k \leq n - 1$, the pair $(k, k + 1)$ is in S.

b) If the successor of rule k is $j_k \neq k$, then the pair (k, j_k) is in S.

c) There are no pairs in S except those arising from (a) and (b).

For each pair (r, s) in S, construct the MA:

$$\text{algorithm } S_{rs}(B); \mathbf{B} \, \rho;$$
$$0: \rho^r \alpha^s \to \alpha^s \rho^r;$$
$$1: \alpha^s \rho^r \to \rho^s \alpha^s;$$
$$2: \qquad \to . \qquad \mathbf{end}$$

Its purpose is to intercept control whenever the contents of R are in alphabet A^r but contain an α^s. The leftmost such α^s is used to convert the entire contents of R to the alphabet B^s. The (nonclosed) algorithm obtained by appending all of these MA's together (in any order, with termination rules deleted) will be called $\widetilde{H}1$. Now replace (in the LMA $\widetilde{H}$) each rule of the form

$$k: Q_1 \to Q_2, j; \qquad \text{(or } j \text{ end)}$$

by
$$\begin{cases} k: Q_1^k \to \alpha^j Q_2^k; & \text{(or end)} & \text{if } j \neq k \\ k: Q_1^k \to Q_2^k \; ; & & \text{if } j = k \end{cases}$$

Each rule with a nonempty left-hand side is thus transformed into a rule which is applicable only if the data are in alphabet B^k; and if it is applicable, with successor statement j, it provides the α^j (when necessary) to convert the data to alphabet B^j (via S_{kj}). Now to make sure that empty left-hand sides don't bypass the selection of applicable rules by choice of alphabet, we replace each rule of the form

$$k: \Lambda \to Q_2, j \; ; \qquad \text{(or } j \text{ end)}$$

by
$$\begin{cases} k: \beta^k \to \alpha^j \beta^k Q_2; & \text{(or end)} & \text{if } j \neq k \\ k: \beta^k \to \beta^k Q_2 \; ; & & \text{if } j = k \end{cases}$$

The MA obtained in this way from $\widetilde{H}$ will be called $\widetilde{H}2$. Now for each $k, 0 \leq k \leq n - 1$, construct the MA

$$\text{algorithm } E_k(B);$$
$$0: \alpha^k \to \alpha^{k+1};$$
$$1: \qquad \to . \qquad \mathbf{end}$$

The nonclosed algorithm obtained by appending all of these E_k algorithms together (again with termination rules deleted) will be called $\widetilde{H3}$. Should the contents of R at some stage be in alphabet B^k, but rule k not be applicable, then one of the rules in $\widetilde{H3}$ will convert α^k to α^{k+1}, one of the pairs of rules in $\widetilde{H1}$ will convert the contents of R to alphabet B^{k+1}, and rule $k + 1$ will be the next available rule because it is the only one in alphabet B^{k+1}.

We must now provide for returning the final contents of R to the alphabet A and getting rid of β^n and the α's. Note that after the invocation of a pair of rules in $\widetilde{H1}$ to convert the data to some alphabet B^k, we always find all of the α's converted to α^k, and they are all at the right end of the data. We therefore define $\widetilde{H4}$ as follows:

> **algorithm** $\widetilde{H4}(A, \alpha, \beta)$; $\mathbf{A} \cup \boldsymbol{\beta}\ \xi$;
> $0: \alpha^n \alpha^n \rightarrow \alpha^n$;
> $1: \xi^n \alpha^n \rightarrow \alpha^n \xi$;
> $2: \alpha^n \beta \rightarrow .$ **end**

All that is needed now is a means of getting started. We will assume that R is initially in alphabet A^{-1} (so that no rules are applicable until we have initialized properly), and we define the nonclosed algorithm $\widetilde{H5}$ as follows:

> **algorithm** $\widetilde{H5}$
> $0: \rightarrow \beta^0 \alpha^0$ **end**

We must make sure that $\widetilde{H5}$ will be applied only once; then $S_{-1,0}$ will switch the contents of R to alphabet A^0, and the original rule 0 of the LMA will be the first rule tested. It should now be clear that the algorithm $\widetilde{H}' = \widetilde{H1}; \widetilde{H2}; \widetilde{H3}; \widetilde{H4}; \widetilde{H5}$ is the MA equivalent to the original LMA $\widetilde{H}$. [Exercise 1.6.2 asks for an MA equivalent to the LMA Copy.]

We have now shown that MA's and LMA's are equivalent representations of algorithmic activities, in that each gives rise in a natural way to the other, and any activity expressible in one is expressible in the other. As a by-product of the process used to go from $\widetilde{H}$ to $\widetilde{H}'$, we can immediately extend our important constructions—appending, composition, two-way branching, and iteration—from MA's to LMA's, as follows:

Let $\widetilde{H0}$, $\widetilde{H1}$, and $\widetilde{H2}$ be LMA's with n_0, n_1, and n_2 rules, respectively, and with their corresponding MA's $\widetilde{H0}'$, $\widetilde{H1}'$, and $\widetilde{H2}'$. Then we define $\widetilde{H1}; \widetilde{H2}$ to be $\widetilde{H1}'; \widetilde{H2}'$, $\widetilde{H1} \circ \widetilde{H2}$ to be $\widetilde{H1}' \circ \widetilde{H2}'$, $\widetilde{H0}(\widetilde{H1}, \widetilde{H2})$ to be $\widetilde{H0}'(\widetilde{H1}', \widetilde{H2}')$, and $\widetilde{H0}(\widetilde{H2})$ to be $\widetilde{H0}'(\widetilde{H2}')$. Since the MA's are LMA's already, there is no reason to change them further. The operations just defined produce LMA's which carry out the desired construction correctly. Unfortunately, the definitions just given involve many alias alphabets, and a great deal of "red tape" manipulations. These manipulations and aliases fall into two classes: Some are used to focus attention on part of the contents of R, and some are used to control the sequencing, i.e., to make sure that certain rules are tested for applicability before (or instead of) others. Using labeled Markov algorithms doesn't help at all in the focusing problem; one still needs punctuation characters. LMA's do help in the sequencing control, however, and that was the main reason for introducing them. The labels designating successor rules do for LMA's the job that aliases do for MA's in controlling sequencing; in fact, they do a better and more economical job. It should be unnecessary, therefore, to incur the overhead implicit in the definitions of appending, composition, two-way branching, and iteration given above. We therefore withdraw these definitions, and we shall introduce independent constructions instead.

1. Appending $\widetilde{H2}$ to $\widetilde{H1}$ is carried out exactly as before; i.e., the combined heading is formed in the same way, it is followed by $\widetilde{H1}$ with its **end** replaced by a semicolon, followed by $\widetilde{H2}$. Now, however, instead of adding only to every label of $\widetilde{H2}$ the number n_1 of rules of $\widetilde{H1}$, we add n_1 to every label *and successor label* of $\widetilde{H2}$. We shall still denote the result by $\widetilde{H1}; \widetilde{H2}$. It should be definitely understood, however, that this is a new Append operation. If the LMA's under consideration happen to be MA's (i.e., all successor labels are null or zero), we do not get the old Append operation again, nor do we obtain an MA as a result. [This difference will be explored further in Exercise 1.6.3.] Henceforth only the new Append will be used.

2. In order to define the composition of two algorithms, we shall find it convenient to use one more notational device. Given an LMA $\tilde{H}$, we write $\tilde{H}_r$ for the algorithm obtained from $\tilde{H}$ as follows:

$$\tilde{H}_r \equiv \frac{\tilde{H}(A,\ Q_1\ '\to'\ Q_2\ '.')}{\tilde{H}_r(A,\ Q_1\ '\to'\ Q_2\ ',' r)}$$

Thus, $\tilde{H}_r$ is obtained by sending control in $\tilde{H}$ to rule r whenever it would otherwise have terminated. The one additional stipulation on the use of this notation is that whenever the algorithm $\tilde{H}_r$ is appended to another algorithm, the substitution of r for the terminal period is to be performed after the translation of successor labels implied by the appending operation. In effect, r is not to be translated. (This will allow the successor designation to be applied to fixed rules within the total construction.)

The composition $\tilde{H3}$ of $\tilde{H1}$ and $\tilde{H2}$ is immediately available:

$$\tilde{H3} = \tilde{H1} \circ \tilde{H2} = \tilde{H2}_{n_2}; \tilde{H1}$$

Remember that the new Append operation is being used here. The operation of composition may be extended immediately to apply to several algorithms. Let $\tilde{H1}, \tilde{H2}, \ldots, H_m$ be LMA's, with $\tilde{Hk}$ having n_k rules, $1 \leq k \leq m$. Let

$$s_k = \sum_{i=0}^{m-k} n_{m-i}$$

so that $s_m = n_m$, $s_{m-1} = n_m + n_{m-1}, \ldots, s_2 = n_m + \cdots + n_2$. Then $\tilde{H1} \circ \tilde{H2} \circ \cdots \circ \tilde{Hm} = \tilde{Hm}_{s_m}; \ldots; \tilde{H2}_{s_2}; \tilde{H1}$.

3. We recall now the "focusing" operation that produced $\sigma\lfloor \tilde{H} \lfloor \tau$ from $\tilde{H}$, so that when $P = Q_1 \sigma Q_2 \tau Q_3$ we have $\sigma\lfloor \tilde{H} \lfloor \tau(P) = Q_1 \sigma \tilde{H}(Q_2) \tau Q_3$. This new focused algorithm was obtained by changing rules in $\tilde{H}$ with empty LHS's, such as $\Lambda \to Q$, to work to the right of σ, that is, to be $\sigma \to \sigma Q$, and composing the modified algorithm between two other algorithms which changed the alphabet outside σ and τ to an alias and back again. Using the new definition of composition, we may retain this construction, and so we retain the focusing notation as well.

4. It will be recalled that a two-way branching algorithm consisted of a control algorithm $\tilde{H0}$ and two branches $\tilde{H1}$ and $\tilde{H2}$, with the result $\tilde{H1}(P)$ if $\tilde{H0}(P) = \Lambda$ and $\tilde{H2}(P)$ if $\tilde{H0}(P) \neq \Lambda$. Remembering that the process of building a branch algorithm began by invoking Copy to produce $P\alpha P$ in R, we next define $\tilde{K0}$ (nonclosed) to recognize whether there are any characters of A to the left of α in R or not.

> **algorithm** $\tilde{K0}(A, \alpha)$; **A** ξ;
> 0: $\xi\alpha \to \beta$, 1;
> 1: $\xi\beta \to \beta$, 1;
> 2: $\beta \to$. ;
> 3: $\alpha \to$, 3 **end**

The algorithm $\tilde{K0}$ deletes α and everything that may be to its left. The difference between the presence or absence of characters to the left of α is reflected in an exit from $\tilde{K0}$ via the termination rule 2, or by dropping through rule 3, once α has been deleted. Now the two-way branch $\tilde{H3} = \tilde{H0}(\tilde{H1}, \tilde{H2})$ is formed as follows:

$$\tilde{H3} = (\tilde{K0}_{n_1+4}; \tilde{H1}; \tilde{H2}) \circ \underline{\Lambda}\lfloor \tilde{H0} \lfloor \alpha \circ \text{Copy}$$

Note that the change in the terminal rule of $\widetilde{K0}$ implied by the subscript $n_1 + 4$ is the key to the entire construction and is greatly facilitated by the use of successor labels. The constant 4 results from the fixed number of rules in $\widetilde{K0}$.

5. For the iteration of $\widetilde{H2}$ under control of $\widetilde{H0}$, we define $\widetilde{H1}$ to be the trivial terminal algorithm

$$\textbf{algorithm } \widetilde{H1}(A);$$
$$0: \rightarrow . \textbf{ end}$$

Then, using $\widetilde{K0}$ as defined in construction 4,

$$\widetilde{H3} = \widetilde{H0}(\widetilde{H2}) = (\widetilde{K0}_5; \widetilde{H1}; \widetilde{H2}_0) \circ \underline{\Delta|}\ \widetilde{H0}\ \underline{|\alpha} \circ \text{Copy}$$

EXERCISES 1.6

1. Give the Labeled Markov Algorithms for the following arithmetic algorithms:
   a) Plus
   b) Diff
   c) Less
   d) Greater
   e) Quot_k
   f) Odd
   g) GCD
   h) The LMA which produces from $n * m$ in R

$$\begin{array}{lll} \Lambda & \text{if} & m \mid n \\ \alpha & \text{if} & m \nmid n \\ \infty & \text{if} & m = 0, n \neq 0 \\ \beta & \text{if} & m = 0, n = 0 \end{array}$$

2. Change the Labeled Markov Algorithm Copy in Section 1.6 into its equivalent Markov Algorithm and then apply the MA to a^{-1} (that is, the element a in alphabet A^{-1}).

3. Let two LMA's (which are also MA's) be defined as follows:

$$\begin{array}{ll} \widetilde{H2}(A, \alpha, \beta); \text{A } \xi; & \widetilde{H1}(A, \alpha, \beta); \text{A } \xi; \\ 0: \alpha \rightarrow \beta ; & 0: \beta \rightarrow \alpha; \\ 1: \xi\beta \rightarrow \beta\xi; & 1: \alpha\xi \rightarrow \xi\alpha; \\ 2: \quad \rightarrow . \textbf{ end} & 2: \quad \rightarrow . \textbf{ end} \end{array}$$

Append the two algorithms as $\widetilde{H}2$; $\widetilde{H}1$ (after deleting the termination rule of $\widetilde{H}2$) first in the old way, not altering successor labels, and then in the new way. Apply both new algorithms to the string $a\alpha b\alpha c$.

1.7. SUBALGORITHMS

A common difficulty in the use of composition of algorithms is that one algorithm must terminate before the other begins. It frequently happens that one would like to insert the execution of an algorithm $\widetilde{H}2$ at several intermediate points of another algorithm $\widetilde{H}1$. More precisely, one should be able to indicate at each of several places in $\widetilde{H}1$ that $\widetilde{H}2$ is to be executed (i.e., *called*), and in each case sequencing should continue afterward from the point in $\widetilde{H}1$ where it happened. An algorithm invoked as $\widetilde{H}2$ in this description is referred to as a *subordinate algorithm*, or *subalgorithm*).† It behaves as if it were a single rule inserted in many places, but it should have to appear explicitly only once.

The principal problem introduced by subalgorithms is that there are several possible successors to the execution of $\widetilde{H}2$; that is, the successor of each rule invoking $\widetilde{H}2$ is a possible successor to $\widetilde{H}2$. Thus we may visualize a typical situation:

algorithm $\widetilde{H}1(A)$;
0: ..., 1 ;
1: ..., $\widetilde{H}2$;
2: ..., 3 ;
3: ..., $\widetilde{H}2$;
4: ....   **end**

If rule 1 is applicable, then $\widetilde{H}2$ is called (i.e., executed), and its successor is rule 2. If rule 3 is applicable, $\widetilde{H}2$ is executed with rule 4 as its successor. If rule 1 (or 3) is not applicable, then $\widetilde{H}2$ is not executed, and rule 2 (or 4) is the successor in the usual way. The following construction sets up the correct returns from $\widetilde{H}2$.

Let $\widetilde{H}2$ have n_2 rules, and let $\widetilde{H}1$ have n_1 rules, including m_2 calls on $\widetilde{H}2$. We shall construct an algorithm $\widetilde{D}2$ (called the *switching directory for $\widetilde{H}2$*), but first we define an alphabet $D = \{\alpha_1, \alpha_2, \ldots, \alpha_{m_2}\}$, consisting of

---

† Another term often used is *subroutine*, perhaps a nostalgic reference to the good old days of vaudeville, in which a sequence of steps to be performed was known as a *routine*.

characters not in the data alphabets of (or used as local variables in) $\tilde{H}2$ and $\tilde{H}1$, to be called the *linking alphabet*. Then we let j_i $(i = 1, 2, \ldots, m_2)$ be the label of the ith calling rule in $\tilde{H}1$, so that the return after execution of the ith call on $\tilde{H}2$ is to be made to rule $j_i + 1$. Then we write:

$$\text{algorithm } \tilde{D}2(A, D); \mathbf{D}\ \xi;\ \mathbf{A}\ \eta;$$

$$
\begin{array}{llll}
0: \alpha_1 & \rightarrow & , j_1 + 1 - (n_2 + n_1); \\
1: \alpha_2 & \rightarrow & , j_2 + 1 - (n_2 + n_1); \\
\quad \vdots \\
m_2 - 1: \alpha_{m_2} & \rightarrow & , j_{m_2} + 1 - (n_2 + n_1); \\
\quad m_2: & \rightarrow \alpha_1 & , 2m_2 & ; \\
m_2 + 1: & \rightarrow \alpha_2 & , 2m_2 & ; \\
\quad \vdots \\
2m_2 - 1: & \rightarrow \alpha_{m_2} & , 2m_2 & ; \\
\quad 2m_2: \xi\eta & \rightarrow \eta\xi & , 2m_2 & ; \\
2m_2 + 1: & \rightarrow & . & \textbf{end}
\end{array}
$$

where the use of negative labels $j_i + 1 - (n_2 + n_1)$ is a temporary device, necessary so that in the relabeling process implied below in the appending of $\tilde{D}2$ after $\tilde{H}1$ and $\tilde{H}2$, the resulting labels will refer back correctly into $\tilde{H}1$. Now the algorithm which has the linkage sufficient to call $\tilde{H}2$ correctly is obtained by the following procedure.

1. In the ith calling rule in $\tilde{H}1$ replace the name $\tilde{H}2$ by $n_2 + n_1 + m_2 + i$ (for $i = 1, \ldots, m_2$).

2. Include D as part of the data alphabet in the headings of $\tilde{H}1$ and $\tilde{H}2$.

3. Then form the desired algorithm:

$$\tilde{H}1;\ \tilde{H}2_{n_2 + n_1};\ \tilde{D}2_{n_1}$$

keeping in mind the following diagram.

Original numbering		New numbering
0 to $n_1 - 1$ - - - $\boxed{\tilde{H}1}$	- - 0 to $n_1 - 1$
0 to $n_2 - 1$ - - - $\boxed{\tilde{H}2}$	- - n_1 to $n_2 + n_1 - 1$
0 to $2m_2 + 2$ - - $\boxed{\tilde{D}2}$	- - $n_2 + n_1$ to $n_2 + n_1 + 2m_2 + 2$

The strategy involved in constructing the above algorithm can be summarized as follows: When a call is to be made on $\tilde{H}2$, a jump is made instead to $\tilde{D}2$, entering at a rule specific to the call involved. A specific character associated with that call is thereby inserted into R, and it is moved to the right end of R just before a jump is made to $\tilde{H}2$. Whenever

$\tilde{H}2$ terminates, a jump is made directly to the first rule of $\tilde{D}2$, where an appropriate rule becomes applicable for the specific α involved, and a return is made to the correct place in $\tilde{H}1$. Figure 1.3 shows more clearly how the switching directory works. [Exercise 1.7.1 asks that a specific example be worked out.]

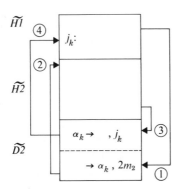

Figure 1.3

Unfortunately, the case we have just considered is too simple. It is usually true that $\tilde{H}2$, being subordinate, is to limit its applicability to a substring of the contents of R. *We establish the convention* that at the left (or right) end of the substring of interest to $\tilde{H}2$ will be placed the character γ (or α), chosen to avoid conflicts with data alphabets already involved; and $\tilde{H}2$ will be expected to focus on the substring set up by $\tilde{H}1$ between γ and α, so that one might have

$$\mu_1^1 \delta_1 \gamma \delta_2 \alpha \delta_3 \mu_2^1$$

where μ_1^1 and μ_2^1 are strings of characters converted to alphabet A^1 by some earlier process, and δ_1 and δ_3 are strings now to be excluded from consideration. The purpose here is to focus attention on the substring δ_2. We shall *establish the additional convention*, however, that if δ_1 (or δ_3) is empty, then γ (or α) need not be used. Since the linkage we are about to develop must work whether γ and α are present or not, it is necessarily more complicated (or potentially so, at least), but in a situation where we are asking the user of our notation to cooperate by inserting γ and α himself, anything we can do to make his life easier will be much appreciated, and it is well worth some additional effort on our part. If, however, an appreciable amount of extra computation results—i.e., if we incur a sizable overhead—we might choose to ask him to carry the burden instead. In this particular case, we shall carry through with the conventions just stated, and we shall have to ensure at all times that the most general case is handled properly. We remark in passing that we cannot use our focusing notation (for example $\sigma|\,H\,|\tau$) in this context, because we never know here where the focusing is to be done *until the algorithm is being executed*.

We must also look very carefully at the situation which arises when the subalgorithm calls in turn on some other subalgorithm to see if any conflicts arise. In particular, we must consider the case in which $\widetilde{H2}$ calls upon itself. (An algorithm which calls on itself as a subalgorithm is said to be *recursive*.) Certainly only one copy of each subalgorithm should have to be included in the construction, so the process of replacing occurrences of the name $\widetilde{H2}$ (as a successor) by integers must include all such occurrences found in all subalgorithms to be included in the construction. As we shall see, at worst this implies an enlargement of the switching directory.

A more likely source of trouble, however, is the multiplicity of characters in D which may appear at various times in R. We must be sure that if we are several calls "deep," (1) the return from $\widetilde{H2}$ is made under the influence of the correct α_k, and (2) the defocusing is performed just to the point where the still focused substring is the correct one for the rule to which the return is made. In other words, as we move down "calling levels" by successive subalgorithm calls, we may visualize a succession of focusings on "nested" substrings. Eventually it will be time to start back up the chain by returning to the point of the most recent call. The focused substring must be restored to that which existed prior to the most recent call, except of course for any modifications caused by the action of the subalgorithm which just finished execution.

Let us follow the appearance of the data in R through several stages, and specify at each step what we wish to have happen. At a typical point in the process some subalgorithm will be working on substrings $\delta_1\delta_2\delta_3$ possibly surrounded by strings of characters in A^1:

$$\mu_1^1\delta_1\delta_2\delta_3\mu_2^1$$

As we shall see shortly, the linkage that will have brought us to this subalgorithm will have inserted a character β^1 (chosen to avoid data alphabet conflicts) at the right end of μ_1^1, so the string above is really of the form

$$\mu_0^1\beta^1\delta_1\delta_2\delta_3\mu_2^1$$

and we shall use this fact later.

Now suppose that this subalgorithm is about to call on another one. Just prior to the call, γ and α are inserted:

$$\mu_0^1\beta^1\delta_1\gamma\delta_2\alpha\delta_3\mu_2^1$$

so the called subalgorithm is to "see" only δ_2, and the call is made. The following steps will occur as part of the linkage. We insert $\beta\alpha_k$ just to the left of δ_1:

$$\mu_0^1\beta^1\beta\alpha_k\delta_1\gamma\delta_2\alpha\delta_3\mu_2^1$$

where α_k is specific to the call. We then move α_k to the right of δ_3, and β to the right of γ:

$$\mu_0^1 \beta^1 \delta_1 \gamma \beta \delta_2 \alpha \delta_3 \alpha_k \mu_2^1$$

and convert $\delta_1 \gamma \beta$ and $\alpha \delta_3 \alpha_k$ to alphabet A^1:

$$\mu_0^1 \beta^1 \delta_1^1 \gamma^1 \beta^1 \delta_2 \alpha^1 \delta_3^1 \alpha_k^1 \mu_2^1$$

Now the called subalgorithm is invoked, and we assume that it replaces δ_2 with a string ϵ:

$$\mu_0^1 \beta^1 \delta_1^1 \gamma^1 \beta^1 \epsilon \alpha^1 \delta_3^1 \alpha_k^1 \mu_2^1$$

(Note that in this process the character just to the left of δ_2 was β^1, as required.) Now the return linkage must replace $\delta_1^1 \gamma^1 \beta^1$ by $\delta_1 \gamma$, and $\alpha^1 \delta_3^1 \alpha_k^1$ by $\alpha \delta_3$, to eliminate the last vestige of the call. We are now back to the level in which the last call was made. Note that if the γ and α are to be eliminated, it is up to the algorithm that introduced them to do it, which is certainly appropriate. The procedure just described traced the action of a single subalgorithm call. It should be clear that this action is independent of the level at which it occurs, since (1) we have restored the contents of R to the same form as before the call and (2) during the action of the called subalgorithm, the contents of R again had the same form, making still deeper calls possible.

We first construct the focusing algorithm $\widetilde{K0}$, assuming that the characters $\beta \alpha_k$ have just been inserted.

algorithm $\widetilde{K0}(A, \alpha, \beta, \gamma)$; $\mathbf{A} \cup \boldsymbol{\alpha} \cup \boldsymbol{\gamma}\ \xi$;	*Comments*
$\mathbf{D}\ \eta$; $\mathbf{A} \cup \boldsymbol{\alpha}\ \tau$; $\mathbf{A} \cup \mathbf{D}\ \sigma, \rho$;	
0: $\beta\eta\xi \rightarrow \xi\beta\eta$, 0;	Move $\beta\alpha_k$ to right of δ_3.
1: $\tau\beta \rightarrow \beta\tau$, 1;	Move β left to γ.
2: $\beta \rightarrow \beta^1$, 3;	
3: $\gamma \rightarrow \gamma^1$, 4;	
4: $\sigma\gamma \rightarrow \sigma^1\gamma^1$, 5;	Convert to the left of γ.
5: $\rho\sigma^1 \rightarrow \rho^1\sigma^1$, 5;	
6: $\alpha \rightarrow \alpha^1$, 7;	
7: $\alpha^1\sigma \rightarrow \alpha^1\sigma^1$, 8;	Convert to the right of α.
8: $\sigma^1\rho \rightarrow \sigma^1\rho^1$, 8;	
9: $\rightarrow$. **end**	(To be changed to jump to $\widetilde{H2}$.)

In order to do the defocusing on the return—but before α_k is deleted, so we don't lose the return indication—we shall insert the defocusing algorithm as the first five rules at the head of the switching directory $\widetilde{D2}$.

algorithm $\tilde{D}2(A, \alpha, \beta, \gamma)$; $\mathbf{D}\,\eta$; $\mathbf{A} \cup \boldsymbol{\alpha}\,\xi$;   *Comments*
$\mathbf{A} \cup \boldsymbol{\gamma}\,\sigma$;

0:	$\eta^1 \rightarrow$	$\phi\eta$, 1;	Restore leftmost α_k, mark with ϕ.
1:	$\xi^1\phi \rightarrow$	$\phi\xi$, 1;	Convert to the left of α_k.
2:	$\beta^1\phi \rightarrow$	$\phi\beta$, 3;	Convert rightmost β.
3:	$\sigma^1\phi \rightarrow$	$\phi\sigma$, 3;	Convert to left of γ.
4:	$\phi \rightarrow$	, 5;	
5:	$\alpha_1 \rightarrow$	, j_1 $+1-(n_2+n_1+10)$	Return to $\tilde{H}1$.
6:	$\alpha_2 \rightarrow$	, j_2 $+1-(n_2+n_1+10)$	

$\vdots$

m_2+4:	$\alpha_{m_2} \rightarrow$	, $j_{m_2}+1-(n_2+n_1+10)$	
m_2+5:		$\rightarrow \beta\alpha_1$.	(To be changed to a jump to $\tilde{K}0$)
m_2+6:		$\rightarrow \beta\alpha_2$.	

$\vdots$

$2m_2+4$: $\rightarrow \beta\alpha_{m_2}$. **end**

If there are calls on $\tilde{H}2$ from within $\tilde{H}2$ (that is, if for some i, j_i is a label in $\tilde{H}2$), then the appropriate rule in $\tilde{D}2$ (for example, $i+4$) should read

$$i+4: \alpha_i \rightarrow , j_i+1-(n_2+10)$$

To set up the new linkage now, we carry out the following steps, keeping in mind the following diagram.

Original numbering		New numbering
0 to n_1-1 - - - $\boxed{\tilde{H}1}$	- -	0 to n_1-1
0 to n_2-1 - - - $\boxed{\tilde{H}2}$	- -	n_1 to n_2+n_1-1
0 to 9 - - - - - $\boxed{\tilde{K}0}$	- -	n_2+n_1 to n_2+n_1+9
0 to $2m_2+4$ - - $\boxed{\tilde{D}2}$	- -	n_2+n_1+10 to $n_2+n_1+2m_2+14$

1. In the ith calling rule in $\tilde{H}1$ replace the name $\tilde{H}2$ by

$$n_2+n_1+m_2+14+i \qquad (i=1,\ldots,m_2)$$

2. Include $D \cup \alpha \cup \beta \cup \gamma$ as part of the data alphabet in the headings of $\tilde{H}1$ and $\tilde{H}2$.

3. In both $\tilde{H}1$ and $\tilde{H}2$ replace all rules with empty left sides

$$j: \quad \to Q, k;$$

by

$$j: \beta^1 \to \beta^1 Q, k;$$

4. Then form the desired algorithm

$$\tilde{H}1; \tilde{H}2_{n_2 + n_1 + 10}; \tilde{K}0_{n_1}; \tilde{D}2_{n_2 + n1}$$

[Exercise 1.7.2. asks that a specific example be worked out.]

Suppose now that we have another subalgorithm $\tilde{H}3$ with n_3 rules, and included in $\tilde{H}1$, $\tilde{H}2$, and $\tilde{H}3$ are m_3 calls on $\tilde{H}3$, in addition to the m_2 calls on $\tilde{H}2$ already discussed. How would the construction have to be modified from that given above? There is really no reason to modify anything already done. It suffices to form a switching directory $\tilde{D}3$ for $\tilde{H}3$, and follow the steps outlined above, using a second copy of $\tilde{K}0$ for focusing. We obtain

$$\tilde{H}1; \tilde{H}2_{n_2 + n_1 + 10}; \tilde{K}0_{n_1}; \tilde{D}2_{n_2 + n_1}; \tilde{H}3_{n_3 + q + 10}; \tilde{K}0_q; \tilde{D}3_{n_3 + q};$$

where $q = n_2 + n_1 + 10 + 2m_2 + 5$ represents the number of rules ahead of $\tilde{H}3$, and plays the same role that n_1 played in the case of $\tilde{H}1$ and $\tilde{H}2$ above. Calls on $\tilde{H}3$ must now be replaced by the successor labels $q + n_3 + m_3 + 14 + j$ $(j = 1, \ldots, m_3)$, just as before.

We may now describe the complete process of packaging a collection of algorithms calling upon one another as subalgorithms in as complicated a way as one can imagine by using the successor notation. There is really no reason to deny $\tilde{H}1$ its own calls as a subalgorithm; we may expect calls from any algorithm on any other. The only special property $\tilde{H}1$ has had is that it starts off the whole process.

Let us construct a "universal starter" $\tilde{H}0$ to call on $\tilde{H}1$ to get started, where $\tilde{H}1$ is to be the first executed of some collection $\tilde{H}1$, $\tilde{H}2, \ldots,$ $\tilde{H}n$ which we wish to package.

> **algorithm $\tilde{H}0$;**
> $0: \to , \tilde{H}1;$
> $1: \to .$ **end**

As we have seen, we must construct for each subalgorithm its own subpackage containing its switching directory, its focusing rules, and the subalgorithm itself, modified to eliminate empty LHS's. Before we can construct the switching directory, however, we must know how many calls will occur for the subalgorithm. This requires that all n algorithms which are to be packaged have been scanned to obtain these counts, and that there are no calls for algorithms not in the collection. (It usually happens that one starts with a smaller collection, and during the initial scan, one finds a number of calls on algorithms not in the collection. These are then brought in from a "library" of algorithms and made part of the collection. We shall assume that this has been done.) During this scanning, we may assume that it is determined that there are m_i calls for algorithm $\tilde{H}i$ (with $m_i > 0$), which consists of n_i rules $(i = 1, 2, \ldots, n)$†. If we agree to order the algorithms in the package $\tilde{H}0, \tilde{H}1, \tilde{H}2, \ldots, \tilde{H}n$, we may compute q_i, the number of rules above $\tilde{H}i$, as

$$q_1 = 2, \quad q_i = 2 + \sum_{j=1}^{i-1} (n_j + 2m_j + 15), \quad i = 2, \ldots, n$$

If we write $\tilde{D}1, \tilde{D}2, \ldots, \tilde{D}n$ for the switching directories of $\tilde{H}1, \ldots, \tilde{H}n$ and assume that the latter no longer have empty LHS's, then each sub-package has the form

$$\tilde{P}i = \tilde{H}i_{n_i + q_i + 10}; \tilde{K0}_{q_i}; \tilde{D}i_{n_i + q_i}$$

The final step is to append $\tilde{H}0, \tilde{P}1, \ldots, \tilde{P}n$ together, but at the same time replace names of algorithms used as successors by labels of the form $q_i + n_i + m_i + 14 + j$. It should be clear that although the algorithmic activity just described is complicated, it may be specified as an algorithm whose data consist of the algorithms in the collection and whose result is the final package. Such a packaging algorithm is usually called a *linking loader*.

By using such methods as have been described, algorithms may be collected and catalogued separately into libraries and then organized among themselves in different ways to form new algorithms, thus forming a growing abstract structure which bears certain interesting similarities to all known organizations. However, the purpose or plan of such an organization of algorithms can be revealed or understood only in terms of the way it is manipulated or—essentially the same thing—in terms of the behavior of some other algorithm operating on it as data. We shall take up this discussion in a later section.

EXERCISES 1.7

1. Let the alphabet $A = \{a, b, c, \beta, \delta, \epsilon, \mu, \rho\}$, and let $\tilde{H}1$ be defined as shown on p. 49.

---

† The call on $\tilde{H}1$ from $\tilde{H}0$ is counted in m_1.

> **algorithm** $\widetilde{H}1(A)$;
> 0: $\epsilon \rightarrow \delta$, 1 ;
> 1: $\delta \rightarrow \beta$, $\widetilde{H}2$;
> 2: $\rho \rightarrow \delta$, 3 ;
> 3: $\delta \rightarrow \beta$, $\widetilde{H}2$;
> 4: $\mu \rightarrow \delta$, 5 ;
> 5: $\delta \rightarrow \beta$, $\widetilde{H}2$;
> 6: $\rightarrow$.   **end**

where $\widetilde{H}2$ is

> **algorithm** $\widetilde{H}2(A)$;
> 0: $\beta \rightarrow$, 1 ;
> 1: $\rightarrow$.   **end**

Construct the switching directory $\widetilde{D}2$, then construct the package

$$\widetilde{H}1; \widetilde{H}2_{19}; \widetilde{K}0_7; \widetilde{D}2_9$$

and apply it to the string $a\epsilon\epsilon b\rho\rho c\mu\mu$.

2. Let the alphabet $A = \{a, b, c, x, y, z\}$, and let $\widetilde{H}1$ be defined as follows:

> **algorithm** $\widetilde{H}1(A)$;
> 0: $x \rightarrow z$, 0 ;
> 1: $b \rightarrow \alpha b$, 2 ;
> 2: $a \rightarrow a\gamma$, $\widetilde{H}2$;
> 3: $a\gamma \rightarrow a$, 4:
> 4: $ab \rightarrow b$, 5;
> 5: $y \rightarrow z$, 5 ;
> 6: $c \rightarrow \alpha c$, 7 ;
> 7: $b \rightarrow b\gamma$, $\widetilde{H}2$;
> 8: $\rightarrow$.   **end**

where $\widetilde{H}2$ is

> **algorithm** $\widetilde{H}2(A)$
> 0: $z \rightarrow w$, 0 ;
> 1: $w \rightarrow$.   **end**

Construct the switching directory $\widetilde{D}2$ and apply

$$\widetilde{H}1; \widetilde{H}2_{21}; \widetilde{K}0_9; \widetilde{D}2_{11}$$

to the string $axxbyyc$.

1.8 ADDRESSABLE STORAGE

We have seen that the introduction of successor labels simplified sequence control considerably, but it was still necessary to employ alias alphabets and special punctuation for focusing attention onto specific substrings in R. In this section we shall introduce a notation, as well as appropriate algorithmic constructions, which will make focusing easier to handle. We select an alphabet $M = \{\Delta, \#\}$, and we denote a Δ followed by a string of m $\#$'s by (m) and refer to it† as the *address* (m). During the execution of an algorithm we shall envision the contents of R to have the form $(1)^1 c_1 (2)^1 c_2 \ldots (n-1)^1 c_{n-1} (n)^1 c_n$, where for $i = 1, \ldots, n$, c_i is a string (possibly empty) in the alphabet A. The string c_i will often be referred to as *the contents of location* (i). (The initial contents of R is always $(1)^1 c_1$, for some string c_1.) The goal here is to make it easy to focus attention on the contents of particular locations.

We extend the form of the LHS and RHS of a rule to allow (but not require) each to be preceded by an address followed by a slash ($/$); and each side of the rule has its own interpretation. Initially, attention is automatically focused on the contents of R, that is, location (1). Execution of rules proceeds in the usual manner until an RHS which is preceded by an address (m) is encountered in an applicable rule. This will be interpreted as follows: (1) If the contents of R contains the address (m), take the string represented by the RHS after the match and append it to the *left end* of c_m to get a new c_m in location (m). (2) If the address (m) does not exist yet in R, append at the right end of R all of the addresses not yet there, up to and including (m), each with null contents, and then apply step (1). When used with an RHS, m must be nonzero.

If, for example, P were initially $(1)^1 aa$ and the rule

$$0\colon a \ \rightarrow \ (3)/b, \ 1\,;$$

were executed, the contents of R would be

$$(1)^1 aa(2)^1(3)^1 b$$

If then the rule

$$1\colon a \ \rightarrow \ (2)/c, \ 2\,;$$

---

† We shall actually maintain all addresses in R in the alphabet M^1, although this will not appear in their use in rules and in the text which follows. Whenever the explicit contents of R is shown, however, we shall indicate the appropriate alphabets.

were executed, we would find in R

$$(1)^1aa(2)^1c(3)^1b$$

Thus we have a way to save partial results of a computation for later handling. It should be emphasized that in this particular usage of "$\rightarrow$" no replacement of a is involved; a is used only to check applicability. If now the rule

$$2 : a \rightarrow (3)/d, 3;$$

were executed, we would have in R

$$(1)^1aa(2)^1c(3)^1db$$

If an address (r) appears to the left of an LHS, then before the rule is even tested for applicability, attention is focused (by changing everything else to the alias alphabet A^1) on the contents of location (r), that is, on c_r. If $r = 0$, we focus on the entire contents (in A) of R. If the nonzero address (r) does not exist in R, the algorithm is incorrect. It is understood that if we were previously focused on location (s), we are no longer focused there when we change to location (r), but we stay focused on location (r) until another change is indicated.

As an example of this new form of algorithm, which we shall call the *addressed labeled Markov algorithm* (ALMA), we construct a set of useful algorithms $\widetilde{nMm}$ over G (the alphabet containing only the character 1); $\widetilde{nMm}$ will append a copy of the contents of (n) to the left end of (m).

algorithm $\widetilde{nMm}(G)$;	*Comments*
$0: (n)/ \rightarrow \tau \qquad , 1;$	Focus on (n), insert τ.
$1: \tau 1 \rightarrow (m)/1 \;, 2;$	Copy a character 1 to (m).
$2: \tau 1 \rightarrow \qquad 1\tau \;, 1;$	Move τ in (n).
$3: \tau \rightarrow \qquad . \qquad$ **end**	Delete τ and stop.

Note that $\widetilde{nMm}$ leaves (n) focused, and it does not erase any addresses or the contents of any locations.

We now wish to show that to each LMA there corresponds an ALMA, and vice versa. Suppose $\tilde{H}$ is an LMA. Let $\tilde{K}$ be derived from $\tilde{H}$ as follows:

$$\tilde{K} \equiv \frac{\tilde{H}(A, \Lambda \, '\rightarrow' \, Q)}{\tilde{K}(A \cup M, \, '\#^1 \rightarrow \#^{1'} \, Q)}$$

Then $\tilde{K}$ is the ALMA which corresponds to the LMA $\tilde{H}$, in the sense that

$$(1)^1\tilde{H}(P) = K((1)^1P)$$

This condition takes into account the fact that we assume an initial address of $(1)^1$ in R for an ALMA.

The converse—i.e., that to each ALMA there corresponds an LMA—is of course more difficult. In what follows, the character β^1 will be used to indicate the current focusing, if any. When (0) occurs with an LHS, the subalgorithm $\widetilde{F0}$ will be invoked.

algorithm $\widetilde{F0}(A, M, \beta)$; **A** ξ;	Comments
$0: \beta^1 \rightarrow \quad , 1;$	Focus on the whole register R.
$1: \xi^1 \rightarrow \xi , 1;$	Change everything in A^1 to alphabet A.
$2: \quad \rightarrow \quad .$ **end**	

The focusing necessary when a nonzero address (m) occurs on the left side is accomplished by the algorithm $\widetilde{Fm}$.

algorithm $\widetilde{Fm}(A, M, \beta)$; **A** ξ, η; **A** δ;	Comments
$0: \beta^1 \qquad \rightarrow \qquad , 1;$	Delete old focus.
$1: \delta \qquad \rightarrow \delta^1 \qquad , 1;$	Change everything to alias alphabet.
$2: (m)^1\xi^1 \rightarrow (m)^1\beta^1\xi , 3;$	Insert new focus.
$3: \xi\eta^1 \quad \rightarrow \xi\eta \qquad , 3;$	Change c_m back to A.
$4: \qquad \rightarrow \qquad .$ **end**	

Note that the occurrence of (m) in rule 2 here does not imply that $\widetilde{Fm}$ is an ALMA. In rule 2, (m) is part of the LHS in the usual sense; i.e., it represents a Δ followed by m #'s, except for the use of aliases in this case. As an example, the effect of $\widetilde{F2}$, given the contents of R to be $(1)^1aa(2)^1c(3)^1db$, is to produce $(1)^1a^1a^1(2)^1\beta^1c(3)^1d^1b^1$.

We also need a control algorithm $\widetilde{Km}$ which determines whether a nonzero address (m), which has occurred with an RHS, exists in R or not.

algorithm $\widetilde{Km}(A, M, \beta)$;	Comments
$\quad\quad \mathbf{A} \cup \mathbf{A}^1 \cup \mathbf{A}^2 \cup \mathbf{M}^1 \cup \boldsymbol{\beta}^1 \delta;$	
$0: (m)^1 \rightarrow \alpha , 1;$	If $(m)^1$, force $\widetilde{Km}(P) = \Lambda.$
$1: \delta\alpha \rightarrow \alpha , 1;$	
$2: \alpha\delta \rightarrow \alpha , 2;$	
$3: \alpha \quad \rightarrow \quad . ;$	
$4: \quad \rightarrow \alpha .$ **end**	If no $(m)^1$, set $\widetilde{Km}(P) \neq \Lambda.$

Now we construct an algorithm $\widetilde{N0}$ which will add one more address at the right end of R.

algorithm $\widetilde{N0}(A, M, \beta)$;	*Comments*
$\qquad \mathbf{A} \cup \mathbf{A}^1 \cup \mathbf{A}^2 \cup \mathbf{M}^1 \cup \boldsymbol{\beta}^1 \, \delta;$	
$\qquad \mathbf{A} \cup \mathbf{A}^1 \cup \mathbf{A}^2 \, \rho; \mathbf{M}^1 \, \xi;$	
0: $\quad \rightarrow \tau \quad , 1;$	
1: $\tau\delta \rightarrow \delta\tau \quad , 1;$	Shift τ to right end.
2: $\rho\tau \rightarrow \tau\rho \quad , 2;$	Shift back to address.
3: $\xi\tau \rightarrow \tau\xi\alpha\xi \, , 4;$	Duplicate.
4: $\alpha\xi\rho \rightarrow \rho\alpha\xi \, , 4;$	Shift new character right.
5: $\alpha\#^1 \rightarrow \#^1 \quad , 3;$	
6: $\tau \quad \rightarrow \qquad , 7;$	
7: $\alpha\Delta^1 \rightarrow \Delta^1\#^1$. **end**	Create address plus one.

The effect of $\widetilde{N0}$ acting on $(1)^1 a^1 a^1 (2)^1 \beta^1 c(3)^1 d^1 b^1$ is to produce

$$(1)^1 a^1 a^1 (2)^1 \beta^1 c(3)^1 d^1 b^1 (4)^1$$

[Exercise 1.8.1 asks how $\widetilde{Fm}$ could be written to be independent of m if the call put (m) in R.] The iteration algorithm $\widetilde{Km}(\widetilde{N0})$ makes sure that (m) exists in R by constructing the addresses up to and including (m), if necessary. We now need an algorithm $\widetilde{N1}$ which will insert an RHS resulting from a match into a specified location, assuming that that location is already in R. In this algorithm we can now see the reason for putting the β^1 after the address of the currently focused location. The string to be put into the specified location must be in alphabet A if the location is the currently focused one or if we are focused on all of R, and in A^1 otherwise. Continuing the earlier example, application of the rule

$$6: \quad \rightarrow (4)/ef, 7;$$

would produce in R

$$(1)^1 a^1 a^1 (2)^1 \beta^1 c(3)^1 d^1 b^1 (4)^1 e^1 f^1$$

We can't rely on the contents of the location to show the desired alphabet, since the location may be empty. Thus, the address itself must show it, and this will be the job of β^1. If β^1 is present in R, but not at the new location, we shall generate a character γ in that location to convert the new string to alphabet A^1. As we shall see, a copy of the RHS in question will have been inserted somewhere in R in alphabet A^2. Moreover, because it would be quite wasteful to put in an entire copy of the algorithm $\widetilde{N1}$ for each m, we shall assume that it follows execution of the shorter algorithm $\widetilde{Lm}$, which marks with a β the location to be changed and inserts γ whenever the string to be inserted at (m) needs to be in alphabet A^1:

algorithm $\widetilde{Lm}(A, M, \beta, \gamma)$;			*Comments*
$A \cup A^1 \cup A^2 \cup M^1 \cup \beta^1 \, \xi$;			
$0: \beta^1$	$\rightarrow \gamma\beta^1$	$, 1;$	If β^1, insert γ,
$1: (m)^1\gamma$	$\rightarrow (m)^1$	$, 3;$	but not at (m).
$2: \xi\gamma$	$\rightarrow \gamma\xi$	$, 2;$	Shift γ to left end.
$3: (m)^1$	$\rightarrow (m)^1\beta$	$, 4;$	Introduce β at (m).
$4: \gamma\xi$	$\rightarrow \xi\gamma$	$, 5;$	Move γ to β.
$5: \gamma\beta$	$\rightarrow \beta\gamma$	$, 6;$	Move γ past β.
$6:$	$\rightarrow$	. **end**	

[Exercise 1.8.2 asks for a revision of $\widetilde{Km}$ to call on $\widetilde{N0}$ directly, so only one copy of $\widetilde{N0}$ is needed, and similarly for $\widetilde{Lm}$ and $\widetilde{N1}$.] Note that if $\widetilde{Lm}$ happens to mark with β the location on which we are currently focused, the address of that location will now be

$$(m)^1\beta\beta^1$$

Otherwise we will have $(m)^1\beta\gamma$ or $(m)^1\beta$, depending on whether β^1 was present in R at all, or not. This is important in the construction of $\widetilde{N1}$.

algorithm $\widetilde{N1}(A, M, \beta, \gamma)$;			*Comments*
$A \cup A^1 \cup M^1 \cup \beta \cup \beta^1 \cup \gamma \, \delta$;			
$A \cup A^1 \cup M^1 \cup \beta^1 \, \rho; A \cup M^1 \, \xi$;			
$0: \delta\xi^2$	$\rightarrow \xi^2\delta$	$, 0;$	Shift the new RHS left.
$1: \xi^2\rho$	$\rightarrow \rho\xi^2$	$, 1;$	Shift it right to β.
$2: \xi^2\beta$	$\rightarrow \beta\xi^2$	$, 2;$	Shift past β.
$3: \xi^2\beta^1$	$\rightarrow \beta^1\xi$	$, 3;$	If β^1, change to A.
$4: \xi^2\gamma$	$\rightarrow \gamma\xi^1$	$, 4;$	If γ, change to A^1.
$5: \xi^2$	$\rightarrow \xi$	$, 5;$	If neither, change to A.
$6: \gamma$	$\rightarrow$	$, 7;$	
$7: \beta$	$\rightarrow$	. **end**	

We now let $\widetilde{Tm} = \widetilde{N1} \circ \widetilde{Lm} \circ \widetilde{Km}(\widetilde{N0})$, which is the algorithm to be invoked for the case of an address occurring with an RHS. Again continuing with our earlier example, but assuming that because of the rule

$$7: c \rightarrow (6)/yz, 8;$$

the characters y^2z^2 have been inserted,

$$(1)^1a^1a^1(2)^1\beta^1cy^2z^2(3)^1d^1b^1(4)^1e^1f^1$$

let us follow the progress of the application of $\widetilde{T6} = \widetilde{N1} \circ \widetilde{L6} \circ \widetilde{K6}(\widetilde{N0})$. The algorithm $\widetilde{K6}(\widetilde{N0})$ leaves

$$(1)^1a^1a^1(2)^1\beta^1cy^2z^2(3)^1d^1b^1(4)^1e^1f^1(5)^1(6)^1$$

Then $\widetilde{L6}$ produces

$$(1)^1a^1a^1(2)^1\beta^1cy^2z^2(3)^1d^1b^1(4)^1e^1f^1(5)^1(6)^1\beta\gamma$$

Applying $\widetilde{N1}$ gives the final result

$$(1)^1a^1a^1(2)^1\beta^1c(3)^1d^1b^1(4)^1e^1f^1(5)^1(6)^1y^1z^1$$

The specific treatment of each occurrence of an address in a rule may now be given: (1) If no addresses occur, no change is made in the rule. (2) If an address (m) occurs with the LHS,

$$k: (m)/Q_1 \to Q_2 ,j;$$

replace rule k by the sequence

$$k: \quad \to \quad , \widetilde{Fm};$$
$$k + 1: Q_1 \to Q_2 ,j \quad ;$$

If Q_1 is null, use $\beta^1 \to \beta^1 Q_2, j$; instead. If Q_2 has an address with it in rule k, the address remains with it in the process. After (2) has been carried out everywhere, then (3) replace each rule which has an RHS address

$$t: Q_1 \to (r)/Q_2 ,j;$$

by the rule

$$t: Q_1 \to Q_1 Q_2^2 , \widetilde{Tr};$$
$$t + 1: Q_1 \to Q_1 \quad ,j \quad ;$$

and (4) renumber all the rules to eliminate duplications introduced in this process. [Exercise 1.8.3 asks what happens to successor labels pointing to duplicated labels in the renumbering.]

We have thus shown that the ALMA is equivalent to the LMA, and hence to the MA. Since we have not changed the control sequencing in this construction (as we did with the LMA), we know that composition, iteration, etc., are unchanged.

One more problem must be handled if we are to have a clean way to construct complicated algorithms out of simpler ones. With all the automatic focusing now at our disposal, we must have some way to be sure that the result of one algorithm (or subalgorithm) is in the proper form for use by another. There must be a convention about the number of addresses in R and the contents of their locations. Otherwise we could easily have the situation in which a subalgorithm could use several locations to save intermediate results, and on the return the calling algorithm would find some unusual strings lying around in R. *We make the following declaration of convention*: Unless specified otherwise, every algorithm will leave its result (if it has one) in location (1) and erase all locations and addresses to the right of it. Thus the result is in proper form for input to another algorithm which was independently written, and for which it might not even have been predicted that it would ever be called as a subalgorithm. In order to facilitate this convention, we provide an algorithm which can be called on termination to delete the address (2)

algorithm Primes$(G, *)$; $\mathbf{G} \cup * \cup \gamma \cup \alpha \; \xi$;		*Comments*
0: $\quad\quad\quad \rightarrow (3)/11$, $\quad 1$;		Set $j = 2$.
1: $(2)/\xi \quad \rightarrow \quad\quad\quad$, $\quad 1$;		Clear out location (2).
2: $\quad\quad\quad \rightarrow (2)/\alpha^1$, $3\widetilde{M}2$;		Form $\gamma j * j\alpha$ in (2).
3: $\quad\quad\quad \rightarrow (2)/*$, $3\widetilde{M}2$;		
4: $(2)/\alpha^1 \rightarrow \alpha \quad$, $\quad 5$;		Call Mult.
5: $\quad\quad\quad \rightarrow \gamma \quad$, Mult;		Compute $\gamma \, j \times j \, \alpha$.
6: $\quad\quad \gamma \rightarrow * \quad$, $1\widetilde{M}2$;		Form $n_k * j \times j \, \alpha$.
7: $(2)/1{*}1 \rightarrow * \quad$, $\quad 7$;		Is $n_k > j \times j$?
8: $*1 \quad\quad \rightarrow \quad\quad$, $\quad 22$;		No, terminate.
9: $\quad\quad \xi \rightarrow \quad\quad$, $\quad 9$;		Yes, form $\gamma n_k * j\alpha$, but first clear out residue.
10: $\quad\quad\quad \rightarrow \alpha^1 \quad$, $3\widetilde{M}2$;		
11: $\quad\quad\quad \rightarrow (2)/*$, $1\widetilde{M}2$;		
12: $(2)/\alpha^1 \rightarrow \alpha \quad$, $\quad 13$;		
13: $\quad\quad\quad \rightarrow \gamma \quad$, Div;		Form $\gamma q * r\alpha$.
14: $*1 \quad\quad \rightarrow * \quad$, $\quad 21$;		Is $r = 0$?
15: $\quad\quad \gamma \rightarrow \quad\quad$, $\quad 16$;		Yes, put j in result.
16: $\alpha \quad\quad\quad \rightarrow \quad\quad$, $3\widetilde{M}4$;		
17: $\quad\quad\quad \rightarrow (4)/*$, $\quad 18$;		Put $*$ in result as separator.
18: $(1)/\xi \quad \rightarrow \quad\quad$, $\quad 18$;		Clear out old n_k.
19: $(2)/* \quad \rightarrow \quad\quad$, $2\widetilde{M}1$;		Set $n_k = q$.
20: $\quad\quad\quad \rightarrow \quad\quad$, $\quad 1$;		Try again with old j, new n_k.
21: $\quad\quad\quad \rightarrow (3)/1$, $\quad 1$;		$r \neq 0$. Try again with new j, old n_k.
22: $\quad\quad\quad \rightarrow \quad\quad$, $1\widetilde{M}4$;		Terminate. Move n_k to result.
23: $(1)/\xi \quad \rightarrow \quad\quad$, $\quad 23$;		Clear out location (1).
24: $\quad\quad\quad \rightarrow \quad\quad$, $4\widetilde{M}1$;		Move result to (1).
25: $\quad\quad\quad \rightarrow \quad\quad$, End;		
26: $\quad\quad\quad \rightarrow \quad\quad$. **end**		

and everything to the right of it. In focusing with (0), it automatically deletes β^1 if it is in R, and sets the contents of location (1) to alphabet A:

$$\textbf{algorithm } \text{End}(A, M); \mathbf{A} \cup \mathbf{M} \cup \mathbf{A}^1 \cup \mathbf{M}^1 \ \xi;$$
$$0: (0)/(2)^1 \rightarrow \sigma(2)^1 \ , 1;$$
$$1: \qquad \sigma\xi \rightarrow \sigma \qquad , 1 \textbf{ end}$$

As an example of the use of the ALMA, we derive the algorithm previously given for finding the prime factors of an integer n (which is in R initially, in location (1)).

In the algorithm for the prime factors of n (facing page), location (2) is used as a "scratch pad," while n (the as yet unfactored integer) and j (the current divisor) are maintained in locations (1) and (3), respectively. In several places α^1 is used temporarily so that $n\widetilde{M}m$ will not focus improperly.

EXERCISES 1.8

1. Describe how the focusing algorithm $\tilde{F}$ could be made independent of m if any time focusing on (m) was desired, (m) was placed in R. For example, if any time we wrote

$$i: (m)/Q_1 \rightarrow Q_2, j;$$

it was changed to

$$i: \qquad \rightarrow (m), \widetilde{H}1;$$
$$i + 1: \qquad Q_1 \rightarrow Q_2, j;$$

what form could $\widetilde{H}1$ have?

2. Rewrite $\widetilde{K}m$ to call on $\widetilde{N}0$ directly as a subalgorithm. Also change the algorithms $\widetilde{L}m$ and $\widetilde{T}m$ so that $\widetilde{L}m$ calls on $\widetilde{N}1$ directly.

3. What happens to successor labels pointing to duplicated labels in the renumbering suggested in the text?

1.9 THE ALGORITHM MACHINE

In preceding sections several important algorithmic activities were described—in particular, converting an LMA to an MA, converting an ALMA to an LMA, replacing rules with empty LHS's by other rules with nonempty LHS's, and so on. We should be able to express these activities as algorithms also, since they can quite clearly be delegated to a machine, just as well as the algorithms being manipulated. To specify these activities as algorithms, however, requires that the algorithms they manipulate be represented in some form as data. During this processing, the data algorithms are not themselves being executed; some other algorithm is being executed on them.

Actually, nothing has been said yet about the mechanics of executing an algorithm $\tilde{H}$. Let us describe this process.

1. The register R must first be initialized to hold the data word P. Rather than include this as part of the activity of executing an algorithm, we merely postulate that at the start of the process P is in R.

2. Rule 0 of $\tilde{H}$ is attempted, then its successor,† and so on. No activity occurs other than the application of rules in the usual way. When a terminal rule is applied, control by the algorithm ceases.

3. All kinds of magic happens; e.g., a "nonalgorithmic agent" may intervene to save the result of the computation just completed, enter a new data word in R, invoke a new algorithm, or call upon a "loader" to package up some subalgorithms. All of this is of course nonalgorithmic, i.e., magical.

This is the way algorithms are invoked, and while we must accomplish these steps, we may attempt to describe them differently to gain some insight into the process.

1′. A word Q is entered in R. This word is some combination of the algorithm $\tilde{H}$, the alphabet A over which $\tilde{H}$ is written, and P, the initial word.

2′. A fixed algorithm U (independent of $\tilde{H}$) is applied to the contents of R.

3′. When U terminates, step (1′) is started, or no further activity occurs.

The fixed activity U is often called *the universal algorithm*. Another way to look at it is as an *algorithm machine*. In order for this description to work, there must be an alphabet A^∞, called the *universal alphabet*, and a word Q in that alphabet, such that $\tilde{H}(P) = U(Q)$ whenever $\tilde{H}$ is

---

† In this section we shall deal only with LMA's as originally introduced, i.e., without subalgorithm calls or addresses, since the ideas developed here do not need such complications, and they will only get in the way.

applicable to P. The construction of Q from $\tilde{H}$, A, and P is an algorithmic activity which we shall discuss. Obviously, Q should not have to be obtained by applying $\tilde{H}$ to P, since then it would be pointless to bring in U. We shall see that Q can be constructed without invoking the algorithmic action of $\tilde{H}$; that is, we will obtain Q by manipulating only the characters used to represent $\tilde{H}$, P, and A.

As an example of such an algorithm machine, consider the dialing of a telephone number. Each complete number to be dialed corresponds to an algorithm to be carried out, i.e., the dialing of each character in turn. The installation of a card-operated dialer amounts to the creation of a machine which will execute the dialing algorithms, and we may start up this machine with a much simpler act than the dialing of a number. The one link we must provide is a representation of the algorithm as data, i.e., the number to be dialed represented as coded punches in a card. This process of abstraction is a device for partitioning complexity into simpler activities. It may be the only effective way we have available to us for coping with complexity.

We first construct the universal alphabet A^∞, and then we shall show how to map the characters of A and its aliases (and the other characters used in writing $\tilde{H}$) into A. For the alphabet A^∞ we use $\{\alpha, \alpha 1, \alpha 1^2, \alpha 1^3, \ldots, \alpha 1^r, \ldots\}$, where 1^r represents r occurrences of the character 1. The character α is used merely as a separator between sequences of 1's. Now we must show how to represent the algorithm and its data alphabet in A^∞. We start by listing all punctuation symbols which we shall need to write an LMA (together with $*$ and $|$, whose role will appear later), and we assign them correspondents in A^∞:

$*$	$\vert$	$:$	$;$	**end**	$\rightarrow$	$,$	$.$
0	1	2	3	4	5	6	7

where the integer i ($0 \leq i \leq 7$) represents $\alpha 1^i$ in A^∞. We call this correspondence T, so that, for example, $T(\mathbf{end}) = 4$; and the table showing the correspondence (i.e., the values of T) will be called the *symbol table*, abbreviated ST. (We shall use the integer i in place of $\alpha 1^i$ in the text, except where we need to be explicit about the actual string of characters in R.) The symbol table will gradually be enlarged to include all of the alphabets and characters needed to write the algorithm and its data. For each character ξ thus entered into the ST, the number r of 1's in $T(\xi) = r$ will be called the *index of the character ξ in the ST*. It is obvious that the second row of the table may now be omitted, since the position of each entry indicates its index, so long as we remember to start with 0. Thus, the ST has so far the form†

	0	1	2	3	4	5	6	7
ST	*	|	:	;	**end**	→	,	.

If T is applied to a string (or substring) of characters, it is understood to apply to each separately, so that $T(\xi_1\xi_2 \ldots \xi_n) = T(\xi_1)T(\xi_2) \ldots T(\xi_n)$, where ξ_i is a substring consisting of one or more characters.

In order to proceed with the representation of an algorithm in A^∞, it is necessary to make precise the form of an algorithm $\tilde{H}$, i.e., the explicit syntax of an LMA. When a syntax is specified, a recognition problem of course follows: Is a given set of characters a form which represents an LMA, or not? To avoid problems in handling two-dimensional objects, we shall linearize the form of $\tilde{H}$; that is, the successor of any character is to its right, rather than up or down. Of course, the semicolons will serve to separate the rules. Thus, the heading and body (i.e., the rules) of an algorithm $\widetilde{K0}$ used earlier

> **algorithm** $\widetilde{K0}(A, \alpha)$; **A** ξ;
> 0: $\xi\alpha \rightarrow \beta$, 1 ;
> 1: $\xi\beta \rightarrow \beta$, 1 ;
> 2: $\beta \rightarrow$.   ;
> 3: $\alpha \rightarrow$, 3 **end**

(with a few minor changes) become

$$A \cup \alpha; A, \xi; 0: \xi\alpha \rightarrow \beta, 1; 1: \xi\beta \rightarrow \beta, 1; 2: \beta \rightarrow . ; 3: \alpha \rightarrow , 3 \text{ end}$$

Now we must describe in a precise way just what constitutes a legal representation of an algorithm.

A very convenient notation for just this kind of situation was introduced by John Backus [5] in 1959. As an example of the use of the Backus notation, let us consider a possible definition of a "string of letters" taken from an alphabet, say $A, B, C, \ldots, Z$. Suppose we mean by a "string of letters" any finite (possibly empty) ordered list of letters of the alphabet, allowing repetitions, and not caring if the resulting string makes any sense at all. A simple way to describe such a string is to say: "To get a

---

† We will continue to number the positions in the table externally for easier reference during the present development.

new string, take any existing string and add another letter at the right. You can get started by choosing any letter of the alphabet." The corresponding statement in the Backus notation is

$\langle \text{letter} \rangle ::= A \mid B \mid C \mid D \mid \cdots \mid Y \mid Z$
$\langle \text{string of letters} \rangle ::= \langle \text{empty} \rangle \mid \langle \text{letter} \rangle \mid \langle \text{string of letters} \rangle \langle \text{letter} \rangle$

Note that objects not enclosed in pointed brackets stand for themselves, while brackets denote a member of the collection of objects having in common the stated property. The first line above defines the collection called $\langle \text{letter} \rangle$, listing the collection explicitly (the vertical bar should be read "or"). The second line describes a $\langle \text{string of letters} \rangle$ just as we indicated above (the bracketed expression $\langle \text{empty} \rangle$ represents the empty string, i.e., the string with no letters in it). Note that objects placed next to each other without a vertical bar between them are to be *concatenated*, i.e., placed side by side to form a new object. This notation makes it convenient, then, to define special strings (or ordered lists) of objects in terms of their constituent parts. In later examples we shall also use some additional notation, which goes beyond the original Backus notation. Alternatives enclosed in braces, such as in

$$\langle a \rangle ::= \langle b \rangle \mid \{\langle c \rangle \mid \langle d \rangle\} \langle e \rangle$$

represent a choice of exactly one of the alternatives. An asterisk (*) following a pair of braces implies an arbitrary number of repetitions (including none) of the object in the braces. If alternatives appear within the braces, then any alternative may appear in any repetition. An example of this use of the asterisk is

$$\langle \text{identifier} \rangle ::= \{\langle \text{letter} \rangle \mid \langle \text{digit} \rangle\} \{\langle \text{letter} \rangle \mid \langle \text{digit} \rangle\}^*$$

An integer appearing below the asterisk indicates a minimum number of repetitions; thus zero is implied if it is omitted. If an integer is used instead of the asterisk, it represents an upper bound for the number of repetitions. Examples:

$$\langle \text{unsigned integer} \rangle ::= \{\text{digit}\}_1^*$$
$$\langle \text{identifier} \rangle ::= \{\langle \text{letter} \rangle \mid \langle \text{digit} \rangle\}_1^*$$

Applying this notation to our present situation, i.e., the syntax of an algorithm expressed as a string of characters, we have

1. $\langle \text{algorithm} \rangle ::= \langle \text{heading} \rangle \langle \text{body} \rangle$
2. $\langle \text{heading} \rangle ::= \langle \text{general alphabet name} \rangle ; \langle \text{generic list} \rangle$
3. $\langle \text{general alphabet name} \rangle ::= \langle \text{alphabet name} \rangle \{\cup \langle \text{alphabet name} \rangle\}^*$
4. $\langle \text{alphabet name} \rangle ::= \langle \text{character} \rangle \mid \langle \text{identifier} \rangle$

5. $\langle \text{identifier} \rangle^\dagger ::= \{\langle \text{letter} \rangle \langle \text{digit} \rangle\}_1^*$
6. $\langle \text{generic list} \rangle ::= \{\langle \text{generic declaration} \rangle;\}^*$
7. $\langle \text{generic declaration} \rangle^\ddagger ::= \langle \text{general alphabet name} \rangle \{,\langle \text{character} \rangle\}_1^*$
8. $\langle \text{body} \rangle ::= \langle \text{open body} \rangle$ **end**
9. $\langle \text{open body} \rangle ::= \langle \text{rule} \rangle \{;\langle \text{rule} \rangle\}^*$
10. $\langle \text{rule} \rangle ::= \langle \text{label} \rangle: \langle \text{Markov rule} \rangle \langle \text{successor} \rangle$
11. $\langle \text{label} \rangle ::= \{\langle \text{digit} \rangle\}_1^*$
12. $\langle \text{Markov rule} \rangle ::= \langle \text{side} \rangle \rightarrow \langle \text{side} \rangle$
13. $\langle \text{side} \rangle ::= \{\langle \text{character} \rangle\}^*$
14. $\langle \text{successor} \rangle ::= . \mid , \langle \text{label} \rangle^\S$

Here $\langle \text{letter} \rangle^{\dagger\dagger}$ and $\langle \text{digit} \rangle$ are primitives, and $\langle \text{character} \rangle$ is arbitrary, except that it must be a uniquely identifiable element of some alphabet. Note that $\langle \text{letter} \rangle$s and $\langle \text{digit} \rangle$s will have to come from an alphabet, but this alphabet itself is not involved in the tableau (or display) of the $\langle \text{algorithm} \rangle$ as a string. Only $\langle \text{identifier} \rangle$s and $\langle \text{label} \rangle$s constructed from $\langle \text{letter} \rangle$s and $\langle \text{digit} \rangle$s become symbols in the tableau. Note also that some additional requirements must be stated in order to ensure that an alleged LMA actually be interpretable as an LMA. For example, every $\langle \text{successor} \rangle$ other than the period must actually appear somewhere (and exactly one time) as a $\langle \text{label} \rangle$ on a rule. Also $\langle \text{character} \rangle$s used as generic variables must not be in any of the general alphabets. Such conditions are not easily formulated formally; this is a topic for current research efforts.

Consider again the algorithm $\widetilde{K0}$ expressed in linear form:

$$A \cup \alpha; A, \xi; 0: \xi\alpha \rightarrow \beta, 1; 1: \xi\beta \rightarrow \beta, 1; 2: \beta \rightarrow . ; 3: \alpha \rightarrow , 3 \text{ end}$$

It should be clear that except for the name $\widetilde{K0}$ (which is really unnecessary), someone familiar with this linear form (and knowing the domains of the alphabet name A) could execute the $\langle \text{algorithm} \rangle$ without any difficulty. This is exactly the role that our universal algorithm U will play. Let us apply the syntax rules to the linear form of $\widetilde{K0}$ to verify that it has the correct form for an LMA. It is an $\langle \text{algorithm} \rangle$ if one can identify a part which is a $\langle \text{heading} \rangle$ and a part which is a $\langle \text{body} \rangle$. We quickly discover

---

† Although we have not used any alphabet names beginning with digits, there is no reason to exclude them.

‡ The comma after the alphabet name, while not normally written, will be used in the linearized form.

§ To simplify the treatment, we shall assume that empty successors are given as explicit zeros.

†† Throughout the remainder of the text the $\langle \ \rangle$ notation, such as in $\langle \text{identifier} \rangle$, will be used to assign a technical intent to the bracketed word "identifier," i.e., a string (not $\langle \text{string} \rangle$) of letters and digits.

that choosing $A \cup \alpha$; as the $\langle$heading$\rangle$ works, but the rest is not a legal $\langle$body$\rangle$ because A, ξ is not a $\langle$rule$\rangle$ (because A is not a $\langle$label$\rangle$, since it does not start with a $\langle$digit$\rangle$). We then find that $A \cup \alpha$; A, ξ; is a legal $\langle$heading$\rangle$, and the rest turns out to be a legal $\langle$body$\rangle$. Each time we apply a partition, such as $\langle$heading$\rangle\langle$body$\rangle$, we have smaller strings to analyze. Eventually each path of partitionings leads to a contradiction or to a legal combination of primitives. For the simpler $\langle$algorithm$\rangle$

$$A \cup \alpha; A, \xi; 0: \xi \rightarrow \alpha \,.\, \textbf{end}$$

we would have the analysis shown in Fig. 1.4 on p. 64.

From the linear representation of the $\langle$algorithm$\rangle$ we can continue to build the symbol table, and at the same time we can convert the string of $\langle$character$\rangle$s in the representation to characters in A^∞. If at all possible, the two activities of building the symbol table and converting $\langle$character$\rangle$s should be accomplished with only one scan of the $\langle$character$\rangle$s. Repeated scans can be very costly in the time of scanning and in the decisions necessary to control them. Since the alphabets under consideration are finite, assigning them correspondents in A^∞ amounts to nothing more than a numbering of their elements, and this can always be accomplished in one scan. We proceed as follows, assuming that we have available a list of the elements of each alphabet mentioned in the $\langle$algorithm$\rangle$; i.e., when we encounter an alphabet name, we can produce a list of its elements.† We proceed to scan the $\langle$algorithm$\rangle$, starting at the left, i.e., with the $\langle$heading$\rangle$.

The function of the $\langle$heading$\rangle$ is to make declarations about alphabets and generic variables. Once the declaration has been assimilated, i.e., understood, with some appropriate action taken to remember the information so declared, there is no need to keep the $\langle$heading$\rangle$ around any longer. The action which is almost always taken when a declaration is encountered is the entry of information into one or more tables, organized so as to make later retrieval of the information as easy as possible. In our case, whenever we come (in our scan) to an alphabet not yet encountered, the elements of that alphabet must be entered into the symbol table and assigned correspondents. Since the name of that alphabet may occur in subsequent declarations with generic variables, and since we must associate with these generic variables certain characters in the alphabet,

---

† We could provide a notation to allow (or require) an explicit list of the characters of each alphabet to appear in the $\langle$heading$\rangle$, but we shall assume instead that the universal algorithm has access to an "alphabet library" from which it can itself retrieve the list of characters.

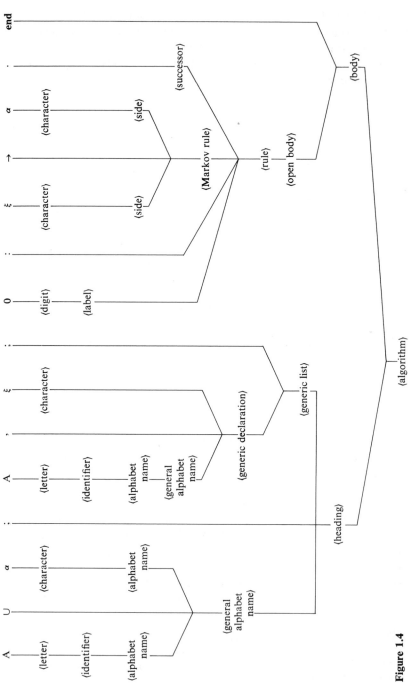

Figure 1.4

we shall build another table, called the *alphabet name table* (ANT), which contains the name of each alphabet so far encountered, and a pair of integers, the first and last indices of its characters in the ST. Thus, if the alphabet $A = \{a, b, c, d\}$ were the first encountered in the heading, the ST and ANT would be changed to

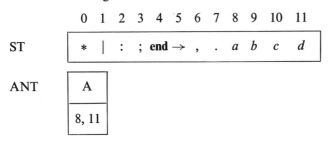

Using this alphabet and the $\widetilde{K0}$ ⟨algorithm⟩

$$A \cup \alpha; A, \xi; 0: \xi\alpha \to \beta, 1; 1: \xi\beta \to \beta, 1; 2: \beta \to . ; 3: \alpha \to , 3 \text{ end}$$

we next find the symbol for set union ∪, which indicates the continuation of the specification of the data alphabet. Then the character α, in a context requiring an ⟨alphabet name⟩,† is to be treated as the name of an alphabet called α and containing only the character α. Then the ST and ANT become

0	1	2	3	4	5	6	7	8	9	10	11	12
*	|	:	;	**end**	→	,	.	a	b	c	d	α

ST

A	α
8, 11	12, 12

ANT

The syntax of a ⟨heading⟩ now guarantees that after the semicolon we will encounter a ⟨general alphabet name⟩, or the ⟨heading⟩ has been exhausted. Each generic variable which follows a ⟨general alphabet name⟩ must be entered into the ST, and we must also remember all of its alphabets so declared. We therefore construct another table, the *generic variable table* (GVT) to record the generic variables and their associated alphabets. Of course, in their use we will not need the names of the alphabets; only their elements will be needed, so that generic variables

---

† This α should not be confused with the α used to build up the alphabet A^∞.

can be tested for matching. We therefore save only the index pairs for the alphabets (which are now available in the ANT). Of course, any generic variable may end up associated with several index pairs. The result of scanning the one ⟨generic declaration⟩ in $\widetilde{K0}$ yields

GVT

ξ
8, 11

The empty position after ξ will be used to remember the "value" of ξ after a successful match is made with an LHS containing ξ. We shall call the contents of this position the *value of* ξ, defined only immediately after a match involving ξ. Of course, since we must always work within the register R, all of these tables must be constructed in R, but they can be isolated from one another (and located when necessary) by suitable punctuation.

It has already become evident that there is no apparent order in which entries are made in the ST (after the first eight entries for the fixed punctuation marks). There is no reason to preserve any order in the ST at all, except that keeping all of the elements of an alphabet together allows us to name the alphabet by one pair of indices. Any assignment of indices to ⟨character⟩s would do, since we will use the mapping T only to represent the ⟨character⟩s in A^∞ and later to decode them back to their original form. The only properties we must insist on for the mapping T are (1) that each ⟨character⟩ be assigned one index in the ST, and (2) that each index be associated with only one ⟨character⟩. This is summarized by saying: "T is a one-to-one mapping from all of the ⟨character⟩s needed to represent the ⟨algorithm⟩ and its data into the alphabet A^∞."

As we scan the ⟨body⟩ of the ⟨algorithm⟩, we will encounter local variables and ⟨label⟩s, and these need merely be entered into the symbol table. We will also encounter aliases of specific ⟨character⟩s in the data alphabet and aliases of generic variables. If they are already in the ST, we may obtain their indices immediately, and no further action need be taken. Suppose that a^m has occurred in the ⟨algorithm⟩ but not yet in the ST, where a is in the alphabet A (that is, it is not a generic variable). We find the index pair for A in the ANT and copy the elements of A, converted to their aliases in A^m, into the first available places in the ST. Then A^m (with its own index pair) is entered into the ANT. Now suppose that a generic variable ξ^n occurs but is not yet in the ST. From the GVT we find the index pair associated with ξ, and in the ANT we find the name of the alphabet, say D, associated with that index pair. If the alias D^n is not already in the ANT, copy the elements of D into the ST, as above, and make an entry for D^n in the ANT. Then enter ξ^n into the ST and into the GVT, with the index pair for D^n. We have thus described the algorithmic activity which guarantees that all the aliases which will be needed for an ⟨algorithm⟩ find their way into the ST.

Every ⟨character⟩ that is encountered in the scan of the ⟨algorithm⟩ either (1) is already in the ST, or (2) is entered in the ST. Thus we are always able to obtain its index. We can now convert every linearly represented LMA into the alphabet A^∞. Henceforth we shall mean by A^∞ the *finite* set of characters α, $\alpha 1$, $\alpha 1^2$, ..., needed to represent an ⟨algorithm⟩ $\tilde{H}$ and its data alphabet (including aliases). In other words, we cut A^∞ down to just that part of it that we need. Then we may define generic variables over A^∞ to be needed by U to process the ⟨algorithm⟩ expressed in the alphabet A^∞. If we continue the example of the ⟨algorithm⟩ $\widetilde{K0}$ with the alphabet $A = \{a, b, c, d\}$, we end up with the following string of characters in A^∞: $\alpha 1^{14}\alpha 1^2\alpha 1^{13}\alpha 1^{12}\alpha 1^5\alpha 1^{15}\alpha 1^6\alpha 1^{16}\alpha 1^3\alpha 1^{16}\alpha 1^2\alpha 1^{13}$ $\alpha 1^{15}\alpha 1^5\alpha 1^{15}\alpha 1^6\alpha 1^{16}\alpha 1^3\alpha 1^{17}\alpha 1^2\alpha 1^{15}\alpha 1^5\alpha 1^7\alpha 1^3\alpha 1^{18}\alpha 1^2\alpha 1^{12}\alpha 1^5\alpha 1^6\alpha 1^{18}\alpha 1^4$, and the tables:

	0	1	2	3	4	5	6	7	8	9	10	11	12	13	14	15	16	17	18
ST	*	|	:	;	**end** $\to$	,	.	a	b	c	d	α	ξ	0	β	1	2	3	

ANT	A	α
	8, 11	12, 12

GVT	ξ
	8, 11

It should be clear that this process of representing an ⟨algorithm⟩ $\tilde{H}$ in A^∞ is in no way dependent on the algorithmic action expressed by $\tilde{H}$.

We turn now to our search for the universal algorithm U, recalling that we shall want it to have the property that $U(Q) = \tilde{H}(P)$, for some Q arising out of $\tilde{H}$, A, and P. We can now be more precise in this statement: Let $Q = T(\tilde{H}) ** T(P)$, where $T(\tilde{H})$ means the linear representation of the ⟨rule⟩s of $\tilde{H}$, preceded by the GVT†. Then we need U such that

$$U(T(\tilde{H}) ** T(P)) = T(\tilde{H}(P))$$

---

† We assume that the ⟨heading⟩ has been processed to produce the ST, the ANT, and the GVT. The ANT is no longer needed once the ST and GVT are constructed; and the ST is needed only for final transcription of the result.

The GVT is represented as follows (continuing the above example):

$$\xi \mid \mid \mid \mid 8 \mid 11 \mid \mid \mid *$$

(converted into A^∞). The vertical bars act as punctuation, so we can distinguish among the contents of the spaces between them. The asterisk (∗) marks the end of the GVT. If there were an additional entry δ in the GVT, ranging over $A \cup \alpha$, for example,

δ
8, 11
12, 12

then the GVT would be represented

$$\xi \mid \mid \mid \mid 8 \mid 11 \mid \mid \mid \delta \mid \mid \mid \mid 8 \mid 11 \mid \mid 12 \mid 12 \mid \mid \mid *$$

with the empty location mentioned above to remember $\langle$character$\rangle$s matched with ξ occurring between the pair of double bars $\mid \mid \mid \mid$ immediately after ξ. Note that the indices 8, 11, etc., are not themselves in A^∞ and will not have representations in the form $\alpha 1^r$. We shall use another alphabet for them, in which $\gamma 1^j$ represents index j. Thus the GVT above, containing only ξ, would be encoded

$$\alpha 1^{13} \alpha 1^1 \alpha 1^1 \alpha 1^1 \alpha 1^1 \gamma 1^8 \alpha 1^1 \gamma 1^{11} \alpha 1^1 \alpha 1^1 \alpha 1^1 \alpha$$

and an empty GVT would appear as an asterisk alone, encoded in A^∞ as α.

Our strategy in specifying U will be to break it up into successively finer parts, according to function. We first view U as an iteration over the $\langle$rule$\rangle$s of $\tilde{H}$. It must isolate one $\langle$rule$\rangle$ after another, test its LHS on P to determine applicability, substitute the RHS if the $\langle$rule$\rangle$ was applicable, and move to the successor, if any. Thus we may write

$$U = U2(UI) \circ U0$$

where $U0$ is an initialization $\langle$algorithm$\rangle$ to make the contents of R look like the general case (even though it is the first $\langle$rule$\rangle$) of the iteration. For the general case, we will suppose that rule $k - 1$ has just been tested for applicability and the RHS substitution carried out (if applicable), and that in the process rule k has been marked (by ψ):

$$\ldots j_1; \psi k : Q_1 \to Q_2, j_2; \ldots$$

(Since the basic punctuation characters $* \mid : ; , \rightarrow$ (and so on) have fixed assignments in the ST for all $\langle$algorithm$\rangle$s, we may use them in writing U; they are always recognizable by U.) We also assume that in the processing of rule $k - 1$ a punctuation mark (i.e., a signal) was inserted into R to indicate whether rule $k - 1$ was applicable or not. We shall specify *by convention* that the characters $\sigma 1^2$ were inserted at the left end of R if rule $k - 1$ was not applicable (so that rule k is to be used now), and the characters $\sigma 1$ were inserted at the left end of R if rule $k - 1$ was applicable (so that rule j_1 is to be used now). It follows that in the initialization $U0$ must insert ψ appropriately and prefix $\sigma 1^2$ to R:

> **algorithm** $U0(B, *, \psi, \sigma)$;
> 0: $\rightarrow \sigma 1^2, 1$;
> 1: 0: $\rightarrow \psi 0$: **. end**

where B is the alphabet $\{\alpha, \gamma, 1\}$.

It is now the job of the control algorithm $U2$ to determine whether rule $k - 1$ (in the general case) was applicable and terminal. If so, the entire $\langle$algorithm$\rangle$ terminates; otherwise $U1$ is invoked.

algorithm $U2(B, *, \psi, \sigma)$; $\mathbf{B} \cup * \cup \psi \cup \sigma \eta$;	*Comments*
0: $\sigma 1^2 \rightarrow \sigma 1^2$. ;	$k - 1$ was not applicable.
	Leave $U2(P) \neq \Lambda$.
1: .;$\psi \rightarrow$, 3 ;	$k - 1$ was applicable and
	terminal.
2: $\rightarrow$. ;	$k - 1$ was applicable and
	not terminal.
3: $\eta \rightarrow$, 3 ;	Force $U2(P) = \Lambda$.
4: $\rightarrow$. **end**	

We now move to a closer look at $U1$, whose job it is to execute the appropriate "next rule" and leave the necessary punctuation (ψ, and $\sigma 1$ or $\sigma 1^2$) in the right places. (Note that the combination ψ **end** cannot occur if $\tilde{H}$ is a closed $\langle$algorithm$\rangle$.) This $\langle$algorithm$\rangle$ will have the form

$$U1 = U6 \circ U3(U4, U5)$$

where $U3$ begins the process by selecting $U4$ (or $U5$) depending on whether rule $k - 1$ was applicable (or not). Then $U4$ or $U5$, as selected, inserts additional punctuation to mark the next $\langle$rule$\rangle$ to be used, and $U6$ executes that $\langle$rule$\rangle$.

algorithm $U3(B, *, \psi, \sigma)$; $\mathbf{B} \cup * \cup \psi \cup \sigma \eta$;   *Comments*
0: $\sigma1^2 \rightarrow$. ;   Not applicable, $U3(P) \neq$
                                                                                  Λ, execute $U5$.
1: $\eta \rightarrow$, 1;   Applicable, force $U3(P) =$
                                                                                  Λ, execute $U4$.

2:    $\rightarrow$. **end**

By convention, both $U4$ and $U5$ will move the ψ to the next rule to set up the next general step, but will mark the current ⟨rule⟩'s left end with θ so $U6$ can find it. The simpler one is $U5$, of course, since it does not involve any search for the successor rule. We recall that before $U5$ is applied ψ is situated as follows:

$$\ldots j_1; \psi k : Q_1 \rightarrow Q_2, j_2; \ldots$$

Then $U5$ is written

algorithm $U5(B, *, \psi, \sigma, \theta)$; $\mathbf{B} \eta$;   *Comments*
0: $\psi \rightarrow \theta\psi$, 1;   Insert θ.
1: $\psi; \rightarrow ;\psi$. ;   Move ψ past next semicolon.
2: $\psi\eta \rightarrow \eta\psi$, 1 **end**   Shift ψ right.

The algorithm $U4$ makes a copy of j_1 preceded by a special punctuation character δ, deletes ψ, moves δj_1 left to the $*$ between the GVT and the ⟨rule⟩s of $\tilde{H}$, then right until a ⟨label⟩ matches j_1, and ends by inserting θ just ahead of that ⟨label⟩ and ψ just after the next semicolon (or **end**). [Its explicit form will be generated in Exercise 1.9.1.]

We have now come to $U6$, whose task is to execute the ⟨rule⟩ bounded on the left by θ and on the right by ψ:

$$\ldots \theta j_1 : Q_1 \rightarrow Q_2, j_2; \psi \ldots$$

We may describe the steps needed to carry out $U6$ as follows: An algorithm $U7$ initializes, and then $U8$ determines if Q_1 can be matched in the current version of $T(P)$. If not, $U9$ is used to terminate; if so, $U10$ computes the value of the RHS by using the assignments to generic variables resulting from the match, and $U11$ substitutes the value of the RHS for Q_1. Thus $U6$ should have the form

$$U6 = U8(U9, U11 \circ U10) \circ U7$$

In thus exhibiting $U6$, there is an example of an error which is commonly made, sometimes under different guises. It is intended that $U10$ should use information derived from the matching process carried out in $U8$. In particular, values assigned to generic variables by the match, and the position in $T(P)$ of the matched substring, are expected to be available to *U10*. Since *U8* is a control ⟨algorithm⟩ involved in a two-way branch, however, its action is on an entirely separate copy of the contents of *R* (see Section 1.4), and any punctuation, insertions, or generic variable assignments made by *U8* are made in that copy. We have been very careful to eliminate all traces of the action of the control ⟨algorithm⟩ before executing one of the branches, and this removes any chance that *U10* can benefit from the action of *U8*.

It is clear that we must manipulate punctuation and make a trial assignment of values for generic variables in a preliminary algorithm (*U12*), then test with *U8* for a match. If *U8* "approves" of the match, we execute *U10* to compute the value of the RHS, and then *U11* to substitute this value for Q_1, as indicated above. Otherwise, we must invoke *U12* for another "setup" and try *U8* again. We thus need an *iteration control algorithm U13*, which terminates when a match is made, or when *T(P)* has been exhausted without success. We can arrange this easily enough by having *U7* (the initializing part of *U6*) delete any $\sigma 1$ or $\sigma 1^2$ that is in *R*. Should *U12* then find a match, it will prefix $\sigma 1$ to *R*. Should *U12* make an attempt to match and fail, no σ will be prefixed. Eventually *U12* may find it impossible to "set up" another try because *T(P)* is exhausted. Then *U12* must prefix $\sigma 1^2$, and *U8* should recognize $\sigma 1^2$ as the signal for a definite failure to match. The presence of σ for either reason in *R* will cause *U13* to exit, terminating the action of *U6*.

$$U6 = U13(U8(U9, U11 \circ U10) \circ U12) \circ U7$$

The lesson here is to separate the control action from any real computation whose results must be used afterwards.

The control algorithm *U13* is of course simple.

algorithm *U13*(B, ∗, ψ, σ, θ);   *Comments*
          B ∪ ∗ ∪ ψ ∪ σ ∪ θ η;
  0: σ → , 2;   Match or *T(P)* exhausted.
  1:   → . ;   Set *U13(P)* ≠ Λ, go to execute *U12*.
  2: η → , 2;   Force *U13(P)* = Λ, terminate.
  3:   → . **end**

Let us see how *U12* will "set up" a match. A character ϵ must be used to point to the "next ⟨character⟩" in Q_1 to be tried in the match, so each entry to *U12* must delete any ϵ left over from a previous trial and insert ϵ to the left of Q_1. Another pointer μ must move through *T(P)*, indicating the place to begin trying for a match. (A match is tried, starting with the first character in *T(P)*, then starting with the second character, and so on.)

A third pointer π must be coordinated with ϵ so long as character-for-character matching has been successful. As soon as ϵ reaches the "$\rightarrow$", a match has been made, and $\sigma 1$ is prefixed to R. The situation during the matching attempt may be visualized as shown in Fig. 1.5, where the γ's and δ's are characters in the alphabet A^∞, and in this case, three characters have been matched successfully. The pointer π must be inserted into $T(P)$ by $U12$ on each entry (just as with ϵ), just to the right of μ. On the other hand, μ must exist in R before and after any particular execution of $U12$, so it must be introduced by $U7$. The removal of ϵ, μ, and π when the action of $U6$ is over may be entrusted to $U9$ on termination, or $U11$ when the RHS substition is made. One other "housekeeping" job $U12$ must do on each entry to set up a match attempt is the deletion of any tentative generic variable assignments left over from previous attempts at matching.

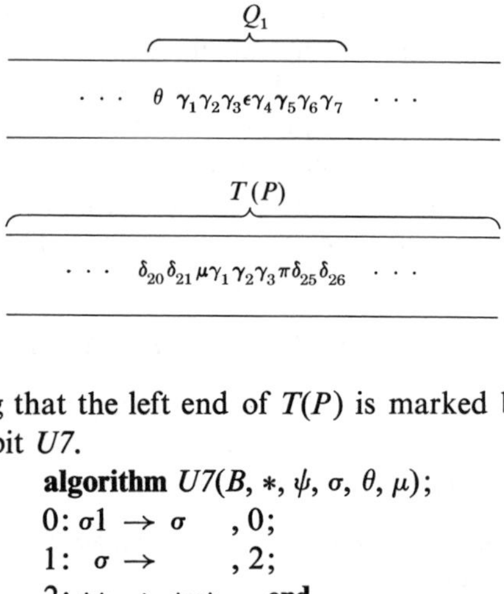

$$Q_1$$

$$\cdots \quad \theta \; \gamma_1\gamma_2\gamma_3\epsilon\gamma_4\gamma_5\gamma_6\gamma_7 \quad \cdots$$

$$T(P)$$

$$\cdots \quad \delta_{20}\delta_{21}\mu\gamma_1\gamma_2\gamma_3\pi\delta_{25}\delta_{26} \quad \cdots$$

Figure 1.5

Remembering that the left end of $T(P)$ is marked by $**$ (see p. 67), we can now exhibit $U7$.

> **algorithm** $U7(B, *, \psi, \sigma, \theta, \mu)$;
> $0: \sigma 1 \rightarrow \sigma \quad , 0;$
> $1: \; \sigma \rightarrow \qquad , 2;$
> $2: ** \rightarrow *\mu* \; , \quad$ **end**

The reason for putting μ before one asterisk is to allow $U12$ to advance μ one ⟨character⟩ on each entry.

The control algorithm $U8$ is also easily written.

algorithm $U8(B, *, \psi, \sigma, \theta, \mu, \epsilon, \pi)$;	*Comments*
$\qquad\qquad B \cup * \cup \psi \cup \sigma \cup \theta \cup \mu \cup \epsilon \cup \pi \, \eta;$	
$0: \sigma 1^2 \rightarrow \qquad , 2;$	Is $T(P)$ exhausted?
$1: \sigma 1 \; \rightarrow \sigma 1 \; . \; ;$	Match, execute
	$U11 \circ U10.$
$2: \eta \quad \rightarrow \qquad , 2;$	Force $U8(P) = \Lambda$,
	execute $U9.$
$3: \qquad \rightarrow \qquad . \;$ **end**	

Similarly, the termination (and cleanup) algorithm $U9$ now appears to be quite simple.

> **algorithm** $U9(B, *, \psi, \sigma, \theta, \mu, \epsilon, \pi)$; $\mu \cup \epsilon \cup \pi \, \eta$;
> $0: \eta \rightarrow , 0$;
> $1: \quad \rightarrow .$ **end**

Our task has now been reduced to specifying $U10$, $U11$, and $U12$. The steps involved in $U12$ may be stated as follows:

1. Delete any previous generic variable assignments, and then advance μ right, past one $\langle$character$\rangle$ in $T(P)$. (If μ cannot move farther to the right, prefix $\sigma 1^2$ to R, signaling a definite failure to match, and terminate $U12$.)

2. Introduce ϵ to the left of Q_1 and π just to the right of μ in $T(P)$.

3. The following action is now repeated.

a) Move ϵ right past one character η in Q_1, and move π right past one character ξ in $T(P)$. If ϵ can't move farther right, a match has been found; so terminate $U12$ after prefixing $\sigma 1$ to R. If π can't move farther right, a failure to match has occurred. In this case, prefix $\sigma 1^2$ to R and terminate $U12$. Otherwise, proceed to (3b).

b) If η is generic (discovered by looking for a match for η in the GVT), then (i) if η has no value assigned as yet, and if ξ is in the range of η (requiring that the index of ξ in the ST lie in one of the ranges recorded for η in the GVT), assign ξ to η, and a match is considered made on these $\langle$character$\rangle$s. Return to (3a). If ξ is not in the range of η, a failure to match has occurred for this position of μ. Terminate $U12$. (ii) If η is generic and has a value η' assigned, then a match on these $\langle$character$\rangle$s has occurred if $\eta' = \xi$, and we return to (3a); otherwise a failure to match has occurred for this position of μ, and $U12$ is terminated. If η is not generic, then a match has occurred if $\eta = \xi$, and we return to (3a); otherwise a failure to match has occurred for this position of μ, and $U12$ is terminated.

[The explicit form of $U12$ is generated in Exercise 1.9.2.]

The algorithm $U10$, which is executed when a match has occurred, must build up an RHS value based on the generic variable assignments made during the match. Remembering that ψ has been inserted just to the right of the semicolon to mark the end of the current rule, we find that the steps here are as follows:

1. Insert a punctuation character τ to the left of ψ and move it left to the beginning of Q_2.

2. Move τ to the right through Q_2. As τ moves past each character η in Q_2, if η is not generic, put a copy of η just to the left of ψ (thus separated from Q_2 and its successor by a semicolon). If η is generic, it must have been assigned a value during the match, and a copy of this value is inserted just to the left of ψ.

3. When τ has moved through Q_2, the appropriate RHS for the substitution lies just to the left of ψ. Delete τ and terminate *U10*.

[The explicit form of *U10* is asked for in Exercise 1.9.3.]

Algorithm *U11*, which is to substitute the value produced by *U10* in place of Q_1, must take advantage of the fact that μ and π were left by *U12* to delimit the part of $T(P)$ that was successfully matched. The steps in *U11* are as follows:

1. Insert a punctuation character τ just to the left of ψ.

2. Delete all of $T(P)$ between μ and π.

3. Move τ left through the substring created by *U10*, moving each $\langle$character$\rangle$ thus identified to the right until it just passes μ. This inserts that substring into the space between μ and π, and ensures that it is no longer to the left of ψ.

4. Delete ϵ, μ, π, and τ. Terminate *U11*.

[The explicit form of *U11* is asked for in Exercise 1.9.4.]

This completes the description of the universal algorithm U, which we wrote originally as $U = U2(U1) \circ U0$, except that R now contains $T(\tilde{H})**T(\tilde{H}(P))$ instead of $T(\tilde{H}(P))$. We shall add one more "cleanup" algorithm *U14*.

> **algorithm** *U14*$(B, *, \psi, \sigma)$; $\mathbf{B} \cup * \cup \boldsymbol{\psi} \cup \boldsymbol{\sigma} \, \eta$;
> $0 : \eta** \;\rightarrow\; ** \,, 0;$
> $1 : \;\; ** \rightarrow \;\;\;\;\;\; . \;\; \mathbf{end}$

so that finally we have

$$U = U14 \circ U2(U1) \circ U0$$

or, in expanded form,

$$U = U14 \circ U2(U13(U8(U9, U11 \circ U10) \circ U12) \circ U7 \circ U3(U4, U5)) \circ U0$$

We are now in a position where we can take any algorithm $\tilde{H}$ and a data word P for $\tilde{H}$, and perform the computation

$$U(T(\tilde{H}) ** T(P)) = T(\tilde{H}(P))$$

The reverse transcription from $T(\tilde{H}(P))$ to $\tilde{H}(P)$ is immediate from the ST, although this is an algorithmic activity which is not included in U.

Since we can represent any LMA as data now, many of the activities we previously performed on ⟨algorithm⟩s to produce useful constructions can now be represented as ⟨algorithm⟩s as well. As an example, let $\tilde{H}3 = \tilde{H}0(\tilde{H}1, \tilde{H}2)$, the two-way branch, which was given in Section 1.4 as

$$\tilde{H}3 = (\tilde{K}0_{n_1+4}; \tilde{H}1; \tilde{H}2) \circ \underline{\Lambda|} \; \tilde{H}0 \; \underline{|\alpha} \circ \text{Copy}$$

where $\tilde{K}0$ is a control ⟨algorithm⟩ which recognizes whether or not there are any ⟨character⟩s to the left of α in R. If we let left and right parentheses be included in A^∞, we define

$$P_1 = T(\tilde{H}0)T(\text{``(''})T(\tilde{H}1)T(\text{``,''})T(\tilde{H}2)T(\text{``)''}) ** T(P)$$

where quotation marks are used to delimit literal character strings. Then we can construct another algorithm $\tilde{K}1$ such that $U(T(\tilde{K}1) ** T(P_1)) = T(\tilde{H}3(P))$. The tasks which $\tilde{K}1$ must perform consist of inserting the ⟨rule⟩s of $\tilde{K}0$ at the left (modified to make it $\tilde{K}0_{n_1+4}$), inserting the ⟨rule⟩s of Copy, focusing $\tilde{H}0$, and so on, What results, however, is a string in R which can be processed by U to compute the result $\tilde{H}3(P)$.

An ⟨algorithm⟩ such as $\tilde{K}1$, which does editing tasks, is known as a *preprocessor* (or *compiler*). Such ⟨algorithm⟩s allow us to introduce many new notational devices, such as the two-way branch, the iteration, etc., without modifying the basic machine, that is, U. We may even introduce new notations within the ⟨rule⟩s of individual ⟨algorithm⟩s, such as the subalgorithm calls, addressable storage, and others, so long as we know that a preprocessor will be invoked to translate them into the machine's language—in this case, into the form of an LMA. If we wish, we can construct a preprocessor $\tilde{K}2$ which allows as input all of the devices we have seen in previous sections (plus others that occur to us en route) and agree to process all input this way, so that we have an enlarged language available for us to use. We may then "build $\tilde{K}2$ into the machine" by using a new machine $U_1 = U \circ \tilde{K}2$ to process all input. Of course, we must be careful to make all of our language changes true extensions, if possible, so that old input is still acceptable; we may have many useful ⟨algorithm⟩s already written which we would not like to make obsolete. We did a little of this in an earlier section, when addressable storage was introduced and R could no longer be assumed to have the null character at the left end. Since all ⟨algorithm⟩s could be converted into new ones easily (in particular, by a simple preprocessor which could be built into the machine), it was considered worth this slight inconvenience to pick up a very useful notation.

More important in some ways than the protection of old ⟨algorithm⟩s is the requirement that the preprocessor should accept its own output— even better, anything written in the language of the machine—as acceptable input. In other words, its action should be "transparent" to an ⟨algorithm⟩ which contains no new constructions; such an ⟨algorithm⟩ should come out unchanged from a trip through the preprocessor. The utility of this requirement lies in our ability to take ⟨algorithm⟩s already processed and embed them in larger ⟨algorithm⟩s which employ the extended language. As stated in Section 1.1, everything must be considered in the light of the larger organization of which it is a part, and this property is what is needed to make that point of view feasible.

There is yet another alternative to the handling of a preprocessor $\widetilde{K2}$. So far we have suggested either (1) allowing $\widetilde{K2}$ to operate on P to produce output which can be processed at a later time by the machine U, or (2) building a new machine $U_1 = U \circ \widetilde{K2}$. In both of these methods, $\widetilde{K2}$ is completely finished before U is used. One may consider a modified version of $\widetilde{K2}$, which would construct the expansion in machine language of each ⟨rule⟩ of an algorithm $\tilde{H}$ written in an extended language and terminate, leaving a pointer in $\tilde{H}$ to mark the preprocessed ⟨rule⟩. Then one may invoke U to execute that ⟨rule⟩ right then, before calling on $\widetilde{K2}$ to process another ⟨rule⟩ in $\tilde{H}$. Such a system is called an *interpreter*. Of course, even without $\widetilde{K2}$, the basic machine U is already an interpreter.

The variety of choices available, such as compilers and interpreters, and the language extensions they facilitate, forms the basis of what is called *computer programming*.

EXERCISES 1.9

1. Give the explicit form of the algorithm *U4*.

2. Give the explicit form of the algorithm *U12*. [Hint: If η is generic with no value assigned, one way to determine if ξ is in the range of η is to define two subalgorithms (a) δ Less τ, which when called upon determines whether the number marked by δ is less than the number marked by τ and leaves a flag accordingly, and (b) δ Greater τ, which acts similarly. Then *U12* sets up δ and τ, calls the appropriate subalgorithm, and checks the flag to determine the next action. Note also that the two subalgorithms which compare numbers of the form $\alpha 1^n$ and $\gamma 1^m$ by shifting δ and τ

through the "ones " must make use of alias alphabets, since δ and τ are themselves of the form $\alpha 1^{\kappa}$.]

3. Give the explicit form of algorithm *U10*.

4. Give the explicit form of algorithm *U11*.

5. One detail not covered in the discussion in the text is the association that must be made between the value of a generic variable ξ after a match and the value of any of its alisaes ξ^n. More generally, there must be an association made between the value assigned to any alias ξ^r by a match and the value used for any other alias ξ^s. Thus, in the rule

$$i: \xi^r \to \xi^s, j;$$

we wish the $\langle$character$\rangle$ in A^r matched to ξ^r to be converted to the corresponding character in alphabet A^s. What changes must be made in the preceding development to handle this association? [Hint: Store as the "value" of ξ^n the name ξ, whenever ξ^n is entered into the GVT. After a match on ξ^n by a^n, store as the actual value of ξ the $\langle$character$\rangle$ a.]

1.10 GENERIC VARIABLES WITH SPECIFIED PROPERTIES—TREE LMA'S

So far in this development, we have required each generic variable ξ to match exactly one $\langle$character$\rangle$ in R, subject only to the condition that the matched $\langle$character$\rangle$ belong to the appropriate alphabet A for ξ. A great deal of convenience and flexibility can be obtained by relaxing the condition that ξ match a single $\langle$character$\rangle$, to allow it to match any substring of elements of A (in particular, the smallest one) such that the entire left-hand side of the $\langle$rule$\rangle$ makes a match. Thus, if a, b, and c are in A and ξ is generic over A, the rule

$$\alpha \xi \beta \to \alpha \beta \xi$$

would transform the contents of R,

$$\alpha abc\beta$$

to $\alpha \beta abc$, with ξ matching the substring abc. When we wish to indicate that a generic variable may match a substring of $\langle$character$\rangle$s in A, we shall write $\mathbf{A}^*\xi$ in the $\langle$heading$\rangle$, instead of $\mathbf{A} \xi$.

The next step, of course, is to specify that ξ may match only certain substrings in R. For example, one might wish to specify that only substrings of length 2 (that is, containing exactly 2 $\langle$character$\rangle$s in A) should be admissible. More generally, one could insist that only substrings for which a particular control algorithm $\tilde{H}$ returns a nonempty register R will be allowed. Thus one could adopt the notations

$$\mathbf{A}(\tilde{H}) \, \xi \qquad \text{or} \qquad \mathbf{A}^*(\tilde{H}) \, \xi$$

for this purpose. [Exercise 1.10.1 asks which part(s) of the machine in Section 1.9 would have to be modified for this to be allowed. Exercise 1.10.2 asks how a particular part of the universal machine would have to be modified using these new ideas. Exercise 1.10.3 asks that a control algorithm $\tilde{H}$ be written which will select out substrings of length 1, thus showing that $A^*(\tilde{H})\ \xi$ includes the original form $A(\tilde{H})\ \xi$ as a special case.]

Another very useful notational device has been adopted in SNOBOL [6] to simplify the use of focusing. In SNOBOL, each ⟨rule⟩ is preceded by the name of a substring of R, and attention is automatically focused on that substring. This procedure is very similar to our use of addresses in ALMA's, but one further step is taken in SNOBOL. When a generic variable is assigned a corresponding substring via a match, that assignment is retained until a new assignment is made, even across ⟨rule⟩s. In other words, once a particular substring has been identified by the context it is in, it does not need to be discovered by context again; it now bears a name. [Exercise 1.10.4 asks that Primes be written with this SNOBOL convention.] Our goal in this chapter was to explore the elementary ideas involved in ⟨algorithm⟩s and languages, and so we did not pursue all possible notational variations. This decision does not lessen the importance of powerful, flexible notation; it is merely a choice of emphasis.

One special choice of the control algorithm $\tilde{H}$ should be mentioned before we leave this topic. As we shall see in the exercises, it is possible to ask via a control ⟨algorithm⟩ that a substring have "balanced parentheses." By definition, a string has "balanced parentheses" if (1) it is not empty, and (2) for every ⟨character⟩ in the string it is true that the number of right parentheses to its left does not exceed the number of left parentheses to its left, and (3) the total number of left and right parentheses are equal. Thus the following strings have balanced parentheses: (a), $(a(bc))$, $(\ )$, ab while the following do not: $)a(, (ab, ((a)))b$. [Exercise 1.10.5 asks for the control ⟨algorithm⟩ $\tilde{H}$.] We shall adopt the special ⟨heading⟩ notation (ξ) if we wish ξ to match only substrings with balanced parentheses. Thus, $A^*(H_1)\ (\xi)$ means that ξ may match substrings of one or more characters in A, but only those which have balanced parentheses and for which, in addition, control algorithm $\tilde{H}_1$ leaves R nonempty. [Exercise 1.10.6 asks what the implications of the notation $A(\xi)$ are.]

The reason for the interest in strings with balanced parentheses is that so many problems are concerned with strings on which a tree structure has been superimposed, and ⟨algorithm⟩s written with this extended notation will be called "tree LMA's." For example, an arithmetic expression, such as

$$((a+b)+(c*d))-e$$

can be represented easily as a tree.

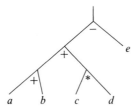

It is the parentheses that impose the tree structure on the string when it is no longer written in two-dimensional form. To be sure, we often omit parentheses, so that the previous example could be written

$$a + b + c * d - e$$

but this is possible only because of a convention, or agreement, as to how missing parentheses must be inserted whenever use is to be made of them. In other words, there is one conventional tree-structure interpretation of such a ⟨character string⟩, and any departures from that one require explicit parentheses. We shall have more to say about such conventions in the next chapter, and in Chapter 3 we shall examine in some detail the treatment of data with particular structures superimposed on them.

As one would expect, some ⟨algorithm⟩s are still appropriate, even if the data acquire some new structure. Thus, for example, the ⟨algorithm⟩ of Section 1.3, which does a ⟨character⟩ for ⟨character⟩ match for equality (after reversing one of the strings), still works on trees, since the parentheses which imply the tree structure are also ⟨character⟩s which must match. However, those activities which specifically deal with elements of the structure are greatly simplified when described in a notation suited to the structure. Consider the problem of merging two lists (represented as fully parenthesized strings) so that their corresponding elements are paired. For example, given the lists $((xyz)(ab)ef)$ and $(gh(kl)m)$, each containing four elements (some of them lists in their own right) we wish to transform the string

$$((xyz)(ab)ef) * (gh(kl)m)$$

into the string

$$(((xyz)g)((ab)h)(e(kl))(fm))$$

An ⟨algorithm⟩ which will do this is presented on the next page. Such manipulations without "tree LMA's" would be formidable indeed.

$$\textbf{algorithm } \text{Merge}(A); \textbf{A}^*(\eta), (\rho), (\phi);$$
$$0: \quad)*(\quad \rightarrow \quad * \qquad , 1;$$
$$1: \quad *\eta \quad \rightarrow \quad \sigma\eta* \quad , 1;^\dagger$$
$$2: \eta\rho\sigma\phi \rightarrow \eta\sigma\phi\rho , 2;$$
$$3: \quad \eta\sigma\phi \rightarrow (\eta\phi) \quad , 3;$$
$$4: \quad * \quad \rightarrow \qquad \quad . \quad \textbf{end}$$

EXERCISES 1.10

1. Which part(s) of the universal algorithm U in Section 1.9 would have to be modified to allow matches of generic varables with substrings, and then only if a control algorithm $\tilde{H}$ returns a nonempty register when applied to the substring?

2. Describe in detail how algorithm $U12$ in Section 1.9 would have to be modified if we allow generic variables to match substrings of any length. What if we required that a control algorithm return a nonempty register when applied to the matching substring?

3. Write a control algorithm $\tilde{H}$ which returns a nonempty register if the substring to which it is applied is of length 1.

4. Write the $\langle$algorithm$\rangle$ Primes using the SNOBOL convention that once a generic variable is assigned a corresponding substring via a match, that assignment is retained until a new assignment is made.

5. Give the explicit form of the control algorithm which will return a non-empty register only if the substring to which it is applied has balanced parentheses, and will return an empty register otherwise.

6. What are the implications for ξ of the notation $A(\xi)$?

1.11 DATA TRANSFORMATIONS

The techniques for deriving the $\langle$rule$\rangle$s which make up a labeled Markov algorithm have not yet been studied here. An $\langle$algorithm$\rangle$ is a creation, and only after it is completely written can it be studied; i.e., only then does it perform the task for which it was created. Thus far very little insight has been provided into the creative activity of constructing the $\langle$algorithm$\rangle$. What follows is still not a complete formal procedure for derivation of $\langle$algorithm$\rangle$s, but rather an approach which can be partially

---

$\dagger$ Remember that η matches the *smallest* substring with balanced parentheses after the asterisk.

automated (perhaps later, fully automated), and which proves useful in creating $\langle$algorithm$\rangle$s.

To begin, consider the LMA

algorithm Even(G, α);
$$
\begin{aligned}
0: &\alpha &\rightarrow\ & \gamma\,, 1;\\
1: &\gamma 11 &\rightarrow\ & \gamma\,, 1;\\
2: &\gamma 1\alpha &\rightarrow\ & \gamma\,, 1;\\
3: &\gamma\alpha &\rightarrow\ & 1\gamma\,, 1;\\
4: &\gamma 1 &\rightarrow\ & .\ ;\\
5: &\gamma &\rightarrow\ & 1\ \ .\ \ \textbf{end}
\end{aligned}
$$

which operates on an initial data word P of the form $\alpha 1^{n_1}\,\alpha 1^{n_2}\ldots\alpha 1^{n_r}$. In order to decide what this $\langle$algorithm$\rangle$ does, it is instructive to write down the transformations induced by the $\langle$rule$\rangle$s of Even in the data word P. The effect of rule 0 may be stated:

$$\alpha: \rightarrow \gamma:$$

where the new notation $\alpha:$ in the LHS means that when and only when the leftmost character is an α, it is changed to γ. (The colon is used to indicate a partition of P into two parts.) The other $\langle$character$\rangle$s in P, being unmentioned, are not examined and are unchanged. Rule 1 can be similarly described:

$$\gamma 11: \rightarrow \gamma:$$

with rule 1 again the successor. Ultimately, one of two states $\gamma 1\alpha$ or $\gamma\alpha$ occurs, except for the rightmost case, when only the terminal states $\gamma 1$ and γ are possible. The transformations used to describe these subsequent situations are

$$
\begin{aligned}
&:\gamma 1\alpha: \rightarrow\ :\gamma: &&\text{(successor is rule 1)}\\
&:\gamma\alpha\ : \rightarrow\ :1\gamma: &&\text{(successor is rule 1)}\\
&:\gamma 1\ \ \rightarrow\ : &&\text{(no successor)}\\
&:\gamma\ \ \ \ \ \ :1 &&\text{(no successor)}
\end{aligned}
$$

(Note how account is taken of possible characters to the left of γ.) The first four $\langle$rule$\rangle$s in Even are able to return to rule 1 because the result of any of their transformations is still in the *general form* assumed to be appropriate input to rule 1:

$$1^q\,\gamma\,1^p\,\alpha\,1^{n_j}\,\alpha\,1^{n_{j+1}} \cdots \alpha 1^{n_r}$$

A brief analysis of these transformations suggests that the $\langle$algorithm$\rangle$ counts the number of the n_i $(i = 1,\ldots, r)$ which are even and leaves the count in R.

It is our goal here to reverse this analysis. Starting with a desirable set of transformations to be performed on a data word given in some general form, we wish to generate the ⟨rule⟩s of *some* LMA—there could be several—which would produce the same transformations on the same initial data word P. It is obvious that we must specify a language in which a *data transformation algorithm* (DTA) may be precisely described. Then we need an ⟨algorithm⟩ (or at least an algorithmic activity) which produces correctly written ⟨rule⟩s from the specified transformations. It will be seen that the activity given below produces rules for an algorithm, but these rules are not exactly in Markov form. We shall call the result a "pseudo-LMA." It will be clear how to proceed after that, but not particularly useful to us to develop all of the necessary detail.

Let us write down the data flow for the same ⟨algorithm⟩, using the language which will be formally introduced shortly.

Even(G, α);

b **form** $\alpha 1^{n_1} \cdots \alpha 1^{n_r} \equiv \alpha: \rightarrow \gamma: = \gamma 1^{n_1}: = a$ **form** $1^a \gamma 1^p \alpha 1^{n_j} \cdots \alpha 1^{n_r}$
$\quad \equiv (:\gamma 11: \rightarrow :\gamma: = a, :\gamma 1\alpha: \rightarrow :\gamma: = a, :\gamma \alpha: \rightarrow :1\gamma: = a,$
$\quad :\gamma 1 \rightarrow :., :\gamma \rightarrow :1.)$ **end**

1. The declarator **form** here indicates that a general data form is about to be given. The role of the declarator and the form after it is that of a comment, i.e., purely informational. They may be omitted (up to, but not including, a comma or $\equiv$) without affecting any part of the process.

2. α: and γ: and other similar constructions are basic data forms which focus attention on particular substrings of the data. An $=$ sign between two such constructions represents a passage to a different view of the data, i.e., a focusing of attention on the data in a new way. (This is not a transformation which changes the data.)

3. The arrow between two forms specifies an actual transformation to be carried out on the data.

4. The use of the colon, as in $:\gamma 1\alpha:$, implies a partition of the data word. In this case the partition is into three substrings, namely, (a) all the characters to the left of the first occurrence of $\gamma 1\alpha$, (b) the substring $\gamma 1\alpha$, and (c) the substring of all the characters to the right of $\gamma 1\alpha$. Similarly, the form $:\beta::\tau:$ may be viewed as $Q_1\beta Q_2\tau Q_3$ where Q_1, Q_2, and Q_3 are substrings (possibly empty) determined by the first occurrence of β and the first occurrence of τ to the right of β. The colon, then, serves merely as a partition delimiter. Such a partition must not be ambiguous when used as a left side of a transformation; that is, $::\gamma 1\alpha:$ would not be allowed as a left side since the two leftmost substrings are not uniquely defined. The transformation indicated by an arrow requires that the number of substrings in the partition on the left equal the number of substrings in the partition on the right. The transformation then carries substrings on the left into corresponding substrings (which may be empty) on the right.

5. $A \equiv$ assigns a label to a state (or general form) of the data so that a return may be made to that label whenever the data have the same form. If **form** is used, the label precedes the symbol **form**.

6. The comma is used to separate elements of a *compound transformation*, i.e., a list of alternative transformations (delimited by left and right parentheses) among which a choice is to be made. The convention here is that the first applicable transformation is chosen, i.e., the first whose left side matches the current state of the data. In the example, the first alternative is

$$:\gamma 11: \ \rightarrow \ : \ \gamma: \ = a$$

the second is

$$:\gamma 1\alpha: \ \rightarrow \ : \ \gamma: \ = a$$

the third is

$$:\gamma\alpha \ : \ \rightarrow \ :1\gamma: \ = a$$

and the fourth and fifth are

$$:\gamma 1 \ \ \rightarrow \ :. \quad \text{and} \quad :\gamma \ \rightarrow \ :1.$$

A particular alternative may contain a sequence of transformations, as in

$$:\mu 1: \ \rightarrow \ :1\mu: \ = \ :\beta: \ \rightarrow \ :1\beta: \ = c$$

which occurs in a later example. The successor to an applicable transformation in such a compound transformation is the next transformation to the right within the same alternative. It is assumed that only the first transformation in an alternative may fail to be applicable; if the first is applicable, the remainder of the alternative must apply also. A label a appearing at the end of an alternative specifies that the successor transformation is to be the one occurring at the point of definition of the label a. If no label appears in this way, or if none of the alternatives is applicable, the successor to an alternative is found immediately after the right parenthesis delimiting the compound transformation.

7. The period indicates a terminal rule, i.e., one having no explicit successor. (This discussion suffices for the first example; the successor rule will be expanded as necessary to accommodate additional notations which will be introduced as we proceed.)

A more complicated example will now be used to show the need for additional constructions. The following set of data transformations on a nonempty initial word of the form $\alpha 1^{n_1} \ldots \alpha 1^{n_r}$ sorts the integers

$n_1 \ldots n_r$ in order of increasing magnitude to the right. [Exercise 1.11.1 asks what happens to duplicates; also what happens to 0, that is, just α.] The strategy here is to reduce by 1 each of the as yet unsorted numbers, keeping track of the number of times just after a character β. When some number $\alpha 1^{n_j}$ is reduced to zero, a copy of the set of 1's after β is made to the left of β to represent a newly sorted number.

Sort$(G \cup \alpha)$;

a **form** $\alpha 1^{n_1} \cdots \alpha 1^{n_r} \equiv \alpha: \to \beta * \alpha \tau: = b$ **form** $\alpha 1^{m_1} \cdots \alpha 1^{m_k}$
$\quad \beta 1^q * \alpha 1^{m_{k+1}} \cdots \alpha 1^{m_{k+j-1}} \alpha \tau 1^{m_{k+j}} \alpha 1^{m_{k+j+1}} \cdots \alpha 1^{m_r} \equiv (:\alpha \tau 1:$
$\quad \to :\alpha \tau:, \text{Count}(:\beta 1^q :: \alpha \tau:) = :\alpha 1^q \beta 1^q :: \tau:) = (:\tau :: \alpha: \to ::: \alpha \tau:$
$\quad = b, :\beta :: \tau: \to :\beta 1 :::= (:*\alpha: \to :*\alpha \tau: = b, :\beta: \to :: \Lambda .))$ **end**

Count$(G \cup \alpha \cup \beta \cup \tau)$;

$:\alpha \tau: \to :\tau: = :\beta: \to :\alpha \beta \mu: = c$ **form** $:\alpha 1^p \beta 1^p \mu 1^{q-p} \equiv (:\mu 1: \to :1\mu:$
$\quad = :\beta: \to :1\beta: = c, :\mu: \to ::.)$ **end**

We continue to list special notational devices which have appeared.

8. The appearance of more than one character string in a left side of a transformation, as in $:\beta :: \tau: \to :\beta 1 :::$, implies simultaneous matching; i.e., all testing for a match on the data (in this case, for β and for τ) is performed simultaneously, and then, only if a total match is found, all transformations are made simultaneously.

9. A subalgorithm "call," such as Count$(:\beta 1^q :: \alpha \tau:)$, means that if the basic data form inside the parentheses is applicable, the DTA Count is applied to produce a new data word of the form following the $=$ sign. The application of a DTA to a basic data form which is partitioned by means of colons carries with it the assumption that only those substrings specifically involved in the test for applicability—i.e., only those explicitly mentioned—are acted upon by the DTA. It is assumed that some sort of focusing of attention (such as change of alphabets) is used to accomplish this.

10. The character Λ denotes the null string, as usual.

As the easiest way to explain what was going on in the sorting transformations shown above, we shall create a pseudo-LMA from them. Since this pseudo-LMA was derived from the data transformations according to the algorithmic activity to be specified later, it may be viewed as an example result of that process.

pseudoalgorithm Sort($G \cup \alpha$);	*Comments*
0: α: $\rightarrow$ $\beta*\alpha\tau$: , 1;	Introduce punctuation.
1: :$\alpha\tau$1: $\rightarrow$:$\alpha\tau$: , 3;	Reduce each α by one.
2: Count(:$\beta1^q$::$\alpha\tau$:) , 3;	If only $\alpha\tau$ left, go to Count.
3: :τ::α: $\rightarrow$ :::$\alpha\tau$: , 1;	Move τ to next α.
4: :β::τ: $\rightarrow$:β1::: , 5;	Let β count reductions.
5: :*α: $\rightarrow$:*$\alpha\tau$: , 1;	Start another cycle.
6: :β: $\rightarrow$ ::Λ . **end**	Delete β and everything to its right.

pseudoalgorithm Count($G \cup \alpha \cup \beta \cup \tau$);	*Comments*
0: :$\alpha\tau$: $\rightarrow$:τ: , 1;	Delete α.
1: :β: $\rightarrow$:$\alpha\beta\mu$: , 2;	Introduce punctuation and new α.
2: :μ1: $\rightarrow$:1μ: , 4;	Move μ through 1^q.
3: :μ: $\rightarrow$ :: .	Terminate.
4: :β: $\rightarrow$:1β: , 2**end**	Duplicate $\beta1^q$ as $\alpha1^q$.

[Exercise 1.11.2 asks that some DTA's be constructed.]

Once the pseudo-LMA is constructed, each rule must be rewritten (in general, expanded) into legitimate Markov notation. Thus rule 5 in the Sort example would become

$$5: *\alpha \rightarrow *\alpha\tau \, , 1;$$

A combination form, such as occurs in rule 3 here, requires more analysis. Clearly, the following sequence will work (since no harm will be done if there is no α to the right of τ).

$$3: \tau1 \rightarrow 1\tau \, , 3;$$
$$3.1: \tau\alpha \rightarrow \alpha\tau \, , 1;$$

However, discovering that this sequence is appropriate is not easy. Clearly one can arrange to put each substring of a partition into a different alias alphabet, apply a sequence of harmless transformations which do nothing but test applicability, follow (if the transformation is indeed applicable) with the rules which carry out the changes, and then finish by returning the whole data word back to the original alphabet. [Exercise 1.11.3 asks that it be done for rule 3.] We would hope to do better than this, but we shall not pursue it here.

Since we are interested in a powerful data transformation language, we now turn to the branching and iterative constructions which proved so useful earlier. Let A be a basic data form (such as $:\beta::\alpha:$), T_1, T_2 arbitrary transformations, and $\tilde{H}$ the name of a control algorithm (either an LMA or a DTA). Consider

$$\tilde{H}(A)(T_1, T_2) \tag{1}$$

This notation means that if A is an applicable data form, then T_1 or T_2 is the next transformation performed, depending on whether $\tilde{H}(A)$ is null or not. (The transformations T_1 and T_2 must be applicable if A is.) If A is not applicable or if either T_1 or T_2 is carried out with no successor indicated by a label, the successor to this construction is the next transformation after the right parenthesis, in the usual way. Note that if A_1 is another data form, then

$$A_1 \rightarrow \tilde{H}(A)(T_1, T_2)$$

is to be interpreted as

$$A_1 \rightarrow A = \tilde{H}(A)(T_1, T_2)$$

so that A is produced, no matter what happens when $\tilde{H}$ is applied. A similar remark applies to the subalgorithm call already discussed (such as Count above) and the iterative construction which follows.

$$\tilde{H}(A)(T_1) \tag{2}$$

Here the transformation T_1 is assumed to be applicable and is to be carried out repeatedly so long as A is applicable and $\tilde{H}(A)$ nonnull.

In each of these constructions, as with the subalgorithm call, the application of an algorithm to a basic data form which is partitioned by means of colons carries with it the assumption that only those substrings specifically involved in the test for applicability—i.e., only those explicitly mentioned—are acted upon by the algorithm. It is assumed that some sort of focusing of attention (such as change of alphabets) is used to accomplish this.

Some of these additional notations will be employed in our next example of a DTA, the decomposition of a number n (represented as 1^n) into its prime factors ($n \geq 4$), as discussed in Section 1.5. (This $\langle$algorithm$\rangle$ was given as an ALMA called "Primes" at the end of Section 1.8.)

Primes($G \cup \alpha$);

a **form** $n \equiv n \rightarrow n\gamma n*2\alpha 2 = b$ **form** $n_k \gamma n_k * j\alpha j\beta m_k \beta m_k - 1 \ldots \beta m_1$
   $\equiv\ :*j: \rightarrow\ :\rho j*j:\ =\ \mathrm{Mult}(:j*j:)\ =\ :n_k\rho j^2: \rightarrow \mathrm{Less}(:n_k*j^2:)(n_k::\alpha j:$
   $\rightarrow \beta n_k: \Lambda: \Lambda:., :n_k*j^2\alpha j: \rightarrow\ :n_k*j\alpha j:\ =\ \mathrm{Div}(:n_k*j:)\ =\ (n_k\gamma q*\alpha j:$
   $\rightarrow q\gamma q*j\alpha j\beta j:\ =\ b, n_k\gamma q*r\alpha j: \rightarrow n_k\gamma n_k*1^{j+1}\ \alpha\ 1^{j+1}:\ =\ b))$ **end**

In order to describe the process of producing a pseudoalgorithm from a set of data transformations, we need a precise specification of the transformation language. We begin with the *data form*, and we use as primitives

(1) ⟨character⟩s, i.e., elements of an alphabet;

(2) ⟨symbol⟩, i.e., an ⟨identifier⟩; and

(3) ⟨alphabet name⟩.

⟨label⟩ ::= ⟨symbol⟩ | ⟨symbol⟩ **form** ⟨free text not containing a comma
    or ≡⟩

⟨character string⟩ ::= {⟨character⟩}$_1^*$

⟨extended character string⟩ ::= ⟨character string⟩ | Λ | ⟨empty⟩

⟨basic data form⟩ ::= ⟨extended character string⟩ {:⟨extended character
    string⟩}*

⟨algorithm call⟩ ::= ⟨symbol⟩ (⟨basic data form⟩)

⟨iteration⟩ ::= ⟨algorithm call⟩ (⟨data form⟩)

⟨branch⟩ ::= ⟨algorithm call⟩ (⟨data form⟩, ⟨data form⟩)

⟨data form⟩† ::= ⟨basic data form⟩ | ⟨iteration⟩ | ⟨branch⟩ |
    ⟨label⟩ ≡ ⟨data form⟩ | ⟨compound transformation⟩

We may now specify the syntax of a *data transformation algorithm* in terms of the ⟨data form⟩:

⟨left side⟩ ::= ⟨data form⟩ = | ⟨data form⟩ →

⟨right side⟩ ::= ⟨data form⟩ | ⟨data form⟩. | ⟨data form⟩ = ⟨label⟩

⟨transformation sequence⟩ ::= ⟨left side⟩ {= ⟨left side⟩ | → ⟨left side⟩}*

⟨transformation⟩ ::= ⟨transformation sequence⟩ ⟨right side⟩

⟨transformation list⟩ ::= ⟨transformation⟩ {, ⟨transformation⟩}*

⟨compound transformation⟩ ::= ⟨transformation⟩ | (⟨transformation
    list⟩)

⟨heading⟩ ::= ⟨symbol⟩ (⟨alphabet name⟩)

⟨labeled compound transformation⟩ ::= ⟨heading⟩; ⟨compound trans-
    formation⟩ **end**

⟨data transformation algorithm⟩‡ ::= {⟨labeled compound transforma-
    tion⟩}$_1^*$

The reader should check that the ⟨DTA⟩s already exhibited conform to this syntax specification.

---

† Note that ⟨compound transformation⟩ occurs here; although it is defined in the next set of specifications, it must occur here as well.

‡ We shall continue to refer to this as a ⟨DTA⟩.

We now return to the generation of a pseudo-LMA from a $\langle \text{DTA} \rangle$. Suppose that we have a $\langle \text{DTA} \rangle$, such as Sort developed earlier:

Sort$(G \cup \alpha)$;

a **form** $\alpha 1^{n_1} \cdots \alpha 1^{n_r} \equiv \alpha: \to \beta * \alpha \tau: = b$ **form** $\alpha 1^{m_1} \cdots \alpha 1^{m_k}$
$\quad \beta 1^q * \alpha 1^{m_k+1} \cdots \alpha 1^{m_k+j-1} \alpha \tau 1^{m_k+j} \alpha 1^{m_k+j+1} \cdots \alpha 1^{m_r} \equiv (:\alpha \tau:$
$\quad \to \; :\alpha \tau:, \; \text{Count}(:\beta 1^q :: \alpha \tau:) = :\alpha 1^q \beta 1^q :: \tau:) = (:\tau :: \alpha: \to ::: \alpha \tau:$
$\quad = b, \; :\beta :: \tau: \to \; :\beta 1 ::: = (: * \alpha: \to \; : * \alpha \tau: = b, \; :\beta: \to \; :: \Lambda \; .)) $ **end**

Count$(G \cup \alpha \cup \beta \cup \tau)$;

$:\alpha \tau: \to \; :\tau: = \; :\beta: \to \; :\alpha \beta \mu: = c$ **form** $:\alpha 1^p \beta 1^p \mu 1^{q-p} \equiv (:\mu 1: \to \; :1 \mu:$
$\quad = \; :\beta: \to \; :1 \beta: = c, \; :\mu: \to \; ::.)$ **end**

We first create a table, called the "symbol table," by listing in some arbitrary order all $\langle \text{label} \rangle$s that occur in the $\langle \text{DTA} \rangle$ (but without any **form**s that might follow them), and assigning each an index in the table, starting with 0. If there are n of them, then n is the index of the next available position in the table. Whenever we wish to enter a new symbol into the table, we shall assign it index n and increase n by 1. The process of inserting into the table an arbitrary symbol distinct from those already in the table and assigning it the next available index will be called *creating a symbol*, and the symbol will be called *a created symbol*.

We now carry out a sequence of modifications of the $\langle \text{DTA} \rangle$ in order to make it easily mapped into a pseudo-LMA.

1. Delete all **form** declarations, including any text which follows, up to but not including a comma or $\equiv$.

2. Replace each occurrence of a $\langle \text{label} \rangle$ by its index in the symbol table.

3. The following substitutions are now carried out in order of occurrence in the list opposite. The symbol $\tilde{H}$ denotes a subalgorithm name, the symbol A a $\langle \text{basic data form} \rangle$, k a $\langle \text{label} \rangle$, and $T, T_1, T_2, \ldots, T_m$ any $\langle \text{compound transformation} \rangle$s. The symbol $\circ$ denotes either $=$, $\equiv$, or $\to$. The symbol n represents a (created) $\langle \text{label} \rangle$ of index n (different for each application of each rule below). It is used to allow pieces of rules to be detached and placed separately in the resulting tableaux, without losing the sequencing relationships. The overall strategy, which will become clearer in the applications which follow, is to build enough *explicit sequencing information* into the text so that it will be possible to break it apart into a different representation, *with a different sequencing discipline*, and still effect the same sequencing on execution of the result.

From	*To*
	$\circledS^\dagger$
$; $	
$\to \tilde{H}(A)$	$\to A\circledS\tilde{H}(A)$
$= \tilde{H}(A)$	$\circledS\tilde{H}(A)$
$\to \tilde{H}(A)(T_1, T_2)^\ddagger$	$\to A\circledS(\tilde{H}(A)\circledS T_1, T_2)$
$= \tilde{H}(A)(T_1, T_2)$	$\circledS(\tilde{H}(A)\circledS T_1, T_2)$
$\tilde{H}(A)(T_1)$	$n \equiv (\tilde{H}(A)\circledS T_1 = n)$
$\circ\ (T_1, T_2, \ldots, T_m) =$	$\circ\ (T_1 = n, T_2 = n, \ldots, T_m = n)\circledS n \equiv$
$\circ\ (T_1, \ldots, T_i \circ A, \ldots, T_m) \to \S$	$\circ\ (T_1 = n, \ldots, T_i \circ A = n, \ldots,$
	$\qquad\qquad\qquad T_m = n)\circledS n \equiv A \to$
$. \ = k$	$.$
$= A =$	$=$
$= A\ \circledS$	$\circledS$
$\equiv A =$	$\equiv$
$= k = T$	$= k$
$\to A \to$	$\to A\ \circledS\ A \to$
$= T$	$\circledS\ T$
$\equiv\ \circledS$	$\equiv$
$= k \equiv$	$= k\ \circledS\ k \equiv$
$A\ \circledS\ T,\ \ (T \text{ not labeled})$	$= n\ \circledS\ n \equiv T$
$k \equiv ($	$(\ k \equiv$

† The symbol $\circledS$ is introduced for this activity, to be interpreted as "successor if successful."

‡ We adopt the convention for pseudorules that the *null* value of a control algorithm is the *successful* case.

§ Note that a compound transformation will not be followed by an arrow if every alternative terminates with a period or a ⟨label⟩.

The ⟨DTA⟩ Sort now has an initial symbol table

$$
\begin{array}{cc}
0 & a \\
1 & b
\end{array}
$$

while Count has the symbol table

$$
\begin{array}{cc}
0 & c
\end{array}
$$

and under these rules they become the modified ⟨DTA⟩s

Sort$(G \cup \alpha)\circledS$

$0 \equiv \alpha: \to \beta*\alpha\tau: = 1\ \circledS\ (1 \equiv :\alpha\tau1: \to :\alpha\tau: = 2,\ \text{Count}(:\beta1^q::\alpha\tau:)$
$\qquad = 2)\ \circledS\ (2 \equiv :\tau::\alpha: \to :::\alpha\tau: = 1,\ :\beta::\tau: \to :\beta1::: = 3\ \circledS\ (3$
$\qquad \equiv :*\alpha: \to :*\alpha\tau: = 1,\ :\beta: \to ::\Lambda.))\ \textbf{end}$

Count$(G \cup \alpha \cup \beta \cup \tau)$

$= 1 \circledS 1 \equiv :\alpha\tau: \rightarrow :\tau: = 2 \circledS 2 \equiv :\beta: \rightarrow :\alpha\beta\mu: = 0 \circledS (0 \equiv :\mu 1:$
$\rightarrow :1\mu: = 3 \circledS 3 \equiv :\beta: \rightarrow :1\beta: = 0, :\mu: \rightarrow ::.)$ **end**

Similarly, the "Primes" $\langle$DTA$\rangle$,

Primes$(G \cup \alpha)$;

a **form** $n \equiv n \rightarrow n\gamma n*2\alpha2 = b$ **form** $n_k \gamma n_k * j\alpha j\beta m_k \beta m_{k-1} \ldots \beta m_1$
$\equiv :*j: \rightarrow :\rho j*j: = \text{Mult}(:j*j:) = :n_k\rho j^2: \rightarrow \text{Less}(:n_k*j^2:) (n_k::\alpha j:$
$\rightarrow \beta n_k: \Lambda: \Lambda:., :n_k*j^2\alpha j: \rightarrow :n_k*j\alpha j: = \text{Div}(:n_k*j:) = (n_k\gamma q*\alpha j:$
$\rightarrow q\gamma q*j\alpha j\beta j: = b, n_k\gamma n_k*r\alpha j: \rightarrow n_k\gamma n_k*1^{j+1} \alpha 1^{j+1}: = b))$ **end**

becomes the modified $\langle$DTA$\rangle$,

Primes$(G \cup \alpha)\circledS$

$0 \equiv n \rightarrow n\gamma n*2\alpha2 = 1 \circledS 1 \equiv :*j: \rightarrow :\rho j*j: = 2 \circledS 2 \equiv :\rho j*j: \rightarrow :j*j:$
$= 3 \circledS 3 \equiv \text{Mult}(:j*j:) = 4 \circledS 4 \equiv :n_k\rho j^2: \rightarrow :n_k*j^2: = 5 \circledS (5$
$\equiv \text{Less}(:n_k*j^2:) = 6 \circledS 6 \equiv n_k::\alpha j: \rightarrow \beta n_k: \Lambda: \Lambda:., :n_k*j^2\alpha j:$
$\rightarrow :n_k*j\alpha j: = 7 \circledS 7 \equiv \text{Div}(:n_k*j:) = 8 \circledS (8 \equiv n_k\gamma q*\alpha j:$
$\rightarrow q\gamma q*j\alpha j\beta j: = 1, n_k\gamma q*r\alpha j: \rightarrow n_k\gamma n_k*j+1 \alpha j+1: = 1))$ **end**

[Exercise 1.11.4 asks for the modified $\langle$DTA$\rangle$ for Even.]

We are now ready to construct the pseudo-LMA from this modified
$\langle$DTA$\rangle$. What we have already created is a simpler $\langle$DTA$\rangle$ built directly
out of pseudorules, such as

$$0 \equiv \alpha: \rightarrow \beta*\alpha\tau: = 1$$

in Sort, which corresponds to the Markov rule

$$0: \alpha \rightarrow \beta*\alpha\tau, 1;$$

The procedure for generating the pseudo-LMA is now quite straightforward. At each stage we shall be dealing with a $\langle$compound trans-
formation$\rangle$, or with a single $\langle$transformation$\rangle$ which we may consider
to be just a special case of a $\langle$compound transformation$\rangle$ containing
one alternative. We begin by writing the $\langle$heading$\rangle$, preceded by the
prefix **pseudoalgorithm**, and we delete any $\circledS$ or $= k \circledS$ which may follow
the $\langle$heading$\rangle$ in the modified $\langle$DTA$\rangle$. Then we write the first alternative
(up to the first comma not contained in another $\langle$compound transforma-
tion$\rangle$) as the first (or next, in the general case) pseudorule.

Below it we write the second alternative, and so on. The step of
writing a $\langle$transformation$\rangle$ as a pseudorule must be carried out in a
special way, however, if it begins with a parenthesized $\langle$compound trans-

formation⟩. In this case, we delete the parentheses and list each of its alternatives as a separate pseudorule. Any part of the original alternative that followed the ⟨compound transformation⟩ is attached to the final alternative of the now separated ⟨compound transformation⟩. Thus a construction such as

$$(T_1, T_2, T_3) \, ⓢ \, (T_4, T_5) \, ⓢ \, A$$

becomes

$$T_1$$
$$T_2$$
$$T_3 \, ⓢ \, (T_4, T_5) \, ⓢ \, A$$

If T_1, T_2, or T_3 had been parenthesized, they would have been expanded in the same way while being written separately. A construction such as

$$((T_1, T_2), T_3, (T_4, (T_5 \, ⓢ \, A), T_6)) \, ⓢ \, B$$

becomes

$$T_1$$
$$T_2$$
$$T_3$$
$$T_4$$
$$T_5 \, ⓢ \, A$$
$$T_6 \, ⓢ \, B$$

We begin, then, by writing the principal alternatives below one another as just described. We then find the first ⓢ symbol from the top, delete it, and write everything to its right as pseudorules below the pseudorules so far written. This process also expands initial parenthesized ⟨compound transformation⟩s while writing them. We continue deleting ⓢ symbols and writing pseudorules in this way until no ⓢ symbols remain. The pseudorules may now be renumbered in the obvious way and converted to the standard notation involving semicolons, etc.

The ⟨DTA⟩ Sort now becomes the following pseudo-LMA (before renumbering).

$$
\begin{aligned}
&\textbf{pseudoalgorithm } \text{Sort}(G \cup \alpha); \\
&0 \equiv \alpha: \quad\quad \rightarrow \beta * \alpha\tau: \quad = 1 \\
&1 \equiv \, :\alpha\tau 1: \, \rightarrow \, :\alpha\tau: \quad = 2 \\
&\quad\quad\quad \text{Count}(:\beta 1^q::\alpha\tau:) \quad = 2 \\
&2 \equiv \, :\tau::\alpha: \rightarrow \, :::\alpha\tau: \quad = 1 \\
&\quad\quad\quad :\beta::\tau: \rightarrow \, :\beta 1::: \quad = 3 \\
&3 \equiv \, :*\alpha: \quad \rightarrow \, :*\alpha\tau: \quad = 1 \\
&\quad\quad\quad :\beta: \quad\quad \rightarrow \, ::\Lambda \quad\quad \textbf{. end}
\end{aligned}
$$

pseudoalgorithm Count($G \cup \alpha \cup \beta \cup \tau$);
$1 \equiv\ :\alpha\tau: \to\ :\tau: \quad = 2$
$2 \equiv\ :\beta: \quad \to\ :\alpha\beta\mu: = 0$
$0 \equiv\ :\mu 1: \to\ :1\mu: \quad = 3$
$\quad\quad :\mu: \to\ ::\ \quad .$
$3 \equiv\ :\beta: \quad \to\ :1\beta: \quad = 0$ **end**

After renumbering and converting to our standard LMA notation, it becomes

pseudoalgorithm Sort($G \cup \alpha$);
$0:\ \alpha: \quad\quad \to\ \beta{*}\alpha\tau:\ ,1;$
$1:\ :\alpha\tau 1: \to\ :\alpha\tau:\ \quad ,3;$
$2:\ \text{Count}(:\beta 1^q::\alpha\tau:)\ ,3;$
$3:\ :\tau::\alpha: \to\ :::\alpha\tau:\ ,1;$
$4:\ :\beta::\tau: \to\ :\beta 1:::\ ,5;$
$5:\ :{*}\alpha: \quad \to\ :{*}\alpha\tau:\ ,1;$
$6:\ :\beta: \quad\quad \to\ ::\Lambda\ \quad .\quad$ **end**

pseudoalgorithm Count($G \cup \alpha \cup \beta \cup \tau$);
$0:\ :\alpha\tau: \to\ :\tau:\ \quad ,1;$
$1:\ :\beta: \quad \to\ :\alpha\beta\mu:\ ,2;$
$2:\ :\mu 1: \to\ :1\mu:\ \quad ,4;$
$3:\ :\mu: \quad \to\ ::\ \quad .$
$4:\ :\beta: \quad \to\ :1\beta:\ \quad ,2$ **end**

[Exercise 1.11.5 asks that Even and Primes be converted to pseudo-LMA's and that the renumbering activity be carried out.]

EXERCISES 1.11

1. In the ⟨DTA⟩ Sort (a) what happens to duplicates? (b) What happens to 0 (that is, α)?

2. (a) Write a ⟨DTA⟩ to find the largest of k integers $\alpha 1^{n_1}, \alpha 1^{n_2}, \ldots, \alpha 1^{n_k}$ by checking the first against the second and deleting the smaller of the two. (b) Generalize on the ⟨DTA⟩ Sort so that it will sort decimal numbers. [Hint: To sort 23, 31, 22, for example, write them as

$$\gamma \alpha 11\alpha 111\gamma \alpha 111\alpha 1\gamma \alpha 11\alpha 11$$

(where γ separates the numbers), and then, starting with the last column first, use a method similar to ⟨DTA⟩ Sort, where the complete number is saved each time in an order depending on the column sorted. After all numbers are sorted according to last column, sort again on the next to last column, etc. Assume that all decimal numbers have the same number of digits by including a preliminary prefixing of α's (that is, leading zeros).]

3. Give the LMA which determines whether $:\tau::\alpha: \rightarrow :::\alpha\tau:$ is applicable, and if so, carries out the transformation, and if not, returns R in its original state.

4. Give the "modified $\langle$DTA$\rangle$" for the $\langle$DTA$\rangle$ Even given at the beginning of this section.

5. Convert Even and Primes to pseudo-LMA's and carry out the renumbering activity.

CHAPTER TWO

LANGUAGE

2.1 INTRODUCTION

We have seen that an algorithm is the appropriate way to describe a solution to a computational problem, and that an algorithm may be viewed as a transformation from one set of symbols to another. Although we have been able to discuss several algorithms already, it has no doubt been quite apparent that the Markov algorithm is not very suitable for the description of some algorithms (in particular, algorithms involving a great deal of arithmetic computation). It is not at all unreasonable, therefore, to ask whether there is some other "language" more suited to the specific task of stating these algorithms so that, at the very least, we may communicate them more easily to others.

This chapter is directed toward a language for computational algorithms. Once such a language is available, one may look toward some sort of standardization of the way in which algorithms are stated, i.e., in terms of such a language. To go even further, one might then consider a machine which could interpret algorithms stated in such a standardized way and actually execute them to solve the corresponding problem. Except for a few minor details, this process has in fact been carried out for this language, much as we did for the LMA in Chapter 1.

Actually, there are several languages, differing in their suitability for stating different kinds of algorithms. One language is very good for stating algorithms of pattern recognition, such as recognizing handwritten or typed characters, while another language is very well suited for describing the simulation of manufacturing processes, and another makes algebraic manipulation of symbolic expressions easy to describe, and so on. No one has as yet designed one language which is equally well suited for all kinds of algorithms. It may be that any such universally useful language must be just a collection of these others. However, the process of combining these many languages into simpler ones is worthwhile and is being done by programmers.

2.2 SPECIFYING A TRANSFORMATION

The obvious way to specify the correspondence between each of the possible inputs I_n for some problem and the corresponding result R_n is to list all pairs (I_n, R_n). Whenever a particular set of input data I_k is encountered, a search of this list of pairs with I_k produces R_k as the result of the transformation, and this is therefore the solution to the original problem. For example, consider the simple mathematical function given by the rule "y is the square of x," where x is an integer, $0 \leq x \leq 3$. This transformation (of x into y) is completely specified by the list of pairs

(0, 0), (1, 1), (2, 4), (3, 9). If the problem to be solved happened to be: "Find the square of an integer which is in the interval [0,3]," this list would immediately imply the algorithm, or transformation, which, when confronted with an integer in the appropriate range, say 3, would yield the square, 9. A telephone book provides a complete solution in the same way to the problem: "What is the telephone number of a particular person in this city?"

Although the problem is stated for one number or person at a time, we cannot tell in advance which input value will occur, and so the list of pairs which provides the answer must have an entry for every possible input value. Another example of such a list would be the solution of the problem: "Given a pair of letters from the collection $a, b, \ldots, z$, write them in alphabetical order." The list would contain 676 entries: (aa, aa), $(ab, ab,), \ldots, (ba, ab), \ldots, (zz, zz)$. If the problem is changed to read "triples" instead of "pairs," the list will contain 17,576 entries, and if the problem reads: "Given a set of not more than 10 letters, arrange them in alphabetical order," the list would be extremely long. The point, of course, is that such lists are completely impractical for a problem of any complexity at all. The strategy that would probably suggest itself next is to remember the procedure that would have generated the list in the first place and, when necessary, generate just that part of the table which contains the entry we need. In fact, we might as well generate just that one entry! In order to pick out the right part of the complete list, however, we must be able to ask questions about the input value. Moreover, the right questions must be asked in the right order, since it can make quite a difference in the amount of work one does if they are not, and questions asked in the wrong order may even give the wrong result.

For example, it is sometimes very important to know whether an integer n greater than 1 is *composite* or *prime*, i.e., whether or not it has divisors other than itself and 1. Prime numbers are important in that branch of mathematics called *number theory* since, as stated earlier, every integer is either a prime or can be expressed in a unique way as a product of primes. One reason this is important is that some properties of numbers can be most easily proved for prime numbers and then generalized to other integers by using their representations as products of primes. In the problem of discovering whether a particular integer is a prime, the list of pairs (I_n, R_n) discussed above would have entries (2, prime), (3, prime), (4, composite), ..., and it would in fact be infinitely long. Our strategy is to generate the entry of the list we need each time we have a specific integer as input value. Of course, as soon as we have a method for generating that entry, we really don't need to mention the list at all, since the problem will then be solved.

What questions do we ask in this case? We need to know, for a number n, whether 2 divides it, whether 3 divides it, and so on, up to the final question, "Does $n - 1$ divide n?" If the answer to all of these questions is "No," n is a prime; otherwise n is composite. A number of short cuts will immediately come to mind. For one thing, as soon as any number is found which divides n, we know that n is composite, and the process should stop. Second, we need try as divisors only *primes* that are less than n, since the existence of a composite number that divides n implies that one of its prime divisors divides n, and we will find that divisor even if we divide only by primes. Third, as we have seen in Chapter 1, we need try only primes r such that $r \leq \sqrt{n}$. Thus, from the original strategy of testing all integers from 2 to $n - 1$, we need now test as divisors only primes not exceeding $\sqrt{n}$. To see whether 61 is a prime, for instance, we see that we need to try only 2, 3, 5, and 7 as divisors, and it follows easily that 61 is a prime. Since there is choice in the selection of an algorithm, it is important to select one which has the right degree of generality and efficiency.

We shall see that the questions which must be asked are primarily concerned with set membership, i.e., with whether a particular number or other object belongs to a particular set. Since the set may be infinite, such as the set of integers that are prime, the membership question may be resolved by testing whether some object possesses some property, but there is always a set of some kind whose membership is involved. It is important that each such membership or property test be itself a finite process, since the overall algorithm of which it is a part must be finite. Of course, asking whether a given object belongs to a set is quite different from discovering the elements of the set directly. For example, we have explicit formulas for the roots of the quadratic equation $ax^2 + bx + c = 0$:

$$x_1 = \frac{-b + \sqrt{b^2 - 4ac}}{2a}$$

$$x_2 = \frac{-b - \sqrt{b^2 - 4ac}}{2a}$$

However, it can be proved that no such formulas exist for the general quintic equation $ax^5 + bx^4 + cx^3 + dx^2 + ex + f = 0$. Therefore, it is very difficult in general to exhibit the set of solutions to a given quintic equation, but it is very easy in principle to test whether or not a particular number is or is not in that set of solutions, since the equation itself furnishes the test.

Another example of an algorithm given in the form of a sequence of questions is the discovery of the largest of n numbers $a_1, \ldots, a_n$. The strategy here is to scan the set of numbers $a_1, \ldots, a_n$. As each number is scanned, it is compared with the first member of the set, and it is copied over (to replace) the first member if it is the larger. We need a way to make such descriptions of strategy more precise and easier to state, e.g., to make explicit the nature and order of questions, and the consequences which ensue from their answers. One very important question which is not explicitly stated in this example is: "Have we scanned all n numbers already?" We shall see that the *flowchart* described below is one way to overcome these difficulties.

2.3 FLOWCHARTS

As we have seen in the previous section, the execution of an algorithm involves a number of questions asked in a particular order, as well as a number of actual computations which may produce symbols (numbers or other objects) about which questions may be asked. A *flowchart* is a representation of an algorithm which explicitly separates the questions and computations from the *control*, that is, the sequence in which questions and computations occur. It consists of several boxes, each containing a question or a computation, connected by arrows which indicate the *flow*, or *control sequencing*. The boxes which one may encounter are shown in Fig. 2.1. There is always exactly one *start* box and at least one *halt* box, and there must be at least one path through every box from the *start* to some *halt*. We shall find it convenient to be able to attach a label to any box and, furthermore, to indicate that the control sequence continues at that labeled box, in the following way.

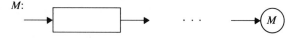

We shall also assume that there are no redundant questions, i.e., questions which are always *true* or always *false*. Such questions serve no purpose, and since computation time is diminished by not asking them, we may as well assume that any boxes for redundant questions have been deleted.

This does raise an interesting point, however. In deleting such a question box, we are actually changing the algorithm, if only in the number of boxes its flowchart contains. Yet we are willing to delete redundant boxes since we know that the resulting flowchart is *equivalent* (in some sense) to the original flowchart. It should be clear that the only sense in which we are interested in equivalent algorithms is their relationship to the original problem to be solved. Two algorithms are *equivalent* if they furnish the same solution to the problem, i.e., if they provide the same

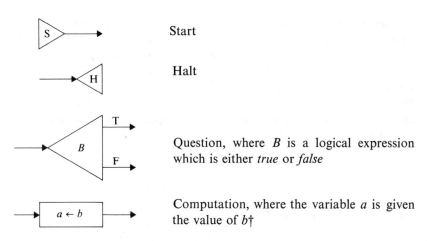

Start

Halt

Question, where B is a logical expression which is either *true* or *false*

Computation, where the variable a is given the value of b†

Figure 2.1

ultimate transformation of the input data. From this point of view, we see that we may indeed delete redundant question boxes.

As an example of an algorithm stated by means of a flowchart, let us consider again the problem of finding the largest of n numbers $a_1, \ldots, a_n$. We scan the numbers $a_1, \ldots, a_n$, retaining at each step the largest number among those already scanned. Let m be the name we give to this largest one. Then the value of m when all numbers have been scanned will be the solution to the problem.

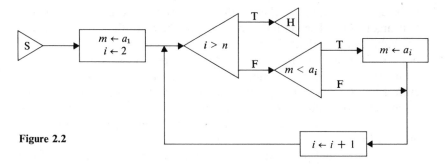

Figure 2.2

Figure 2.2 is a complete flowchart for this algorithm. We begin by letting m have the value a_1, and we set i to 2. The variable i will play the role of a pointer, each time pointing toward the value a_i, which is being scanned and hence is to be compared with m. It will also enable us to

---

† This is a new use of the arrow and can be thought of as "the value of b goes into a" or "the value of a is replaced by the value of b."

terminate the algorithm correctly, since its value must reach n, but no more. Note that this algorithm will work correctly if $n = 1$. It is easy to overlook such special cases and create algorithms which appear to be correct but which fail to take such cases into account. Thus the above algorithm is undefined if $n = 0$, for then what is a_1? We shall assume that the set of n numbers is not empty, i.e., that $n \geq 1$. One could of course include the case $n = 0$ as a special case if there were reason to expect that such an application of this algorithm might occur.

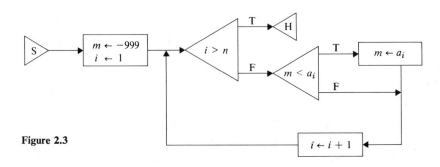

Figure 2.3

Figure 2.3 shows a slightly different flowchart for solving the same problem. It is assumed here that -999 is less than or equal to all of the a_i that might appear as input data to the problem. Figure 2.3 differs from Fig. 2.2 in that m is initially set to -999 and i is set to 1, forcing even a_1 to be compared with m, whereas this comparison was unnecessary in the first algorithm. The computation time for the algorithm of Fig. 2.2 will be slightly shorter than the computation time for the second algorithm, but the algorithm of Fig. 2.3 is somewhat more elegant, in that all of the numbers $a_1, \ldots, a_n$ are treated in the same way, and it gives a result even if $n = 0$. The two algorithms are *equivalent* for $n \geq 1$, in the sense discussed above, but there are computational differences between them which might lead us to choose one over the other; e.g., the case $n = 0$ might arise.

The clarity and precision we have achieved in representing algorithms by means of flowcharts leads one to ask what it is about flowcharts that makes them so much clearer than the verbal description we saw earlier. Probably the most important feature is the distinguishability of the question boxes and of the paths of control. The two-dimensional layout of the boxes may appear to be an essential feature, but Fig. 2.4 is the algorithm of Fig. 2.3, with explicit control arrows always pointing to the right and implicit control using labeled boxes.

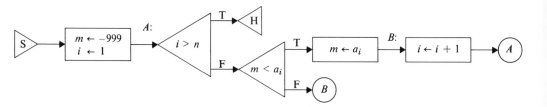

Figure 2.4

From Fig. 2.4 it is but a step to Fig. 2.5, in which the control is understood to pass to the next listed line unless explicitly indicated otherwise
by "halt" or "go to," the latter representing a command to continue the
algorithm at the labeled line specified. Since the control does not allow
more than one computation or question to be processed at a time, a linear
representation of the algorithm, such as in Fig. 2.5, carries as much
information as the flowchart, and we see that the two-dimensional layout
is not really essential.

$$m \leftarrow -999$$
$$i \leftarrow 1$$

$A:$ if $i > n$, then halt

       if $m \not< a_i$, then go to B

       $m \leftarrow a_i$

$B:$ $i \leftarrow i + 1$

Figure 2.5   go to A

It is not obvious that control must necessarily restrict the computation
so that only one question or computation is processed at a time. In some
problems it might be true that several computations are independent of
each other and could in fact be accomplished simultaneously if the control would allow it. (Solving several different problems at the same time
would be a good example.) This simultaneous computation could occur
actually within one algorithm, since it might happen that two different
values u and v are needed to compute w, but u and v are independent of
each other, as in Fig. 2.6. The flag on the box in which w is computed
indicates that the box is not to be processed until two control sequences
have arrived at the box. This approach can be generalized to allow more
than two sequences, and at least one computer has been built to incorporate some concurrent processing. It is interesting to speculate on the
possibilities for using such a facility when, for example, the flag indicates

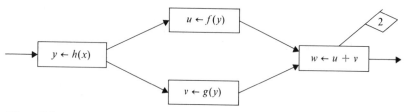

Figure 2.6

that only *m* out of *n* ($m < n$) arrivals are needed. One could postulate that any later arrivals should be queued, or perhaps ignored, or subject to some other scheduling strategy. A flag setting of 1 would then indicate (if other arrivals are queued, for example) that the facility is to be shared by all paths, but only one at a time. Clearly, the behavior of an algorithm containing such a box becomes very difficult to predict. Because the control hardware becomes much more complicated, most computers allow only a very limited amount of such concurrent operation, and for simplicity we shall assume that our control allows only one box to be processed at a time.

We note in passing that almost every algorithm represented in linear form, such as that in Fig. 2.5, will contain at least one label indicating a *loop*, or a return of control to an earlier point in the algorithm, which implies that some part will be repeated. The algorithms we can write with a given set of marks and without labels are quite restricted, though they do raise some interesting questions. It is not surprising that labels play an important role in the representation of algorithms, used as they are to indicate control behavior. With the use of labels, as in Fig. 2.4, we find that an algorithm may be represented in the form of a *rooted tree with directed branches*, i.e., a set of nodes (or boxes) connected by arrows, with one special node, the *root*, having no arrows entering it

and with the additional property that each node other than the root has one arrow entering it. This guarantees that there will be no *cycles*; i.e., a connected path which leaves a node cannot return to it. We shall discuss this point again in the next section.

As further illustrations of the use of flowcharts, we find in Fig. 2.7 the algorithm which will test whether an integer $n \geq 2$ is prime, and in Fig. 2.8 an algorithm for the *bisection method*, or *half-interval method*, for finding a zero of a continuous function. Figure 2.7 represents the algorithm $P(n)$, for integer $n > 1$, with the value *true* if *n* is a prime, and *false* if *n* is composite. The notation $m \mid n$ means "*m* divides *n*." Note

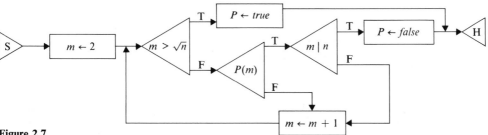

Figure 2.7

that P is executed "recursively"; i.e., an invocation of the algorithm P
may occur from within the algorithm itself. We will use the notation

$$P(n) \quad \text{is} \quad \boxed{S} \longrightarrow \boxed{m \leftarrow 2} \longrightarrow \quad \cdots$$

or alternatively,

$$P \quad \text{is} \quad \lambda(n) \; \boxed{S} \longrightarrow \boxed{m \leftarrow 2} \longrightarrow \quad \cdots$$

where n is called a "formal parameter." We shall return to this notation
later in the chapter. The reader should interpret and execute the algorithm for several values of n before continuing, in order to ensure a reasonable familiarity with flowcharts.

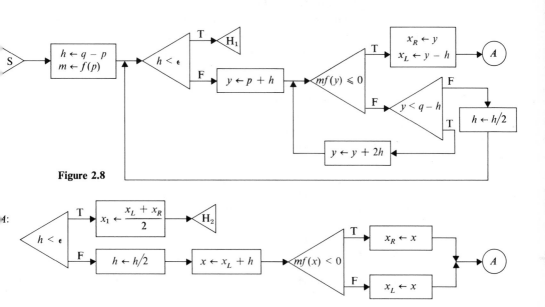

Figure 2.8

The algorithm in Fig. 2.8 is concerned with finding a zero of the continuous function f in some closed interval $[p, q]$, i.e., a value x_0 such that $f(x_0) = 0$. Since this method will in general find only an approximate value, we cannot expect that the computed value x_1 will have the property $f(x_1) = 0$, but rather that $|x_1 - x_0| < \frac{1}{10}$, or $|x_1 - x_0| < \frac{1}{100}$, or $|x_1 - x_0| < 10^{-5}$, depending on the error one is willing to tolerate. Since f is continuous, we know that if x_1 is close enough to x_0, then $f(x_1)$ is close to $f(x_0)$; i.e., $f(x_1)$ will be close to zero, and x_1 will be a good approximation to the zero for which we are looking. Usually algorithms are written in such a way that the tolerance ($\frac{1}{10}$, $\frac{1}{100}$, etc.) may be specified as part of the input data to the problem, and we will designate the tolerance by ϵ.

The algorithm uses the important property of continuous functions that if, for some values x_L and x_R, $f(x_L)$ and $f(x_R)$ have opposite signs (for example, $f(x_L) < 0$ and $f(x_R) > 0$), then for some value x_0 *between* x_L *and* x_R, $f(x_0) = 0$. The first part of the algorithm finds values x_L and x_R such that $f(x_L)$ and $f(x_R)$ have opposite signs. We assume that the input data (besides ϵ) specifies an interval $[p, q]$ containing an odd number of zeros of the function. The algorithm begins by scanning the interval $[p, q]$, looking for a change in sign from $f(p)$. (Since the value of $f(p)$ is constant throughout the entire algorithm, we compute it once at the beginning. Its value is saved as the value of the variable m. Also, once $f(q)$ is computed and used, it is not computed or tested again.) Each time the interval $[p, q - h]$ is scanned unsuccessfully, the size h of the step used to move along the interval is halved, and the interval is scanned again, using only values of y not tested before. If the step size ever becomes less than ϵ, the search terminates with an indication (H_1) that no zero exists in the interval $[p, q]$.† If a sign change (or a zero) is found,‡ control advances to the second part of the algorithm. (Note that in Fig. 2.8 a difference of sign is recognized by the occurrence of a negative product.) The interval $[x_L, x_R]$ is identified on the way to the second part of the algorithm by observing that since y is the first value for which $mf(y) \leq 0$, it must have been true that $mf(y - h) > 0$, so that the interval $[y - h, y]$ must contain at least one zero of f. Thus we set $x_L = y - h$ and $x_R = y$.

In the second half of the algorithm (starting with the question box labeled A), we know that an interval $[x_L, x_R]$ exists such that $f(x_L)$ and $f(x_R)$ have different signs. Then the midpoint of the new interval becomes

---

† Actually, the difficulty could be caused by having sets of the zeros clustered, but we will ignore this possibility.

‡ Since the probability of hitting a value of y such that $f(y) = 0$ is very small, it is probably not worth the time to test for it each time $f(y)$ is computed. It is included in the inequality $mf(y) \leq 0$.

the new x_L or the new x_R, depending on whether it agrees or does not agree in sign with $f(p)$. Since h is halved each time such a change of interval is made, the midpoint of the interval $[x_L, x_R]$ is most easily found as $x_L + h$. The process repeats, with h getting smaller by a factor of 2 each time. When finally $h < \epsilon$, then x_L and x_R differ by no more than ϵ, and since the zero x_1 is between them, x_1 differs by less than $\epsilon/2$ from $(x_L + x_R)/2$. We can therefore choose $(x_L + x_R)/2$ as the final answer x_1. (The reader can verify that if the second half of the algorithm is reached because $f(y) = 0$, a value of x_1 is reached that may not coincide with the correct solution but is within ϵ of it, as required.)

Assuming a zero can be found, how effective is this algorithm? To answer this we need to establish a measure of "effectiveness." If the function f is fairly complicated, we would probably like to minimize the number of times f must be evaluated. Let us consider the first half of the algorithm. Since f must be evaluated once when $h = q - p$, then once when $h = (q - p)/2$, then twice when $h = (q - p)/4$, and so on until a change is found, the number of evaluations of f is

$$N_1 = 1 + 1 + 2 + 2^2 + \cdots + 2^{r-2}$$

where we will assume that a sign change is discovered on the rth scan. (We might as well assume the worst case, i.e., that in which the sign change is found at the end of the rth scan. This implies that the last term above is 2^{r-2} instead of something less.) Treating this as 1 plus the sum of a geometric progression, we obtain

$$N_1 = 1 + (2^{r-1} - 1) = 2^{r-1}$$

In the second half of the algorithm, we start with $h = (q - p)/2^{r-1}$, since we have assumed that a sign change was found on the rth scan. Since we now have one evaluation of f each time h is halved, we need to know how many divisions by 2 will bring $(q - p)/2^{r-1}$ down to ϵ or below. We therefore need for N_2 (the number of function evaluations in the second half of the algorithm) the smallest n such that

$$\frac{1}{2^n} \left(\frac{q - p}{2^{r-1}} \right) \leq \epsilon$$

It follows that n should be chosen so that

$$\frac{q - p}{\epsilon} \leq 2^{n+r-1}$$

or

$$\log_2 \left(\frac{q - p}{\epsilon} \right) \leq n + r - 1$$

or

$$n \geq \log_2 \left(\frac{q - p}{\epsilon} \right) - r + 1$$

If we let $w = [\log_2 (q - p)/\epsilon + 1]$, that is, the next highest integer above $\log_2 (q - p)/\epsilon$, we may choose $N_2 = w - r + 1$. We see then that the total number of evaluations of f in this algorithm is

$$N = N_1 + N_2 = 2^{r-1} + (w - r + 1)$$

For example, if $f(p)$ and $f(q)$ have different signs, so the sign change is found on the first scan (that is, $r = 1$), then we have $w + 1$ evaluations. This is to be expected, since there would be one evaluation in the first half of the algorithm, and w more in the second half.

Now that we have a measure of effectiveness, namely, the number of evaluations of f, how can it be used? There are two ways. It can be applied to other algorithms which solve the same problem, so that one may have a way of choosing among them, and second, one may try to improve the effectiveness of this algorithm. To pursue the latter idea further, we note that $N = 2^{r-1} + w - r + 1$ increases with r, since 2^{r-1} grows faster than r for $r > 2$. To minimize its value, then, we need to minimize r, and we see that the minimum value of N occurs when $r = 1$, namely, $w + 1$. This means that the algorithm is most effective when a sign change is found on the first scan, i.e., when $f(p)$ and $f(q)$ have opposite signs. Moreover, the smaller $q - p$ is, the smaller w will be. It follows that p and q should be chosen as close together as possible, on either side of the zero point, that is, with $f(p)$ and $f(q)$ of opposite signs. Perhaps this was intuitively obvious from the description of the algorithm, but the formula

$$N = 2^{r-1} + w - r + 1, \quad \text{for } w = [\log_2 \left(\frac{q - p}{\epsilon} \right) + 1]$$

shows the cost of a poor choice of p and q. There are many techniques, such as careful plotting of the function f in the neighborhood of the zero, which can be used to obtain good estimates for p and q. The formula for N may help decide how much effort should be expended on such techniques.

2.4 REPRESENTATION OF FLOWCHARTS

It was pointed out in the preceding section that a flowchart can be written (using labels) without any arrows which go backward (Fig. 2.4). This led to the comment that a flowchart could also be considered a rooted tree with directed branches. One very convenient property of such trees is

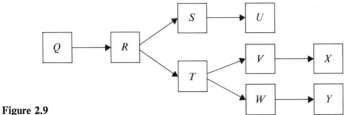

Figure 2.9

that one may represent them by *parenthesized lists*. For example, the tree in Fig. 2.9 can be represented by the parenthesized list:

$$(Q(R(S(U),T(V(X),\ W(Y))))))$$

The strategy here is to follow each box name by a list of items (enclosed in parentheses and separated by commas if necessary), representing the arrows emanating from that box. The correspondence between the tree and the parenthesized list can best be explained by showing how to construct each from the other. Once this is done, we will add the use of labels. Then we will be in a position to represent algorithms not only as flowcharts, but also as parenthesized lists whenever it is convenient to do so.

If we start with a rooted tree, such as that in Fig. 2.9, and we wish to construct the corresponding list, the first step is to begin the list with a left parenthesis. Each box† encountered, starting with the root, may have no exit, one exit, or two or more exits. The appropriate action to be taken in each of these cases is indicated below. No comma is added to the list if it would be immediately preceded by a left parenthesis. The comma is simply dropped in that case. If a box has two or more exits, we shall assume that they are numbered in some standard way—such as from top to bottom if the tree is drawn from left to right, as in Fig. 2.9. Whenever we wish to choose one of a box's exit arrows which has some particular property, we shall *by convention* choose that one with the lowest number, according to the standard numbering.

1. If the box has one exit arrow, add the contents of that box to the list, preceded by a comma and followed by a left parenthesis. Mark the arrow "done." Then proceed to the box designated by the exit arrow.

---

† The branch points and other significant points of a tree are usually called *nodes*, but we shall refer to them as *boxes*, in anticipation of our application of these ideas to flowcharts.

2. If the box has two or more exit arrows, add the contents of that box to the list, preceded by a comma and followed by a left parenthesis. Choose one of the exit arrows from that box, mark it "done," and proceed along that arrow to the next box.

3. If the box has no exit arrows, add the contents of that box to the list. Then follow in reverse order the arrows leading to that box, until a box is reached with at least one arrow not yet marked "done." For each arrow so traversed in the reverse direction, add a right parenthesis to the list being constructed. When a box is reached with an arrow not yet marked "done," delete the last right parenthesis added, choose the first unmarked arrow, mark it, and follow that arrow to the next box.

4. When all arrows are marked "done"—discovered by following a reverse path all the way back to the root and adding the appropriate number of right parentheses—terminate the process by adding one more right parenthesis to match the starting left parenthesis.

The reader should verify that the procedure for constructing a list does produce the correct list for Fig. 2.9. Note that we have just described an *algorithmic activity* for the construction of a list. [Exercise 2.4.1 asks for a flowchart of this activity.]

Now let us consider the other construction, namely, that of the tree from a parenthesized list. We shall make one scan of the list from left to right, and at the end, the tree should be completely done. We shall imagine a pointer (called the *list pointer*) moving across the list, pointing to the next comma, parenthesis, or element (such as Q, R, etc.) whenever necessary. We shall sometimes refer to the *next item*, meaning the next comma, parenthesis, or element, whichever happens to occur. As soon as the item has been handled according to the rules given below, the list pointer moves one item forward. The list pointer is to start at the first element, *after the outermost parentheses are deleted.* When this element is added to the tree, it is to be marked as the root of the tree.

There will also be a pointer (called the *tree pointer*), which indicates the next position at which something may be added to the tree. Except at the beginning of the process, when the tree pointer indicates the (empty) root of the tree, it will always point to the head of some arrow (or an element just added at that arrow head). Whenever an arrow is added to a box to which one or more arrows are already attached, the new one is added in the position determined as next available according to the standard numbering of arrows which was specified earlier.

1. If the list pointer indicates an *element*, attach that element to the tree as indicated by the tree pointer.

2. If the list pointer indicates a *left parenthesis*, attach an arrow to the element to which the tree pointer is currently pointing, and move the tree pointer to the head of that arrow.

3. If the list pointer indicates a *right parenthesis*, move the tree pointer back to the box at the tail of the arrow to whose head it is pointing.

4. If the list pointer indicates a *comma*, move the tree pointer back to the box at the tail of the arrow to whose head it is pointing. Attach another arrow at that box (according to the standard numbering), and move the tree pointer to the head of that new arrow.

5. The process stops when the list pointer moves past the last list item.

[Exercise 2.4.2 calls for the flowchart of this activity.]

There is one flaw in the discussion of algorithms for transformations between trees and parenthesized lists. Although we know quite well what a tree is, we do not really know what a parenthesized list is in this context. For example, is any collection of parentheses, elements, and commas a parenthesized list? Is it enough that the number of left parentheses and the number of right parentheses agree? Does any such collection correspond to a tree?

If we look at the rule for constructing the parenthesized list from the tree, we can begin to get an answer to this question. Suppose that we start with a list L_1 and construct the tree T that corresponds to it, and then in turn, we construct the parenthesized list L_2 that corresponds to T. Then L_1 and L_2 should be identical. It follows from this that the only lists we can allow are those which can arise from our rule for constructing them from trees.

How are we to describe such lists? To put it another way, what properties distinguish acceptable lists from unacceptable lists? Looking at our algorithm, we see that the leftmost item is always a left parenthesis, and the next item must be an *element* (the root), and so on. Again we find that we need more formal notation than English if we are to describe these lists, especially since any of the alternatives—no exit arrow, one exit arrow, or more than one exit arrow—may arise at any time.

What are the constituent parts of parenthesized lists? We have already seen that each list must begin with a left parenthesis and the root element. After this, however, we could find a right parenthesis (in the trivial case), or a left parenthesis followed by another element, and so on. The definition may be stated as follows:

1. $\langle\text{node}\rangle ::= A \mid B \mid C \mid \ldots \mid Y \mid Z$

2. $\langle\text{sublist}\rangle ::= \langle\text{node}\rangle \{(\langle\text{sublist}\rangle \{, \langle\text{sublist}\rangle\}^*)\}_0^1$

3. $\langle\text{parenthesized list}\rangle ::= (\langle\text{sublist}\rangle)$

In the example used earlier, $(Q(R(S(U), T(V(X), W(Y))))))$, we see a $\langle\text{sublist}\rangle$ of the form $Q(\ldots)$, which contains a $\langle\text{sublist}\rangle$ of the form $R(\ldots)$, which in turn contains the $\langle\text{sublist}\rangle$s $S(U)$ and $T(V(X), W(Y))$. Each of these may be further analyzed. [Exercise 2.5.1 will illustrate how lists which do not satisfy this definition fail to correspond to trees.]

All that remains now is to add the use of labels to $\langle\text{parenthesized list}\rangle$s. Then we may use either flowcharts or $\langle\text{parenthesized list}\rangle$s to represent algorithms.

The following obvious modification of the first two lines of the definition given above should suffice.

1a. $\langle\text{node}\rangle ::= A \mid B \mid C \mid \ldots \mid Y \mid Z$

1b. $\langle\text{label}\rangle ::= A \mid B \mid C \mid \ldots \mid Y \mid Z$

1c. $\langle\text{element}\rangle ::= \{\langle\text{label}\rangle:\}_0^1 \langle\text{node}\rangle$

2. $\langle\text{sublist}\rangle ::= \langle\text{element}\rangle \{(\langle\text{sublist}\rangle \{, \langle\text{sublist}\rangle\}^*)\}_0^1$

3. $\langle\text{parenthesized list}\rangle ::= (\langle\text{sublist}\rangle)$

If we wish to apply this notation to the description of flowcharts, we must make the obvious generalization of the discussion above to allow $\langle\text{element}\rangle$s to be simple sentences or mathematical relations. Thus the flow chart of Fig. 2.4 may now be written as a $\langle\text{parenthesized list}\rangle$, as follows:

$$(\text{Start } (m \leftarrow -999 \ (i \leftarrow 1 \ (A: i > n \ (\text{Halt}, m < a_i \ (m \leftarrow a_i \ (B: i \leftarrow i + 1$$
$$(\text{go to } A)), \text{ go to } B))))))$$

EXERCISES 2.4

1. Draw the flowchart for the algorithmic activity which gives a $\langle\text{paren-}$ thesized list$\rangle$ when applied to a rooted tree with directed branches.

2. Draw the flowchart for the algorithmic activity which gives a rooted tree with directed branches when applied to a $\langle\text{parenthesized list}\rangle$.

2.5 RECOGNITION BY SYNTAX

Now that we have described ⟨parenthesized list⟩s both intuitively and more formally, there is a very interesting problem that we should consider, i.e., deciding whether a miscellaneous collection of ⟨element⟩s, parentheses, and commas actually is or is not a legal ⟨parenthesized list⟩ according to these descriptions. This is not an easy task when the number of ⟨element⟩s gets to be rather large. For example, at the end of Section 2.4, a list was exhibited that corresponded to Fig. 2.4. If this list were incorrectly written

(Start (($m \leftarrow -999$) ($i \leftarrow 1$ ($A : i > n$ (Halt, $m < a_i$ ($m \leftarrow a_i$ ($B : i \leftarrow i + 1$

(go to A)), go to B))))))

how would one know that it is incorrect? The error introduced here (extra parentheses) gives this list an incorrect *syntax*, or *form*, which could not be generated by repeated applications of the Backus notation description given above. This incorrect list starts with what is apparently a ⟨sublist⟩, but it doesn't contain a ⟨sublist⟩ after the left parenthesis, since a ⟨sublist⟩ must begin with an ⟨element⟩.

How then do we manage the recognition of legitimate ⟨parenthesized list⟩s, using the Backus notation as a guide? We shall see that the description given in Backus notation is itself the basis of a recognition procedure. Following the method used by Floyd [7], we shall introduce a *pointer* Δ which shall move from left to right, each time examining the next character to the right and taking some appropriate action. Most often, the action taken will depend on one or more characters just to the left of Δ. We will assume, however, that the list of characters to the left of Δ is a *push-down list*. This means that one adds new characters to the list only at the right end, next to Δ, and one removes characters only from the right end. Moreover, the last character added is the first to be removed.

The action to be taken by our recognition procedure will be described partly by means of *productions*, which specify a transformation to be performed on the list being examined. Thus the production

$$\Delta(\rightarrow (\Delta$$

means: "Whenever the character just to the right of Δ is a left parenthesis, move it to the left of Δ, adding it thereby to the push-down list." In the production

$$\Delta A : \rightarrow \langle L \rangle : \Delta$$

we shall understand by the notation $\langle L \rangle$ that we mean a set named L.

Implicit in this notation is the occurrence of A as the representative of the set L in the present application. If one applies soon after that production the following one,

$$\langle L \rangle : \langle N \rangle \Delta \rightarrow \langle E \rangle \Delta$$

where the representative for $\langle N \rangle$ is G, then associated with $\langle E \rangle$ as its representative is the specific representative $A:G$. Thus, if we use the set of productions given below for a $\langle$parenthesized list$\rangle$, by the time we actually recognize the overall form as a $\langle$parenthesized list$\rangle$, we shall have parsed it into all of the constituent parts, such as $\langle$label$\rangle$s, $\langle$node$\rangle$s, etc. To simplify the termination of the process, we shall append a special character $\dashv$ to the right end of the candidate sequence. This character appears in Fig. 2.10 in the production numbered (8).

Number	Production		Comment
(1A)	$\Delta A:$	$\rightarrow \langle L \rangle : \Delta$	Find a $\langle$label$\rangle$ if possible.
(1B)	$\Delta B:$	$\rightarrow \langle L \rangle : \Delta$	
$\vdots$	$\vdots$		
(1Z)	$\Delta Z:$	$\rightarrow \langle L \rangle : \Delta$	
(2A)	ΔA	$\rightarrow \langle N \rangle \Delta$	Otherwise, find a $\langle$node$\rangle$.
(2B)	ΔB	$\rightarrow \langle N \rangle \Delta$	
$\vdots$	$\vdots$		
(2Z)	ΔZ	$\rightarrow \langle N \rangle \Delta$	
(3A)	$\langle L \rangle : \langle N \rangle \Delta \rightarrow \langle E \rangle \Delta$		Find an $\langle$element$\rangle$.
(3B)	$\langle N \rangle \Delta$	$\rightarrow \langle E \rangle \Delta$	
(4)	$\Delta ($	$\rightarrow (\Delta$	Find a $\langle$parenthesized list$\rangle$.
(5)	$\langle E \rangle \Delta$	$\rightarrow \langle S \rangle \Delta$	$\langle$Sublist$\rangle$.
(6A)	$\langle S \rangle \Delta ,$	$\rightarrow \langle S \rangle , \Delta$	Collect components.
(6B)	$\langle S \rangle , \langle S \rangle \Delta \rightarrow \langle S \rangle \Delta$		
(7)	$\langle E \rangle (\langle S \rangle \Delta) \rightarrow \langle S \rangle \Delta$		
(8)	$(\langle S \rangle \Delta) \dashv$	$\rightarrow \langle P \rangle \Delta$	Stop—success.
(9)		$\rightarrow$	Error.

Figure 2.10

In Fig. 2.10 we have a set of productions corresponding to the definition of the $\langle$parenthesized list$\rangle$. The rule in processing a sequence of characters, using a set of productions, is to apply always the first production from the top that can be applied. In every case, the search begins again at the top of the list. Thus the sequencing rule is precisely that of the Markov Algorithm of Chapter 1.

The following two sequences illustrate the process for a correct ⟨parenthesized list⟩ and an incorrect ⟨parenthesized list⟩, respectively. The first is the list of Figure 2.9 with a ⟨label⟩ added, while the second is the incorrect list discussed earlier in this section, with single letters replacing more general elements. In a few obvious cases, several productions are indicated in one step.

I. $(Q(A:R(S(U),T(V(X),W(Y)))))\dashv$

Production used	Result†	
(4)	$(\Delta Q(\ldots$	
(2Q)	$(\langle N\rangle\Delta(A\ldots$	
(3B)	$(\langle E\rangle\Delta(A\ldots$	
(4)	$(\langle E\rangle(\Delta A:\ldots$	
(1A)	$(\langle E\rangle(\langle L\rangle:\Delta R(\ldots$	
(2R)	$(\langle E\rangle(\langle L\rangle:\langle N\rangle\Delta(\ldots$	
(3A)	$(\langle E\rangle(\langle E\rangle\Delta(S\ldots$	
(4)	$(\langle E\rangle(\langle E\rangle(\Delta S(\ldots$	
(2S)	$(\langle E\rangle(\langle E\rangle(\langle N\rangle\Delta(U\ldots$	
(3B)	$(\langle E\rangle(\langle E\rangle(\langle E\rangle(\Delta U)\ldots$	
(2U)	$(\langle E\rangle(\langle E\rangle(\langle E\rangle(\langle N\rangle\Delta),\ldots$	
(3B)	$(\langle E\rangle(\langle E\rangle(\langle E\rangle(\langle E\rangle\Delta),\ldots$	
(5)	$(\langle E\rangle(\langle E\rangle(\langle E\rangle(\langle S\rangle\Delta),\ldots$	
(7)	$(\langle E\rangle(\langle E\rangle(\langle S\rangle\Delta, T\ldots$	
(6A)	$(\langle E\rangle(\langle E\rangle(\langle S\rangle, \Delta T(\ldots$	
(2T)	$(\langle E\rangle(\langle E\rangle(\langle S\rangle, \langle N\rangle\Delta(\ldots$	
(3B)	$(\langle E\rangle(\langle E\rangle(\langle S\rangle, \langle E\rangle\Delta(\ldots$	
(4)	$(\langle E\rangle(\langle E\rangle(\langle S\rangle, \langle E\rangle(\Delta V(\ldots$	
(2V)	$(\langle E\rangle(\langle E\rangle(\langle S\rangle, \langle E\rangle(\langle N\rangle\Delta(\ldots$	
(3B)	$(\langle E\rangle(\langle E\rangle(\langle S\rangle, \langle E\rangle(\langle E\rangle\Delta(\ldots$	
(4)	$(\langle E\rangle(\langle E\rangle(\langle S\rangle, \langle E\rangle(\langle E\rangle(\Delta X),\ldots$	
(2X), (3B), (5)	$(\langle E\rangle(\langle E\rangle(\langle S\rangle, \langle E\rangle(\langle E\rangle(\langle S\rangle\Delta),\ldots$	
(7)	$(\langle E\rangle(\langle E\rangle(\langle S\rangle, \langle E\rangle(\langle S\rangle\Delta, W(\ldots$	
(6A), (2W), (3B)	$(\langle E\rangle(\langle E\rangle(\langle S\rangle, \langle E\rangle(\langle S\rangle, \langle E\rangle\Delta(Y)\ldots$	
(4), (2Y), (3B), (5)	$(\langle E\rangle(\langle E\rangle(\langle S\rangle, \langle E\rangle(\langle S\rangle, \langle E\rangle(\langle S\rangle\Delta))\ldots$	
(7), (6B)	$(\langle E\rangle(\langle E\rangle(\langle S\rangle, \langle E\rangle(\langle S\rangle\Delta))))\dashv$	
(7), (6B)	$(\langle E\rangle(\langle E\rangle(\langle S\rangle\Delta)))\dashv$	
(7)	$(\langle E\rangle(\langle S\rangle\Delta))\dashv$	
(7)	$(\langle S\rangle\Delta)\dashv$	
(8)	$\langle P\rangle\Delta$	Success.

† Only the nearest characters will be shown on the right of Δ at each step. The entire left part will be shown at all times.

II. $(S((M)(I(A:N(H, L(F(B:P(G)), K))))))\dashv$

Production used	Result
(4)	$(\Delta S(\ldots$
(2S), (3B)	$(\langle E \rangle \Delta((\ldots$
(4)	$(\langle E \rangle (\Delta M) \ldots$
(4)	$(\langle E \rangle ((\Delta M) \ldots$
(2M), (3B)	$(\langle E \rangle ((\langle E \rangle \Delta) \ldots$
(5)	$(\langle E \rangle ((\langle S \rangle \Delta) \ldots$
(9)	Error.

Such a recognition procedure is very powerful. One can also add to each rule a secondary process to be carried out whenever that rule is successfully applied, thus providing for remembering the sequence of events, applying additional transformations when various combinations occur, and so on. The *application* of such a set of productions can of course be carried out by an algorithmic activity and even as an algorithm by some machine, once the data and the productions are suitably represented as data, but we shall not elaborate on this here.

EXERCISE 2.5.1

Apply productions (1A) to (9) of Fig. 2.10 to the following lists to see if in fact they are $\langle$parenthesized list$\rangle$s and thus correspond to rooted trees.
   a) $(A(B(C), D(E)))$
   b) $(A(B(C), D(E(F))))$
   c) $(A(B(C), (D(E(F)))))$

2.6 CONSTITUENTS OF BOXES

We have so far been considering the external structure of an algorithm, i.e., the sequence of control as it appears in the form of a flow diagram, a rooted tree, or a $\langle$parenthesized list$\rangle$. Throughout the discussion, however, we avoided looking closely at the elements inside the boxes of a flow diagram. In fact, most of the time we replaced these elements with single letters. Now let us see what kinds of elements actually occur in algorithms. Figure 2.8, the flow diagram for the bisection method, illustrates several of the more important kinds.

   One of the most common boxes is the rectangle, which contains an *assignment* statement, i.e., a statement of the form $h \leftarrow q - p$, in which the value of the expression on the right becomes the new value of the variable on the left. The assignment statement exists specifically to perform the necessary transformations on the data. Of course, these data may subsequently be involved in decisions which affect the sequence of control, but at the time of the assignment, the sequence of control is not affected. Each assignment box always has exactly one arrow entering it and one arrow leaving it.

In Fig. 2.8 some of the assignment boxes contain more than one statement. Such combining of statements is allowed only when they are *independent*; i.e., no statement computes a new value for a variable which appears on the right side of another. An example of *dependent* statements is the pair

$$t \leftarrow s + r$$
$$r \leftarrow r + 1$$

Here it clearly makes a difference in the value of t whether r is increased by 1 before or after t is computed. Since the flowchart exists specifically to emphasize sequence of control, we shall insist that the sequence implicit in dependent assignments be made explicit in the flowchart. This is the basis for the requirement that only independent assignments be placed in one box; putting dependent assignments in separate boxes makes their order of computation explicit.

Another box frequently encountered contains a question which determines sequence of control by choosing among several subsequent paths. This kind of box is usually referred to as the *conditional*, since the subsequent behavior of the algorithm is conditional on the answer to the question it contains. Although the usual question has two alternatives, *true* and *false*, leading to two exit arrows, one often encounters questions with three or more possible answers. Thus, in the solution of the quadratic equation $ax^2 + bx + c = 0$, one might compute the discriminant, $d \leftarrow b^2 - 4ac$, and then choose one of three alternatives, as shown in Fig. 2.11. The exits have the following meanings.

H_1: $a = b = 0$; not an acceptable problem.†
H_2: Linear equation; the value of x_1 is the root.
H_3: $(d < 0)$ Complex roots; not found in this particular algorithm.
H_4: $(d > 0)$ Two real, distinct roots x_1 and x_2.
H_5: $(d = 0)$ A double root; that is, $x_1 = x_2$.

(The cases distinguished by labels A and B could have been combined if we were not interested in recognizing the double-root case, since the path labeled A is valid for $d = 0$, also.)

We may note here that if we wished, we could restrict question boxes to two exits each by "cascading" them, as is done in Fig. 2.12 to the

---

† If $c = 0$, then every value of x is a solution. If $c \neq 0$, then no value of x is a solution.

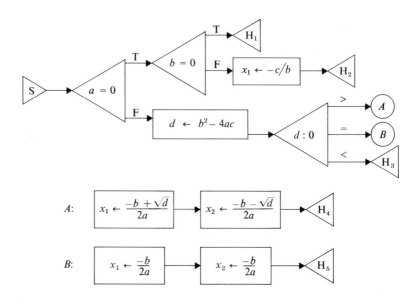

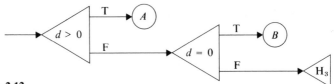

Figure 2.11

Figure 2.12

three-way decision of Fig. 2.11. This is sometimes done, but allowing multiple exits can simplify the diagram considerably.

Two more kinds of boxes specify input and output and are usually referred to as *I/O* boxes. In Fig. 2.11 we pictured the algorithm as rather abstract, without any thought as to where a, b, and c came from, and without worrying about what happened to x_1 and x_2. (The value of d, used only internally, is seldom of interest to the user of the algorithm.) Since the algorithm of Fig. 2.11 does not depend on a particular choice of a, b, and c, it will work for *every* choice of these variables. We must therefore ask for the specific values of the input—that is, a, b, and c— which are to be used each time the algorithm is executed. The *input* box is shaped like a punched card, since data are often (but not necessarily) punched on such cards to provide input values for algorithms. It has one arrow entering and one leaving, since it doesn't affect the sequence of control. The normal interpretation of such a box in a flowchart is that there is a stream of input values, such as a_1, b_1, c_1, a_2, b_2, c_2, a_3, ... in the quadratic equation example. The box

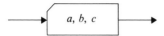

would indicate that a_1, b_1, and c_1 are brought in as the values of a, b, and c at that point in the algorithm. These values are no longer in the input stream, and if the sequence of control happens to be such that this box is executed again, then a_2, b_2, and c_2 are brought in, and so on. Eventually the input stream will be exhausted, and *the conventional interpretation* is that when an attempt is made to execute an input box and there are no further values in the input stream, then the algorithm terminates. Note that under these circumstances an algorithm can terminate without having the sequence of control arrive at an explicit *halt* box. There is actually an implicit *halt* in the input box, as if

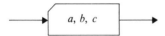

were really an abbreviation of the flowchart

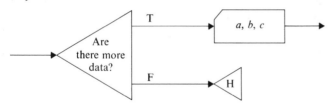

and this can be made explicit whenever necessary.

There is also a need for an *output* box, since the algorithm must communicate its results to the external world, i.e., to the one who invoked the algorithm to carry out his task. We shall use a box shaped like a torn piece of paper, with one arrow entering and one leaving. (Since we shall assume an infinite supply of paper, there is no need here for the implicit halt described above for input. Furthermore, output need not be recorded on paper; it can just as well be displayed on the face of a television tube.) The output box for the quadratic equation algorithm would be

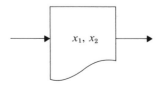

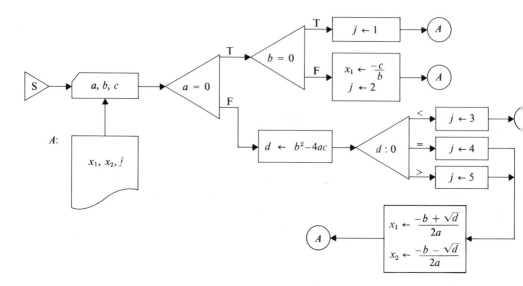

The one remaining problem with this example is that there is no indication in the output as to which of the five possible halting situations $H_1, \ldots, H_5$ actually occurred. For example, if only x_1 was printed as the output, was the halt H_2 (the linear equation) or H_5 (the double root)? The problem exists because implicit in the description of the output box above is the idea that what is printed as output is the value of a variable. Although we may easily extend the output box to allow values of expressions in the box:

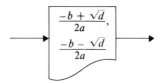

there is still no variable or expression in this algorithm whose value indicates which halt occurred. We could take care of this by an assumption that an occurrence of a halt box automatically causes the numerical designation of the halt to be printed. This is sometimes considered undesirable, however, since such automatic printing might disturb an otherwise carefully formatted and planned printed sheet. A way to retain control over what is printed and when it occurs is to introduce an additional variable, j. As soon as there is enough information to indicate which type of halt is to occur, we shall give j a value from 1 to 5; and then we may print the value of j as the desired halt indicator. Figure 2.13, a revised version of Fig. 2.11, contains provisions for input (with the

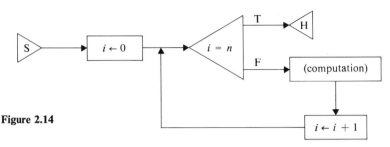

Figure 2.14

implicit *halt*), output, and the use of the new halt indicator variable, *j*. To simplify the algorithm, all output may now go through a single box, but we shall need to be aware that for some types of *halts*, i.e., for some values of *j*, the printed values of x_1 and/or x_2 may be *meaningless*. For example, if $j = 3$, neither x_1 nor x_2 will have any meaning, although both will print. [Exercise 2.6.1 asks that the flowchart be modified so that only the meaningful values occur as output.]

The assignment, conditional, and input/output (*I/O*) boxes are the most useful components of which flowcharts are constructed. Occasionally a particular combination of elements occurs so often that a single package is invented and a special box introduced as an abbreviation for the combination. We shall consider two, that for the *loop*, or *iteration*, and that for the *subroutine call*.

We have already seen that an algorithm (or part of an algorithm) may be executed many times by calling for more input data and then repeating the computation for the new values. In fact, this ability to execute parts of algorithms repeatedly makes it possible to deal easily with data which consist of many similar pieces. An example of such data is the string of characters manipulated in Chapter 1. The Markov form of algorithm has certain kinds of repetition included implicitly, in that the sequence of control goes back each time to the beginning—or elsewhere, as directed by a label—and thus the same decision process is executed over and over. In the flowchart representation there is no implicit repetition, so it must be provided explicitly. The principal components of such a repetitive execution of part of an algorithm, usually called a *loop* or *iteration*, are the computation to be performed, called the *body* or *scope* of the loop, and the decision process which controls the number of times the repetition occurs. Sometimes it is a simple matter of counting the number of times the body of the loop has been executed and stopping at some predetermined number. Very often, however, the decision as to when the repetition stops depends on the outcome of the computation going on within the body of the loop, as we saw in the iteration construction of Chapter 1.

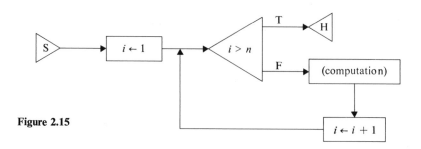

Figure 2.15

For the simple case in which one merely counts *n* repetitions of some computation, the flowchart may be written as shown in Fig. 2.14. An equivalent variation appears in Fig. 2.15. Which of these (or other) versions one chooses is largely a matter of taste, but the role played in the computation by *i*, called the *index variable*, can sometimes be facilitated by the choice. Another form frequently used (Fig. 2.16) is *not* equivalent to the others. Should an occasion arise in which $n = 0$, that form would behave differently. (How?) The major point of difference is of course the placement of the *conditional*, or *decision*, box relative to the computation and the incrementing of the index variable. Since the form in Fig. 2.14 treats the case in which $n = 0$ consistently with those for other values of *n*, we shall adopt it as our standard form.

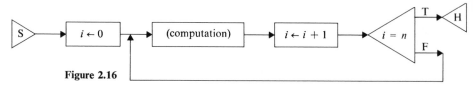

Figure 2.16

Referring to Fig. 2.14, we may now identify the components of the combination of boxes called the *loop*. There is an *initialization* of an index variable, a *conditional* (usually involving the index variable), the *body*, and the *modification* of the index variable. In one way or another, these parts are always present when a loop occurs in an algorithm. Of course, any of these components may be more complicated than in the simple case of Fig. 2.14. The right side of the assignment in the initialization

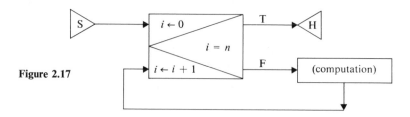

Figure 2.17

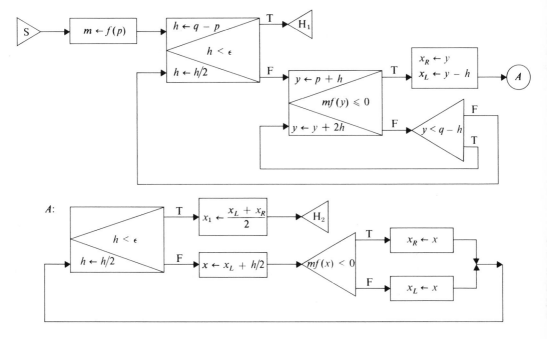

Figure 2.18

may be a long expression, the question in the conditional box may depend
on many variables in a complex way, and the modification assignment
statement may involve a complicated computation as well. The form of
the loop occurs so often, however, that a special box for it is often introduced into the flowchart (Fig. 2.17). The understanding is that the
conditional is the successor of each of the boxes adjoining it at the left.
Adopting this new means of simplification, we can now present in Fig. 2.18
the algorithm shown earlier in Fig. 2.8. The empty part of the iteration
box in the second part of the algorithm indicates that h already has its
initial value as determined by the first part of the algorithm, so no initialization is necessary. Note the occurrence of one loop within another,
referred to as *nesting*. As another example of a loop simplified by means
of the iteration box, the algorithm of Fig. 2.4 is shown in Fig. 2.19.
[Exercise 2.6.2 asks for a similar modification of Figs. 2.3 and 2.7.]

    The second special flowchart box, that for the *subroutine call*, has
one arrow entering and one leaving. In this box, f is the name of the
subroutine, and x, y, and $z + w$ are the expressions whose values are to
be used as parameters for this occurrence of the subroutine call.

$$\longrightarrow \boxed{f(x,\, y,\, z + w)} \longrightarrow$$

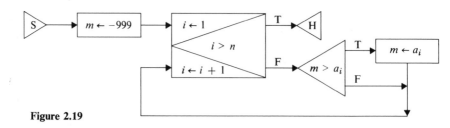

Figure 2.19

Some subroutines determine alternative exits, so, depending on the results of the computation, we shall use only one exit arrow and assume that if an alternative exit is needed, the subroutine will set the value of some variable to be tested after the return to the calling program. An example of a subroutine with alternative exits might be a logarithm algorithm which normally returns the logarithm of the call parameter, but which provides for a separate return if the call parameter is not a positive number. We have already seen (Fig. 2.13) that an algorithm with multiple exits may be transformed easily into one with a *halt*-indicating variable and one exit, i.e., the implicit exit of the input box.

Implicit in the use of the subroutine call box is the idea that, at the point of its occurrence, control moves to the flowchart of the subroutine named, with appropriate substitutions for the parameters of the call. After the called subroutine has completed the task for which it was called, control returns to the successor of the box which called the subroutine. We shall look at this process in some detail later in this section.

As an example of a subroutine call, let us suppose that the algorithm of Fig. 2.18, which finds a zero of a continuous function, has been given the name Z and modified slightly to set the first of two arguments, z_1, to 0 if the exit H_1 is taken and to 1 if the exit H_2 is taken, and to set the second argument, z_2, to the value of the zero whenever $z_1 = 1$. (z_2 is meaningless if $z_1 = 0$.) [Exercise 2.6.3 asks for the necessary modifications.] There are four other arguments also, namely, f, p, q, and ϵ. Then Fig. 2.20 shows how an algorithm might be constructed to use Z to find n zeros of a function, given n intervals $(p_1, q_1), \ldots, (p_n, q_n)$ in which to look.

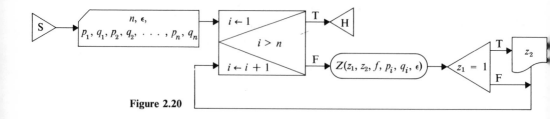

Figure 2.20

In more complicated algorithms, of course, the same subroutine may be called in several different places, each time with parameter expressions appropriate to that call.

Many subroutines return a value as the result of a call. For example, subroutines for the square root, sine, and cosine would each compute a single value. As in the box

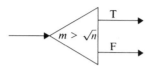

which appeared in Fig. 2.7, or the box

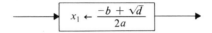

which appeared in Figure 2.11, the value is most often used directly in an expression. (Although there is a special symbol for the square root, we might just as correctly have written

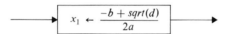

where *sqrt* is the name of a square root subroutine.)

EXERCISES 2.6

1. Modify Fig. 2.13 so that only meaningful values occur as output.

2. Modify Figs. 2.3 and 2.7 to include the iteration box.

3. Modify Fig. 2.18 (the algorithm which finds a zero of a continuous function) so that two arguments, z_1 and z_2, are set as follows, depending on the path taken:
   a) $z_1 = 0$ if $h < \epsilon$ and no change of sign is found.
   b) $z_1 = 1$ if $h < \epsilon$ after the first change of sign is found.
   c) $z_2 = $ the zero of the function if $z_1 = 1$.

2.7 ELEMENTS WITHIN BOXES

At the beginning of Section 2.6, we suggested looking not only at the kinds of boxes that occur in flowcharts, but also at the elements of the computation that occur within the boxes. For example, in assignment boxes we found names of variables on the left and expressions on the right. What kind of data would we expect to be manipulating and computing in such expressions? We have already seen examples of several kinds of data, such as letters, numbers, and special characters (i.e., punctuation symbols and mathematical operations). From these one may also construct more complicated forms of data. In Section 2.4 we discussed an activity for constructing a ⟨parenthesized list⟩ from a tree. For that activity the data consisted of the root, nodes, and branches of a tree; and the output, which was treated internally as data until it became output, consisted of a string of letters, parentheses, and commas.

One can also expect to combine these structures, so that we should be able to use as data such structures as lists in which the letters are replaced by expressions, or even by other lists or collections of lists. (For the latter we would probably expect to attach a label, or name, to the collection and use the name in the list.) The elements of a tree need not be only single letters or simple expressions. We should expect to encounter algorithms for which the most appropriate data are in the form of a tree whose nodes contain names of other trees, lists of lists, or lists of trees, etc.

We shall discuss such structures more completely in the next chapter. Of more immediate interest here is the understanding of the internal representation of data. Some of the manipulations of data may depend on their representation, which we shall need to specify quite carefully. Such specification is particularly important when constructing algorithms that must be interpreted and executed by others—or by devices. Everyone concerned must have a clear understanding of the conventions employed with respect to data representation. The point of view we shall take is to specify the form of most basic forms of data, such as letters, integers, other kinds of numbers, and so on; and then we shall consider the process of constructing more complicated forms of data from these.

Since the goal will be very general constructions, the rules for carrying them out—and for their subsequent interpretation during the execution of algorithms—must be simple and natural. Otherwise their interpreters will be mired in a morass of details. In fact, a fairly general rule is: Whenever you find that the development of a structure requires many restrictive and controlling rules—especially rules to cover exceptional cases—look for a more general overall approach to the task. Because initial goals are often too low and too specific, opportunities for general constructions are missed. For example, when the output box was introduced, we saw the need for printing values of variables as output, but sooner or later we are certain to want to print a constant. Is this legal? If not, the output box was poorly planned. Once we extend the output box to allow expressions, however, the difficulty with constants disappears since, as we shall see shortly, even simple constants are considered expressions, and hence they are automatically eligible for the output box. Generalizing the rule for this box thus makes it unnecessary to consider a long stream of apparently exceptional cases. In terms of the point made above, the appearance of such a stream of exceptions to the existing rules should trigger a search for simpler, more general rules which encompass these cases as well. The search is successful surprisingly often.

We shall start our data representations with the simplest one, the unsigned integer. *By convention*, we shall allow any finite string of digits to be an unsigned integer. Examples: 0, 5, 160241, and 16.

Along with this specification of the form of an unsigned integer, we shall assume a familiarity with (and a facility for implementing) the standard operations and relations on integers, provided the operations are restricted to those that produce nonnegative integer results. Thus addition and multiplication are defined in the usual way on the entire set K of unsigned integers; $m - n$ is defined only if $m \geq n$, and m/n is defined only for $n \neq 0$. Moreover, we shall assume that it is possible to attach one of the values *true* and *false* to such statements as $m \geq n$, $n \neq 0$, and $m = n$.

Now we wish to move on to a new kind of number, a signed integer, which we shall construct out of the kind we already have, i.e., the unsigned integer. We define an integer as a pair (s, k), where $s = 0$ or 1, and $k \in K$. Associating $s = 0$ with the plus sign and $s = 1$ with the minus sign, we define addition of two such pairs as

$$(s, k) = (s_1, k_1) + (s_2, k_2)$$

where s and k are determined in the following way.

If $s_1 = s_2$, then $s = s_1$ and $k = k_1 + k_2$. Otherwise, assume that $s_1 = 0$, and let $q_1 = max(k_1, k_2)$ and $q_2 = min(k_1, k_2)$. Let h be the value of j such that $10^{j-1} \leq q_1 < 10^j$, and compute $t = (10^h - k_1) + k_2$. Writing $t = s \cdot 10^h + k_3$ with $k_3 < 10^h$, we determine s; and we put $k = q_1 - q_2$. As an example, the computation

$$300 + (-200) = 100$$

would appear to be

$$(s, k) = (0, 300) + (1, 200)$$

and we would have $q_1 = 300$, $q_2 = 200$, $h = 3$, $t = (1000 - 300) + 200 = 900 = 0 \cdot 1000 + 900$, so $s = 0$, and $k = 300 - 200 = 100$. On the other hand, if

$$(s, k) = (0, 300) + (1, 500)$$

then we would have $q_1 = 500$, $q_2 = 300$, $h = 3$, $t = (1000 - 300) + 500 = 1200 = 1 \cdot 1000 + 200$, and $s = 1$, $k = 500 - 300 = 200$.

The operation of subtraction, previously restricted to nonnegative results, may now be defined for all pairs in terms of addition:

$$(s_1, k_1) - (s_2, k_2) = (s_1, k_1) + (1 - s_2, k_2)$$

Defining

$$s_3 = \begin{cases} 0 & \text{if } s_1 = s_2 \\ 1 & \text{if } s_1 \neq s_2 \end{cases}$$

we may easily define multiplication,

$$(s_1, k_1) \times (s_2, k_2) = (s_3, k_1 \times k_2)$$

and division,

$$(s_1, k_1) / (s_2, k_2) = (s_3, k_1 / k_2), \quad k_2 \neq 0$$

Note that there is an obvious correspondence between a subset of the integers represented as pairs and the unsigned integers; for example, $k \leftrightarrow (0, k)$. There is one exceptional case, however, in that both of the pairs $(0, 0)$ and $(1, 0)$ behave like 0 in the arithmetic we have just defined. In particular, $(0, k) + (1, k) = (1, 0)$, but $(s, k) \times (s, 0) = (0, 0)$ and $(s, k) \times (1 - s, 0) = (1, 0)$. Aside from this inconvenient behavior of zero, however, there are some important properties of this correspondence which we shall find useful whenever we construct new kinds of data out of old:

1. The arithmetic of each component of the pair is defined only in terms of the arithmetic of the base set (K) from which it comes.

2. Each element m of the base has a representation $R(m)$, unique except for zero, in the extended set.

3. If m and n are in the base set, θ is an operation defined for m and n, and $R(\theta)$ is the corresponding operation on the new kind of data, then

$$R(m) \ R(\theta) \ R(n) \ [2] = m \ \theta \ n$$

where the notation [2] denotes the selection of the second element of the pair. In this sense, the arithmetic of the base set has been "preserved" in the extension.

Because of these properties, we can revert to the notation and arithmetic of the base set K whenever the signed integers involved represent unsigned integers. Thus the first step of notation simplification we may take is to write $+m$ for $(0, m)$, and $-m$ for $(1, m)$; but we can go even further and write m for $+m$. That there is no confusion between this notation and that used for the unsigned integer m is a direct consequence of the above properties. Each extension of our data will provide for these properties, and we shall continue to write m for unsigned integers as we move on; but we must be careful to verify this fact each time.

We now consider the representation of a class of signed *real* numbers. Each number x in this class must be representable as a pair (m, p), where m and p are signed integers such that $x = m \times 10^p$. Thus, what we actually have is

$$x = ((s_m, k_m), (s_p, k_p))$$

To make the representation unique, we specify that the least significant digit of m (that is, the rightmost digit) must be nonzero unless $x = 0$. As an example, from the possible representations of the number -12.73, such as -12730×10^{-3} and -127300×10^{-4}, we choose

$$-1273 \times 10^{-2}$$

and write it as

$$((1, 1273), (1, 2)) \qquad \text{or} \qquad (-1273, -2)$$

To make the representation of zero unique, we specify further that if $x = 0$, then $m = p = 0$. [Exercise 2.7.1 asks for the representations of various real numbers.]

We observe that a different representation could have been chosen for x, for example, as a quadruple,

$$x = (s_m, k_m, s_p, k_p)$$

In this case, selection of the first component $x[1]$ would yield s_m rather than m. If this notation were used to represent x, however, the arithmetic of signed real numbers would have to be specified in terms of s_m, k_m, s_p, and k_p, duplicating the earlier definitions for signed integers. It is much more convenient to build on what we have already accomplished.

Suppose now that (m_1, p_1) and (m_2, p_2) are two real numbers, and we wish to define the sum $(m, p) = (m_1, p_1) + (m_2, p_2)$. Assume that $p_1 \geq p_2$. Then

$$m = m_1 \times 10^{(p_1 - p_2)} + m_2$$
$$p = p_2$$

As an example, consider $(m, p) = (5, 1) + (12, -1)$, which corresponds to the sum $50 + 1.2$. We have

$$m = 5 \times 10^2 + 12 = 512$$
$$p = -1$$

so the sum is (512, −1), corresponding to 51.2, as expected. [Exercises 2.7.2 and 2.7.3 ask for the other appropriate arithmetic definitions for real numbers and verification of the properties discussed above.]

Have we now represented all real numbers in this way? Unfortunately, an important property of computers is that all data must have finite representations; i.e., they must be describable in a finite number of digits. This clearly rules out real numbers like $\frac{1}{3} = .333\ldots$ and implies that extremely long integers must be ruled out as well. In general, on the assumption that the internal representation is via binary integers, there will be M binary digits available. However, even when M is large (perhaps 48 or 60), some numbers cannot be handled.

If we are limited to a fixed maximum number of digits that can be retained, we must, for example, represent 11/9 as (122222, −5). Every computation in which such a representation is subsequently used will reflect this approximation error (often called *round-off error*), and particular care must always be taken to ensure that such errors don't grow too rapidly. In many cases, the cumulative effect of such errors completely overshadows the correct digits, and the results—though they look legitimate—have no relation to the correct solution to the problem. The branch of computer science that studies these problems is called *numerical analysis*.

Let us turn our attention now to the complex numbers. A typical complex number can be written $x + yi$, where $x \equiv (x_1, x_2)$ and $y \equiv (y_1, y_2)$ are real numbers. As our representation we shall use

$$x + yi \equiv (x, y)$$

Then the arithmetic for complex numbers may be expressed in terms of the arithmetic of real numbers, as follows:

$$(x + yi) \times (r + si) \equiv (x, y) \times (r, s)$$
$$\equiv (xr - ys, yr + xs)$$
$$(x + yi) \pm (r + si) \equiv (x \pm r, y \pm s)$$

[The definition of division is asked for in Exercise 2.7.4.] The representation of a complex number as a pair of real numbers allows us to use the same notation as before to select one of its components. Thus, if $z = (x, y)$ is a complex number, we call $z[1]$ and $z[2]$ the *real* and *imaginary* parts, respectively, and

$$z[1] = x \quad \text{and} \quad z[2] = y$$

[Exercise 2.7.5 asks for verification of the properties discussed above for the complex numbers.]

It is clear that the notation needed for numbers will very quickly grow in complexity if we continue at this rate. Yet much of it is really unnecessary for such simple numbers as integers. We shall therefore *adopt the convention* that whenever a number to be written belongs to a special, easily recognized subset of the numbers under consideration, and when the result is clear and unambiguous, we shall use the simpler notation as an abbreviation for the complete notation. It is essential, of course, that no information be lost in thus suppressing what amounts to punctuation; we must in every case be able to interpret the result exactly as if the complete notation were provided. Moreover, when a convenient and unambiguous conventional notation is available, we shall feel free to use it; but an internal representation such as that here described will always be assumed.

Thus we have already begun to use the minus sign for negative signed integers. Similarly, we shall write -3.21 for $(-321, -2)$, and even 4.256×10^6 for $(4256, 3)$, if convenient. Remembering the internal representation, we will be able to write $-3.21[2]$ and obtain the value -2 as well, though we are more likely to apply this selector notation to complex numbers. The conventional notation for complex numbers is $x + yi$, and as we remarked above, $(x + yi)[2] = y$. (Note that convention requires the extra parentheses in this case because of the usual application of the selector function before addition.)

In later chapters, we shall provide a notation for building new kinds of data from previously defined ones, just as we have been doing here. In doing so, we shall not restrict ourselves to pairs, but will allow n-tuples with arbitrary n, so long as we then specify how such n-tuples are to be treated. Since there will then be several kinds of n-tuples occurring, we shall need a notation to distinguish among them, and our standard notation will consist of a prefix followed by the n-tuple. Thus, if complex numbers were not already defined, we could write them:

$$\textbf{complex}(x, y)$$

Similarly we could write **matrix**(a, b, c) or **column**$(p, q, r + s, j, k)$, and so on.

EXERCISES 2.7

1. Express the following real numbers as unsigned integers only: $1, 0, 0.0,$ $-.12456, .0012$.

2. Define subtraction, multiplication, and division for real numbers in terms of signed integers.

3. Verify that the three properties discussed above for definitions of new types of data are present in the definition of real numbers.

4. Define division for complex numbers in terms of the arithmetic for real numbers.

5. Verify that the three properties discussed above for definitions of new types of data are present in the definition of complex numbers.

2.8 REPRESENTATION OF ALPHABETS

In the preceding section we developed a set of numerical alphabets: the integer alphabet, the real number alphabet, and the complex number alphabet. It is really immaterial whether the commas and parentheses actually appear in any physical device in which these numbers are to be handled. What is important is that "characters" from each alphabet be recognized and treated appropriately when the data need to be manipulated. There are several ways in which such recognition can be organized. To begin with, the data are in the register R. We have already seen in Chapter 1 that parts of the data can be accessed by interspersing special punctuation marks to act as separators. One method of recognizing elements from different alphabets consists in having enough different separating punctuation marks so that each one not only separates, but also indicates the alphabet of the preceding (or following) item. Unfortunately, this technique uses up a fairly large number of punctuation marks, which can then have no other meaning. Another method consists in combining all the alphabets into one large one. This doesn't really solve the problem, however, since it is almost always necessary to discover which alphabet the number came from in order to manipulate it properly.

Sometimes the difficulty is avoided by distorting the individual representations so that they all appear to be the same; then a common set of manipulations is used. For example, if all numbers were written as complex numbers, we could use only complex arithmetic every time. But what time and energy would then be wasted on the most frequently performed calculations, those involving integers! What emerges from this analysis is a realization that there is a kind of basic cost to a computation. Part of it may be expended in recognizing the alphabet, after which specific, cheap, and effective operators may be used. Or one can avoid the work of recognition and apply nonspecific, less efficient operators. Between these extremes lie intermediate positions, where some time—but not much—is spent in classification, etc. The search for the best balance has led to many different organizations for computing devices.

Still another method of recognition is used. Suppose that there are several alphabets and that whenever the algorithm specifies a certain action to be performed, the data to be accessed are always guaranteed to be in the proper alphabet for that action. Now one can dispense with the recognition phase and still apply operators specific to the assumed alphabet. This method is quite efficient, compared with those discussed above, but the check on the computation, which makes sure that the right operators are being applied to the right alphabet, is now being bypassed. Should anything go wrong, we may find ourselves working with the imaginary part of a string of alphabetic characters, whatever that means! When this happens, there is often no obvious difficulty, and the computer continues its computation furiously, using completely meaningless information.

Let us move on now to letters and special characters, such as parentheses, commas, etc. Here we may just as well use each character to represent itself. Thus, when we wish to write $A + B$, we use precisely those three characters.† Now we run full tilt into the age-old problem of distinguishing between an object and its name: the difference between California and "California." For as soon as strings of letters may be used as data and also as names, we must always have enough information to allow us to tell which we have. Let us discuss this problem in some detail.

In the algorithm for the quadratic equation we used the symbols a, b, and c. It was clear then that these were *names* representing *values*; with each symbol—that is, each *name*—we associated a value at each instant in time. Several distinct names could have the same value at any time, and a name could have different values at different times. What are the rules for forming a name? *By convention*, we stipulate that a name may consist of any number of small or capital letters and/or digits, at least one of which is a letter. (Usually the first character must be a letter, but only because this rule contributes to the ease of parsing expressions; there is no need for us to require it here.) Examples of names are *3A, A3, bad, Alice,* and *and.* Note that special characters such as + are not allowed, since we must be able to distinguish between the sum $A + B$ and what otherwise would be the name of a variable $A + B$!

Why must at least one character of a name be a letter? This requirement is forced on us by our desire to write the integer 12 using only the digits 1 and 2. If a name could consist entirely of digits, we could not distinguish an occurrence of the *name* 12 from an occurrence of the

---

† We shall have to include the blank space as a character, of course, so we can distinguish (when we need to) between $A + B$ and $A + B$.

integer 12. If we extend this reasoning to strings of letters, however, we run into trouble. Since any string of letters qualifies as a name, we cannot write a string of letters as a constant in the same sense in which the integer 12 is a constant. Our only hope is to put a special indicator mark either on all names or on all constant alphabetic strings so that we may then know which we have. Since the latter usually occur less often, we shall agree to put an apostrophe at the beginning of a string that is to be considered an alphabetic constant and not a name. For convenience, we shall call this character a *left apostrophe*.

Our problems are not yet all solved, however. It would be quite foolish to restrict constant strings of characters to letters only, since we then couldn't write even a house address or a telephone number. Obviously, every character in the basic alphabet should be allowable. But then, when does a constant string stop, once it has begun with the occurrence of a left apostrophe? Obviously, we also need a right apostrophe, just as a right terminator is needed in parentheses, quotation marks, and the notation for absolute value. Examples of legal constant strings are now:

$$\text{`A + B', `3', `A', `   ',   and   `and'}$$

With right apostrophes thus preempted for use as indicators, they become the only characters in the basic alphabet that cannot occur as part of a string. This difficulty is overcome with *the convention* that two consecutive right apostrophes represent a single right apostrophe occurring as a character within a string. (We assume that the input device we are using distinguishes between two consecutive apostrophes and double quotation marks. This is usually true.)

As we have seen, a name is associated with a value. The value occupies a place in the *R* register (that is, in *storage*) from which we can retrieve it in order to use it in a computation. Retrieval is sometimes done by searching out some special punctuation associated with the name. More commonly the storage capacity is divided into many small compartments called *locations*—usually all of the same size—which are then numbered. With each name we associate one of these numbers, called its *address*, which we may use to facilitate the search for the value associated with the name. Of course, sometimes we may want the address itself, rather than the value. In general, with each name there will be associated various kinds of information: its address, its value, the name of the alphabet in which its value is expressed, and so on. Operators will usually be available (sometimes implicit in other operators) for retrieving different items from this collection of information associated with each name. But a constant—numeric or alphabetic—has many of the same properties as a name, and with it we may associate all the same kinds of information, such as value, address, etc. All we really lack is a name for the constant. If we had a name for it, we could henceforth treat constants and variables in a unified way, with an expected simplification in subsequent descriptions of operators, etc. The most natural name for the integer constant 12 is of course the two-character symbol 12 itself. Thus a constant may now be thought of as a variable whose value is so fixed that the name is allowed to exhibit it.

A rather startling consequence of this point of view is that it is now legal to write the assignment statement: $12 \leftarrow 3$. Applying the usual interpretation to the form of an assignment statement, we are to find the *value* of the expression on the right side and the *address* of the "variable" on the left side, and substitute the former as the new value of the latter. Now the variable which so clearly proclaims its value as 12 really has the value 3. Some people consider this procedure dangerous and rule out constants on the left side of an assignment statement. If used with care, however, it is sometimes convenient. In any case, novices beware!

2.9 THE PHYSICAL REPRESENTATION

So far we have not been too concerned with the *actual representation* of characters and numbers used in physical devices, but some discussion of it may now be in order. Suppose a device were to be constructed in which it would be necessary to use a basic alphabet consisting of the 26 letters, the digits 0 through 9, and the special characters: $+, -, (,), =, .$, the blank, and the comma. These characters represent 44 different, distinguishable states which may occur in any position in the storage of the device. It is physically impossible to measure 44 different levels of voltage, for example, or 44 levels of magnetic flux, with any degree of accuracy and reliability. Even early attempts to code just the ten decimal digits for separate recognition were given up. By far the most reliable—and least expensive—device is one required to distinguish between only two states, such as positive or negative voltage, absence or presence of current, high or low level of magnetic flux, etc. Since six such simple devices can be used in 2^6, or 64, different combinations, with six we have more than enough to handle our 44 characters. If we represent the two states that each device can recognize by 0 and 1, then the table in Fig. 2.21 shows one way of encoding these characters.† One column has the heading "6-bit code" in Fig. 2.21 since the binary digits 0 and 1 are usually referred to as *bits*. The simpler form obtained by converting these six-bit numbers to two-character octal numbers will also be used when convenient. The table

---

† Note that the codes, which are strings of zeros and ones, may be interpreted also as the decimal integers 0 to 43 represented in the binary number system. We shall assume a familiarity with both the binary and the octal systems.

Character	6-bit code	Character	6-bit code	Character	6-bit code	Character	6-bit code
0	000000	B	001011	M	010110	X	100001
1	000001	C	001100	N	010111	Y	100010
2	000010	D	001101	O	011000	Z	100011
3	000011	E	001110	P	011001	+	100100
4	000100	F	001111	Q	011010	−	100101
5	000101	G	010000	R	011011	(	100110
6	000110	H	010001	S	011100	)	100111
7	000111	I	010010	T	011101	=	101000
8	001000	J	010011	U	011110	.	101001
9	001001	K	010100	V	011111	(blank)	101010
A	001010	L	010101	W	100000	,	101011

Figure 2.21

in Fig. 2.22 contains the same assignment of codes as that in Fig. 2.21, expressed in the more economical octal system. Note that in both tables, the codes are ordered by increasing value, considered as binary or octal integers. In octal the character string 'AB + CD.5' would be coded 12134414155105. By using 8-bit codes, one may have 256 distinct characters, and such expanded alphabets are used on many computers.

There really isn't any reason to give all codes the same number of digits. In other words, there is no special reason that exactly two octal digits are used for each character. In any largely numeric text, there will be a great many leading zeros whose only role is to make it possible to convert the text back to characters. For example, in the string of octal

Character	Octal code	Character	Octal code	Character	Octal code	Character	Octal code
0	00	B	13	M	26	X	41
1	01	C	14	N	27	Y	42
2	02	D	15	O	30	Z	43
3	03	E	16	P	31	+	44
4	04	F	17	Q	32	−	45
5	05	G	20	R	33	(	46
6	06	H	21	S	34	)	47
7	07	I	22	T	35	=	50
8	10	J	23	U	36	.	51
9	11	K	24	V	37	(blank)	52
A	12	L	25	W	40	,	53

Figure 2.22

Character	Code	Probability	Character	Code	Probability
0	101^20	.025	M	0^21010	.020
1	10^31	.025	N	0^3101	.020
2	10^4	.025	O	010^3	.040
3	10^21^2	.025	P	0^310^2	.020
4	10^210	.025	Q	01^20^310	.005
5	1^301	.025	R	01^301	.015
6	1^30^2	.025	S	0101^2	.035
7	1^5	.025	T	01^201	.030
8	1^40	.025	U	0^41	.040
9	1^20^21	.025	V	101^30^21	.005
A	0^21^3	.040	W	101^30^3	.005
B	1^20^3	.025	X	101^301	.005
C	1^201^2	.025	Y	$01^20^31^20$	.004
D	1^2010	.025	Z	$01^20^31^3$	.001
E	0^21^20	.040	+	01010	.035
F	0^51	.025	−	0^6	.025
G	0^210^21	.020	(	0^31^3	.020
H	0^210^3	.020	)	0^31^20	.020
I	010^21	.040	=	01^4	.025
J	01^20^4	.010	.	01^30^2	.015
K	101^4	.010	(blank)	1010	.050
L	0^2101^2	.020	,	01^20^21	.015

Figure 2.23

code digits 01021103040510, which represents the character string '1293458', five of the octal zeros are merely "place-holders." Sometimes codes are devised in which one of the goals is minimization of the expected number of digits needed to represent information. For such a code the characters of the alphabet are first listed in order of expected frequency of use. Then codes are assigned in such a way that no code is an initial part of another. The usual assignment is made by using a method suggested by D. Huffman.† In Fig. 2.23 a hypothetical ordering is shown for our 44-character alphabet, with codes assigned (in binary). The notation is similar to that used in Chapter 1, with 01^r an abbreviation for a 0 and r ones (r written in decimal), and typical probabilities of occurrence for a language somewhat like English.

---

† Huffman, D. "A Method for Construction of Minimum Redundancy Codes," *Proc. IRE*, Vol. 40, No. 9, September 1952.

Character	Code	Probability	Character	Code	Probability
0	010^2	.092	M	01010^410^2	.001
1	0^31	.092	N	01010^41^3	.001
2	0^4	.092	O	01010^41^20	.001
3	0^21^2	.092	P	01010^61	.001
4	0^210	.092	Q	01010^7	.001
5	101	.092	R	01010^511	.001
6	10^2	.092	S	01010^510	.001
7	1^3	.092	T	0101^30101	.001
8	1^20	.092	U	0101^3010^2	.001
9	01^2	.092	V	0101^301^3	.001
A	0101^4010	.001	W	0101^301^20	.001
B	0101^401^2	.001	X	0101^30^41	.001
C	0101^40^3	.001	Y	0101^30^5	.001
D	0101^40^21	.001	Z	0101^30^31	.000
E	0101^60	.001	+	01010101	.005
F	0101^7	.001	−	0101010^2	.005
G	0101^50^2	.001	(	010101^3	.005
H	0101^501	.001	)	010101^20	.005
I	0101^30^210	.001	=	01010^31	.005
J	$0101^30^21^20$	.001	.	0101^201	.010
K	$0101^30^21^3$	.001	(blank)	0101^20^2	.010
L	01010^4101	.001	,	01010^21	.010

Figure 2.24

Once these probabilities are determined, one can compute an expected code length for the alphabet by multiplying each individual code length by its probability, and summing. For the codes assigned in Fig. 2.23, the expected code length is then 5.31 bits (1.77 octal digits). For a word like "auto," the bit length is now 20 instead of 24. For the string 'AB + CD.5' used as an example above, the coded form in binary is $0^21^50^31^201^4010^2$ $1^30^21^301$, which has a total of 31 bits, compared with 42 bits in the encoding of Fig. 2.21. It should be clear by now that such a scheme is feasible only when a few characters in the alphabet are expected to be used with a very high frequency relative to the rest of the alphabet, so that only the shortest codes appear most of the time. If the text were to be almost entirely numeric, for instance, the shortest codes could have been assigned to the digits, as in Fig. 2.24, and now the expected code length is 3.891 bits (1.297 octal digits). The string '1293458,' which previously required 42 bits, now has the representation $0^310^51^20^21^20^210101^30$, with only 25 bits.

One serious disadvantage encountered with the variable-length codes we have just discussed is the difficulty in parsing a string of bits to find its parts (for example, the separate digits). The only way to find the fifth digit of a number is to start at the left end and count the codes as they are passed. Arithmetic on numbers represented in this way is extremely difficult to mechanize and is inevitably slow. In any system in which arithmetic is to be done (rather than manipulation of textual material), one would probably not expect to find such a system of codes.

On the other hand, though a coding scheme that uses 6-bit codes, as in Fig. 2.21, is more convenient for manipulating characters, especially since all the characters are treated in a uniform way, it is still not very efficient for ordinary arithmetic. For example, when a decimal carry is generated, it is not a trivial process to recognize it and handle it properly. As an example, the reader should try adding 5 (i.e., 000101) and 6 (i.e., 000110) to get 11 (i.e., 000001000001).

In short, a binary representation is employed, but the convenience of binary arithmetic is being ignored. In order to simplify and speed up arithmetic processes, therefore, numbers are usually represented in pure binary notation, without any attempt to keep the decimal digits separated. (The binary digits are of course explicit.) Thus the number 178_{10} would be represented internally as 10110010. Now full advantage may be taken of the extremely simple arithmetic of the binary number system, and the only problem is the communication with the person for whom the computation is being done. He would like to deal with decimal digits, both as input from him to the machine, and as output from the machine back to him. Somewhere, then, an algorithmic activity must be used to convert his decimal digits into a binary number; and the binary results of the computation must also be converted into decimal digits for use as output.

Devices are readily available which can "read" holes in punched cards or in paper tape or magnetized spots on magnetic tape and create a pattern of bits internally which corresponds to the pattern of holes or spots read. Similarly, devices are available which print or display on a screen the characters corresponding to specific patterns existing internally. In general, such input and output devices make use of character-by-character codes, such as those in Fig. 2.21. For this reason some machines do their arithmetic on character strings, in spite of the difficulties with arithmetic mentioned above. For scientific work, in which one normally expects a great deal of arithmetic to occur per input or output action, the binary form of numbers is commonly used. In this case, as part of the action to be attributed to an input or output (I/O) box in a flowchart, we must include the conversion of the decimal digit characters to and from the binary number representation.

We now have the situation in which a string of bits stored internally no longer has a unique interpretation. When the string 000101000011001001

occurs, does it represent the decimal character string '539' (viewing it as
000101 000011 001001), or is it the binary number whose decimal form is
20,681? Unless an extra bit is allocated just for this purpose, i.e., as a
"flag," there is no way to know which interpretation to use. As mentioned
earlier, the machine is usually built to assume that the string of bits it
finds is what it expects to find, and the algorithm, rather than the data,
specifies the interpretation—with possible (but, we hope, improbable)
chaotic results.

2.10 EXPRESSIONS

We now have at our disposal names of variables and names of constants,
as well as some operators (such as selection operators) which can be applied
to them. What other operators do we expect to encounter? The answer
depends largely on the form of the data and the kinds of manipulations
specified by the algorithm to be invoked. For example, if the data consist
of numbers, we would expect to find the usual arithmetic operators and the
comparison operators (or *relations*): $=$, $\neq$, $>$, $\geq$, $\leq$, and $<$. If the data
are composed of strings of characters, the most appropriate operators are
probably *concatenation* and the relations of *equality* and *nonequality*. Often
the relation "the string x is a substring (or *head or tail*) of the string y" is
useful, too. We shall eventually want to provide appropriate operators for
data represented as lists and trees as well, such as relations for *equality*,
sublist, and so on.

Note that a relation always produces an expression, such as $x < y$,
which for particular values of x and y has a *truth value*, i.e., *true* or *false*,
rather than a numeric value. Our definitions should therefore be extended
to include variables whose values can be *true* or *false*. Such variables are
often said to be of type *Boolean*† rather than *integer* or *real*. We shall
also find it convenient to combine relational expressions into more
powerful truth-valued expressions by using $\wedge$ (and), $\vee$ (inclusive-or),
and $\neg$ (not). Thus the condition which guarantees two distinct, real
roots to the quadratic equation $ax^2 + bx + c = 0$ is

$$a \neq 0 \wedge b^2 - 4ac > 0$$

Some years ago (1958), representatives of several countries met to
specify a language for stating algorithms. It was hoped that this new
language (now revised and called ALGOL—for Algorithmic Language)

---

† After George Boole, a famous logician who gave impetus to the use of logical
operators.

[8] would be complete enough and convenient enough to satisfy the needs of most people. To some extent it has succeeded, though one effect of ALGOL has been to stimulate the generation of still more powerful languages. Because ALGOL has been used extensively for publication and machine computation in several countries, and because it is built on the philosophical foundation of generality espoused earlier in this chapter, this language will be the basis for much of the notation used here. There will be departures and extensions from ALGOL when needed, of course, but such modifications will generally be indicated. For example, there is no provision in ALGOL for complex numbers, lists (other than arrays), or trees. Any forms used here involving these constructs are therefore extensions of ALGOL. In Fig. 2.25 (pp. 140–141) the specification of "expressions" is written in Backus notation and closely parallels part of the ALGOL specification. Lists, trees, and arrays are not yet included. [Exercise 2.10.1 asks for examples of the application of these forms.] By means of Fig. 2.25 we now have a complete, unambiguous description of the forms in which ⟨arithmetic expression⟩s and ⟨Boolean expression⟩s may be written. According to this description, the following are examples of ⟨arithmetic expression⟩s.

$$(Ab + 2_{10}3/p \uparrow (c - d)), \qquad 1, \qquad -1/2.3, \qquad 2 + 3i - x + yi - 2.3_{10}4i$$

The following are ⟨Boolean expression⟩s.

$$x \leq y \wedge \neg x > y, \qquad p \vee q \vee r, \qquad p$$

Note that in the first example of ⟨arithmetic expression⟩s, two kinds of notation were used which have not yet been introduced, the subscript $_{10}$ and the $\uparrow$. In spite of the total absence of meaning to attach to these characters, it was quite possible to assert (from Fig. 2.25) that the expression given there is a legitimate example of an ⟨arithmetic expression⟩, *merely by its form*. These rules for constructing admissible combinations of the characters in the basic alphabet are called the rules of *syntax* of the language. The meanings which govern the subsequent interpretation (usually called the *semantics* of the language) have yet to be provided. Until they are, the character $\div$, for example, may be used in an expression such as $4 \div 3$, but we have no idea about how we are to interpret it. It was chosen to remind the user of a division process, but there is also the character $/$, so we must have in mind two kinds of division! The appropriate interpretation of each of these division signs must therefore wait for the statement of the semantics. Meanwhile, we may construct as many *syntactically correct* expressions—ignoring their meanings—as we like.

Let us proceed then to the statement of semantics.

1. The logical values **true** and **false** shall have the obvious meanings, as in ordinary usage.

2. The blank space which occurs in the printed representation of any construction, as well as the space created by starting a new printed line, shall have no effect and convey no additional meaning.

3. ⟨Identifier⟩s have no inherent meaning but serve for the identification of arithmetic and Boolean variables, which have numerical and logical values, respectively.

4. Numbers have their conventional meanings. The exponent part of a number is a scale factor expressed as an integral power of 10.

Identifiers, Declarators, and Operators

⟨letter⟩ ::= $a \mid b \mid c \mid d \mid e \mid f \mid g \mid h \mid i \mid j \mid k \mid l \mid m \mid n \mid o \mid p \mid q \mid r \mid s \mid t \mid$
    $u \mid v \mid w \mid x \mid y \mid z \mid A \mid B \mid C \mid D \mid E \mid F \mid G \mid H \mid I \mid J \mid K \mid L \mid M \mid$
    $N \mid O \mid P \mid Q \mid R \mid S \mid T \mid U \mid V \mid W \mid X \mid Y \mid Z$

⟨digit⟩ ::= $0 \mid 1 \mid 2 \mid 3 \mid 4 \mid 5 \mid 6 \mid 7 \mid 8 \mid 9$

⟨logical value⟩ ::= **true** | **false**†

⟨logical operator⟩ ::= $\vee \mid \wedge \mid \neg$

⟨relational operator⟩ ::= $< \mid \leq \mid = \mid \neq \mid > \mid \geq$

⟨arithmetic operator⟩ ::= $+ \mid - \mid \times \mid / \mid \div \mid \uparrow$

⟨operator⟩ ::= ⟨arithmetic operator⟩ | ⟨relational operator⟩ | ⟨logical operator⟩

⟨type⟩ ::= **Boolean** | **integer** | **real** | **complex** | **character**‡

⟨declaration⟩ ::= ⟨type⟩ ⟨type list⟩

⟨identifier⟩ ::= $\{$⟨letter⟩ | ⟨digit⟩$\}^*_1$ | **r** §

⟨type list⟩ ::= ⟨identifier⟩$\{,$⟨identifier⟩$\}^*$

Numbers

⟨unsigned integer⟩ ::= $\{$⟨digit⟩$\}^*_1$

⟨integer⟩ ::= $\{+ \mid -\}^1_0$ ⟨unsigned integer⟩

⟨exponent part⟩ ::= $_{10}$⟨integer⟩

⟨floating point number⟩ ::= ⟨unsigned integer⟩$\{ . \{$⟨unsigned integer⟩$\}^1_0\}^1_0$ |
    $.$⟨unsigned integer⟩

⟨unsigned real number⟩ ::= ⟨floating point number⟩ | ⟨exponent part⟩ |
    ⟨floating point number⟩ ⟨exponent part⟩

⟨imaginary number⟩ ::= ⟨unsigned real number⟩ i

---

† Boldface words are to be regarded as additional basic characters in the alphabet.
‡ The use of **character** will be seen in Chapter 3.
§ The use of **r** will be seen in Section 2.15.

Figure 2.25

5. Logical values and variables so declared are of ⟨type⟩ **Boolean**. Numbers involving *i* and variables so declared are of ⟨type⟩ **complex**. ⟨Integer⟩s and variables so declared are of ⟨type⟩ **integer**. All other numbers and variables are of ⟨type⟩ **real**. The property of "⟨type⟩" refers to the value of the entity named.

6. The value of an expression is obtained by executing the indicated operations. The ⟨operator⟩s +, −, and × have the conventional meaning. The value of an ⟨arithmetic expression⟩ which involves one of these operations and for which both operands are of the same ⟨type⟩ is also of that ⟨type⟩. If they are not of the same ⟨type⟩, then the value of the ⟨arithmetic expression⟩ has the "higher" ⟨type⟩ of the two, according to the

---

⟨real number⟩ ::= {+ | −}$_0^1$⟨unsigned real number⟩
⟨complex number⟩ ::= ⟨real number⟩{{+ | −}⟨imaginary number⟩}$_0^1$ |
　　{ + | − }⟨imaginary number⟩

Strings
⟨open string⟩ ::= ⟨any sequence of symbols in the basic alphabet such that
　　right apostrophes occur only in pairs⟩
⟨string⟩ ::= '⟨open string⟩'

Arithmetic Expressions
⟨add operator⟩ ::= + | −
⟨multiply operator⟩ ::= × | / | ÷
⟨primary⟩ ::= ⟨unsigned real number⟩ | ⟨imaginary number⟩ | ⟨identifier⟩ |
　　(⟨arithmetic　expression⟩)
⟨factor⟩ ::= ⟨primary⟩ | ⟨factor⟩ ↑ ⟨primary⟩
⟨term⟩ ::= ⟨factor⟩ | ⟨term⟩ ⟨multiply operator⟩ ⟨factor⟩
⟨arithmetic expression⟩ ::= ⟨term⟩ | ⟨add operator⟩ ⟨term⟩ |
　　⟨arithmetic expression⟩ ⟨add operator⟩ ⟨term⟩

Boolean Expressions
⟨relation⟩ ::= ⟨arithmetic expression⟩ ⟨relational operator⟩ ⟨arithmetic
　　expression⟩
⟨Boolean primary⟩ ::= ⟨logical value⟩ | ⟨identifier⟩ | ⟨relation⟩ |
　　(⟨Boolean expression⟩)
⟨Boolean secondary⟩ ::= ⟨Boolean primary⟩ | ¬⟨Boolean primary⟩
⟨Boolean factor⟩ ::= ⟨Boolean secondary⟩ | ⟨Boolean factor⟩
　　∧ ⟨Boolean secondary⟩
⟨Boolean expression⟩ ::= ⟨Boolean factor⟩ | ⟨Boolean expression⟩
　　∨ ⟨Boolean factor⟩

Figure 2.25 (continued)

ordering: **integer** < **real** < **complex**. The value of a ⟨Boolean expression⟩ is of ⟨type⟩ **Boolean**.

7. The operations ⟨term⟩ / ⟨factor⟩ and ⟨term⟩ ÷ ⟨factor⟩ both denote division, to be understood as a multiplication of the term by the reciprocal of the ⟨factor⟩. The ⟨operator⟩ / is defined for all combinations of ⟨type⟩s among **integer, real**, and **complex**, with the ⟨type⟩ of the value of the division determined as in (6) above, except that an expression of the form

$$\langle integer \rangle \, / \, \langle integer \rangle$$

has ⟨type⟩ **real**. The ⟨operator⟩ ÷ is defined only for operands of ⟨type⟩ **integer** and yields a value computed by the rule:

$$a \div b \equiv \operatorname{sgn}(a/b) \times [|a/b|]$$

where the brackets denote the greatest-integer function, i.e., the greatest ⟨integer⟩ not exceeding $|a/b|$.

8. The operation ⟨factor⟩ ↑ ⟨primary⟩ denotes exponentiation, where the ⟨factor⟩ is the base and the ⟨primary⟩ is the exponent. Thus, for example, $a \uparrow b \uparrow c$ is usually written $(a^b)^c$.

9. The sequence of operations within one expression is determined by the order of composition according to the syntax. In general, it is from left to right for ⟨operator⟩s of equal precedence, and otherwise subject to the rule of precedence, as follows:

first: ↑   fifth: ¬
second: × / ÷   sixth: ∧
third: + −   seventh: ∨
fourth: < ≤ = ≠ > ≥

10. An expression enclosed by matching parentheses is always evaluated by itself, and the value thus obtained is used in subsequent calculations.

11. ⟨Relation⟩s take the value **true** when the corresponding ⟨relation⟩ is true for the expressions involved, otherwise **false.**

12. The evaluation of the Boolean ⟨operator⟩s ∧, ∨, and ¬ is based on the following table:

$b1$	false	false	true	true
$b2$	false	true	false	true
¬ $b1$	true	true	false	false
$b1 \wedge b2$	false	false	false	true
$b1 \vee b2$	false	true	true	true

EXERCISE 2.10.1

Give an example of the application of each syntax definition of Fig. 2.25, showing all possible ways of satisfying the definition. As an example of ⟨identifier⟩ we might have: $g \mid 7 \mid 7c \mid g6$. Omit, of course, examples of definitions for those given explicitly, e.g., ⟨letter⟩, ⟨declarator⟩, etc.

2.11 STATEMENTS

We have thus specified both the syntax and semantics of ⟨arithmetic expression⟩s and ⟨Boolean expression⟩s. As yet there is no apparent use for ⟨Boolean expression⟩s, however. What is missing in this language is a way to express decisions; without them, all we can do is specify a sequence of ⟨assignment statement⟩s. It is obvious from even the simplest of flowcharts, however, that the decision (or conditional) box is at least as important as the assignment box. Let us then extend the syntax description to include the conditional statement, as well as the assignment statement, as follows:

⟨variable⟩ ::= ⟨identifier⟩
⟨left part list⟩ ::= {⟨variable⟩ :=}$_1^*$
⟨expression⟩ ::= ⟨arithmetic expression⟩ | ⟨Boolean expression⟩
⟨assignment statement⟩ ::= ⟨left part list⟩ ⟨expression⟩
⟨basic statement⟩ ::= ⟨assignment statement⟩
⟨if clause⟩ ::= **if** ⟨Boolean expression⟩ **then**
⟨unconditional statement⟩ ::= ⟨basic statement⟩ | ⟨compound state-
    ment⟩
⟨statement⟩ ::= ⟨unconditional statement⟩ | ⟨conditional statement⟩
⟨compound tail⟩ ::= {⟨statement⟩;}$_0^*$ ⟨statement⟩ **end**
⟨compound statement⟩ ::= **begin** ⟨compound tail⟩
⟨if statement⟩ ::= ⟨if clause⟩ ⟨unconditional statement⟩
⟨conditional statement⟩ ::= ⟨if statement⟩ | ⟨if statement⟩ **else** ⟨state-
    ment⟩
⟨program⟩ ::= ⟨compound statement⟩

[Exercise 2.11.1 asks for examples of the above.] The semantics needed here are:

1. A ⟨compound statement⟩ allows a collection of ⟨statement⟩s to appear in a construction (such as in the ⟨conditional statement⟩), in which a single ⟨statement⟩ occurs. The sequence of execution of the constituents of a ⟨compound statement⟩ is from left to right.

2. In an ⟨assignment statement⟩ the value of the ⟨expression⟩ is computed and then assigned to all the ⟨variable⟩s of the ⟨left part list⟩. The ⟨type⟩ associated with each of the ⟨variable⟩s of a ⟨left part list⟩ must be such that there exists a "transfer function" for the value of the ⟨expression⟩ to that ⟨type⟩. The transfer functions allowed are summarized in Fig. 2.26; an entry of x signifies that the value is unchanged externally, but the internal representation may be changed according to the ⟨type⟩s involved.

x \\ y	integer	real	complex	string	Boolean
integer	x	x	x	NA	NA
real	$[x + 0.5]$	x	x	NA	NA
complex $x = a + bi$	$[\sqrt{a^2 + b^2} + 0.5]$	$\sqrt{a^2 + b^2}$	x	NA	NA
string	NA	NA	NA	x	NA
Boolean	NA	NA	NA	NA	x

Figure 2.26   Transfer functions for $y: = x$ (NA ≡ not allowed).

3. ⟨Conditional statement⟩s cause certain ⟨statement⟩s to be executed or skipped, depending on the values of the ⟨Boolean expression⟩s involved. The ⟨unconditional statement⟩ of an ⟨if statement⟩ will be executed if the ⟨Boolean expression⟩ of the ⟨if clause⟩ is true. Otherwise it will be skipped, and the operation will be continued with the next ⟨statement⟩.

4. Since the ⟨statement⟩ in a ⟨conditional statement⟩ may be a ⟨conditional statement⟩ again or an ⟨unconditional statement⟩, two cases arise:

> **if** B_1 **then** S_1 **else if** B_2 **then** S_2 **else** S_3; S_4
> **if** B_1 **then** S_1 **else if** B_2 **then** S_2 **else if** B_3 **then** S_3; S_4

where B_1, B_2, and B_3 are ⟨Boolean expression⟩s, and S_1, S_2, and S_3 are ⟨unconditional statement⟩s, while S_4 is whatever ⟨statement⟩ follows the complete ⟨conditional statement⟩. The expression of a ⟨conditional statement⟩ may then be described as follows: The ⟨Boolean expression⟩s of the ⟨if clause⟩s are evaluated one after the other in sequence from left to right until one yielding the value **true** is found. Then the ⟨unconditional statement⟩ immediately following this ⟨Boolean expression⟩ is executed, and then the next ⟨statement⟩ to be executed is S_4. The construction

> **else** ⟨unconditional statement⟩

is equivalent to

> **else if true then** ⟨unconditional statement⟩

If none of the ⟨if clause⟩s is true, no computation results from the ⟨conditional statement⟩, and the next ⟨statement⟩ to be executed is S_4.

Let us now see what we have accomplished. First of all, we have a very complete facility for writing ⟨expression⟩s. Since an ⟨expression⟩ can be embedded repeatedly in more complicated ones, we can construct whatever ⟨expression⟩ is needed to compute an arithmetic value or make a logical decision—though later we shall need to add as well the facility for *calling* upon (or *invoking*) subroutines (also referred to as *functions* or *procedures*). Thus we can write ⟨arithmetic expression⟩s such as $a + b \uparrow c - e \uparrow f/(d - f) + 4.25$, as well as ⟨Boolean expression⟩s such as $x < y + 1 \lor x \uparrow 2 < y + p - 3 \lor Q \land \neg R$.

With the ⟨assignment statement⟩s and ⟨conditional statement⟩s now available to us, we can write

$a := b := c := d + e + g;$
$P := Q := x \leq y \land z \neq m;$ (assuming that P and Q are of ⟨type⟩ **Boolean**)
if $x \leq y$ **then** $x := y$ **else if** $x \leq y + 5$ **then** $x := y + 5;$
if $x \leq y$ **then begin** $x := y;$ $y := y + 1;$ $z := y$ **end**;

In fact, all we need in order to be able to write the simple but complete ⟨program⟩s discussed earlier in this chapter is the ability to specify the transfer of control which the arrows in the flowchart show explicitly. In other words, now that we have agreed on ways of writing the ⟨expression⟩s that can occur inside boxes of the flowchart—our earlier goal—it has been but a short step to replace the flowchart entirely by providing in our "language" ways of expressing decisions and, as we shall now specify, transfer of control, i.e., to change from the normal successor of a ⟨statement⟩ to a different successor.

As seen earlier, the appropriate device for specifying the sequence of control is the *label*. We need a way to indicate that a transfer is to be made to some label. But if we are to allow sufficient flexibility in this procedure, there should be some choice as to which label is to be selected at the time the transfer is to be made. In fact, based on earlier computations, a complicated decision process might occur at this point. What is needed is a computation which results in (i.e., has as a value) a label. We call such a computation a ⟨designational expression⟩, and in ALGOL these are usually listed as entries in a sequence called a **switch**. For example, one might write

$$\text{\textbf{switch} } S := S1, S2, Q[m], \text{ \textbf{if} } v > -5 \text{ \textbf{then} } S3 \text{ \textbf{else} } S4$$

where *S1*, *S2*, *S3*, and *S4* are labels, and *Q* is itself a **switch** in which the *m*th entry (i.e., the *m*th ⟨designational expression⟩) is to be evaluated to produce a label if the third entry in the **switch** *S* is selected. The declaration for *Q* might be

$$\text{\textbf{switch} } Q := p, q, r$$

We must add this to our growing syntax and semantics specifications. (Henceforth, we shall understand that *any construction which expands or otherwise modifies an earlier specification supersedes the earlier one.*)

⟨declarator⟩ ::= **Boolean** | **integer** | **real** | **complex** | **character** | **switch**
⟨label⟩ ::= ⟨identifier⟩
⟨switch identifier⟩ ::= ⟨identifier⟩
⟨switch designator⟩ ::= ⟨switch identifier⟩ [⟨arithmetic expression⟩]
⟨simple designational expression⟩ ::= ⟨label⟩ | ⟨switch designator⟩ |
    (⟨designational expression⟩)
⟨designational expression⟩ ::= ⟨simple designational expression⟩|
    ⟨if clause⟩ ⟨simple designational expression⟩ **else** ⟨designational
    expression⟩
⟨switch list⟩ ::= {⟨designational expression⟩}$_1^*$
⟨switch declaration⟩ ::= **switch** ⟨switch identifier⟩ := ⟨switch list⟩
⟨unlabeled basic statement⟩ ::= ⟨assignment statement⟩
⟨basic statement⟩ ::= ⟨unlabeled basic statement⟩ | ⟨label⟩ : ⟨basic
    statement⟩
⟨unlabeled compound⟩ ::= **begin** ⟨compound tail⟩
⟨compound statement⟩ ::= ⟨unlabeled compound⟩ | ⟨label⟩ :
    ⟨compound statement⟩
⟨statement⟩ ::= ⟨unconditional statement⟩ | ⟨conditional statement⟩ |
    ⟨label⟩ : ⟨statement⟩

[Exercise 2.11.1 asks for examples of the above.] The semantics specifications in this case would be:

1. Each of the ⟨label⟩s appearing immediately before a ⟨statement⟩ is considered to apply to the beginning of that ⟨statement⟩.

2. The value obtained by evaluating a ⟨designational expression⟩ is a label of a statement. A ⟨switch designator⟩ refers to the corresponding ⟨switch declaration⟩, and by the actual numerical value of its ⟨arithmetic expression⟩, which must be an integer, selects one of the ⟨designational expression⟩s listed in the ⟨switch declaration⟩ by counting from left to right.

Now all we need is the statement which actually transfers control:

⟨go to statement⟩ ::= **go to** ⟨designational expression⟩

Here the semantics are:

1. A ⟨go to statement⟩ interrupts the normal sequence of operations by defining its successor explicitly by the ⟨label⟩ obtained by the evaluation of its ⟨designational expression⟩. The next ⟨statement⟩ to be executed is the one with this ⟨label⟩.

2. A ⟨go to statement⟩ which is executed during the normal execution of a ⟨conditional statement⟩ has the immediate effect of naming a successor to its execution, thus overriding whatever further sequencing was implied by the unexecuted part of the ⟨conditional statement⟩. For example, in the ⟨compound statement⟩

begin if $x \leq y$ **then go to** L; **if** $x \leq y + 5$ **then** $x := y$ **end**

for $x = 3$, $y = 4$, the next ⟨statement⟩ executed would be the one labeled L (elsewhere in the program), and x would not be set to the value of y. However, if $x = 5$ and $y = 4$, then control would go as usual to the ⟨statement⟩ following the ⟨conditional statement⟩, after x has had its value changed to the value of y by the execution of the assignment statement $x := y$.

As a complete example, Fig. 2.27 shows how a program for Fig. 2.13 would now appear, using our modified version of the ALGOL language. Note how indentation of the lines makes the conditional structure stand out clearly.

```
begin integer j;
    B: Read(a, b, c);
    if a = 0 then begin
        if b = 0 then begin j := 1;
            A: Print(x1, x2, j);   go to B end
        else begin x1 := −c/b;   j := 2;   go to A end
    else begin d := b↑2 −4 × a × c;
        if d < 0 then begin j := 3;   go to A end
        else if d = 0 then begin j := 4;
            D: x1 := (−b + sqrt(d)/(2 × a);
            x2 := (−b − sqrt(d)/(2 × a);   go to A end
        else begin j := 5;   go to D end end
```

Figure 2.27

The process of laying out the lines in a printed algorithm may be regarded as a necessary evil, something which must be done so that the algorithm may be exhibited. However, we take a more positive view here, and we shall take as much advantage of the layout available to us as we can—in particular, the indentation—to make the algorithm as clear as possible. Since the key to understanding an algorithm is the flow of control, especially that implied by the scope of ⟨if clause⟩s and other constructions which group ⟨statement⟩s together, we shall use indentation to make this as explicit as possible. A full statement of the use of indentation will be found in Section 2.13.

EXERCISE 2.11.1

Give an example of each syntax definition in Section 2.11, again showing all possible ways of satisfying the definition.

2.12 THE ITERATION STATEMENT

In Fig. 2.17 we introduced the iteration box. As yet, however, we have not provided an analogous construction in our formal ALGOL-like language. There are two main ways in which iterations are used. In one a ⟨variable⟩ is used as a counting device to control the number of iterations.† The other main use of the iteration structure—to repeat a computation until some condition is satisfied—may not be a simple counting procedure at all. An example occurred in the half-interval method for finding a zero of a continuous function (Fig. 2.18), where h was halved on each iteration until $h < \epsilon$. Although the counting form of iteration may be viewed as a special case of the more general second form, it occurs so often that a special notation for it has been established in ALGOL. Thus we have, as an example of the iteration statement,

$$\textbf{for } i := 0 \textbf{ step } 1 \textbf{ until } n \textbf{ do } S;$$

where S is the ⟨statement⟩ (usually a ⟨compound statement⟩) which is the body of the iteration (corresponding to Fig. 2.17), and

$m := f(p); \textbf{ for } h := q - p, h/2 \textbf{ while } h \geq \epsilon \textbf{ do}$
   $\textbf{begin for } y := p + h \textbf{ step } 2 \times h \textbf{ until } m \times f(y) \leq 0 \textbf{ do}$
      $\textbf{if } y \geq q - h \textbf{ then go to } L;$
         $xR := y; \quad xL := y - h; \quad \textbf{go to } A;$
         $L: \textbf{end};$
   $\textbf{go to } H1;$

---

† As we shall see later, this variable is also useful as an *index*, or pointer, to the specific entry under consideration in an array of values; as the index changes, attention is focused on successive elements of the array.

expresses the first part of the half-interval algorithm of Fig. 2.18. In the
process of specifying the syntax of the **for** statement, we should of course
be as general as possible. Thus we shall allow a list of control clauses
consisting of individual values to be used (in order) by the index variable,
as well as the **step–until** form and the **while** form which we have just seen.
The syntax of the **for** statement then is

⟨for list element⟩ ∷= ⟨arithmetic expression⟩ {⟨empty⟩|
    step ⟨arithmetic expression⟩ **until** ⟨arithmetic expression⟩|
    while ⟨Boolean expression⟩}
⟨for list⟩ ∷= ⟨for list element⟩ {,⟨for list element}*
⟨for clause⟩ ∷= **for** ⟨variable⟩ := ⟨for list⟩ **do**
⟨for statement⟩ ∷= ⟨for clause⟩ ⟨statement⟩
⟨statement⟩ ∷= ⟨unconditional statement⟩ | ⟨conditional statement⟩ |
    ⟨for statement⟩ | ⟨label⟩ : ⟨statement⟩

[Exercise 2.12.1 asks for examples of the above.] The semantics are:

1. A ⟨for clause⟩ causes the statement S which follows it to be repeatedly
executed zero or more times. In addition it performs a sequence of assignments to its index ⟨variable⟩. After all assignments have been made,
execution continues with the successor to the ⟨for statement⟩ (unless
control has been explicitly transferred out of the scope of the ⟨for state-
ment⟩, i.e., out of the ⟨statement⟩ to be executed).

2. The ⟨for list⟩ gives the rule for obtaining the values which are consecutively assigned to the index ⟨variable⟩. The ⟨for list element⟩s are
invoked from left to right, and they generate values as described in (3),
(4), and (5) below. Thus a ⟨for clause⟩ of the form

$$\textbf{for } A := L_1, L_2, L_3, \ldots, L_k \textbf{ do } S$$

where $L_1, \ldots, L_k$ is a ⟨for list⟩ and L_i, $1 \le i \le k$, are ⟨for list element⟩s,
has the same effect as the ⟨compound statement⟩

$$\textbf{begin for } A := L_1 \textbf{ do } S; \textbf{ for } A := L_2 \textbf{ do } S; \ldots; \textbf{ for } A := L_k \textbf{ do } S \textbf{ end}$$

3. The ⟨arithmetic expression⟩ occurring alone as a ⟨for list element⟩
gives rise to one value, namely, the value of that ⟨arithmetic expression⟩
as computed immediately before the corresponding execution of the
⟨statement⟩ S in the scope.

4. A ⟨for list element⟩ of the form E_1 **step** E_2 **until** E_3, where E_i is an
⟨arithmetic expression⟩, generates values in such a way as to yield

$$v := E_1;$$
$$L1: \quad \textbf{if } (v - E_3) \times E_2 > 0 \textbf{ then go to } L2;$$

$$S;$$
$$v := v + E_2;$$
$$\textbf{go to } L1;$$
$$L2:$$

We note that almost all of the ⟨for list element⟩s which occur in programs are of the form E_1 **step** E_2 **until** E_3 where the values of E_2 and E_3 are constant during the execution of the ⟨for statement⟩. In such cases the interpretation given just above can be made more efficient by rewriting it as

$$v_1 := E_1; \quad v_2 := E_2; \quad v_3 := E_3;$$
$$L1: \quad \textbf{if } (v_1 - v_2) \times v_3 > 0 \textbf{ then go to } L2;$$
$$S;$$
$$v_1 := v_1 + v_2;$$
$$\textbf{go to } L1;$$
$$L2:$$

so that the ⟨arithmetic expression⟩s E_2 and E_3 are evaluated only once. This is an example of our ability to achieve efficiencies if we are willing to "bind" certain values so that they cannot change.

5. The execution generated by a ⟨for list element⟩ of form E_4 **while** B, where E_4 is an ⟨arithmetic expression⟩ and B is a ⟨Boolean expression⟩ is

$$L3: \quad v := E_4$$
$$\textbf{if } \neg B \textbf{ then go to } L4;$$
$$S;$$
$$\textbf{go to } L3;$$
$$L4:$$

6. The value of the index ⟨variable⟩ on exit from the execution of the ⟨for statement⟩ is the value it had at the time of the implicit or explicit ⟨go to statement⟩ that caused the exit.

7. ⟨Go to statement⟩s are not allowed from outside the scope of the ⟨for statement⟩ to ⟨label⟩s in the scope. (The difficulty here is the determination of the appropriate value of the index ⟨variable⟩ at the time of entry, as well as the choice of the next element of the ⟨for list⟩ to be invoked.)

The algorithm for the half-interval method of Fig. 2.18 uses iteration statements heavily. [Exercise 2.12.2 asks for a correct statement of this algorithm in ALGOL.]

EXERCISES 2.12

1. Give an example of each syntax definition in Section 2.12, showing all possible ways of satisfying the definition.

2. Write the algorithm of Fig. 2.18 in ALGOL.

2.13 INDENTATION

In this section we describe the conventions to be used in indenting printed algorithms. The reason for making these conventions quite explicit and precise is that indentation can be closely linked to the flow of control and can therefore become (1) a guide to an author of an algorithm as to whether he has handled his control sequencing correctly and as intended, and (2) a guide to a reader of the algorithm as to how the conditional sequence control may be understood. The consequences of having precise rules for indentation might very well include the possibility of an algorithm (carried out by a machine) which performs the indentations automatically.† The goals of such an indentation convention:

1. Changes of level of indentation should coincide with important and recognizable constructions in the algorithm.

2. Needless indentation, resulting in crowding of the algorithm to the right and/or elongation, should be avoided.

3. The rules of the convention should be simply stated and easy to carry out.

We assume that we have a standard amount of indentation, depending on the style and size of type, column width, etc., to be called here the *indentation unit*. We shall also refer to the leftmost column in which characters may be printed as the (current) *primary origin*. (This is initially some fixed column to the right of the left margin). Certain constructions in our ALGOL will move the primary origin to the right; others will move it to the left. The column situated one indentation unit to the right of the current primary origin is called the *secondary origin*.

The symbols **if** and **for** preceded by a ⟨label⟩ are regarded as occurrences of **if** and **for**, respectively. Also, **else if** and **else for** are regarded as occurrences of **else**. The rules then are as shown on p. 152.

---

† This is being done already in some places, but usually with local indentation conventions.

a) All lines after the first commence at or to the right of the current secondary origin.

b) The occurrence of a ⟨for clause⟩ or an ⟨if clause⟩ establishes a new primary origin at the column in which the initiating **for** or **if** occurred (including any ⟨label⟩s that may precede).

c) Each **else** establishes a new primary origin without moving it right or left; i.e., it is printed at the primary origin established by its initiating **if**, and subsequent lines have the usual secondary origin, one indentation unit to the right.

d) A semicolon terminating an ⟨if statement⟩ or a ⟨for statement⟩ reestablishes the primary origin at the setting in force when the **if** or **for** construction began. The next line must commence as far left as permitted by the new origin.

e) ⟨Label⟩s, except when occurring after an **else**, must start a new line.

f) The page is considered to extend indefinitely to the right in leaves. The first column of the page holds the current leaf number. This number is changed and printed whenever a column to be employed occurs past the right or left margin of the current leaf. Each new leaf is printed at or to the right of the second column of the page. The initial leaf number, assumed to be 1, need not be printed.

The reader should verify in detail that the algorithm printed in Fig. 2.27 satisfies these conventions.

We now observe that there is enough information contained in the indentation to permit the suppression of all occurrences of **begin** and **end**. In other words, if one starts with an ordinary ALGOL algorithm indented according to the above conventions, and if one suppresses occurrences of **begin** and **end**, then an algorithmic activity can be given which introduces the symbols **begin** and **end** to produce a representation of the original algorithm "equivalent to" the original indented representation. (In fact, it must differ at most in the elimination of redundant occurrences of **begin** and **end**.) This reintroduction activity (if we assume a correctly indented representation) may be stated as follows:

1) Insert a **begin** at the beginning of the algorithm.

2) Reading from left to right, insert a **begin** after each occurrence of a **then** or a **do**, and after each **else** not followed immediately (except possibly for a ⟨label⟩) by an **if** or a **for**.

3) Whenever a line of print is followed by a line which starts no farther to the right than the current primary origin, append *n* occurrences of the

symbol **end** at its right end (but in front of any final semicolon that might be there). Here n is the difference between the number of occurrences of **begin** already introduced for origins at or to the right of the next line's primary origin and the number of occurrences of **end** already introduced for origins at or to the right of the next line's primary origin. The last line may be treated in the same way by assuming a fictitious next line starting at the extreme left margin.

4) After step (3) is completed, delete every **begin–end** pair which bounds a ⟨basic statement⟩.

[Exercise 2.13.1 asks for applications of these algorithmic activities in both directions, i.e., indentation and subsequent suppression of **begin** and **end** symbols, and the introduction into indented programs of missing **begin** and **end** symbols on the basis of the indentation.] In this text we shall abide by these conventions. The **begin** and **end** symbols will be used, in spite of the fact that they may be suppressed, to facilitate comparisons with other occurrences of ALGOL text and to reassure readers in their understanding of our text.

EXERCISE 2.13.1

a) Indent and suppress **begin** and **end** symbols.

> **begin if** B_1 **then begin if** B_2 **then begin for** F_1
> **while** B_3 **do begin** S_1; S_2 **end end else begin**
> **for** F_2 **while** B_4 **do begin** S_3; S_4 **end end end else begin**
> **if** B_5 **then** S_5 **else** S_6 **end end**

b) Provide missing **begin** and **end** symbols.

> **for** F_1 **while** B_1 **do**
>   **if** B_2 **then** S_1
>   **else if** B_3 **then**
>   **if** B_4 **then** S_2
>   **else** S_3
>   **else for** F_2 **while** B_5 **do** S_4

2.14   THE BLOCK

We have already seen how several ⟨statement⟩s can be grouped together to form a ⟨compound statement⟩. The scope of the combination is determined by the use of **begin** and **end**, which act like parentheses at the level of ⟨statement⟩s, rather than ⟨expression⟩s. Sometimes it is very convenient to have a way of naming ⟨variable⟩s which exist only over the current

execution of the ⟨compound statement⟩, perhaps for temporary storage
or as a counter or index variable, as in a ⟨for statement⟩. Since the
begin and **end** are available, we can use them to create and eliminate
⟨variable⟩s without any confusion. *We make the following convention:*
(1) If a ⟨variable⟩ is "declared," i.e., given a ⟨type⟩, immediately after a
begin symbol, then storage is reserved for it from that point on, until the
corresponding **end** occurs, at which point the storage disappears. (2) If a
⟨variable⟩ with the same name occurs outside the scope of that **begin–end**
pair, its value will be preserved "on ice" while the new interpretation of the
name is in use, and only the new interpretation will be used until the **end**
occurs. At that time the previous interpretation will be reinstated.

A ⟨compound statement⟩ with such ⟨declaration⟩s after the **begin** is
called a *block*. The syntax needed to accommodate the block is:

⟨unconditional statement⟩ ::= ⟨basic statement⟩ |
    ⟨compound statement⟩ | ⟨block⟩
⟨block head⟩ ::= **begin** ⟨declaration⟩ {;⟨declaration⟩}*
⟨block⟩ ::= ⟨block head⟩; ⟨compound tail⟩

An example of a ⟨block⟩ would be:

begin integer *i*;   **real** *x, y*;   *x* := (*w* + *1*)/2;   *i* := 0;
    for *y* := (*x* + *w*/*x*)/2 **while** *i* ≤ *100* ∧ *abs*(*x* − *y*) ≥ *epsilon*
        do begin *x* := *y*;   *i* := *i* + *1* **end**;   *z* := *y* **end**

This is a Newton-Raphson computation for the square root of a number
w to within a tolerance given as the value of a variable called *epsilon*.
[Exercise 2.14.1 asks for the derivation of the formula *y* := (*x* + *w*/*x*)/2
from the Newton formula.] Here *x, y*, and *i* are *local* to the ⟨block⟩;
i.e., they have no meaning outside it; and *w*, *epsilon*, and *z* are *global*
to the ⟨block⟩. The global variables must have been declared somewhere
in a ⟨block⟩ which contains the example above. For this outer ⟨block⟩,
these variables are local; for our example, they are global. Note that
within the ⟨block⟩ a second **begin–end** pair occurred because a ⟨compound
statement⟩ was needed as the one ⟨statement⟩ to which the iteration
could be applied. This ⟨compound statement⟩ is not a ⟨block⟩, however,
since there are no ⟨declaration⟩s immediately after the **begin**. As with
parentheses, the first **end** after a **begin** closes off that ⟨block⟩ or ⟨compound
statement⟩.

An interesting question arises when the ⟨go to statement⟩ is used to
jump into, out of, or within a ⟨block⟩. The problem is whether or not the
⟨label⟩ will have the appropriate meaning. Since attaching a ⟨label⟩
to a ⟨statement⟩ is quite analogous to declaring it to be a ⟨label⟩, we
may treat it as if it were declared in the smallest ⟨block⟩ containing its

"declaration." Then it clearly has the desired meaning for a **go to** jump within the same ⟨block⟩. But what about a jump into that ⟨block⟩ from outside? Clearly, since the ⟨label⟩ has no existence outside that ⟨block⟩, such a jump is meaningless and cannot occur. There are also other implications of this restriction on jumps into a ⟨block⟩. As soon as we prohibit such jumps, we can assume that every ⟨block⟩ is entered "through the top," i.e., by processing the ⟨declaration⟩s first and then the text. We can then arrange for that part of the processing that allocates storage and assigns ⟨type⟩s to symbols, etc., to reside at the head of the ⟨block⟩, and this step has been taken in most ALGOL processors. In a later chapter, however, we shall see that this procedure is too restrictive. Without allowing jumps into the ⟨block⟩, i.e., without upsetting the assumption of coming in "through the top," we shall still need to avoid the necessity of having all ⟨declaration⟩s right up at the head of the ⟨block⟩. It will be seen in Chapter 3, which deals with data structures, that it is very convenient to allow ⟨declaration⟩s to occur later in the ⟨block⟩ as well. To be sure, they must occur before the name being declared is used in the text, but we shall see that we must be able to intermix text with ⟨declaration⟩s. Thus the syntax of ⟨block head⟩ should be given, not as we gave it earlier in the ALGOL form, but as follows:

⟨block head⟩ ::= **begin** {⟨statement⟩;}* ⟨declaration⟩ {{;⟨statement⟩}*;
    ⟨declaration⟩}*

When we move on to the consideration of a ⟨go to statement⟩ from within a ⟨block⟩ to a ⟨label⟩ in an outer ⟨block⟩, the problem is a little more difficult. Conceptually, there should be no complications at all. We may visualize the situation as follows:

begin...L:...
    begin... **go to** L;... **end**;... **end**

If the inner ⟨block⟩ contained a "declaration" of a ⟨label⟩ L, that would be the ⟨label⟩ to which the jump would be made. Here we are really considering the other case, in which no "declaration" of a ⟨label⟩ L occurs in the inner ⟨block⟩. In this case, it is clear that the jump is made to the ⟨statement⟩ labeled L in the outer ⟨block⟩.

Where then is the difficulty? Let us examine the bookkeeping implied by the use of ⟨block⟩s, especially the case in which several ⟨variable⟩s, x, y, z, etc., are declared in both the outer and the inner ⟨block⟩s. While we are executing the ⟨statement⟩s in the inner ⟨block⟩, we must give these ⟨variable⟩s their "inner ⟨block⟩" interpretation with regard to ⟨type⟩, value, storage requirements, and so on. As soon as we leave the inner ⟨block⟩ and begin to execute ⟨statement⟩s in the outer ⟨block⟩, these

⟨variable⟩s must be given an "outer ⟨block⟩" interpretation. While this bookkeeping is quite straightforward and expected at the end of a ⟨block⟩, we now see that it must be invoked as well in the case of a jump via a ⟨go to statement⟩ from the inner ⟨block⟩ to the outer one. [Exercise 2.14.2 gives examples of jumps to ⟨label⟩s with several occurrences and asks to which statement the jump is to be made. Exercise 3.5.10 will discuss this bookkeeping in terms of a particular data structure which may be used.]

What about the **begin–end** pairs used in ⟨block⟩s when it comes to the indenting of programs? We were able to argue earlier that indentation according to our rules preserved enough information to allow **begin–end** pairs to be suppressed. This feature is certainly worth preserving, so we should add appropriate conventions for including ⟨block⟩s in the indentation scheme. Since a ⟨block⟩ usually represents a smaller, self-contained computation, we shall maintain its identity by indenting it completely one additional indentation unit to the right. Specifically, the indentation rule to be added to the others in Section 2.13 should be:

g) The declarators for a ⟨block⟩ (i.e., the ⟨block head⟩) establish a new primary origin one unit to the right of the current *secondary* origin.

In the reverse process of reintroducing **begin–end** pairs to show the original ALGOL form, we restate the rules as follows, with changes only in (2) and (4):

1) Insert a **begin** at the beginning of the algorithm.

2) Reading from left to right, insert a **begin** after each occurrence of a **then** or a **do**, and after each **else** not followed immediately (except possibly for a ⟨label⟩) by an **if** or **for**. Also, insert a **begin** to the left of any ⟨declaration⟩ which starts a doubly indented line.

3) Whenever a line of print is followed by a line which starts no farther to the right than the current primary origin, append n occurrences of the symbol **end** at its right end (but in front of any final semicolon that might be there). Here n is the difference between the number of occurrences of **begin** already introduced for origins at or to the right of the next line's primary origin and the number of occurrences of **end** already introduced for origins at or to the right of the next line's primary origin. The last line may be treated in the same way by assuming a fictitious next line starting at the extreme left margin.

4) After step (3) is completed, delete every **begin–end** pair which bounds a single ⟨block⟩ (which already includes its own **begin–end** pair), or a ⟨basic statement⟩.
[Exercise 2.14.3 asks how the indentation rules now work.]

EXERCISES 2.14

1. Newton's iteration formula can be stated as follows:

$$x_{n+1} = x_n - \frac{F(x_n)}{F'(x_n)},$$

where F is a function whose zero is sought by consecutive iterations. Derive the formula

$$x_{n+1} = \left(x_n + \frac{w}{x_n}\right)\Big/2$$

from Newton's iteration formula, when $F(x) = x^2 - w$.

2. In the example below, to which statements are the jumps made? Which ⟨go to statement⟩s are meaningless?

> **begin real** y; $L1$: **go to** $L3$; ...; $L2$: **go to** $L4$;
>   **begin real** x; $L1$: **go to** $L3$; ...; $L2$: **go to** $L1$;
>   **begin** $L3$: **go to** $L4$; ...; $L4$: **go to** $L2$ **end**;
> $L3$: **go to** $L2$; ...; $L4$: **go to** $L1$ **end end**;

3. Indent and suppress unnecessary **begin–end** symbols.

> **begin integer** I_1, I_2; **real** R_1, R_2;
> A: **if** B_1 **then begin** S_1; S_2; **go to** E **end else if** B_2
> **then begin** S_3; S_4; **go to** A **end else if** B_3 **then begin**
> S_5; S_6; **go to** A **end else**
> **begin integer** I_3, I_4; **real** R_3, R_4;
> U: **if** B_4 **then begin** S_7; S_8; **go to** U **end**; S_9; S_{10}; S_{11};
> **for** F_1 **while** B_5 **do begin** S_{12}; S_{13}; S_{14} **end end**;
> E: S_{15} **end**

2.15 PROGRAM EXPRESSIONS

Since the ⟨block⟩ represents a self-contained computation, as we have seen, a natural extension of the ALGOL ⟨block⟩ concept is to allow this computation to produce a result, or *value*. This value can then be used in further computation, just as if the entire ⟨block⟩ were replaced by a ⟨variable⟩ with that value. As an example, consider the ⟨block⟩ representing the square root computation shown in the preceding section:

begin integer i;   **real** x, y; $x := (w + 1)/2$; $i := 0$;
    for $y := (x + w/x)/2$ **while** $i \leq 100 \wedge abs(x - y) \geq epsilon$
       do begin $x := y$; $i := i + 1$ **end**; $z :=$ y **end**

If we use the symbol **r** for the result of the new kind of expression we have in mind, we may simply replace the variable z by **r**. Now we could write, for $q = s + \sqrt{t + 1}$, the ALGOL statement

$q := s + $ **begin integer** $i;$ **real** $x, y;$ $x := ((t + 1) + 1)/2;$ $i := 0;$
   for $y := (x + (t + 1)/x)/2$ **while** $i \leq 100 \wedge abs(x - y) \geq epsilon$
     do begin $x := y;$ $i := i + 1$ **end**;   **r** $:= y$ **end**

Note that a more complete treatment would include a test to see if the iteration terminates because i reached 100, as well as some corrective action to be performed in this case.

At present there may not appear to be much need for such "⟨block⟩ expressions" (or "program expressions"), but we shall see them used heavily in Chapter 4. There, for example, we shall look into such possibilities as defining a new operator, such as *square root*, directly into the language. It will turn out that program expressions are exactly the forms needed to make such definitions. We content ourselves here with the remark that the syntax of a program expression is almost exactly that of a ⟨block⟩ or ⟨compound statement⟩, except that there must be an assignment of a value to a "variable" **r** somewhere in the ⟨block⟩, and there may be a ⟨type⟩ specification preceding the **begin** symbol to specify the ⟨type⟩ of the value produced by the program expression. The syntax is then:

⟨program⟩ ::= ⟨block⟩ | ⟨compound statement⟩
⟨program expression⟩ ::= ⟨program⟩ | ⟨type⟩⟨program⟩

with the added condition that there be exactly one occurrence of **r**, and that must be in the ⟨left part list⟩ of an ⟨assignment statement⟩. The value of the ⟨program expression⟩ is the value of **r** at the time the computation of the ⟨block⟩ is completed. Of course, if there is one ⟨program expression⟩ within another, each will have its own occurrence of its own **r**.

2.16 PROCEDURES

The one problem with ⟨program expression⟩s is that, although they provide a convenient notation for embedding a "package computation" into an expression, there is no simple way to use a ⟨program expression⟩ from another part of the algorithm. If it must be evaluated in two separate places, a copy must appear in each place. What is needed is the ability (i.e., a notation) to give a name to a ⟨program expression⟩, and then to use the name in an ⟨expression⟩ to stand for the occurrence of the ⟨program expression⟩. This is just the subroutine idea introduced for LMA's in Chapter 1 and already mentioned several times in this chapter.

The basic subroutine concept is commonly used in an extended form not yet discussed. Consider, for example, the square root algorithm given in the preceding section as a typical ⟨program expression⟩. While we might not wish to compute the square root of $t+1$ more than once in an algorithm, it is quite possible that we would need to compute two square roots (of different expressions) in one algorithm. The point is that we may wish to reproduce almost all of a ⟨program expression⟩ in another part of an algorithm, but we need to be able to specify in each case that some variable (or a set of variables) internal to the ⟨program expression⟩ is to have a particular value. Since we must make this specification at the point where the reference to the ⟨program expression⟩ occurs, it is necessary that this variable's name have the same meaning outside the ⟨program expression⟩ as within it. Such a variable is called "global" with respect to the ⟨program expression⟩. Variables which are meaningful only within the ⟨program expression⟩ are called "local" with respect to the ⟨program expression⟩. On each entrance to the ⟨program expression⟩ all local variables are assumed to be undefined. There is no provision for saving any previous value that may have been generated at an earlier time, except through an explicit assignment of a value to a global variable.

The set of global variables provides a means of communication between the context where the name of the ⟨program expression⟩ occurs and the definition of the ⟨program expression⟩. We shall refer to the occurrence of the name as a "call," and the occurrence of the ⟨program expression⟩ (i.e., its definition) as a "declaration." Then a call, occurring within some ⟨expression⟩, must cause the following sequence of actions:

1. Some of the global variables of the ⟨program expression⟩ are assigned values.

2. The evaluation of the current ⟨expression⟩ is interrupted, with provision made for its continuation later (after the evaluation of the ⟨program expression⟩).

3. The ⟨program expression⟩ is evaluated.

4. The evaluation of the ⟨expression⟩ is continued, with the value of **r** (in the ⟨program expression⟩) used in place of the name of the ⟨program expression⟩.

It is obvious that all of this could be achieved within the syntax of the ALGOL language, but if we wished to avoid writing the entire ⟨program expression⟩ in place of its name each time, it would become rather cumbersome. Since this "subroutine call" construction occurs so often and is so useful, the syntax of languages like ALGOL is always extended to include a specific notation for this purpose. We then call the occurrence of the ⟨program expression⟩ a "procedure declaration," since in ALGOL the term "procedure" has been used for the programming construct "subroutine."

Now access to the procedure from different contexts within the calling program requires in each case a setting of the global variables. Thus, in the square root example, we might decide that the initial value a, the maximum number of iterations N, and *epsilon* are to be specified at each call. These variables, known in this context as "⟨formal parameter⟩s" or "arguments," must then be designated as special among the global variables for the ⟨program expression⟩ for the square root procedure. In general, a fixed subset of the global variables of a ⟨program expression⟩ are designated as ⟨formal parameter⟩s, gathered together into a list, and attached to the name of the ⟨program expression⟩ in the ⟨declaration⟩. The usual treatment of ⟨formal parameter⟩s is to regard all of their occurrences outside the ⟨program expression⟩ as completely unrelated to occurrences within it. The ⟨identifier⟩s may be the same, but all attributes of one are independent of the attributes of the other. In fact, following ALGOL,† we insist that each ⟨formal parameter⟩ have its attributes declared as if it were occurring for the first time (as it is, in fact). Of course, once the execution of the ⟨program expression⟩ is completed, the external meaning of the ⟨identifier⟩ is in effect again. Thus the square root computation may be defined as a procedure:

procedure *square root*(*a, N, epsilon*); **real** *a, epsilon*; **integer** *N*;
    begin integer *i*; **real** *x, y*; *x* := (*a* + *1*)/2; *i* := 0;
        for *y* := (*x* + *a*/*x*)/2 **while** *i* ≤ *N* ∧ *abs*(*x* − *y*) ≥ *epsilon*
            do begin *x* := *y*; *i* := *i* + *1* **end**; **r** := *y* **end**

At a call on a procedure, the actions of (1) and (2) above need not be programmed; both of these actions are implied by the call itself. We write the call $f(x_1, x_2, \ldots, x_n)$, where $x_1, \ldots, x_n$ are called the "⟨actual parameter⟩s." These are the values to be used to set the ⟨formal parameter⟩s for the specific computation desired by that call. The correspondence is understood to be according to position in the list of parameters. For the example used earlier,

$$q = s + \sqrt{t + 1}$$

we could write

$$q := s + \textit{square root}(t + 1, 100, .00001)$$

if the tolerance was to be 10^{-5}.

---

† Other languages specify "default" attributes which apply to variables not otherwise declared. This is convenient for the user, but eliminates a possible check for errors.

Actually, we have departed from the ALGOL procedure† in one small detail. In ALGOL there is no special notation for the result **r**. Instead, the name of the procedure is used as a variable to which a value is assigned, and the value it has on exit from the computation for that procedure is the value used. Thus, in the square root example, the last statement would be

$$square\ root := y$$

Since there is no desire here to depart from the ALGOL forms unnecessarily, we shall adopt the ALGOL convention and use the procedure name instead of **r**. Since a ⟨program expression⟩ has no name, however, we shall continue to use **r** in that case.

It should be pointed out that since a ⟨program expression⟩ is merely a ⟨block⟩ which yields a single value (i.e., the value of **r**), we could just as well use a ⟨block⟩ and its global variables as a ⟨procedure⟩ throughout the preceding discussion. In this case, we must require the call to appear only in contexts where a ⟨block⟩ could occur. An example of such a ⟨procedure⟩ would be a ⟨block⟩ which sorts the items in a file. Global variables for such a ⟨procedure⟩ might be A (the name of the file to be sorted), B (the name of the file in which the resulting sorted information is to be put), and n (the number of items in the file). If all of these global variables are to be ⟨formal parameter⟩s, they might be listed as follows:

$$Sort(A, n, B)$$

and a call might be

$$Sort(X, r + s, Y)$$

If the file A were to remain the same on every call, one could choose to leave it as a global variable—not as a ⟨formal parameter⟩. In this case, it would have to be named A in the ⟨procedure⟩ also, and no ⟨declaration⟩ would be made for it (so it would not become a local variable). Then only n and B would be ⟨formal parameters⟩, and the call would only contain two ⟨actual parameter⟩s.

Suppose, on the other hand, that the name of the ⟨procedure⟩ occurs in contexts other than the ⟨left part⟩ of an ⟨assignment statement⟩. Here there is a source of confusion, since a *call* for a procedure which happens to have no parameters but does produce a value cannot be distinguished from an occurrence of the procedure name as a ⟨variable⟩. If a procedure were somehow prevented from calling on itself, this would

---

† Note that ALGOL does have procedures which return values, but not the equally useful ⟨program expression⟩.

settle the question, since then the name would always represent the value currently being computed. But for some purposes it is very useful to allow "recursive" procedures, i.e., procedures that call upon themselves. At the very least, one should not rule out recursion to settle this ambiguity problem; it would be simpler to bring the result **r** in again. ALGOL settles it by the stipulation that *every* occurrence of the procedure name is a call for the procedure unless it is in the ⟨left part⟩ of an ⟨assignment statement⟩. This is actually almost equivalent to the use of **r**, since a call cannot occur in a ⟨left part⟩, and we have already restricted **r** so that it can occur only in ⟨left part⟩s (in fact, only once).

Assuming that every procedure is potentially recursive, as ALGOL does, brings in its own problems, however, and we might decide to rule out recursion, anyway. Even a little experience with recursion shows that rather elaborate machinery is needed to provide for it. [Exercise 2.16.1 looks into the example of Ackerman's formula.] The complexity occurs because a procedure must be able to save everything pertaining to a particular call on it (including the location of the call so that the return can be made, as well as all parameters) each time it calls on itself, since the parameters may be different each time. In any event, the return will surely be different, since after the original call from outside the procedure, subsequent calls are made from within the procedure. Each time the procedure ends its computation, it must return to the last point of call. At this time, everything that could have changed must be restored to the state in which it existed at the time of that call. Thus, while using a recursive procedure may simplify the algorithm, the bookkeeping introduced may cost too much in computation time when the algorithm is executed. For this reason, some languages other than ALGOL [9] provide no automatic machinery for saving parameters, etc., but instead provide statements such as

> 1)   'SAVE' X, Y, Z, 'EXIT'
> 2)   'RESTORE' 'EXIT', Z, Y, X

where (1) puts the current values of X, Y, Z, and the return indicator on a list in the order given, and (2) brings them back in a last-in-first-out order. Such a list is called a "push-down stack," since two successive executions of SAVE cause the first set of values to be "pushed down" to make room for the second set of values. The second ones are the first to be restored, of course. (The discerning reader will quickly point out that a push-down stack could be used quite effectively to handle the bookkeeping involved with recursion automatically. If it is done automatically, not only the ⟨formal parameter⟩s must be pushed down, but the local variables and temporarily computed values must be saved as well.) Having thus pointed

out the costs, we shall adopt the ALGOL form, primarily because we shall
not need it very much here! A commonly used example of a recursive
procedure is the computation for the factorial. If $f(n) = n!$ for $n \geq 0$,
we may represent the definition of f as follows, emphasizing its recursive
nature:

$$f(n) = \begin{cases} n \times f(n-1) & \text{if} \quad n \geq 1 \\ 1 & \text{if} \quad n = 0 \end{cases}$$

The procedure definition is written as follows:

procedure *factorial*(*n*); **integer** *n*;
    if *n* = *0* **then** *factorial* := *1* **else** *factorial* := *n* × *factorial*(*n* − *1*);

We have seen that the ⟨actual parameter⟩s provide communication
between the context of the call and the ⟨declaration⟩. Normally, one would
expect all of the ⟨actual parameter⟩s to be evaluated and assigned as
values to their corresponding ⟨formal parameter⟩s before the computation of the ⟨procedure⟩ is initiated. An interesting question arises, however, when one of the ⟨actual parameter⟩s in the call is itself an ⟨expres-
sion⟩ which must be evaluated over and over as the computation within
the ⟨procedure⟩ is carried out. For example, suppose we wish to compute

$$x = \sum_{n=0}^{100} n \uparrow 2$$

which, in conventional mathematical notation, would be

$$x = \sum_{n=0}^{100} n^2$$

but the ⟨procedure⟩ is to be written so that among the ⟨formal para-
meter⟩s is the ⟨expression⟩ $n \uparrow 2$ itself. This will allow the same procedure
(which we shall call *Sigma*) to compute

$$x = \sum_{n=L}^{U} f(n)$$

for any L, U, and f. Clearly, as n takes on its values from L to U, we
must continue to reevaluate $f(n)$. In this case, we cannot evaluate f once
and for all at the time the computation of the ⟨procedure⟩ is initiated.

For each parameter, then, the communication between the context
of the call and the declaration defining the ⟨procedure⟩ may be of two
kinds: (1) *by value*, in which a value is assigned to the ⟨formal parameter⟩
once and only once, on entry to the ⟨procedure⟩; and (2) *by name*, which
may be viewed as copying the entire ⟨actual parameter⟩ into the place
occupied by each occurrence of the corresponding ⟨formal parameter⟩,

and evaluating that ⟨actual parameter⟩ *in the original context of the call.*
The declaration fixes, for each parameter, which kind it shall be; all
calls must conform to this specification. Note that a call (of a ⟨formal
parameter⟩) by value implies that this parameter can never be an ouput
of the ⟨procedure⟩; i.e., it cannot occur as a ⟨left part⟩ of an ⟨assignment
statement⟩.

   We shall indicate which ⟨formal parameter⟩s are called by value, as
in the following example; other ⟨formal parameter⟩s are called by name.

procedure *Sigma*(*L*, *U*, *k*, *f*, *y*);   **value** *L*, *U*;   **integer** *L*, *U*, *k*;   **real** *f*, *y*;
   begin *y* := *0*;   **for** *k* := *L* **step** *1* **until** *U* **do** *y* := *y* + *f* **end**;

With this procedure, the call *Sigma*(0, 100, *n*, *n* ↑ 2, *x*) would compute

$$x = \sum_{n=0}^{100} n \uparrow 2$$

but this depends directly on the convention that the ⟨procedure⟩ named
as the ⟨actual parameter⟩ for *f* is reevaluated for each value of *n*. It is
quite clear from this example that one will almost always have the ⟨actual
parameter⟩ for *f* dependent on the ⟨actual parameter⟩ for *k* in calls on
Sigma. This "dependence" is understood in the sense that the ⟨actual
parameter⟩ for *k* (in our example, *n*) is to be regarded in turn as a ⟨formal
parameter⟩ in the definition for *f*. In fact, the only reason for making
k a ⟨formal parameter⟩ for *Sigma* at all is that we must be able to associate its ⟨actual parameter⟩ with the ⟨procedure⟩ *f*. Otherwise, it is
quite clear that *k* would be just a local variable for the ⟨procedure⟩ *Sigma*.
The declaration would be written

procedure *Sigma*(*L*, *U*, *f*, *y*); **value** *L*, *U*; **integer** *L*, *U*;   **real** *f*, *y*;
   begin integer *k*; *y* := *0*;
      for *k* := *L* **step** *1* **until** *U* **do** *y* := *y* + *f*(*k*) **end**;

and the call would be

$$Sigma(0, 100, \lambda(\textbf{integer } n)\, n \uparrow 2, x)$$

where the notation λ(**integer** *n*) *n* ↑ 2 designates *n* ↑ 2 to be a ⟨procedure⟩
which needs no name other than the ⟨expression⟩ itself, but which has one
⟨formal argument⟩, the **integer** variable *n*. The ⟨body⟩ of the ⟨procedure⟩
is the ⟨expression⟩ *n* ↑ 2. In the declaration for *Sigma*, there is a call on
this ⟨procedure⟩ in the occurrence of *f*(*k*), and the ⟨actual parameter⟩ in
this call is the value of *k*. Somewhere, however, we must specify whether
the ⟨formal parameter⟩ *n* for the nameless ⟨procedure⟩ above is called by
value or by name. According to our preceding convention, should this

occur in the declaration of the ⟨procedure⟩. Thus we should write

$$\lambda(\textbf{value } n; \textbf{integer } n)\ n \uparrow 2$$

but this is not very satisfactory, since we would expect the ⟨procedure⟩ *Sigma* to dictate all of the parameter substitution rules, although it could certainly be made to work properly for us.

Suppose now that we wished to compute

$$y = \sum_{n=0}^{100} \sum_{m=0}^{n} m \uparrow 2$$

The natural method is by "composition" of *Sigma* with itself. Unfortunately, we have been writing *Sigma* as a ⟨procedure⟩ whose ⟨body⟩ is a ⟨block⟩, rather than a ⟨program expression⟩, and there is no value to be attached to *Sigma* as an output value, or result. [Exercise 2.16.2 asks for a version of *Sigma* based on a ⟨program expression⟩.] One way to overcome this difficulty is to postulate a "value operator" ν, such that

$$\nu(z)\ Sigma(L,\ U,\ k, f,\ z)$$

specifies that the value of z on return from the computation of *Sigma* is the "value" of the call on *Sigma*.† Then the call representing the composition would be

$$Sigma(0,\ 100,\ n,\ \nu(z)\ Sigma(0,\ n,\ m,\ m \uparrow 2,\ z),\ y)$$

Since this call invokes *Sigma* within itself, it is referred to as a "recursive call." The ⟨procedure⟩ *Sigma* could also have been written recursively, i.e., so that it would call on itself within its ⟨body⟩.

procedure *Sigma*(L, U, f, y);   **value** L, U;   **integer** L, U;   **real** f, y;
    begin real z; $y := f(L) +$ **if** $L < U$ **then**
        $\nu(z)\ Sigma(L + 1,\ U, f,\ z)$ **else** 0 **end**;

[Exercise 2.16.3 asks for an evaluation of a call on this version of *Sigma*.]

We return now to an earlier remark, which probably didn't seem suspicious at the time, but which does allow several quite different interpretations. In describing the role of parameters for a procedure, we asserted that the ⟨expression⟩s listed in a call for a procedure (the *actual parameters*‡) would be put in one-to-one correspondence with the

---

† One could clearly apply ν to any ⟨block⟩, but there is little point in pursuing this further, since one can always use a ⟨program expression⟩ instead.

‡ Throughout the rest of this chapter the terms ⟨actual parameter⟩ and ⟨formal parameter⟩ occur so often that we shall suppress the enclosure symbols ⟨ and ⟩ to improve readability.

parameters in the definition for that procedure (the *formal parameters*), and then the actual parameters would be "substituted for the formal parameters." One interpretation of this substitution process can be summarized as follows: (1) Compute the values of the various actual parameters and save them in a temporary storage area. (2) Whenever a reference is made to a formal parameter, find and use the corresponding value. As we have seen, this is referred to as a "call-by-value." Note that with this interpretation one cannot change the value of any actual parameters; the actual parameters are treated only as a kind of input to the procedure. Some advocates of the call-by-value argue that it is necessary to "protect" actual parameters from inadvertent destruction. For example, if x is a formal parameter, the statement

$$x := x + 1$$

in the definition could change the value of a ⟨variable⟩ given as the actual parameter corresponding to x in a call. Others say, "Users beware!" and argue that if properly used, the ability to change the value of an actual parameter as one product of the computation of the ⟨procedure⟩ can be very beneficial. The answer depends, as always, on the experience and maturity of the people to whom the language is made available.

Another objection to call-by-value is that, if an actual parameter names a collection of values (as we shall see in Chapter 3, where one could use as an actual parameter the name of an array of values), then storing the "values" of actual parameters in a temporary storage area could mean the physical movement of a great many values, a time-consuming activity.

A different interpretation for the substitution of actual parameters for formal parameters is the "call-by-name." Here the actual parameter is literally substituted for the formal parameter *as an expression*, and the computation represented by the actual parameter is carried out on every reference to the corresponding formal parameter. (The actual parameter doesn't have to be physically substituted into the procedure. There are other ways to refer to and carry out the original encoding of the computation without actually making a copy of it. The effect is the same [10].)

The difference between the call-by-value and the call-by-name is that in a call-by-value, actual parameters are evaluated only once, at the time of entry to the ⟨procedure⟩. In a call-by-name, the actual parameter is evaluated each time, producing possibly different results. As a simple example, suppose the expression

$$1 + \text{Random}$$

is used as an actual parameter in a call on a function F, where Random is the name of a procedure which produces a sequence of uniformly distributed **real** numbers on the interval $(0,1)$, a new number on each call. If this actual parameter corresponds to the formal parameter y appearing in the definition of F, then a call-by-value would use the same value for every occurrence of y in the definition, but a call-by-name would produce a new value for each reference to y.

As another example, suppose that both x and $G(x)$ are actual parameters in a call-by-name on a procedure $H(z,w)$:

$$H(x, G(x))$$

Suppose also that in the definition for H there is the sequence of statements

$$u := w; \quad z := z + 1; \quad v := w;$$

Then each time this sequence is executed, say with $x = x_0$, the value of x is increased by 1, and the values of u and v are $G(x_0)$ and $G(x_0 + 1)$, respectively. If one now combines a call on H of this kind with other occurrences of x,

$$t := x + H(x, G(x)) + x * s$$

then, since the call on H changes the value of x as a "side-effect," it is important to know the order in which the expression on the right of this assignment statement is evaluated. This is often pointed to as a danger of the call-by-name interpretation. As with the call-by-value, this interpretation has its advocates and opponents, and only time will tell which is the more useful interpretation.

Actually, the interpretation most commonly used to date differs from both of those already mentioned. Often called the "call-by-simple-name," the "call-by-reference", or the "FORTRAN-call-by-name"—the last because of its introduction to the general user in the IBM FORTRAN II supervisory system—it is based on the use of names (actually, machine addresses) for all parameters. All expressions are evaluated at the time of entry to the procedure, but the values are put, if necessary, into temporary locations. Then the addresses of these locations are given as the parameters. If a value already exists in a storage cell, such as for a ⟨variable⟩ or constant, that cell's address is used. For more complicated expressions, this method acts like a call-by-value. For simple expressions, however, it behaves like a call-by-name. Its greatest advantage over call-by-value lies in the use of an address for the base of a large array of values, rather than the transfer of all the values into some temporary area.

The one aspect of call-by-simple-name that still varies from system to system is the treatment of an actual parameter which is an array name with an expression for a subscript. This construction will be developed more fully in the next chapter; a brief description will suffice here. If an array of n values is designated A, then we may select among the elements of the array by providing "subscripts," i.e., selection parameters. For example, if we superimpose a "linear" structure on the array, it amounts to numbering all the elements, say from 0 to $n - 1$. Then A_i (or, in ALGOL notation, $A[i]$) selects one of them if i satisfies the condition: $0 \leq i < n$. If we visualize a two-dimensional, lattice-like structure on the elements of A, then two subscripts are needed to select an element, much as the x and y coordinates select a point in a plane, once a coordinate system has been chosen. In this case, one writes $A[i, j]$ in ALGOL for A_{ij}.

Now, if $A[i + 3 \times k + 17]$ happens to be a parameter in a call to a procedure, the call-by-value computes the subscript, finds the value in the array A, and passes the value to the procedure, perhaps in a special parameter array. The call-by-name passes the entire parameter designation to the procedure (or at least the address of a small auxiliary procedure which finds the value of $A[i + 3 \times k + 17]$ each time it is called). The call-by-simple-name could either (1) treat $A[i + 3 \times k + 17)$ as one complicated $\langle$expression$\rangle$ and put its value into a temporary location, or (2) treat only the subscript as an $\langle$expression$\rangle$ and pass as the parameter the address of the selected element of the array A. One can find examples of both methods in use. Method (2) is usually considered better, since one can always find the value from the address, but not the address from the value in a temporary location. Since $A[i + 3 \times k + 17]$ might very well be meant to point to the base of a subarray which needs processing, the address may be far more important than the value.

It is interesting to observe that in a process of translating such ALGOL constructions as $A[i + 3 \times k + 17]$ into some machine language, both the call-by-value and call-by-name methods allow the translator to assign all necessary addresses for temporary storage, etc., well in advance of the computation. The call-by-simple-name cannot allow this if (2) is used, however, since the address that must be passed must be determined as the computation is progressing. Thus small headaches are built into translators!

We note in passing that we have not dealt with input-ouput features of the language. Certainly this is very important, but a full discussion would lead us far from our current discussion. We shall simply note that one can build rather elaborate statement structures into a language for this purpose, or one can provide a set of $\langle$procedure$\rangle$s. We shall assume that the latter is the case, as we did in an earlier example in writing $Print(x1, x2, j)$. Similarly, one needs a way to stop a computation, and one can simply assume the existence of a $\langle$procedure$\rangle$ named $Stop$.

Before we leave procedures, we shall specify their syntax. We do not include the syntax of the v notation since, as we have seen, it is not necessary for the ALGOL language once the ⟨program expression⟩ is included. The reader should verify that the examples already given are indeed constructed according to this syntax specification. The syntax for the ⟨procedure declaration⟩ is:

⟨formal parameter⟩ ::= ⟨identifier⟩
⟨formal parameter list⟩ ::= ⟨formal parameter⟩ {,⟨formal parameter⟩}*
⟨formal parameter part⟩ ::= ⟨empty⟩ | (⟨formal parameter list⟩)
⟨identifier list⟩ ::= ⟨identifier⟩ {,⟨identifier⟩}*
⟨specifier⟩ ::= **string** | ⟨type⟩ | **label** | **procedure** | ⟨type⟩ **procedure** |
    switch
⟨specification part⟩ ::= ⟨empty⟩ | ⟨specifier⟩⟨identifier list⟩; |
    ⟨specification part⟩ ⟨specifier⟩ ⟨identifier list⟩;
⟨procedure identifier⟩ ::= ⟨identifier⟩
⟨value part⟩ ::= **value** ⟨identifier list⟩; | ⟨empty⟩
⟨λ heading⟩ ::= λ(⟨value part⟩ ⟨specification part⟩)
⟨procedure heading⟩ ::= ⟨procedure identifier⟩ ⟨formal parameter part⟩;
    ⟨value part⟩ ⟨specification part⟩
⟨procedure body⟩ ::= ⟨program⟩
⟨prefix⟩ ::= ⟨empty⟩ | ⟨type⟩
⟨procedure declaration⟩ ::= ⟨prefix⟩ **procedure** ⟨procedure heading⟩
    ⟨procedure body⟩ | ⟨λ heading⟩ ⟨expression⟩

The syntax for the ⟨procedure statement⟩ is:

⟨actual parameter⟩ ::= ⟨string⟩ | ⟨expression⟩ | ⟨procedure identifier⟩
⟨actual parameter list⟩ ::= ⟨actual parameter⟩ {,⟨actual parameter⟩}*
⟨actual parameter part⟩ ::= ⟨empty⟩ | (⟨actual parameter list⟩)
⟨procedure statement⟩ ::= ⟨procedure identifier⟩ ⟨actual parameter part⟩

Since we can also embed procedure calls in ⟨expression⟩s now, we need to modify the syntax specification for ⟨expression⟩s as well. Following the ALGOL terminology, a procedure call used in this way is referred to as a *function designator*.

⟨function designator⟩ ::= ⟨procedure identifier⟩ ⟨actual parameter part⟩
⟨primary⟩ ::= ⟨unsigned number⟩ | ⟨variable⟩ | ⟨function designator⟩ |
    (⟨arithmetic expression⟩)

EXERCISES 2.16

1. Ackerman's formula defined for nonnegative integers can be stated as follows:

   a) $A(M, N) = A(M - 1, A(M, N - 1))$

b) $A(M, 0) = A(M - 1, 1)$
c) $A(0, N) = N + 1$

As an example of the complexity involved when recursion is allowed, evaluate $A(2,3)$.

2. Rewrite the final (recursive) version of *Sigma* so that it is based on a ⟨program expression⟩ instead of a ⟨block⟩. [Hint: Drop the formal parameter y and include an assignment to the symbol "*Sigma*."]

3. Find the final value of y in the following calls on the final version of *Sigma* in the text:

a) *Sigma*$(1, 4, \lambda(\textbf{integer } m) \, 2 \times m + 1, y)$
b) *Sigma*$(1, 4, \nu(z) \, Sigma(0, 3, m \uparrow 2, z), y)$

2.17 ENUMERATED EXPRESSIONS

Just to illustrate how the language could be extended even further, we give the syntax for ⟨enumerated expression⟩s, which could play the role of explicit arrays, such as we shall develop in the next chapter. Except for some additional remarks on p. 257, however, we shall not expand on this syntax or its implications.

⟨structured expression⟩ ::= ⟨expression⟩ | ⟨program expression⟩ |
    ⟨function designator⟩ | ⟨enumerated expression⟩ |
    (⟨structured expression⟩)
⟨list of structured expressions⟩ ::= ⟨structured expression⟩
    {,⟨structured expression⟩}*
⟨enumerated expression⟩ ::= ⟨prefix⟩ (⟨list of structured expressions⟩)

CHAPTER THREE

DATA STRUCTURES

3.1 INTRODUCTION

It is impossible to create an algorithm without knowing the form of the data. This basic fact confronts one at every step; it is most easily appreciated when the punctuation, the alphabet, or the amount of some data is changed, and an algorithm which used to work no longer does. [Exercise 3.1.1 asks about a sorting $\langle DTA \rangle$ for integer and decimal data.]

Once the data have "arrived"—i.e., become available to the algorithm—additional punctuation may be inserted to imply new organization to the data, and special "addresses" and other structural information may be added. The choices involved in this activity are endless. They must be determined by (1) the *questions* to be asked about specific items of data (and their relationships), and (2) the *changes* which must subsequently be made to these items, to their relationships, and even to the overall structure and organization of the data.

The data always have structure, i.e., punctuation and/or organization which govern the accessing and modification of parts of the data. On the one hand, the algorithm must obey the constraints imposed by the structure, and on the other hand, it may take advantage of the structure to do some of its manipulations more efficiently. To the extent that we take advantage of the known structure, however, we incur the risk—and the cost—of subsequent changes in the data which modify the structure.

In this chapter we shall explore some of the commonly used data structures and their properties. Along the way we shall develop a rather formal notation for describing structures, and we shall at the same time be concerned with the processing of this notation so that operations on the structures become natural extensions of the ALGOL language. We are thus concerned throughout the rest of this book with the way in which our initial language can be made more useful—by the user of the language—for his personal applications.

EXERCISE 3.1.1

Consider the $\langle DTA \rangle$ Sort of Chapter 1 which sorted integers of the form $\alpha 1^n$. Describe in detail the changes which must be made to sort decimal numbers of the form

$$\gamma \alpha 1^{n_1} \gamma \alpha 1^{n_2} \dots \gamma \alpha 1^{n_k}$$

3.2 THE LMA DATA STRUCTURE

The LMA of Chapter 1 assumes almost no structure in the data. Only the following assumptions are made.

1. The data consist of a string of characters from some alphabet.

2. There is a first character in R, which may be taken to be the null character Λ.

3. A properly identified substring may be replaced by another substring, possibly of a different length.

If an algorithm prefers any other structure in the data, it can only resort to the use of additional alphabets, such as punctuation characters and aliases. We saw this in the Primes example, when we used γ, $*$, α, and β to structure the data:

$$n_k \gamma q * r \alpha j \beta m_k \beta m_{k-1} \ldots \beta m_1$$

The unstructured string, which is all the LMA processor assumes it has, will be called the *primitive* data form *for that processor*. It is primitive in the sense that any superimposed structure must be manipulated by explicit rules, the results of which will be the data form allowed by the basic processor. These rules may be viewed as converting *defined* (or *higher level*) data structures into primitive structures. We shall be concerned with such definitions and conversions throughout this development.

Though the primitive data form of the LMA is quite unstructured, the LMA is still a very useful data manipulator, because of the powerful *selector rule*, which is available for the identification of specific substrings. This selector rule focuses attention on substrings, and the basic LMA rule then provides for a substitution of another substring, usually defined in terms of the selected one. For example, let Φ be an arbitrary string, and ξ a generic variable for an alphabet A. Then we could write three algorithms which use Φ to replace the entire string in R, the leftmost character in R, and the rightmost character in R, respectively:

> **algorithm I**(A); **A** ξ;
> $0 \colon \xi \;\rightarrow\; , 0$;
> $1 \colon \quad \rightarrow \Phi$.   **end**

> **algorithm II**(A); **A** ξ;
> $0 \colon \xi \;\rightarrow\; \Phi$.   **end**

> **algorithm III**(A); **A** ξ;
> $0 \colon \quad \rightarrow \beta, 1$;
> $1 \colon \beta\xi \rightarrow \xi\beta, 1$;
> $2 \colon \xi\beta \rightarrow \Phi$.   **end**

As we have seen many times before, the scope of these simple algorithms can be easily extended by embedding some punctuation characters in the data. As they stand, they are independent of the alphabet A, and they could be added as new elementary LMA rules:

$$k: \text{ I } \Phi \quad , m;$$
$$k: \text{ II } \Phi \quad , m;$$
$$k: \text{III } \Phi \quad , m;$$

to give an extended LMA "language" in which I, II, and III are primitive, provided the basic LMA processor is extended to recognize the new forms and interpret them correctly.

In passing, we note that the original selector rule for the MA and LMA could have required the less powerful forms:

		Comments
(I)	$\xi \uparrow \rightarrow \uparrow v$	Move ξ right and replace with v
(II)	$\uparrow \xi \rightarrow v \uparrow$	Move ξ left and replace with v

where $\uparrow$ is a fixed character representing a pointer into the data, and not belonging to any data alphabet, and ξ and v are single (generic or local) characters in the algorithm's data alphabet. These two rules could also be written

$$(\text{I}') \; \xi \, R \, v$$
$$(\text{II}') \; \xi \, L \, v$$

respectively, and with the MA or LMA restricted to their use, we would have the familiar Turing machine on a semi-infinite tape, particularly when the data alphabet is taken to be $\{0, 1\}$.

Returning to the standard LMA, we recall that in Section 1.8 we did superimpose a structure on the data by means of *addresses*, so that we could more easily select the portion of the data to be handled. In that system, we put one standard numbering on the entire contents of R—i.e., on all of the storage available to us—and "(m)" meant "the mth location after the beginning of R." We could easily extend this notation now to allow subsequences or groups of locations (usually called *vectors*) to be given names early in the ALMA, so that

$$Q \textbf{ from } (m) \textbf{ to } (n) \qquad (m \leq n)$$

would be a declaration meaning that the vector Q is the set of locations starting with (m) and ending with and including (n). Then in the ALMA language, we could write $Q[3]$ (or $Q[i]$), meaning the third (or ith) location from the beginning of Q, respectively. The number in brackets is called a *subscript*. The ALMA processor would then interpret $Q[3]$ as

$(m + 2)$, and $Q[i]$ as $(m + i - 1)$. The preceding sentence is then the conversion process, indicated above as necessary when a higher-level structure is superimposed on a lower-level one.

Note that it is implied here that a higher-level structure need not be defined in terms of (or converted to) the primitive structure directly. In fact, we reduced the vector notation to the ALMA notation, and while we may regard this as primitive for the ALMA processor, it is still a higher-level structure for the MA and LMA processors. We see then that it is possible to move up through many levels of structures, each time building up more complicated ones from simpler ones. The reverse process of *interpreting* the notation of higher-level structures need not proceed to the primitive forms in one stage, either; it may also move through intermediate levels. We shall exploit this point of view later in our specification of higher-level structures. It is also instructive to recall that this was exactly how the definition of *complex* arithmetic was handled in Chapter 2, with a promise there that similar methods would be employed here!

Let us return to the vector notation and consider some ways of making it more useful. In some situations, such as a person's age, S, which starts at 0, or ranges of temperature, T, which may run from $-10°$ to $+20°$, it is useful to be able to write $S[0]$ or $T[-10]$. We shall therefore change our *vector declaration* to be

$$S[0:100] \textbf{ from } (s)$$
$$T[-10:20] \textbf{ from } (t)$$

The processor, which must then interpret subscripts used with S and T, would associate (s) with $S[0]$ instead of $S[1]$, and (t) with $T[-10]$ instead of $T[1]$. In each case a simple relationship may be stated.

$$S[i] \text{ corresponds with } (s + i)$$
$$T[i] \text{ corresponds with } (t + i + 10)$$

[Exercise 3.2.1 asks for the general case.]

We may also imagine that the contents of a single location $S[i]$ has a structure superimposed on it, perhaps (but not necessarily) of the same kind. In other words, we may find it useful to punctuate the string $S[i]$— that is, the string between $(s + i)$ and $(s + i + 1)$—by means of some additional characters representing addresses (counting from the beginning of that string). Now, to select the jth part of $S[i]$, one would write $S[i, j]$, which is interpreted as if it had been written $(S[i])[j]$. This double-level structure is known as an *array*, or more specifically, a *two-dimensional array*. (A vector is sometimes called a *one-dimensional array*.) One may now picture the selection of $S[3]$ as follows:

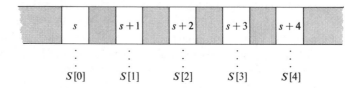

$$S[0] \qquad S[1] \qquad S[2] \qquad S[3] \qquad S[4]$$

where the shaded areas are the contents of the locations indicated. The selection of $S[3, 2]$ would then appear as

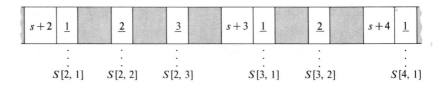

$$S[2, 1] \qquad S[2, 2] \qquad S[2, 3] \qquad\qquad S[3, 1] \qquad S[3, 2] \qquad\qquad S[4, 1]$$

where the underlined addresses are the punctuation characters used to provide the higher-level structure. Note that in thus selecting $S[3, 2]$ it was necessary to search first for the address $S[3] = (s + 3)$ before the second subscript could be used. Essential use is made of the two distinct levels of structure. One advantage of this organization is that additional locations and their addresses, such as $S[3, 3]$, $S[3, 4]$, etc., could be inserted before $(s + 4)$ without disturbing any other addresses, i.e., without causing any other addresses to be recomputed. We shall call each substring of the first level a *row*. Thus $S[3]$ names the row consisting of the substring between the addresses $(s + 3)$ and $(s + 4)$. In this particular two-dimensional array, as we have just seen, the rows need not have the same *length*; i.e., the number of second-level addresses can vary from row to row.

Let us consider now a different two-dimensional array structure, which does not have the property of easy modification mentioned above. We now assume that our rows have a known, fixed length, say 3. No second-level addresses or special punctuation marks are used here; instead, we might declare the range of each of the subscripts of S to be

$$S[1 : 100, 1 : 3] \textbf{ from } (s)$$

The addresses $S[1, 1]$, $S[1, 2]$, $S[1, 3]$, $S[2, 1]$, ..., would then correspond with (s), $(s + 1)$, $(s + 2)$, $(s + 3)$, ..., respectively, according to the rule (sometimes called the *storage function*):

$$S[i, j] \text{ corresponds with } (s + 3(i - 1) + (j - 1))$$

Thus $S[2, 1]$ corresponds with $(s + 3(2 - 1) + (1 - 1)) = (s + 3)$, as we have seen. In general, if the length of each row is n, then $S[i, j]$ corresponds with $(s + n(i - 1) + (j - 1))$. [Exercise 3.2.2 asks that the storage function be found if rows are not of fixed length but have an easy summation formula.] This data structure has the advantage of a simpler selector than the earlier one, but at the cost of having to have constant row lengths.

It is important to notice that even in the two-level structure, any insertion of new addresses other than at the end of a row involves a renumbering of the remaining addresses in the row. This kind of insertion, or substitution, where the number of elements inserted is allowed to be different from the number being deleted, we will call *string substitution*, and we will always assume a renumbering of the elements involved so that the result contains no hint that anything has happened. String substitution is precisely that used in Markov algorithms.

In the other structure for the two-dimensional array, in which a fixed length row structure is superimposed and no second-level addresses are used, any substitution which affects only a single location is still a string substitution. However, if even one new location is created (other than at the end), the entire structure is affected. In general, in a structure not specifically set up for string substitution, we will restrict substitutions to those which do not force a renumbering.

EXERCISES 3.2

1. If V is a vector which varies from (m) to (n), $m \leq n$, that is, $V[m:n]$ **from** (v), what is the general relationship for $V[i]$?
2. Give the storage function for $S[i, j]$ if S is an array with a triangular shape, that is, if row i has length i, and row $i + 1$ follows immediately after row i.

3.3 BASIC DATA STRUCTURES

We are now ready to describe specific data structures in terms of which more general ones may be specified. The structures discussed in the previous section will serve as useful examples, but we are not necessarily dealing with LMA's here. The initial concept is that of a named sequence of elements from an alphabet A, together with two operations: (1) identification of a subsequence, and (2) substitution of a sequence for an identified subsequence. Identification is determined by a position in the sequence, and possibly by what appears in that position as well. For example, if the contents of an identified element turn out to represent the name of another sequence, the selection process might dictate a subsequent selection from the sequence thus named. Depending on the regime of use of a sequence (i.e., the context in which a reference to it appears), the subsequent substitution of another sequence for one so selected may be a string substitution, or it may not. In the case of a string substitution, subsequent selections are made only after a renumbering occurs based solely on position in the sequence. Other renumberings are possible, or there may be none at all. This choice, determined always by the intended use of the information contained there and by the expected variability (in time) of the structure itself, leads to a variety of useful data organizations.

We assume a basic alphabet A. It is often useful to partition A into two disjoint subalphabets: (a) the primitive characters, and (b) a set of symbols to be used as names for the structures being defined. In this way, we may allow as elements in the structure the names of other structures. Thus we have:

1. *String structure.* A sequence over the alphabet A, that is, a sequence of characters from A, with string substitution.

2. *String.* A string structure whose elements are taken only from the primitive characters in the alphabet A.

For example, let $A = \{a, b, \ldots, z, s_1, s_2, \ldots\}$, where it is intended that $s_1, s_2, \ldots$ shall be used only as names. Then $s_1 \equiv (a, b, z)$, $s_2 \equiv (a)$, and $s_3 \equiv \Lambda$ (that is, the null string) are strings with assigned names, while $s_4 \equiv (a, s_1, b)$ and $s_5 \equiv (s_4, s_5)$ are string structures. It is assumed that in designating an alphabet as the basic alphabet for a string structure, enough information is provided so that it is possible to tell, by looking at an element of a string structure, whether it is a name or a primitive character.

3. *Array.* A sequence over the alphabet A, with substitution which is always made for a subsequence of length 1, without a renumbering of the positions in the sequence. Identification of subsequences is also restricted to those of length 1, that is, to individual elements identified by position number.

4. *Vector.* An array in which the elements are taken only from the primitive characters in A.

Thus the only difference between a string structure and an array (and between a string and a vector), is the type of substitution and identification of elements which is allowed.

A string structure or an array will be called *regular* if its elements are either all primitive characters (so that it is a string or a vector), or all names. The purpose of such a classification is to eliminate whenever possible the extra effort involved in determining whether a selected element is a name or not; for a regular structure, this question always has a fixed answer known in advance. Sometimes one has additional ways to partition the primitive characters of A. Then further economies might be gained by knowing that certain structures are built up in uniform ways with respect to the disjoint sets produced by that partition. For example, if the primitive characters consisted of the integers and the floating point numbers (which need different internal representations), it could be very helpful to know that a vector contained only one kind of number.

It is quite possible, and often desirable, to mix the types of structures we have described. Thus we may now describe the standard ALMA data structure as a vector over an alphabet whose basic characters are strings. These strings are structures in their own right over some basic alphabet which is quite general, and which is usually designated as an input to the ALMA. The two-dimensional array structures which we superimposed on the ALMA data also have mixed types. In each case we have a regular vector of rows. However, in the first case, where we used second-level addresses, we retained the identity of each row by allowing it to be identified by a single subscript, and this led to the separate application of the subscripts. In the other structure we described, we gave up the ability to identify an entire row as a single component. Instead we took advantage of the uniformity of the rows and the regularity of the array to represent the entire array as a single sequence, using the mapping $S[i, j] \rightarrow (s + n(i - 1) + (j - 1))$, where (s) is the *base address* for the array S. This mapping relates the selector function of the two-dimensional array to the selector function of the single sequence which is primitive to the ALMA processor. [Exercise 3.3.1 shows that the primitive single sequence is really structured as a string of arrays, and one can discuss even another level to get to the primitives.]

We may very well consider how we shall take advantage of regularity in general, as we did in the previous example. Given a regular array, we must distinguish between the case in which (a) all of the components are primitive characters, and (b) all of the components are names. The case in which the components are all primitive characters is easily disposed of, since it is nothing more than a vector. However, we may go somewhat further by considering the situation that arises when these components, although primitive in A, may actually have structure with respect to some other alphabet, say B. In fact, we have just seen an example of this, since the two-dimensional array was described as a vector, each of whose components (which we called *rows*) in turn were vectors.

In general, then, we may visualize several levels, each level being, for example, a vector whose components are vectors, eventually encountering a truly primitive alphabet. It should be noted that a structure is actually a collection of all those data elements that satisfy the description of the structure. Thus a vector of n elements of $\langle type \rangle$ **real** is the set of all sequences of n **real** elements, each sequence properly being called an "instance" of the vector. In general, we shall use the term "structure" rather loosely, since the context will always make it clear. A useful notation for such structures may be built out of a basic symbol $\sum_n$, which stands for a vector of n components. Thus, $\sum_m \sum_n \langle string \rangle$ will represent a two-dimensional array over an alphabet whose primitive characters are $\langle string \rangle$s, and which is structured as a vector of m components, each of which is a vector of n components, each of which in turn is a $\langle string \rangle$. We might wish to specify a string structure as well. For this we shall use the symbol $\int_r^s$, where r and s are the lower and upper limits, respectively, on the length (i.e., the number of elements) of the string. Thus the collection of all strings over an alphabet A would be

$$\int_0^\infty A$$

while the set of strings of length 2 would be $\int_2^2 A$, which we shall usually write as $\int_2 A$. The previous example: $\sum_m \sum_n \langle string \rangle$, could now be written

$$\sum_m \sum_n \int_0^\infty A$$

if arbitrary strings are allowed, or

$$\sum_m \sum_n \int_k A$$

if only strings of length k are allowed.

If a regular array consists entirely of names, we may represent this as

$$\sum_n \textbf{name-of}\,(A)$$

Again we may consider the case in which the characters of A are structures over a lower-level alphabet B. The general regular structure will have some mixture of "characters" and "names," such as

$$\sum_{n_1} \textbf{name-of} \left(\sum_{n_2} \sum_{n_3} \textbf{name-of} \left(\int_{2} A \right) \right)$$

What is still missing from this notation is the assignment of a name (i.e., **row**) to the second level structure, so that it is clear that one might wish to select an entire row by means of only one subscript. Thus we shall write

$$\textbf{two-level-array} := \sum_{m} (\textbf{row} := \sum_{n} A)$$

$$\textbf{one-level-array} := \sum_{m} \sum_{n} A$$

where A is the primitive alphabet (the alphabet of strings, in the ALMA case). This naming of a substructure such as **row** will have implicit in its use that when it does not appear (as in the **one-level-array** above), one cannot assign any meaning to a single subscript; two subscripts must be used. Of course, it is understood that such a construction as is given here for the **two-level-array** is merely an abbreviation for

$$\textbf{row} := \sum_{n} A$$

$$\textbf{two-level-array} := \sum_{m} \textbf{row}$$

and nothing more than this is to be inferred from its use. We note also that we might have written

$$\textbf{one-level-array}(m, n) := \sum_{m} \sum_{n} A$$

and thus made m and n ⟨formal parameter⟩s, in the terminology of the preceding chapter. Since we did not do so, m and n are to be regarded as *global variables* relative to this structure definition; i.e., their values are determined outside the definition and are fixed at the time the definition is made, as the then current values of these variables.

Another useful structure is

$$\textbf{standard-array} := \sum_{m} (\textbf{row} := \textbf{name-of} (\sum_{n} A))$$

which consists of a vector of m row names. Each component is the name of an n-component vector, so that while there are $m \times n$ primitive characters of A in this array, the structure implies a grouping of these characters into m rows of n characters each. Two subscripts are still necessary to select one of the characters, although one subscript will select (the name of) a row, and the selector functions involved are quite different from the selector functions for other structures we have considered. We now have the selector function:

Structure of an array B	Selector function for $B[i, j]$
two-level-array	$(B[i])[j]$
one-level-array	$B[n(i - 1) + (j - 1)]$
standard-array	$(\text{vc-of } (B[i]))[j]$

The operator **vc-of**† is necessary because the row $B[i]$ in the standard array is a *name* (or *identifier*) of a vector. Before a subscript can be applied to the vector, we must obtain the vector which is the contents of the name $B[i]$. The standard array is most useful in situations where one expects some variability in the array; in particular, it is easy to replace a row by another row, since it involves the change of only one name. It is also true that some physical processors can evaluate the selector function for the standard array more efficiently than the selector function for the one-level array.

EXERCISE 3.3.1

When we considered $S[i, j] \to (s + n(i - 1) + (j - 1))$, we were really considering two transformations, one which mapped $S[i, j] \to S[r]$, and one which mapped $S[r] \to (s + r)$. What is r for the example above and for the case of the triangular array?

3.4 LISTS

The degree and kind of variability which one expects to need in a structure will greatly influence a choice of internal representation for it. Because a vector allows no variation of its structure, we may expect a simple internal representation, such as placing all of its components consecutively and contiguously. However, in string structures, one often wishes to perform string substitution (to vary the number of elements) but still access individual elements, and we should expect to need a more flexible representation. Since string substitutions incur the cost of a renumbering, in which the position of any element in the sequence may change, we do want to take advantage of the fact that in a string substitution the relation "a is the successor to b" (to be denoted $a \otimes b$) remains unchanged for all but one

---

† This is an abbreviation for "value contents of." By "contents" we mean the item whose name it is. Later we shall see other kinds of contents of names which are not values.

pair of the list. For example, let us represent a string $S = (a, b, c, d, e)$ as a table of values, with another sequence (f, g, h) also in the table at some other point, as follows:

index	1	2	3	4	5	6		n_1	n_2	n_3	
value	a	b	c	d	e	Λ	...	f	g	h	...

If the sequence (f, g, h) is to be moved so that it occurs in the string between a and b, then the resulting table is

index	1	2	3	4	5	6	7	8	9		n_1	n_2	n_3	
value	a	$*f$	$*g$	$*h$	$*b$	$*c$	$*d$	$*e$	Λ	...	Λ	Λ	Λ	

but the cost is the displacement of the seven starred elements. Suppose instead that the string is represented via an "explicit successor" notation, as follows:

name	s_1	s_2	s_3	s_4	s_5	s_6		s_7	s_8	s_9	s_{10}
value	a	b	c	d	e	Λ	...	f	g	h	Λ ...
successor	s_2	s_3	s_4	s_5	Φ	Φ		s_8	s_9	Φ	Φ

with Φ a special character that means "no successor." Now the insertion of the sequence (f, g, h) between a and b leads to the table

name	s_1	s_2	s_3	s_4	s_5	s_6		s_7	s_8	s_9	s_{10}
value	a	b	c	d	e	Λ	...	f	g	h	Λ ...
successor	$*s_7$	s_3	s_4	s_5	Φ	Φ		s_8	s_9	$*s_2$	Φ

where it is clear that only two of the explicit successors were changed, and none of the elements themselves were displaced. For this reason, the "explicit successor" notation is often employed when string substitutions are expected. There is a cost even here, of course, since selection by subscript cannot now assume that the ith component is in the position with index i (that is, with name s_i). It is necessary to employ a "successor" operator (which we shall denote **cdr**†), which can be applied $i-1$ times to the name of the string to get the ith component. Thus, for the final sequence shown above (with two starred elements), we would interpret $s_1(6)$ as

---

† A notation begun in LISP by J. McCarthy [11]. It arose from the particular implementation of LISP on the IBM 704 computer but has since left this interpretation behind. We will also see **car** and **cons** used later.

$\mathbf{cdr}^5(s_1) = s_3$, the name of the subsequence whose first element is c.† Another cost, of course, is the additional storage needed for the successors.

We may now describe a representation for a string which shall be referred to as a *list representation*. It should be emphasized that it is not necessary—only more convenient and efficient—to represent strings this way. A *list* is a sequence such that: (1) its elements are named ordered pairs; (2) the second component of each pair is either the name of another ordered pair or the character Φ; (3) if s_1, s_n are two (names of) pairs in the sequence, then there exists a chain $s_2, \ldots, s_{n-1}$ of pairs in the sequence such that either $s_1 \oslash s_2 \oslash \cdots \oslash s_{n-1} \oslash s_n$ or $s_n \oslash s_{n-1} \oslash \cdots \oslash s_2 \oslash s_1$; (4) there is exactly one pair in the sequence, called the *head* of the list, which has no *predecessor* (i.e., it is not the successor to any pair); and (5) there is exactly one pair, called the *end* of the list, whose second component is Φ. The name of a list is the name of its head. The empty list will be assumed to have one pair in it: (Φ, Φ). The notation for a (**real**) string (with at least n and at most m elements), will then continue to be

$$\int_{n}^{m} \mathbf{real}$$

but now it is implicitly understood, when talking about strings, that the elements are represented as ordered pairs, and that the second component is of a new type **name**.

It is perfectly natural to have an array (i.e., a vector, except that some of its elements may be names), which is represented as a list, while the structures whose names it carries are not lists—and vice versa. Such decisions are made on the expected variation of structure, as remarked earlier. We already have the notation $\int_m^n$ to describe a string represented as a list, but we are now considering a vector to be represented as a list, with at least m and at most n components. What is needed here—in order to allow the number of components to vary but still have an efficient subscription process based primarily on indexing—is an initial vector of length m, and a fixed-size block of p additional components that can be added repeatedly as needed, up to a maximum of n elements. Thus we would have a list of vectors, which we may picture as shown in Fig. 3.1. We note in passing that another picture could be drawn as well (Fig. 3.2), where the name of the next item is located last in each contiguous block. This is much less efficient for answering the question: "Given the name of

---

† In LISP the notation **cddddr** would be used for $\mathbf{cdr}^5$, but we shall not continue that, especially since we shall need such constructions as $\mathbf{cdr}^n$.

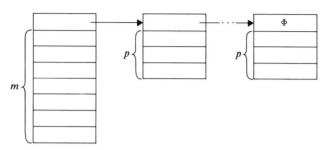

Figure 3.1

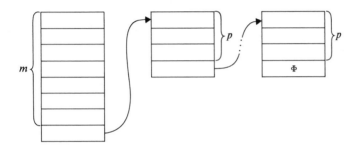

Figure 3.2

a block, what is the next block?" In general, under the second organization, one would have to provide, with each block, a way of determining
how long it is, so the name of the next block could be found. We will still
consider the successor name to be the (logically) second component of an
element of the list. The notation for this type of list will be

$$\sum_{m(p)}^{n} A$$

If $p = 1$, we will usually omit it. The case $\sum_{n}^{n}$ coincides with our previous
notation $\sum_{n}$, and we shall know that an ordinary vector is intended, but
when $n \neq m$, we shall use a list representation as additional blocks are
needed. Of course, $\int_{0}^{N} A$ and $\sum_{0}^{N} A$ describe the same structure, but the
former allows string substitution.

    While we introduced a notation **cdr** earlier for extracting the name of
the successor of a list element, e.g., its second component, we have not
yet provided an extractor for its first component. This is written **car,**†
so that the value of the ith element of list x is **car cdr**^{i-1}x.

---

† Also from LISP.

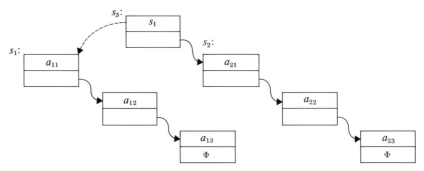

Figure 3.3

There is another operator which is often very useful in manipulating lists. Just as in Chapter 2 it was found necessary to build up structures as well as to take them apart, we need to be able to combine two objects into a pair. For example, if s_1 and s_2 are names of lists, then one might wish to create the pair

$$s_3 \equiv (s_1, s_2)$$

If this is done, s_3 is a list which contains s_2 as a sublist, and whose first element's first element (that is, **car** s_3) is s_1. This can be represented as shown in Fig. 3.3. We name the operator which creates pairs **cons**,† so that we could have written

$$s_3 := \mathbf{cons}(s_1, s_2)$$

For any lists x and y it follows that

$$\mathbf{cons}(\mathbf{car}\ x, \mathbf{cdr}\ x) = x$$
$$\mathbf{car}(\mathbf{cons}(x, y)) = x$$
$$\mathbf{cdr}(\mathbf{cons}(x, y)) = y$$

3.5 THE SPECIFICATION OF DATA STRUCTURES

As we move now to the specification of general data structures, it is important to realize that the organization of the data is an integral part of creating the algorithm for manipulating it. While it is not true that the proper choice of the data organization guarantees a trivial algorithm for

---

† Also from LISP.

each problem, it is true that the wrong choice of structure can make an algorithm so cumbersome or so inefficient in its execution that it may be useless. For example, an unwarranted indication of expected variability in a data structure may imply the use of a set of operations for its manipulation that slows its algorithm down beyond tolerable limits. Furthermore, since programming is the creation of algorithms to be executed by a machine, all data organizations must ultimately be represented as data capable of manipulation by a machine. Naturally, algorithms written to be manipulated by one machine may be executed by others via translation programs (or algorithms). It follows that the choice of *primitive structures* is always determined by the existence of machines and translation programs. We will choose the ALGOL language as representing the machine on which algorithms will ultimately be run, though we have not resisted the temptation to tinker slightly with the machine which was delivered to us as the "official" ALGOL. We will call our ALGOL "the background machine." Since this machine does not routinely handle as wide a range of data structures as programmers would like to use for their algorithms, it is necessary to provide (1) a language for defining a wide range of useful data structures and (2) a translation program to produce the ALGOL statements in which the intent of these structures is preserved and the operations on them are correctly performed.

We have already begun to develop the notation which will be useful in specifying structures. Let us summarize it here:

$$\sum_{m(p)}^{n}$$

means a vector whose components number between m and n (represented as a list of vectors, the first vector having m components and each one after the first having p elements);

$$\sum_{n}$$

means a vector of n components;

$$\int_{m}^{n}$$

means a string whose elements number between m and n (represented as a list); and

$$\int_{n}$$

means a string of n elements. We may include another obvious notation, grouping by means of commas and parentheses, to cover vectors which are not homogeneous. Thus

$$(\textbf{real}, \sum_n \textbf{integer}, \textbf{character})$$

is a vector of three components, one of which is itself a vector.

Since the data structures **real**, **integer**, **Boolean**, **character**, and now **name** are considered primitive in ALGOL, they shall be assumed to be primitive here. All other structures will be constructed (via $\sum$ and $\int$) from them. We shall use the following definition of equality of structures:

1. Primitive structures are equal if they are equal as sets.

2. Two structures (not both primitive) are equal if and only if they have the same selector functions and corresponding components name equal structures.

The selector functions on vectors will be indicated by the application of subscripts to the name of the vector. The selector functions on strings will be indicated by using *range pairs* as subscripts. Thus, if v has the string structure $\int_{10} \textbf{real}$, then $v[3:10]$ selects the last eight (**real**) components of the string v. For a string v, the notation $v[j]$ will mean $v[j:j]$.

The selectors are intimately associated with finding, or accessing, components. Therefore, a selector has as its value the **name-of** (or "a pointer to") the component selected. The operations to which the component is to be subjected determine how it is treated once the selection is made. For example, if the component has a structure of its own, and another subscript is to be applied to select a component from within that structure, the result of the first selection is maintained as a name, and then the next selector is applied. On the other hand, if the first selector comes up with the name of a primitive character, say a **real** number, then its value will most likely be needed, and the name selected will be used to access the number itself. It is an important property of languages like ALGOL that this determination of whether to use the name or the value of a selected component is made by the "machine" on the basis of context. The person writing the algorithm is generally able to ignore these decisions, but when it is necessary to overrule the interpretation imposed by some context, operators such as **vc-of** are available.

It will be instructive to exhibit here some examples of common data structures, including some of those we have already seen:

a) A **real** vector of length n:

$$\sum_n \textbf{real}$$

b) A **real** square array with n^2 elements:

$$\sum_n \sum_n \textbf{real}$$

c) A standard array of n^2 **complex** numbers:

$$\sum_n \textbf{name-of} \left(\sum_n (\textbf{complex} := \sum_2 \textbf{real}) \right)$$

d) A master file containing up to 5000 entries, each entry consisting of a 10-character part number, a list of up to 20 previous numbers used for this part, a list of up to 25 parts with which it is interchangeable, an integer reorder threshold, and an integer current amount on hand:

$$\sum_0^{5000} \left(\int_{10} \textbf{character}, \sum_0^{20} \int_{10} \textbf{character}, \sum_0^{25} \int_{10} \textbf{character}, \textbf{integer}, \textbf{integer} \right)$$

e) A list of vectors, each having n **real** components:

$$\sum_0^{\infty} \sum_n \textbf{real}$$

This can be pictured as shown in Fig. 3.4. Note that it is not the same as the structure given by the specification

$$\sum_{n(n)}^{\infty} \textbf{real}$$

which was illustrated earlier (except that here $p = n$), though the pictures look the same. If A is given the latter structure, we would expect to select components of A by using only one subscript, such as $A[73]$, and the selector function would automatically find the correct block and index into it for the desired component. On the other hand, if B is given the structure

$$\sum_0^{\infty} \sum_n \textbf{real}$$

shown above, a quite different selector function is implied. In this case, we would have to write the **cdr** explicitly to move from one component

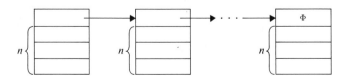

Figure 3.4

vector of the list to the next, and we would then use single subscripts to index directly into the current vector. The structure used on A is useful for a single vector whose number of components is expected to change dynamically, while the structure used on B here allows one to deal with a collection of individual vectors. Each has its advantages and disadvantages.

f) A triangular **real** array, with the ith row having i elements. This represents the lower triangle plus the diagonal, of a square array:

$$\sum_{i \to n} \sum_{i} \textbf{real}$$

Here we introduce an extension, $\sum_{i \to n}$, of the notation $\sum_n$.† This form is interpreted as follows: "The variable i, which starts with 1 and moves in steps of 1 to n, is an index over the components of this vector." As in the triangular **real** array considered here, the index i may be used as a parameter in the lower limit of the $\sum$ specification of the structure of the ith component. Should the range of i be from a to b instead of from 1 to n, we shall write $\sum_{i \to [a:b]}$ instead. [Exercise 3.5.1 asks that the notation $\sum_{i \to [a:b](p)}^{N}$ be explored.]

An alternative structure for the triangular **real** array (as a standard array) would be

$$\textbf{t} := \sum_{i \to n} \textbf{name-of}(\sum_{i} \textbf{real})$$

Here we have again expanded our notation to indicate an assignment of a structure specification to a ⟨boldface symbol⟩. (The symbol **t** was used to suggest the triangular array.) As we shall see, this ⟨boldface symbol⟩ will then be used very much like a new ⟨type⟩.

The selector functions defined on a triangular array A with one of these structures (for example, after a declaration **t** A) will be defined as long as one writes $A[i, j]$ only when $i \geq j$. It often happens, however, that references are made to elements of the array which would lie in the upper triangle, and that the value 0 is desired when this happens. It would be wasteful to store a great many 0 values for this purpose, so one would wish to provide a conditional subscription function:

$$\textbf{if } i \geq j \textbf{ then } A[i, j] \textbf{ else } 0$$

One could actually insert this conditional explicitly at each point in the algorithm, but it would be much better (from the point of view of the person

---

† We shall from time to time expand the structure specification notation during this development. A complete formal syntax of these specifications is given in Section 3.6.

writing the algorithm), if this could be done automatically.† In the next chapter we shall introduce a method of defining strings of ALGOL text to be used in place of various special constructions which may occur in an algorithm. Thus, if we must have an interpretation of $A[i, j]$ which is different from the ordinary one, as is the case here, we would specify that when the following context occurs:

$$\textbf{real } X \downarrow \textbf{ [integer } p \textbf{, integer } q]$$

(where $\downarrow$ represents subscription),‡ some particular text would replace it, such as

$$\textbf{if } p \geq q \textbf{ then } X[p, q] \textbf{ else } 0$$

Then, when $A[i, j]$ occurs in the algorithm, the desired conditional subscript function would be used. This is developed in great detail in Chapter 4; here we shall go only one step further. We shall see, in the subsequent development, that after the replacement text is inserted into the algorithm, it is itself scanned for replacements that may need to be made. Thus it would be necessary to avoid having $A[i, j]$ introduced again as part of the replacement string. Moreover, we probably don't want every **real** array to have all of its subscripted occurrences subjected to this replacement throughout the algorithm. We give here a brief description of the solution to this dilemma, but only to illustrate what is done more slowly later.

The way to accomplish what we wish is to assign to A the triangular structure, and to another symbol, B, a special $\langle$type$\rangle$ involving A as a parameter, say $\textbf{w}(A)$, but no structure (and hence no storage for values). Thus we have the declaration $\textbf{w}(A) B$. Then it will be necessary to specify how symbols of type $\textbf{w}(A)$ must be treated when they are encountered, since we will henceforth write $B[i, j]$ in the algorithm instead of $A[i, j]$. The one context in which this $\langle$type$\rangle$ will be encountered *in this example* is $B[i, j]$, or, if we include the $\langle$type$\rangle$s,

$$\textbf{w}(A) B \downarrow \textbf{ [integer } i \textbf{, integer } j]$$

---

† One might wish to incorporate checking for illegal subscript values into the subscription function also:

$$\textbf{if } max(i, j) > n \textbf{ then } Signal$$
$$\textbf{else if } i \geq j \textbf{ then } A[i, j] \textbf{ else } 0$$

where *Signal* is a procedure which might return a value of "undefined" and record the occurrence of the event for later analyses, etc.

‡ One can normally understand juxtaposition of an $\langle$identifier$\rangle$ and square brackets to represent subscription, as in $A[i, j]$. Although perhaps more cumbersome, for the sake of clarity, we shall make the subscription operator explicit in this way whenever it occurs in certain special contexts.

One will then specify the value to be assigned this context, i.e., the string of text to be substituted for it (delimited by ' '), preceded by the ⟨type⟩ of the result:

w(Y) $X \downarrow$ [**integer** p, **integer** q] := **real** 'if $p \geq q$ then $Y[p, q]$ else 0';

Then an occurrence of this context involving B, say $B[i + 1, 3]$, would be transformed to

$$\textbf{if } i + 1 \geq 3 \textbf{ then } A[i + 1, 3] \textbf{ else } 0$$

Should we be dealing with a symmetric array A (instead of a triangular array), so that $A[i, j] = A[j, i]$ for all i, j, then one could give instead either

w(Y) $X \downarrow$ [**integer** p, **integer** q] := **real** ' $Y[max(p, q), min(p, q)]$';

where *min* and *max* are ⟨procedure⟩s which yield the minimum and maximum values, respectively; or else the conditional

w(Y) $X \downarrow$ [**integer** p, **integer** q] := **real** 'if $p \geq q$ then $Y[p, q]$ else $Y[q, p]$';

The point is that while we will be able to generate automatically the selector functions for the structures specified by means of the $\sum$ and notation, it will be necessary to give explicitly any selector functions which must differ from these standard ones. As indicated above, the complete syntax and processing of such "context definitions" is the subject of Chapter 4.

g) A ring list. One question we have not yet discussed is: "What happens when you come to the end of a list while applying a successor operator?" At the purely mechanical level, the answer is: "There is no successor, as is indicated by the Φ in the second component of the last pair." But in the context of a particular problem for which the list is a useful data structure, this terminal aspect of reaching the end of the physical list may be inappropriate. For example, suppose that the items on the list were the names of pictures to be displayed on a television screen in such rapid succession that there is no observable flicker. A list is quite useful here, since changes in the composite picture thus produced are most easily effected by string substitutions. Because of the need for rapid repetition, the most sensible way to treat the end of this list is to make its successor the head of the list. Then, while it may still be useful to remember which pair is the head—so that its first component can be used to point to a list of attributes of the picture currently being displayed—the display algorithm need not be bothered with asking after each subpicture whether

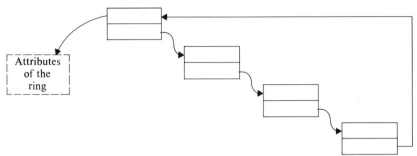

Figure 3.5

another follows. Such a list, in which the terminal element points to the head, is called a "ring." It can be pictured as shown in Fig. 3.5.

The *structure* of a ring is that of a list, but once the list has been created,† it is necessary to find the end of it and replace the Φ by the name of the list (i.e., the name of the first element). The following program in our version of ALGOL shows how this is accomplished for a list x (where **list** $:= \int_{m}^{n}$ **real**):

list x; **name** y; $y := x$;
     L: **if** **cdr(vc-of(** y **))** $\neq \Phi$ **then**
          begin $y := $ **cdr(vc-of(** y **))**; **go to** L **end**
     else **cdr(vc-of(** y **))** $:= x$;

Note here the implicit assumption that an assignment of the value of a list x to a variable y of $\langle$type$\rangle$ **name** amounts to assigning the name of the first pair of the list x to y. The specification of structure for a ring, then, will consist of an ordinary list structure assignment, which we shall write

$$\textbf{ring} := \int_{m}^{n} \textbf{real}$$

plus the small program given here, called the *initialization*. The syntax for specifying an initialization will be given in Section 3.6.

h) A two-way list. In some situations, such as in the display ring of example (g), it is necessary to perform many string substitutions very rapidly, and the time needed to identify the substring to be deleted or replaced must be kept at a minimum. Thus one might keep an independent set of pointers so that when it is decided that subpicture A is to be deleted

---

† A newly created list may have more elements than (Φ,Φ); that is, it may have an initial set of (empty) components. This is the role of m in the notation $\int_{m}^{n}$. If $m = 0$, the algorithm which follows can be made much simpler.

from the display, one immediately obtains the pointer to (or the name of) the entry in the display ring that represents A. Now, however, one must make the ring bypass the entry for A:

The way to do this is to set **cdr** B to C instead of A. But it is probably not known, from the decision to delete A from the display, that the predecessor in the display is B. From A's entry, one can find only its successor C. A common solution to this problem is the two-way list, in which each entry "remembers" its predecessor as well as its successor. A structure that will do this is

$$\textbf{two-way-list} := \int_1^\infty \sum_2 \textbf{name}$$

which puts a two-component vector at each first component of the implicit list pair implied by the $\int_1^\infty$ notation. This vector will have two components, the name of its predecessor, and the pointer to the subpicture A, respectively. A pictorial representation is given in Fig. 3.6. The initialization

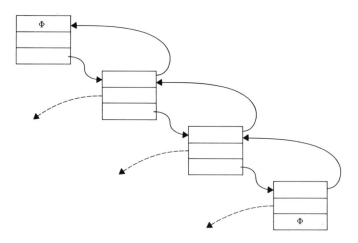

Figure 3.6

needed to insert predecessor pointers into the two-way list is

two-way-list x; **name** y; **(car** x)[1] := Φ; y := x;
    L: **if cdr(vc-of(** y **))** $\neq$ Φ **then**
        begin (car cdr(vc-of(y **)))**[1] := y; y := **cdr(vc-of(** y **))**;
        go to L **end**

It should be noted that in such two-way lists the standard appending process which can be assumed to exist for combining lists is not enough. [Exercise 3.5.2 asks that a standard "append" program be written, as well as an "insert" program and a "prefix" program for (one-way) lists.] Someone defining a new structure like these two-way lists will have to provide his own "append" program, as well as the initialization. In this case, the "append" program (to append the two-way list b to the two-way list a, assuming the availability of the standard "append" program) could look as follows:

two-way-list a, b; **name** y; *append*(a, b); y := a;
    L: **if (car cdr(vc-of(** y **)))**[1] $\neq$ Φ **then**
        begin y := **cdr(vc-of(** y **))**; **go to** L **end**;
        (car cdr(vc-of (y **)))**[1] := y;

A useful way to understand what is happening here is to visualize the list as a sequence of pairs. In this case, each pair has a first element which is itself a pair. The pairs involved in the appending program above, just after the standard "append" is invoked, appear as shown in Fig. 3.7, where

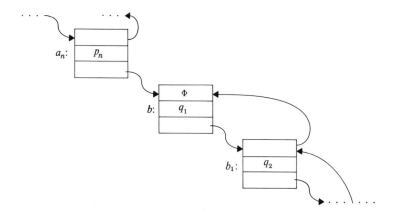

Figure 3.7

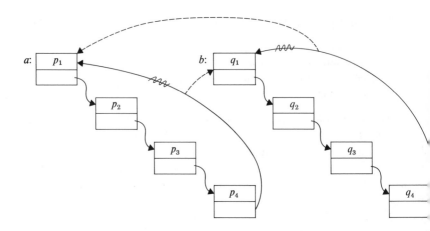

Figure 3.8

p_j and q_j are the "content items" in the lists, and $a, a_1, \ldots, a_n, b, b_1, \ldots,$ are the names of the list pairs. The program just given searches out the pair labeled b,† which is found because of the Φ it contains, and replaces the Φ with the name a_n.

It is unfortunate that in the last example so much time is spent traversing the list, since the standard append does it to find the end of the list a in order to append b, and our superimposed append program traverses the entire list a again immediately afterward. All of this could be avoided by constructing *two-way rings* instead. We first consider the appending of two one-way rings, however.

Since we are dealing with rings, the standard append can no longer be invoked at all, since it depends on finding a terminating Φ; but the append we need can now be written very easily. The process for two one-way rings (Fig. 3.8) involves changing only two components, the successors to the two end elements (from a, b to b, a, respectively). [Exercise 3.5.3 asks for the program.] In the one-way rings, this still involves traversing them to find the end elements; but in the two-way rings, we need change only two names for the forward pointers and two names for the backward pointers, and no traversing is needed at all. The append program for two-way rings is

two-way-ring a, b; **name** y; $y := (\textbf{car } a)[1]$;
   $(\textbf{car } a)[1] := (\textbf{car } b)[1]$; $(\textbf{car } b)[1] := y$;
   $\textbf{cdr}((\textbf{car } b)[1]) := b$; $\textbf{cdr}((\textbf{car } a)[1]) := a$;

---

† Although the name b is known, its new predecessor in a is not known.

[Exercise 3.5.4 asks for a diagram. Exercise 3.5.5 asks that it be done without using y for temporary storage.]

It should be clear by now how insertions and deletions have been simplified by the use of two-way pointers. [Exercise 3.5.6 explores this procedure further.] The one thing that still involves traversing the list is the question: "What ring am I on?" More generally, since it is possible to have first contact with a ring by a reference to one of its elements, such as arriving at the subpicture entry for A by considerations involving features of A other than its display, it is natural to want to proceed directly to the head of the ring† to obtain other (more global) information about the ring, such as its name, its current length and status, and so on. With our present ring structure one must traverse the ring, applying at each step some test appropriate to that particular ring which recognizes the head.

A ring structure especially constructed to facilitate "head-finding" was first designed by L. Roberts [12] for use with the CORAL language, and we shall call it a C-ring. In a C-ring each element also carries an integer code—0, 1, or 2—so that in our notation we have

$$\textbf{C-ring} := \int_{1}^{\infty} (\textbf{integer, name, real})$$

Code 0 will mean the head of the list, code 1 will mean that the pointer which appears as the second component is a backward pointer to the most recent element of type 1, and code 2 means that the second component is the name of (i.e., a pointer to) the head of the list (Fig. 3.9). Now, given the name of any element, one can find the head of the list by moving forward (via **cdr**) to an element of type 2,‡ which has a second component that furnishes a pointer to the head. Finding the predecessor of an element, in order to make an insertion or deletion, requires a forward move to a type-1 element, then a move along the backward pointer to the first element of type 1 preceding the element to be deleted, then forward again until an element is found whose successor is the original element. [Exercise 3.5.7 asks for the programs on deletion.] When a new element is to be inserted, a decision must be made as to whether to make it a type-1 or type-2 element. A good strategy here would be to keep the type-1 and type-2 elements evenly distributed, although it certainly does no harm if they do not strictly alternate. [Exercise 3.5.8 asks for the programs to insert different types of elements.]

---

† "Take me to your header."
‡ One can watch for type 0 along the way, but it isn't necessary.

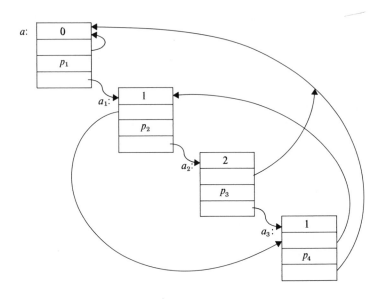

Figure 3.9

As an example of the use of such rings, let us consider the representation of the display of a triangle. One can imagine a man seated before a display screen selecting three points in turn with a special photosensitive pen. By pushing a special button or pointing to one of several alternatives on the display screen, he specifies that the three points are to be taken as the vertices of a triangle. By means of other signals, he specifies that the three sides are to be displayed and named separately for future use, and that the three sides are to be considered an alternative definition for the triangle. If he causes a side to move or change length, the change will then be reflected in the display of the triangle, even though the triangle was originally determined by the three vertices. One can visualize an interlocking network of rings as shown in Fig. 3.10. Of course, the boxes in the figure contain only pointers—to successors in various rings and to the data associated with each point, line, etc. Should L_2 move, for example, it is immediately clear from following one of the two rings through L_2 that P_1 and P_3 are affected, and from the other ring that the picture of the triangle is affected. Secondary effects could then be explored by moving along rings passing through elements encountered in the first rings named.

i) A stack. One simple data structure that has proved very useful is the "push-down stack," named after a famous example of it, the cafeteria

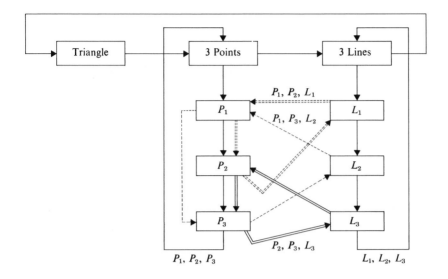

Figure 3.10

tray stack. It is usually referred to as a last-in-first-out (LIFO) list.† From the point of view of data structures, a stack is a string for which string substitutions are restricted to: (a) a "push," which consists of replacing the null character at the left by one character, and (b) a "pop," which replaces the leftmost character by the null character. [Exercise 3.5.9 asks what is left after a particular series of pushes and pops.] As far as a data structure is concerned, then, we have

$$\mathbf{stack} := \int_0^\infty A$$

where A is some alphabet. To use this structure as a stack requires only that no string substitutions other than those described above be used;

---

† One example of its use occurred in Chapter 1, where we developed the linkage mechanism which allowed one algorithm to call upon another as a subalgorithm. The device was used there to prefix specific recognition characters $\alpha_1, \alpha_2, \ldots$, at the left end of the register R on each call and remove them afterward. The last one prefixed was the first removed. The "push-down" characteristic of this device was made completely automatic, since the entire string in R always moved far enough to the right to accommodate new characters prefixed at the left. The LIFO discipline has nothing to do with either the nature of the string in R or the Markov "machine." It is simply a convention of use.

one would probably provide standard "push" and "pop" programs for this purpose.

In some cases it has been found more convenient to provide additional "utility programs" as well. In the IPL-V language [13], for example, it is very often necessary to make a new copy of the leftmost character and insert it at the left. This allows the copy to be used in various ways without losing the original.† In IPL-V this is called *preserving* the current contents of the stack. It is actually an ordinary "push," in which the new character being inserted at the left end of the string is a copy of the leftmost character. [Exercise 3.5.10 asks how symbol tables in a block structure can be "pushed down."]

j) A queue. Another string which one encounters often is the first-in-first-out (FIFO) queue. Subject to some distribution of arrivals, characters from some alphabet A are appended at the right end of the queue, and the discipline of use dictates that the only way to obtain characters from the queue is to remove them one at a time from the left end. We have

$$\textbf{queue} := \int_0^\infty A$$

and we would expect a standard utility program to be available called "next," which would deliver as its value the next character from the queue, while deleting it from the queue as well. It is necessary to provide here for some standard behavior on the part of the "next" program if the queue is (or becomes) empty, perhaps changing the value of some variable from zero to nonzero. [Exercise 3.5.11 asks for the "next" program.]

k) A threaded-list structure. There are several ways to represent a structure like the following:

$$((x, y), (z, w, t), e, ((a, b), c))$$

One way is the tree shown in Fig. 3.11. The parentheses are included in the tree to indicate the original notation, although the structure would be fully preserved in the tree representation even if they were omitted. In our data-structure notation, we could write

$$(\sum_2 \textbf{real}, \sum_3 \textbf{real}, \textbf{real}, (\sum_2 \textbf{real}, \textbf{real}))$$

Unfortunately, we have done such a good job of preserving the structure here, that we must have exactly the right number of subscripts in

---

† We also used this copy technique to implement the two-way branch in Chapter 1. In fact, we had an algorithm called "Copy" just for that purpose.

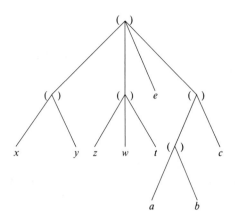

Figure 3.11

order to reach any particular component. For example, if the structure
is named A, we would refer to e as $A[3]$, but we would have to refer to
c as $A[4, 2]$. For some purposes it might be necessary to represent all
parts of the structure in some uniform way so one could move across the
information "more gently," i.e., without bumping into structural barriers
at every step.

    In [14] a proposal was made for a different data structure which would
facilitate moving across a set of data in such a way that its structure didn't
get in the way of the selector that wished to access elements in it. The idea
is to represent the data and the structure together in a uniform way, so
that the original structure itself becomes part of the data. The new structure in which the old is represented is called a *threaded list*:

$$\textbf{threaded-list} := \int_{1}^{\infty} (\textbf{integer, name})$$

with an initialization:

      threaded-list x; $(\textbf{car } x)[1] := 3$; $(\textbf{car } x)[2] := x$;

The initialization produces a list of the form

$$x: ((3, x), \Phi)$$

The threaded list which would represent the parenthesized form

$$(-, (*, (+, a, b), e), (+, f, g))$$

would be

$$x: ((3, x_1), \Phi) \qquad\qquad x_7: ((0, +), x_8)$$
$$x_1: ((0, -), x_2) \qquad\qquad x_8: ((0, f), x_9)$$
$$x_2: ((1, x_4), x_3) \qquad\qquad x_9: ((2, g), x_3)$$
$$x_3: ((3, x_7), x) \qquad\qquad x_{10}: ((0, +), x_{11})$$
$$x_4: ((0, *), x_5) \qquad\qquad x_{11}: ((0, a), x_{12})$$
$$x_5: ((1, x_{10}), x_6) \qquad\qquad x_{12}: ((2, b), x_5)$$
$$x_6: ((2, e), x_2)$$

where an element on the threaded list, such as a, b, or $+$, is understood to be represented (in the second component of an entry) by its name, i.e., by a pointer. [Exercise 3.5.12 asks for the program to create this list from the parenthesized form by direct construction.] The interpretation of this representation, as given below, is quite straightforward, and it will be seen immediately that the use of threaded lists need not be restricted to parenthesized forms. The sequence represented as a tree at the beginning of this discussion of threaded lists is also easily represented in this way. [Exercise 3.5.13 asks for this threaded list.]

Suppose the left parentheses are numbered from the left, starting with 1. The "*group number*" of an element z is defined to be the number m of the rightmost left parenthesis such that it and its matching right parenthesis contain z. Thus, in the form given as an example above, the three elements: $-$, $(*, (+, a, b), e)$, and $(+, f, g)$ all have group number 1, while $*$, $(+, a, b)$, and e all have group number 2, g has group number 4, and so on.

For the threaded-list interpretation, if the integer part of a list element y—that is, (car y)[1]—is 0 or 2, the element y contains as its second component—that is, (car y)[2]—the name of an actual list item, which is the next item with the same group number. If the integer is 1 or 3,† the second component is the name of the sublist which occurs as the next item with the current group number. Of course, the contents of this sublist have a new group number. Either a 2 or a 3 indicates that the item (either an actual list item or a sublist) is the last with the current group number. If (car y)[1] is either a 0 or a 1, then **cdr** y is the name of the next list element whose name component—either an actual list item or a sublist—has the current group number. If (car y)[1] is either a 2 or a 3, then **cdr** y is the name of the list element whose sublist was just completed. The reader should check that the threaded list given above does represent the form used as an example.

---

† In the use of the integer 3 and in some other aspects we differ from [14].

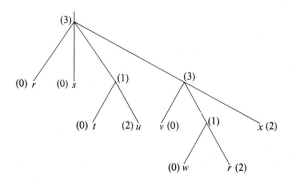

Figure 3.12

As another example, the form

$$y: \ (r, s, (t, u), (v, (w, r), x))$$

has the group number assignments

r	1
s	1
(t, u)	1
$(v, (w, r), x)$	1
t	2
u	2
v	3
(w, r)	3
x	3
w	4
r	4

and the tree shown in Fig. 3.12, where the parenthesized integers are those needed to represent the tree as the following threaded list. As can be seen by taking the rightmost branch from any node, one eventually reaches either a 2 or a 3 (the last item or the last sublist with the current group number, respectively). Each node also gives rise to a new group number.

$$y: \ ((3, y_1), \Phi) \qquad\qquad y_6: \ ((2, u), y_3)$$
$$y_1: \ ((0, r), y_2) \qquad\qquad y_7: \ (0,(v), y_8)$$
$$y_2: \ ((0, s), y_3) \qquad\qquad y_8: \ ((1, y_{10}), y_9)$$
$$y_3: \ ((1, y_5), y_4) \qquad\qquad y_9: \ ((2, x), y_4)$$
$$y_4: \ ((3, y_7), y) \qquad\qquad y_{10}: ((0, w), y_{11})$$
$$y_5: \ ((0, t), y_6) \qquad\qquad y_{11}: ((2, r), y_8)$$

Now we can see that to obtain all the elements with group number 1, for example, one would always take the normal **cdr** as the successor (after the first pair). To sequence through the list in such a way that one finds each time the next actual item (in this example, r, s, t, u, v, w, r, and x), the following strategy would be used (with z containing on entry the name of the head of the list or the name of the last item found, and at exit the name of the next item or Φ):

In the special case of starting at the head of the threaded list, we must simply select the **name** component of z—that is, $z := (\mathbf{car}\ z)[2]$. Otherwise, z will contain the name of a type-0 or type-2 element, the last one found. In general, we wish to move (via **cdr**) to the next element of the list. Since this next element might be the beginning of a sublist, however, we must be careful to move down that sublist, provided we have not already been there. In the program which follows, s is the signal for having already traversed a sublist. If $s = 0$, the next sublist encountered is to be traversed. When $s = 1$, we have just finished a sublist, and we should move to the next item with the same group number, if it exists. The program is then

threaded-list y; **name** z; **integer** s; $s := 0$;
    if $(\mathbf{car}\ z)[1] = 2$ **then** $s := 1$;
    if $(\mathbf{car}\ z)[1] = 3$ **then** $z := (\mathbf{car}\ z)[2]$ **else** $z := \mathbf{cdr}\ z$;
    L: **if** $(\mathbf{car}\ z)[1] = 1\ \vee\ (\mathbf{car}\ z)[1] = 3$ **then**
        begin if $s = 0$ **then begin** $z := (\mathbf{car}\ z)[2]$; **go to** L **end**
            else if $(\mathbf{car}\ z)[1] = 1$ **then** $s := 0$; $z := \mathbf{cdr}\ z$;
            if $z \neq \Phi$ **then go to** L **end**

The exercises will explore other ways of sequencing through a threaded list [3.5.14], and a way to determine if two threaded lists are equal [3.5.15].

It will also be necessary to provide programs to prefix and append one threaded list to another. The following simple program prefixes a threaded list y to a threaded list x in such a way that y becomes the first component (i.e., sublist) of x.

  threaded-list x, y; **cdr** $y := (\mathbf{car}\ x)[2]$; $(\mathbf{car}\ x)[2] := y$; $(\mathbf{car}\ y)[1] := 1$;

The append program is slightly more complicated, and is left to be done as an exercise [3.5.16].

l) A higher-dimensional array. It may happen that one wishes to generate a very regular structure from repeated applications of a basic one. Consider the specification

$$\mathbf{integer}\ j;\ \mathbf{u} := \sum_m \mathbf{real};\ \mathbf{for}\ j := 2\ \mathbf{step}\ 1\ \mathbf{until}\ n\ \mathbf{do}\ \mathbf{u} := \sum_m \mathbf{u};$$

If $n = 2$, one has **u** specifying a vector of m elements, each of which is an m-element vector; hence, **u** specifies an $m \times m$ array. If $n = 3$, we obtain an $m \times m \times m$ array. If we declare x to have type **u** for $n = 3$, we would need three subscripts to select a **real** element of x, and we would interpret $x[i, j, k]$ as $((x[i])[j])[k]$. To make this construction more general, so that we can specify a $p \times q \times r$ array, for example, we should allow some variability in the lower (and upper) limits on $\sum$. Thus we might represent the dimensions of a vector as $A = (p, q, r)$, and write

$$\textbf{integer } j; \textbf{u} := \sum_{A[1]} \textbf{real}; \textbf{for } j := 2 \textbf{ step } 1 \textbf{ until } 3 \textbf{ do u} := \sum_{A[j]} \textbf{u};$$

It is also clear that the same specification should be available for defining **Boolean** higher arrays, and it would be unfortunate if we could not just substitute **Boolean** for **real**. What we need is a list of "parameters" to go with **u**; i.e., we should be able to write **u**(3, A, **real**) and obtain the specification just above. On the other hand, if we write **u**(t, B, **Boolean**), we should obtain

$$\textbf{integer } j; \textbf{u} := \sum_{B[1]} \textbf{Boolean}; \textbf{for } j := 2 \textbf{ step } 1 \textbf{ until } t \textbf{ do u} := \sum_{B[j]} \textbf{u};$$

While we are improving things, we should also arrange to have the name **u** reflect the choice of arguments. Let us agree that boldface brackets (**[** , **]**) in a $\langle$type$\rangle$ name imply a parameter substitution into the name. Thus we could write something like

procedure *higher-array*(n, X, z); **integer** n; **array** X;† **begin integer** j;

$$\textbf{[}z\textbf{]-array} := \sum_{X[1]} z; \textbf{for } j := 2 \textbf{ step } 1 \textbf{ until } n \textbf{ do}$$

$$\textbf{[}z\textbf{]-array} := \sum_{X[j]} \textbf{[}z\textbf{]-array};$$

$$\textit{higher-array} := \textbf{[}z\textbf{]-array end}$$

and then we could make the assignment

$$\textbf{u} := \textit{higher-array}(3, A, \textbf{real})$$

In this case, we have also generated a definition for **real-array**.

EXERCISES 3.5

1. What is meant by the following notation?

$$\sum_{i \to [a:b](p)}^{n} \textbf{real}$$

---

† Since the array structure of X is determined by the actual parameter for X in a call, none is given in the procedure definition.

2. Write programs

    a) to append list y to list x;

    b) to insert list y after the ith element of list x; and

    c) to prefix list x to list y.

3. Write the program to append the one-way ring y to the one-way ring x.

4. Give the diagram showing what changes are needed to append one two-way ring to another.

5. Write the append program for two-way rings without using y as temporary storage.

6. Given the one-way list x, write the programs

    a) to delete the element with name x_k (not necessarily the kth element of the list); and

    b) to insert an element with name x_j in place of the element with name x_k.

    Write the same two programs, assuming that x is a two-way list.

7. Write a program to delete an element with name x_k from the C-ring x (assuming that x_k might be either type 1 or type 2).

8. Write the program to insert the element with name x_j after the element with name x_k in the C-ring x (assuming that x_k might be either type 1 or type 2).

9. What is left in the stack after the series: "Push" a, "Push" b, "Push" c, "Pop", "Push" d, "Pop"?

10. Explain in detail how a push-down stack can be used to advantage in keeping a symbol table while assembling a language with a block structure such as ALGOL. In particular, how are blocks within blocks handled? What happens if a transfer is requested to a label defined in both the current block and an outer block? What about a transfer to a label defined only in an outer block?

11. Write a labeled Markov subalgorithm "next in," which inserts a value into the queue delimited by the characters α and β, the value having been previously placed in the temporary location delimited by γ and α. Write a subalgorithm "next out," which deletes a value from the queue on a first-in-first-out basis and puts it in the temporary location delimited by γ and α. (Thus, if the queue is empty, the temporary location will be empty on return.)

12. Write an LMA which creates a threaded list from a parenthesized form by direct construction. Check it on $(-, (*, (+, a, b), e), (+, f, g))$. [Hint: Scan through the parenthesized form, each time creating $n+1$: $((,),)$ and then deciding whether to assign type 0, 1, 2, or 3. If 1 or 3 (i.e., a sublist), assign (**car** $(n+1)$)[2] and remember the address $(n + 1)$ in a push-down stack. The next type 2 must assign (**car** $(n+1)$)[1] and **cdr** $(n+1)$.]

13. Give the threaded list that corresponds to the form $((x, y), (z, w, t), e, ((a, b), c))$.

14. Write an ALGOL program that when called obtains the name of the next list item (either actual list item or sublist) from a threaded list.

15. Using the program of Exercise 3.5.14, write an ALGOL ⟨program expression⟩ which has **Boolean** result **true** if two threaded lists are equal, and **false** otherwise. Use the fact that two threaded lists, when you are sequencing through them concurrently, are equal if at each step, both of them point to the same actual list item or both point to a sublist. (Why is it not sufficient to sequence through, each time finding the next actual list item and comparing?)

16. Give the program to append threaded list y to threaded list x.

3.6 THE SYNTAX OF S-EXPRESSIONS

It is now time to formalize the language in which structures may be specified. We wish to generate expressions that, when evaluated, yield structures as values. They are called *S-expressions*, and in general we shall use the prefix S- with words normally used in arithmetic situations.

Since S-expressions are to be embedded into our version of ALGOL, we do not need to give the entire syntax of the language here. It is necessary to give only the syntax of ⟨S-expression⟩ and ⟨S-assignment⟩, together with the stipulation that once a symbol has been assigned an S-value, it is eligible to serve as a ⟨type⟩ in declarations for ordinary variables and procedures. The syntax follows.

⟨boldface character⟩ ::= **a** | **b** | ... | **z** | **A** | **B** | ... | **Z** | -
⟨boldface symbol⟩ ::= ⊔{⟨boldface character⟩}$_1^*$ †
   Example: x-array

---

† It is sometimes a source of confusion that certain sequences of characters, such as **begin**, already exist in ALGOL, but are apparently allowed here as ⟨boldface symbol⟩s also, leading to conflicts. Actually, there is no real conflict, since **begin, end, go to,** and other symbols like them in ALGOL are always considered to be single characters in some other alphabet, not sequences of characters in the boldface alphabet at all. Thus we could replace them with α, β, γ, etc., using some fixed correspondence, and no conflict need ever occur. Another possible solution to this apparent problem is to agree beforehand that those sequences of ⟨boldface character⟩s which resemble ALGOL "characters" are not allowed as ⟨boldface symbol⟩s. This solution leads to a list of "reserved" words, which is always an annoyance. Given the problem and the two cited solutions, however, we must choose one, and "reserved words" appear to be more palatable for our purposes. We shall therefore use **begin, end,** etc., only with their ALGOL meanings. The leading character (⊔) representing the blank will be suppressed where no ambiguity is possible.

⟨S-identifier⟩ ::= ⟨boldface symbol⟩
   Example: table
⟨S-id parameter⟩ ::= [⟨identifier⟩]
   Example: [*table*]
⟨S-id name generator⟩ ::= {⟨S-identifier⟩ | ⟨S-id parameter⟩}$_1^*$
   Example: array [*z*] table
   Example: [*s*] [*r*] array [*z*] complex
⟨basic S-primary⟩ ::= **character** | **real** | **integer** | **Boolean** | **name** |
   ⟨S-id name generator⟩ | (⟨S-assignment⟩) | (⟨S-expression⟩) |
   name-of (⟨basic S-primary⟩)
   Example: (complex := $\sum_2$ real)
⟨S-primary list⟩ ::= ⟨basic S-primary⟩ {,⟨basic S-primary⟩}*
   Example: real, complex
⟨S-primary⟩ ::= ⟨basic S-primary⟩ | (⟨S-primary list⟩)
   Example: (real, complex)
⟨lower limit⟩ ::= ⟨arithmetic expression⟩ | [⟨arithmetic expression⟩:
   ⟨arithmetic expression⟩]
   Example: [0:199]
⟨iterative limit⟩ ::= ⟨lower limit⟩ | ⟨lower limit⟩(⟨arithmetic expression⟩)
   Example: [*m*:*n*](*p* × *q*)
⟨iterative $\sum$ limit⟩ ::= ⟨iterative limit⟩ | ⟨identifier⟩ → ⟨lower limit⟩
   Example: $i \to [a:b](p)$
⟨upper limit⟩ ::= ⟨arithmetic expression⟩ | ∞ [†] | ⟨empty⟩
   Example: $d + e + f$

⟨S-factor⟩ ::= ⟨S-primary⟩ | $\displaystyle\int_{\langle\text{iterative limit}\rangle}^{\langle\text{upper limit}\rangle}$ ⟨S-primary⟩ [‡]

   Example: $\displaystyle\int_{[a:b]}^{\infty}$ real

⟨simple S-expression⟩ ::= ⟨S-factor⟩ | $\displaystyle\sum_{\langle\text{iterative }\Sigma\text{ limit}\rangle}^{\langle\text{upper limit}\rangle}$ ⟨simple S-expres-
   sion⟩

   Example: $\displaystyle\sum_{i \to n} \int_{[a:b]}^{\infty}$ (real, complex)

---

† The symbol ∞ represents the largest available integer, hence is understood to have
ype **integer**.
   Since input to most computers is still in the form of a single line at a time, this
ˈructure might have to be linearized in some way, a task we leave to the imagination
ˈ the reader.

$\langle$S-expression$\rangle$ ::= $\langle$simple S-expression$\rangle$ | $\langle$if clause$\rangle$ $\langle$simple S-expression$\rangle$ **else** $\langle$S-expression$\rangle$

    Example: if $x = y$ **then Boolean else integer**

$\langle$S-left side$\rangle$ ::= {$\langle$S-id name generator$\rangle$:= }$_1^*$

    Example: u := v := complex :=

$\langle$S-assignment$\rangle$ ::= $\langle$S-left side$\rangle$ $\langle$S-expression$\rangle$ | $\langle$S-left side$\rangle$ $\langle$S-expression$\rangle$ **initialization** ($\langle$identifier$\rangle$) $\langle$program$\rangle$

    Example: ring := $\int_m^n$ **real initialization** (x) **begin** ... **end**

Finally, we allow the designation of a $\langle$procedure$\rangle$ definition (along with **real procedure, Boolean procedure,** etc.) as an **S-procedure,** meaning that its value, if any, is structure-valued. Similarly, the symbol **S** used as a $\langle$type$\rangle$ means that the $\langle$variable$\rangle$ so declared is structure-valued.

    The definition of the procedure *higher-array* given at the end of the previous section would now be written correctly in this syntax as follows:

S-procedure *higher-array*(n, A, z); **integer** n; **array** A; **S** z;

    begin integer j, $[z]$**array** := $\sum_{A[1]} z$;

        for j := 2 **step** 1 **until** n **do** $[z]$**array** := $\sum_{A[j]} [z]$**array end**;

    higher-array := $[z]$**array end**

The specification for **threaded-list** given earlier now becomes

threaded-list := $\int_1^\infty$ **(integer, name) initialization**(x) **begin (car x)**$[1]$:= 3;

    (car x)$[2]$:= x **end**;

The $\langle$identifier$\rangle$ after the symbol **initialization** names the $\langle$identifier$\rangle$ being declared a threaded list, thus allowing the name to appear in the initialization program. If two or more variables, e.g., y and z, were declared to be **threaded-list,** then an initialization program would be generated for each:

begin (car y)$[1]$:= 3; **(car** y)$[2]$:= y **end**;
begin (car z)$[1]$:= 3; **(car** z)$[2]$:= z **end**;

The interpretation to be given $\sum_{[m:n](j)}^k$ or $\int_{[m:n](j)}^k$, which the syntax allows, is the following: An initial vector or list, respectively, of $n - m + 1$ elements is to be provided whose components are numbered m, $m + 1$, ..., n. If a reference is ever made to a component farther out in the list than position n, then j additional elements are to be added, and this is to be repeated until position k is reached. It is expected that

$$k - (m - n + 1)$$

will be a multiple of j. For example, one might work with a table of values which will ordinarily contain fewer than 200 entries of the form (**integer,** $\sum_2$ **real**), numbered 0, 1, 2, ..., 199. Should it fill up, however, additional spaces are to be added, 50 at a time, up to 399. Then the structure will be

$$\textbf{table} := \sum_{[0:199](50)}^{399} (\textbf{integer}, \sum_2 \textbf{real})$$

As before, if j is omitted, we take it to be 1.

3.7 THE PRIMITIVE MACHINE STRUCTURES

It is certainly possible to have "machines" in which all data are stored in lists (see [11], for example), or in strings, or in vectors, and so on. For example, in ALGOL the **primitive structures** are the individual variables of type **character, real, integer, Boolean,** and **name,** and arrays of an arbitrary (but fixed for each array) number of dimensions. Whatever the primitive structures may be for a particular machine, we must find a way to describe a structure generated by an ⟨S-assignment⟩ in terms of those primitive structures. Moreover, it is important that an algorithmic activity (or even better, an algorithm) be given for generating such descriptions. In fact, we shall wish to write entire ⟨program⟩s in the notations appropriate to our structures, and we shall expect that each of the following steps should be carried out automatically:

1. Each defined structure should be expressed in terms of its primitive representation; i.e., when a variable is declared to have that structure, appropriate ALGOL text is substituted instead of the ⟨declaration⟩.

2. Storage allocation should be provided for ⟨variable⟩s declared to have these structures.

3. ⟨Arithmetic expression⟩s, ⟨Boolean expression⟩s, and ⟨assignment statement⟩s involving ⟨variable⟩s declared to have new ⟨type⟩s and/or structures should be recast in terms of primitive operations on the corresponding primitive structures.

It should be clear that step (3) can be carried out only if the person (or machine!) who defines the structures spells out in some detail the arithmetic he wishes to carry out on them. The arithmetic is not determined by the structure alone. This fact is clear as soon as one person defines the appropriate arithmetic on the structure $\sum_2$ **real** to obtain the complex numbers, and another person defines a different arithmetic on the same structure to obtain the rational numbers. In the next chapter, a notation will be provided for expressing such definitions of arithmetic, and there an exercise will explore this distinction between complex number arithmetic and rational number arithmetic. [Exercise 4.3.7.] Our goal in the development which follows is to describe an algorithmic activity which will carry out steps (1) and (2). The strategy will be to process ⟨S-expression⟩s and declarations that involve them in such a way that they are replaced ultimately by text suitable for processing by the basic machine.

Let us leave unresolved for the moment the decision as to what the primitive machine structures are. If we can describe new structures in terms of arrays and lists in a convenient way, then whenever we choose a particular basic machine representation, we need merely represent arrays and lists in terms of the primitive structures of that machine. For example, if we choose ALGOL, with its arrays and individual variables, as our basic machine, we can represent lists in terms of arrays, say as two-element vectors, and then any structures already expressed in terms of lists and arrays are easily given ALGOL representations.

We turn then to the reduced problem of describing general structures in terms of lists and arrays. First, we observe that every structure definable by the syntax given in the previous section (except for the initializing ⟨program⟩) will be built up from one or more of the individual primitives **character, name, real, Boolean,** or **integer**† by repeated use of $\sum$ and/or $\int$, together with **name-of.** Even those structures obtained by evaluating an ⟨S-procedure⟩—which may be quite complicated in terms of the decisions needed to construct them—are built out of $\sum$ and $\int$, once they are determined. We shall thus deal explicitly with the following basic structures:

1) $\sum_{n_1} \cdots \sum_{n_r} \mathbf{y}$, with $r \geq 1$

2) $\int_{m(n)}^{N} \mathbf{y}$

3) $(\mathbf{y}_1, \ldots, \mathbf{y}_r)$, with $r \geq 1$

4) $\sum_{m(n)}^{N} \mathbf{y}$

5) $\sum_{i \to n} \sum_{A[i]} \mathbf{y}$

where $\mathbf{y}, \mathbf{y}_1, \ldots, \mathbf{y}_r$ are arbitrary structures.

---

† Here we are already anticipating our later particularization to ALGOL.

Consider first the example of an $m \times n$ array of complex numbers:

$$\mathbf{u} := \sum_m \sum_n (\mathbf{complex} := \sum_2 \mathbf{real})$$

When a declaration $\mathbf{u}\ a$ is encountered, we should expect it to be replaced by **complex array** $a[1:m, 1:n]$. It is the job of the activity we are interested in to determine that this is the appropriate interpretation for $\mathbf{u}\ a$, and this must come directly from the $\langle$S-assignment$\rangle$ above. The activity will in fact be assumed to generate the following:

$$\mathbf{u}\ a := \text{'}\mathbf{complex\ array}\ a[1:m, 1:n]\text{'};$$
$$\mathbf{complex}\ a := \text{'}\mathbf{real\ array}\ a[1:2]\text{'};$$

The single quotation marks indicate strings; the string to the right of the $:=$ is to replace the declaration on the left, i.e., act as its "definition." Such a definition is called a "declaration-context definition"; it is used for storage allocation and initialization. The syntax for these and other definition facilities will be developed in the next chapter. By the obvious substitution of the **complex** declaration into the **u** declaration, with a convention that $\langle$bound pair list$\rangle$s introduced in this way are appended to the right end of the existing list, and that all but one of a collection of consecutive occurrences of **array** are eliminated, we have

$$\mathbf{u}\ a := \text{'}\mathbf{real\ array}\ a[1:m, 1:n, 1:2]\text{'};$$
$$\mathbf{complex}\ a := \text{'}\mathbf{real\ array}\ a[1:2]\text{'};$$

We must also produce a definition for an occurrence of $a[i, j]$ or $a[i, j, k]$ in an $\langle$expression$\rangle$, if a has a structure such as $\mathbf{u}$. We call these the "path functions," or "accessing functions," since they represent the path through the structure which is needed to reach a particular element. In this example, $a[i, j]$ produces a **complex** number, while $a[i, j, k]$ produces a **real** number. We need do very little to specify the path function in these cases if the basic machine we are using is based on arrays (such as the ALGOL machine). We will see later, however, that the path functions for structures involving the $\int$-construction will be fairly complicated on an ALGOL machine. If the basic machine had lists as primitives, and not arrays, the tables would be turned. *We now declare* that we will henceforth use the ALGOL machine for our examples. Then the path functions can be expressed as follows:

$$\mathbf{u}\ a \downarrow [\mathbf{integer}\ i, \mathbf{integer}\ j] := \mathbf{complex}\ \text{'}a[i, j]\text{'};$$
$$\mathbf{u}\ a \downarrow [\mathbf{integer}\ i, \mathbf{integer}\ j, \mathbf{integer}\ k]^\dagger := \mathbf{real}\ \text{'}*a[i, j, k]\text{'};$$
$$\mathbf{complex}\ a \downarrow [\mathbf{integer}\ i] := \mathbf{real}\ \text{'}*a[i]\text{'};$$

---

† We shall no longer make any distinction between $a[i, j, k]$ and $a[i, j][k]$.

We shall provide in the next chapter a complete syntax for writing such "context definitions," as we shall call them. For the present, it is sufficient to point out that the left side of these apparent "assignment statements" represents a "context," or a pattern of text, usually involving one or more operators and one or more "typed variables." The right side starts with a "type," which is intended to be the ⟨type⟩ of the value produced by the left-side context whenever it occurs. The string which follows (indicated by single quotation marks), is the text to be substituted for the context in order to express it in terms of the basic machine, although in some cases no change in notation is needed. (This is true in the first context definition above.†) The asterisk which appears in the other two strings is used to indicate that the reduction to the basic machine is now complete for the variable a, and its ⟨type⟩ is to be considered **real** in subsequent processing, rather than its declared ⟨type⟩ **u**.

A more elaborate example, which we shall see shortly, gives rise to a path function represented by the context definition

$$\mathbf{w} \; a \; \downarrow \; [\textbf{integer} \; i] := \mathbf{y} \; \text{'}listfind(a, 5, 3, \infty, i)\text{'};$$

For example, if a ⟨program⟩ contained

$$\ldots B[j + 3] := 6; \ldots$$

where B had ⟨type⟩ **w**, then our activity would produce

$$\ldots listfind(B, 5, 3, \infty, j + 3) := 6; \ldots$$

for further processing on the ALGOL machine.

The definitions given above for declarations and the context definitions just described are examples of the more general concept of definition mentioned earlier. More specifically, context definitions will be used in the next chapter to define appropriate operators for the new data structures, and even to redefine the behavior of existing operators on existing data types. In this chapter we are more concerned with the derivation of appropriate definitions for declarations and path functions for the general data structures we have been describing.

Our first example was concerned with the case of one or more $\sum$'s of fixed dimension (i.e., no ⟨upper limit⟩ present). The next example shows how we handle structures built out of dissimilar elements, some of which may even involve other defined structures. Let **u** be given as in the last example, and let $\mathbf{v} := (\sum_3 \mathbf{u}, \textbf{Boolean})$. We then face the problem that in ALGOL all of the elements of a vector must have the same ⟨type⟩; i.e.,

---

† Henceforth, if no change is needed, and the string would merely repeat the left-side context, it will be omitted. This is necessary to avoid having our activity get into an endless repetition of the substitution of the right side for the left side.

all must be **real**, or all **integer**, etc. In such heterogeneous cases, we shall represent the structure as a vector of components of ⟨type⟩ **name**, and thus we trade the problem at hand (i.e., dissimilar elements) for another, the accessing of elements along paths involving the names so introduced. By looking at the structure of **v** as a two-component vector, we can see that the following declaration-context definitions can be produced by our activity:

> **v** a := '**name array** $a[1:2]$; **v.1** $a.1$; **Boolean** $a.2$; $a[1]$:= **name-of**$(a.1)$;
> $a[2]$:= **name-of**$(a.2)$';
> **v.1** a := '**u array** $a[1:3]$';

Here we have also had to introduce another device, the "created symbol." In this example, we created a ⟨type⟩ symbol, **v.1**, and two symbols representing ⟨variable⟩s, $a.1$ and $a.2$. If we had stopped with declaring **v** a to be '**name array** $a[1:2]$', then a declaration **v** x would generate

> **name array** $x[1:2]$

and x would be allocated only two storage locations. It is not only necessary to have two additional storage areas (i.e., for $\sum_3$ **u** and **Boolean**) allocated to x, but we must arrange to generate (or create) names for these storage areas and have them planted into the vector x. The definitions given above generate, for the declaration **v** x,

> **name array** $x[1:2]$; **u array** $x.1[1:3]$;
> **Boolean** $x.2$; $x[1]$:= **name-of**$(x.1)$;
> $x[2]$:= **name-of**$(x.2)$;

Since **u array** $x.1[1:3]$ is again a declaration, it expands further with the substitution of the definition for a **u** declaration:

> **u** a := '**real array** $a[1:m, 1:n, 1:2]$';

into

> **real array** $x.1[1:3, 1:m, 1:n, 1:2]$;

remembering that ⟨bound pair list⟩s are appended at the right.

While the symbol **v.1** eventually disappears, the symbols $x.1$ and $x.2$ must remain as a permanent part of the program, so that storage will actually be allocated for them. Created symbols are often encountered in situations where text is processed by one "evaluator" or processor, with output intended as symbolic input to another processor. In such cases, it is necessary to create names which are acceptable to the next processor, but which cannot conflict (i.e., cannot coincide) with names which may have been used in the original text and are still present. The usual device to guarantee no conflicts is to reserve one or more characters (or particular sequences of characters) for use in creating symbols. Such characters or sequences are then made illegal in symbols in the original syntax, but acceptable in the syntax of the next processor's language. Thus we now assume that ALGOL can accept a period between two otherwise legal characters as a legal character in an ⟨identifier⟩, but we do not make this use of the period available to anyone else who may be writing programs in ALGOL. We know now that symbols such as $x.1$ and $x.2$ cannot duplicate symbols already present in a program. To allow for the created ⟨type⟩ symbol **v.1**, we do not need additional assumptions about ALGOL, since **v.1** disappears before the text is handed over to the ALGOL processor. We do have to modify the syntax definition for ⟨boldface symbol⟩, however:

⟨boldface digit⟩ ::= **0** | **1** | **2** | **3** | **4** | **5** | **6** | **7** | **8** | **9**
⟨boldface integer⟩ ::= {⟨boldface digit⟩}$_1^*$
⟨boldface symbol⟩ ::= ⊔{⟨boldface character⟩}$_1^*$ {.⟨boldface **integer** ⟩}*

The path functions for **v** are now given by the following context definitions:

$$\textbf{v}\, a \downarrow [\textbf{integer}\; i] := (\textbf{v.1},\, \textbf{Boolean})[i](`a.1', `a.2')[i];$$
$$\textbf{v.1}\, a \downarrow [\textbf{integer}\; i] := \textbf{u};$$

where the two occurrences of the subscript i on the right of the first context definition are used to select a ⟨type⟩ and a string. In a particular program using **v**, if we have

$$\textbf{v}\; y; \ldots ; x := y[2]; \ldots$$

then for $y[2]$ we would be led by these path function definitions to generate $y.2$, with ⟨type⟩ **Boolean**. Similarly, for an occurrence of $y[1]$, we would generate $y.1$. But should we find $y[i]$, we would have to generate

$$(y.1, y.2)[i]$$

In this last case, there is no way to tell in advance what ⟨type⟩ to assign this expression; it will have to be considered a legal ⟨expression⟩ in contexts which need **Boolean** operands as well as in those which expect contexts of ⟨type⟩ **v.1**. Any checking for correct ⟨type⟩s in these situations will have to be delayed until the program is actually executed.

Before we move on to the next case, we should consider whether we could produce any other useful context definitions directly from the structure expression. Two additional contexts that arise very often in the use of such structures will be suggested here. These are the **Boolean**

⟨expression⟩ $a = b$, and the function evaluation $f(x)$. The ⟨expression⟩ $a = b$ will be taken as **true** if a and b have the same structure, and if corresponding elements in the structure are equal. Of course, if these elements have structure in turn, their equality is determined by the appropriate equality test for that structure.

For the structure **u** introduced above, our proposed activity can generate immediately the following context definitions.

u a = **u** b := **Boolean** 'Boolean begin Boolean t; integer i, j;
    $i \to m$ **do** $j \to n$ **do begin** $t := a[i, j] = b[i, j]$;[†]
        if $\neg t$ **then go to** L **end**; L: **r** $:= t$ **end**';
complex a = **complex** b := **Boolean** 'Boolean begin Boolean t; integer i;
    $i \to 2$ **do begin** $t := a[i] = b[i]$;
        if $\neg t$ **then go to** L **end**; L: **r** $:= t$ **end**';[‡]

It is important to understand that the values of m and n here are fixed at the time that the structure **u** is defined. If the person defining the structure had wanted m and n to be arguments, he could have written **u**(m, n). We shall see several uses of this in the next chapter. For the structure **v**, we have

$\quad$ **v** a = **v** b := **Boolean** '$a.1 = b.1 \wedge a.2 = b.2$';
$\quad$ **v.1** a = **v.1** b := **Boolean** 'Boolean begin Boolean t; integer i;
$\quad\quad$ $i \to 3$ **do begin** $t := a[i] = b[i]$;
$\quad\quad\quad$ **if** $\neg t$ **then go to** L **end**; L: **r** $:= t$ **end**';

Note that the definitions for **u**, **complex**, and **v.1** are exactly analogous, which is not surprising since all are of the $\sum$ family. One could treat $\sum_2$ and $\sum_3$ as special cases, however, by writing for **complex**, for example,

$\quad$ **complex** a = **complex** b := **Boolean** '$a[1] = b[1] \wedge a[2] = b[2]$';

We shall usually not give these special cases, except as exercises, since we are developing a general facility here. [Exercise 3.7.1 asks for $\sum_3$.] One could modify a general procedure to handle special cases for increased efficiency at a later time, but to dwell too soon on these cases would obscure the overall view.

We turn now to function evaluation. Here we envision the need to apply the function f to each element of the structure. Such a need arises,

---

† We shall use the notation $i \to m$ to mean **for** $i := 1$ **step** 1 **until** m.

‡ Although the ⟨expression⟩ $a[i, j] = b[i, j]$ in the context definition for **u** a = **u** b needs the context definition for **complex** a = **complex** b for its interpretation, the order in which they occur is unimportant, since the ⟨expression⟩ is not interpreted until after both context definitions are processed. This will be clear in the development of the next chapter.

for example, with functions which are to count occurrences of elements with certain properties, or for functions which need to modify some or all of the elements. It follows that if such a function is to be applied, then all elements of the structure which have a primitive ⟨type⟩ must have the same ⟨type⟩, namely, that which the function expects as an argument.†
Such a structure is called *homogeneous*. The structures **u** and **complex** given above are homogeneous (of primitive ⟨type⟩ **real**) but **v** is not. For homogeneous structures we can provide a context definition automatically, as follows:

real $f \oplus$ **u** $a := $ **u** 'u **begin integer** i, j;
    $i \to m$ **do** $j \to n$ **do** $r[i, j] := f \oplus a[i, j]$ **end**'; ‡
real $f \oplus$ **complex** $a := $ **complex** 'complex **begin integer** i;
    $i \to 2$ **do** $r[i] := f \oplus a[i]$ **end**';

The corresponding context definition for **v.1** is left as an exercise [3.7.2].

Suppose now that we have a structure $\mathbf{w} := \int_{5(3)}^{\infty} \mathbf{y}$, where **y** is some other structure. Since the symbol $\int$ implies the need to make string substitutions, we shall use a pure list representation. According to the lower limit on the symbol $\int$ in the ⟨S-expression⟩ for **w**, additional elements must be added to an existing **w**-list in groups of three, as needed. We therefore need a utility procedure called *getlist*(n), whose task is to generate a list of n elements and return the name of the first list element as its value. The contents (or **car**) of the list elements so generated remain undefined until they are assigned values. [Exercise 3.7.3 is concerned with the form of the *getlist* function.] We shall also need to take advantage of the way a ⟨program expression⟩ is allocated storage for its result whenever it is executed. Even if there is no result value produced, storage of the appropriate kind will be available. Thus the ⟨program expression⟩

y begin end;

does no computation, but creates a structure of ⟨type⟩ **y** into which values can subsequently be deposited. We may now exhibit the declaration-context definition for **w**.

w $a := $ 'name $a, a.1$; **integer** $a.0$; $a.1 := a := getlist(5)$;
    $a.0 \to 5$ **do begin** $car(\text{vc-of}(a.1)) := $ **y begin end**;
    $a.1 := cdr(\text{vc-of}(a.1))$ **end**';

---

† One could extend ALGOL further, as in GPL [15], to allow a function to interrogate the ⟨type⟩ of its arguments and act accordingly, but we shall not do that here.
‡ The operator symbol for function evaluation is $\oplus$.

This declaration-context definition starts off each **w**-structured variable as a list of five **y**-structured variables. The ⟨assignment⟩ whose right side is the ⟨program expression⟩

$$\textbf{y begin end}$$

assigns the name of the **y** structure thus created to the first component of the list element in each case.

Another utility procedure we shall need is the one which looks through a list x of m elements, then through additional groups of n elements, until the element with index i (from the beginning of the list) is found, or until the upper limit N is reached:

name procedure *listfind*(x, m, n, N, i); **name** x, **integer** m, n, N, i;
    begin name t; $t := x$; **if** $i > N$ **then go to** *Error*;
        if $i \le m$ **then go to** *out*;
        $i := i - m$; $t := \textbf{cdr}^{m-1}(t)$;†
        L: **if cdr**$(t) \neq \Phi$ **then begin**
            $L1$: **if** $i \le n$ **then begin** $t := \textbf{cdr}(t)$; **go to** *out* **end**
                 else $t := \textbf{cdr}^n(t)$; $i := i - n$; **go to** L **end**;
        else cdr$(t) := getlist(n)$; **go to** $L1$;
        out: *listfind* := $(\textbf{cdr}^{i-1}(t))$ **end**

Now we may give the path function for **w**:

$$\textbf{w } a \downarrow [\textbf{integer } i] := \textbf{y } \text{`}listfind(a, 5, 3, \infty, i)\text{'};$$

The equality context for **w** is given below, and the function evaluation context is left as an exercise [3.7.5].

It has probably been obvious to the reader that the simple list is a poor data structure for **w**, since the procedure *listfind* can reach the next group of n elements only by traversing the elements of the previous group one at a time. A much better structure would be one that retained, at the start of each group, the name of the next group. Since a trivial comparison between the current subscript and the group size suffices to decide between searching a particular group or bypassing it, the *listfind* procedure would be greatly improved. The structure just described, which is a list whose elements are sublists, is another case where the threaded-list representation would be very appropriate. [Exercise 3.7.6 will explore this point further.]

---

† The notation $\textbf{cdr}^{m-1}(t)$ is an abbreviation for either a function call $mcdr(m-1, x)$, which will take the **cdr** of x, $m-1$ successive times, or a ⟨program expression⟩ involving an internal iteration [Exercise 3.7.4].

The equality context for **w** is

w a = **w** b := **Boolean** 'Boolean begin name p, q; **Boolean** t; $p := a$;
    $q := b$;
    $L: t :=$ **car**(**vc-of**(p)) = **car**(**vc-of**(q)) $\land$ (**cdr**(**vc-of**(p))) = Φ $\equiv$
        cdr(**vc-of**(q)) = Φ); [†]
    if $t \land$ **cdr**(**vc-of**(p)) $\neq \Phi$ **then begin** $p :=$ **cdr**(**vc-of**(p));
        $q :=$ **cdr**(**vc-of**(q)); **go to** L **end**; **r** := t **end**';

In this definition, p and q start out being assigned the names of the lists a and b. To access the parts of these lists via **car** and **cdr**, we must therefore apply the function **vc-of** to p and q. The assignment to t computes the value **true** if the first components of the lists are equal (as defined for their ⟨type⟩s), and if both **cdr**'s are Φ or both are not Φ. Note that this definition is so constructed that the computation terminates as soon as any **false** value occurs. [Exercise 3.7.7 asks: Why test only **cdr** of p in the **if**?]

We have now seen how to generate appropriate declaration, path, equality, and function-evaluation context definitions for the following basic structures:

1) $\sum_{n_1} \cdots \sum_{n_r} \mathbf{y},$ with $r \geq 1$

2) $\int_{m(n)}^{N} \mathbf{y}$

3) $(\mathbf{y}_1, \ldots, \mathbf{y}_r),$ $r > 1$

where $\mathbf{y}, \mathbf{y}_1, \ldots, \mathbf{y}_r$ are arbitrary structures. We must still account for the cases which involve the **name-of** procedure explicitly [Exercise 3.7.8], the structure $\sum_{m(n)}^{N} \mathbf{y}$, and the structure $\sum_{i \to n} \sum_{A[i]} \mathbf{y}$.

If $\mathbf{z} := \sum_{m(n)}^{N} \mathbf{y}$, it is again wise to employ a threaded-list structure (as we remarked above for **w**). Since we do not have to provide for string substitutions in this case, we may allocate a vector of $m + 1$ elements initially, i.e., m locations plus one for the thread. We also need a procedure called *getvec*, which will obtain a vector of storage for us and return the name of the vector as its value:

name procedure *getvec*(m); **integer** m;
    getvec := **name-of array** $[1:m]$ **begin end**;

[†] The **Boolean** operator $\equiv$ (read "if and only if") yields the value **true** exactly when the **Boolean** values of its operands agree, i.e., when both are **true** or both are **false**.

Here we again take advantage of the ability of a structured ⟨program expression⟩ to have storage allocated for its value. In this case the "value" is indicated as having the structure of a vector, with subscript range $[1:m]$. As before, it is also necessary to have a search procedure: *vector-find*(x, m, n, N, i). This procedure will be the one to set up the threaded-list structure whenever a new vector of n components is added. Once *getvec* and *vectorfind* are available, the four basic context definitions mentioned above can be written. [Their details are developed in Exercise 3.7.9.]

Finally, suppose that we have the structure $t := \sum_{i \to n} \sum_{A[i]} y$, where A is a vector of n integers† and y an arbitrary structure not dependent on i. We shall use the term "first level of storage for y" to mean that storage pointed to when given the name of a structure of ⟨type⟩ y. We arbitrarily assume one unit (or location) of storage for each of the primitive structures, such as **real, integer,** etc., although in physical machines there may be differences in this respect. Let k be the number of storage locations needed for the first level of storage for the structure y. Thus, for the examples considered so far,

y	k
u	$2mn$
v	2
w	1
z	$m + 1$

Our strategy will be to lay out the structure t as a single vector. The first $A[1] \times k$ locations will contain the first component of the t structure, i.e., $A[1]$ copies of the first-level storage for a y structure. Then will come $A[2] \times k$ locations, etc. For the special case of a triangular **real** array, $\sum_{i \to n} \sum_i$ **real**, we have $k = 1$, and the array is simply stored "by rows," first one element, then two, etc. The total number of locations needed for the one long vector for a t structure is $k \times \sum_{i=1}^{n} A[i]$. We see then that we can generate for each y the following declaration-context definition:

$t\ a := $ 'y **array** $a[1:$**begin integer** $i, c;\ c := 0;\ i \to n$ **do**
$\quad c := c + A[i];\ \mathbf{r} := k \times c$ **end**]';

The path-function context definition from this vector layout also follows.

$t\ a \downarrow$ [**integer** i, **integer** j] $:= y$ 'a[**integer begin integer** $m, c;\ c := 0;$
$\quad m \to (i - 1)$ **do** $c := c + A[m];\ \mathbf{r} := c + j - 1$ **end**]';

---

† We could just as well use $\sum_{f(i)} y$, where f is an integer-valued ⟨procedure⟩.

The equality and function evaluation context definitions are considered in Exercise 3.7.10.

The one item not yet mentioned is the initialization program. If an initialization program is provided with a structure expression, it is understood that this program is appended to the string on the right of the declaration-context definition for that structure (after the specified ⟨variable⟩ is changed in an obvious way). [Exercise 3.7.11 asks about conflicts of names.]

We have thus made it possible to specify quite general structures and, through the mechanism of the context definition, reduce them to ⟨expression⟩s and declarations in the "basic machine language," in this case our version of ALGOL. In the next chapter we shall show, as part of an example, how **car** and **cdr** may also be defined in terms of ALGOL structures.

Before we move on to the more general problem of definitions, so that operations on these new data structures may be included as well, it is necessary to point out a source of difficulty which we have so far ignored. If a data structure is to be generated by the evaluation of an ⟨S-procedure⟩ at the time of entry to a block, the specific structure which results may very well depend on values of variables computed outside the block. While it is certainly true that during the execution of the ⟨program⟩, all such values are known, they are not necessarily known until then, i.e., until execution time. It makes a difference, therefore, whether we visualize (a) a step-by-step process in which (1) all structures are replaced by context definitions, then (2) all context definitions are replaced by "basic machine language," and (3) the program is then executed; or (b) a process in which all of these steps take place during a single step of "program evaluation." In (a), the values of variables determined outside the block are not known during step (1), while in (b) they are always known. Such questions of "evaluation time" must eventually be faced. We can certainly say at this point that any structures given explicitly, such as **t**, **u**, **v**, **w**, and **z** above, do not involve such questions and are treated the same way under either point of view.

EXERCISES 3.7

1. Give the context definition for **triple** a = **triple** b where **triple** x := 'real array $x[1:3]$'.

2. Give the context definition for functional evaluation applied to ⟨type⟩ **v.1**.

3. Write the program for the *getlist* function which generates a list of n elements and returns the name of the first list element as its value.

4. Give the procedure $mcdr(n, x)$ which will take the **cdr** of x for n successive times.

5. Give the context definition for function evaluation applied to type **w**.

6. Using a threaded-list representation for the structure $\mathbf{w} := \int_{m(n)}^{\infty} \mathbf{y}$, give the following:

  a) the procedure *getthreadedlist*(n);

  b) the procedure *threadedlistfind*(x, m, n, N, i);

  c) a declaration-context definition for **w**;

  d) a path function for **w**.

7. In the equality context definition for **w**, why is it unnecessary to test

$$\textbf{if } t \wedge \textbf{cdr(vc-of}(p)) \neq \Phi \wedge \textbf{cdr(vc-of}(q)) \neq \Phi \textbf{ then} \ldots$$

to determine when to end?

8. Suppose that $\mathbf{v} := (\sum_3 \textbf{name-of(u)}, \textbf{Boolean})$ and $\mathbf{z} := \int_{3(5)}^{\infty} \textbf{name-of(y)}$. Give the declaration-context definitions for **v** and **z**.

9. For the structure $\mathbf{z} := \sum_{m(n)}^{N} \mathbf{y}$, give the following:

  a) the procedure *vectorfind*(x, m, n, N, i);

  b) a declaration-context definition;

  c) a path function;

  d) an equality context definition;

  e) a function-evaluation context definition.

10. For the structure $\mathbf{t} := \sum_{i \to n} \sum_{A[i]} \mathbf{y}$, give the following:

  a) an equality context definition;

  b) a function-evaluation context definition.

11. Suppose that we want to append an initialization program of the form

$$\textbf{initialization } (a) \textbf{ begin integer } b, c; \ b \to m \textbf{ do } c \to n \textbf{ do } a[b, c] := 0 \textbf{ end}$$

to the declaration-context definition $\mathbf{s}\, a := \text{`} \textbf{real array } a[1:m, 1:n]\text{'}$. What happens if we come across a declaration $\mathbf{s}\, b$ or $\mathbf{s}\, c$? What must be changed in the initialization program?

CHAPTER FOUR
DEFINITIONS

4.1 INTRODUCTION

In Chapter 3 we described an algorithmic activity which replaced structure expressions by context definitions, and thus allowed ultimate processing by an ALGOL processor. We now need to formalize the form and processing of context definitions so that they become part of a general definition facility within which many kinds of changes can be introduced into the ALGOL language.

Definitions have always been used to suppress the reiteration of constant information. The use of the word "equilateral" allows one to discuss a collection of triangles without mentioning each time that the three sides are equal. Similarly, the historian introduces the term "feudal" to imply a large body of social and economic conditions prevalent in some areas at certain times. In this same spirit we have written $\mathbf{u} := \sum_m \sum_n (\mathbf{complex} := \sum_2 \mathbf{real})$ so that a declaration $\mathbf{u}\ x$ will imply a great deal of information about x without our having to write it explicitly. The detail of the iteration needed to compute $f(x)$, where f is a **real** procedure and x has structure $\mathbf{u}$, is always of the same form (see Chapter 3), and we are able to suppress it when we write simply $f(x)$.

On the other hand, if everyone always used the structure $\mathbf{u}$, we could have built it into the ALGOL language permanently. It is precisely because one cannot predict in advance which information is to be constant —and therefore suppressed—that one needs a general facility for constructing definitions. Each problem area will find its own natural data structures,† and the detail involved in using these structures will be so constant as to demand suppression by definitions. Beyond the definitions which we were able to generate directly from the structure expression, however, it must be possible to write new definitions easily for ⟨arithmetic expression⟩s and other contexts as well. At the very least, we must provide a way to escape from the possible tyranny represented by such automatic generation of definitions; we must be able to specify alternatives to them. We must also make it possible to specify alternatives to the initial specifications of ALGOL itself, since these too represent a form, however benevolent, of tyranny.

There are two distinct stages in the use of definitions: (1) the specification of the new context to be recognized, together with the ⟨string⟩ to be used as its definition; and (2) the handling of occurrences of the newly defined context in subsequent text. These two stages are quite analogous to the "definition" and "call" of a ⟨procedure⟩, and we shall sometimes refer to (2) as a "call" for a defined context. But what language is to be

---

† Just as we were led to the use of threaded lists for $\mathbf{w}$ and $\mathbf{z}$ in the preceding chapter.

used to specify definitions? Even worse, since definitions are introduced precisely for the purpose of changing the language, what is the language in which newly defined contexts are to be called? Finally, what is the scope of a definition? For how long is it in effect?

It is clear from the syntax of ALGOL that we cannot write a context definition in that language. We must extend the syntax of ALGOL at least far enough to allow context definitions. With regard to scope, it is most convenient to use the existing ⟨block⟩ structure of ALGOL, since there are already several parts of the language dependent on the ⟨block⟩ structure. To be more specific, we shall follow the **begin** symbol of each ⟨block⟩ by whatever ⟨S-assignment⟩s are necessary, then by any explicit context definitions we need for the arithmetic of the new structures, and then by the usual ⟨declaration⟩s and other text. Whenever we exit from a ⟨block⟩, the language reverts to what it was on entry to that ⟨block⟩. In other words, if definitions change the language for the computation in a ⟨block⟩, the change is undone when that ⟨block⟩ is terminated.

We must provide for the transition period, however. Which language is in effect during the processing of new definitions that change the language? In order to prevent chaos, *we stipulate that* definitions and structure assignments are written and understood in the language that is in force at the moment of entry to the ⟨block⟩. Only after all such definitions and structure assignments have been processed, and a new language is completely specified thereby, does that new language take effect. The ⟨declaration⟩s and other contexts which follow may (and probably will) require interpretation via the definitions just processed, i.e., as contexts in the newly defined language. It is the purpose of this chapter to describe in some detail the processing of definitions which define a new language for a ⟨block⟩, and the processing of subsequent "calls" to produce ALGOL text.

4.2 THE NEW SYNTAX ELEMENTS

In the previous chapter we saw how ⟨S-assignment⟩s could be replaced by definitions; and we now assume that some sort of "evaluator" or "processor" has preceded us, and that it has in fact eliminated ⟨S-assignment⟩s in favor of definitions. We have already indicated that definitions will be introduced at the beginning of a ⟨block⟩, i.e., as part of the ⟨block head⟩. Now it is necessary to revise the syntax of the ⟨block head⟩ to provide for such definitions, whether generated from ⟨S-assignment⟩s or written by the person who wrote the original ⟨program⟩.

⟨declaration list⟩ ::= {⟨statement⟩;}* ⟨declaration⟩ {{;⟨statement⟩}*;
    ⟨declaration⟩}*
⟨new syntax element⟩ ::= ⟨declaration-context definition⟩ | ⟨context
    definition⟩ | ⟨set definition⟩ | ⟨new operator declaration⟩
⟨new syntax list⟩ ::= ⟨new syntax element⟩ {;⟨new syntax element⟩}*
⟨block head⟩ ::= **begin** ⟨new syntax list⟩; ⟨declaration list⟩; |
    begin ⟨declaration list⟩; | **begin** ⟨new syntax list⟩;

The syntax of the ⟨declaration list⟩ just given may look slightly complicated; it is intended to allow any sequence of ⟨statement⟩s and ⟨declara-
tion⟩s which terminates with a ⟨declaration⟩. The reason we intermixed
⟨statement⟩s with ⟨declaration⟩s in the ⟨declaration list⟩ is that initialization sequences resulting from declaration-context definitions may introduce ⟨assignment statement⟩s (and others) before subsequent ⟨declara-
tion⟩s occur. The new syntax units ⟨set definition⟩ and ⟨new operator
declaration⟩ will be discussed shortly.

We will now move toward the formal syntax for introducing definitions. The underlying motivation throughout is to make it possible to
name a new ⟨type⟩ and, if desired, new arithmetic or logical operators.
Once these have been named, it must be possible to assimilate them into
the ALGOL language. For a new ⟨type⟩, assimilation means that one
can specify appropriate interpretations for occurrences of the ⟨type⟩
name in ⟨declaration⟩s and for occurrences of ⟨variable⟩s declared to
have that ⟨type⟩ within ⟨expression⟩s. For new operators, assimilation
means that one can specify appropriate interpretations for occurrences
of the new operator name in various contexts, such as within ⟨expres-
sion⟩s. Since we usually relate operators to other operators occurring in
the same ⟨expression⟩ by means of relative precedence, it is also necessary
to specify the precedence level of a new operator.

We shall also introduce some devices for economizing on the number
of definitions which must be provided. For example, if a number of
definitions are the same except that a particular operator is a + in one, a −
in another, a × in a third, and a new operator, **times**, in yet another, a
set can be defined:

$$\mathbf{Q} := (+, -, \times, \textbf{times})$$

and then **Q** can be used in place of the operator in a single statement of that
definition. Another example of economizing is the provision for parameters as part of a new ⟨type⟩ name. Thus one might specify a new
⟨type⟩ **polygon**(n) to represent objects intended to behave like polygons
of n sides. While we may interpret an object of ⟨type⟩ **polygon**(3) to be a
triangle, and one of ⟨type⟩ **polygon**(4) to be a quadrilateral (or, if we so

define its behavior in various contexts, a square), we may find it possible
to define some (or all) of its behavior with a few definitions given in terms
of n. We shall see various examples of this later. Of course, in declaring
a variable to have such a ⟨type⟩, a specific value of n must be specified, as
in

$$\textbf{polygon}(4) \; y; \; \textbf{polygon}(3) \; z;$$

The ⟨declaration⟩

$$\textbf{polygon}(r) \; z;$$

would certainly be permitted if r already had a value from its occurrence
outside the ⟨block⟩ containing this ⟨declaration⟩.

   With this as motivation, we shall present the syntax which is needed,
and follow that with a more detailed discussion.

   The syntax for introducing ⟨type⟩s:

⟨fixed type⟩ ::= **real** | **Boolean** | **integer** | **name** | **character**
⟨basic new type⟩ ::= ⟨boldface symbol⟩ | ⟨fixed type⟩
   Example: matrix
   The syntax for ⟨new syntax element⟩:

1. for ⟨new operator declaration⟩:

⟨precedence relation⟩ ::= ⟨ | = | ⟩
⟨operator⟩ ::= ⟨boldface symbol⟩ | ⟨arithmetic operator⟩ |
      ⟨logical operator⟩ | ⟨relational operator⟩ | , | ↓ | ⊕
   Example: T
⟨current operator⟩ ::= ⟨operator⟩
⟨new operator⟩ ::= ⟨operator⟩
⟨new operator declaration⟩ ::= ⟨new operator⟩ ⟨precedence relation⟩
      ⟨current operator⟩ | ⟨operator set name⟩ ⟨precedence relation⟩
      ⟨current operator⟩
   Example: T = ÷

2. For ⟨set definition⟩:

⟨operator set name⟩ ::= ⟨boldface symbol⟩
⟨operator list element⟩ ::= ⟨operator⟩ | ⟨operator set name⟩
   Example: R1
⟨operator list⟩ ::= ⟨operator list element⟩ {,⟨operator list element⟩}*
   Example: B, <
⟨operator set definition⟩ ::= ⟨operator set name⟩ := (⟨operator list⟩)
   Example: R1 := (>, <, =, ≥, ≤, ≠)

⟨context type set name⟩ ::= ⟨boldface symbol⟩

⟨context type list element⟩ ::= ⟨context type⟩ | ⟨context type set name⟩
> **Example: arith**

⟨context type list⟩ ::= ⟨context type list element⟩ {,⟨context type list element⟩}*
> **Example: real, integer**

⟨context type set definition⟩ ::= ⟨context type set name⟩ := (⟨context type list⟩)
> **Example: any := (arith, Boolean)**

⟨set definition⟩ ::= ⟨operator set definition⟩ | ⟨context type set definition⟩
> **Example: any := (arith, Boolean)**

3. For ⟨context definition⟩:

⟨formal type parameter⟩ ::= ⟨formal parameter⟩ | ⟨basic new type⟩
> **Example: v**

⟨formal type parameter list⟩ ::= ⟨formal type parameter⟩ {,⟨formal type parameter⟩}*
> **Example: u, v, integer**

⟨context type⟩ ::= ⟨basic new type⟩ | ⟨boldface symbol⟩ (⟨formal type parameter list⟩) | ⟨context type set name⟩
> **Example: matrix(p, u, v)**

⟨result type⟩ ::= ⟨context type⟩
> **Example: matrix(p, u, v)**

⟨context typed identifier⟩ ::= ⟨context type⟩⟨identifier⟩
> **Example: matrix(p, u, v) b**

⟨current context operator⟩ ::= ⟨operator⟩ | ⟨operator set name⟩
> **Example: A**

⟨basic context⟩ ::= ⟨context typed identifier⟩ | (⟨context⟩)
> **Example: (real a ↓ [integer i])**

⟨subscripted context⟩ ::= ⟨basic context⟩ | ⟨subscripted context⟩ ↓ [⟨context typed identifier⟩]
> **Example: complex** a ↓ **[integer i]**

⟨context⟩ ::= ⟨subscripted context⟩ | ⟨current context operator⟩ ⟨subscripted context⟩ | ⟨subscripted context⟩ ⟨current context operator⟩ ⟨subscripted context⟩ | **if** ⟨context⟩ **then** ⟨subscripted context⟩ **else** ⟨context⟩
> **Example: if Boolean** a **then integer** b **else integer** c

⟨left side⟩ ::= ⟨context typed identifier⟩ | ⟨left side⟩ ↓ [⟨context typed identifier⟩]
> **Example: real** b ↓ **[integer i]**

⟨assignment context⟩ ::= ⟨left side⟩ := ⟨context⟩
  Example: matrix a := **matrix** b
⟨context definition⟩ ::= {⟨context⟩ | ⟨assignment context⟩} := ⟨result
  type⟩ {⟨string⟩ | ⟨empty⟩}
  Example: complex a := **complex** b := **complex** 'begin $a[1]$:= $b[1]$;
  $a[2]$:= $b[2]$ **end**'
⟨declaration-context definition⟩ ::= ⟨context typed identifier⟩ :=
  ⟨string⟩
  Example: complex a := '**real array** $a[1:2]$'

As we indicated earlier, the use of set names is a device for allowing
one ⟨context definition⟩ to apply to many cases. Set names are allowed
as ⟨formal type parameter⟩s, as ⟨operator⟩s in ⟨context definition⟩s,
etc., with the understanding that the processing of a ⟨new syntax element⟩
which involves one or more set names always begins by generating all of
the possible copies of that ⟨new syntax element⟩ which can be obtained
by replacing all occurrences of a set name by an element of its set, chosen
in all possible ways. If a particular set name occurs in several places in
one ⟨new syntax element⟩, the same representative is used for each occurrence.† As an example, suppose that we define the set **A** by the set definition **A** := (+, −). Then the ⟨context definition⟩

  complex a **A complex** b := **complex** '**complex**$(a[1]$ **A** $b[1], a[2]$ **A** $b[2])$';

generates two ⟨context definition⟩s which are used in its stead:

  complex a + **complex** b := **complex** '**complex**$(a[1] + b[1], a[2] + b[2])$';
  complex a − **complex** b := **complex** '**complex**$(a[1] - b[1], a[2] - b[2])$';

Note the form of each of these context declarations: (1) a ⟨context⟩,
e.g., **complex** a + **complex** b; (2) a ⟨result type⟩, e.g., **complex**; and (3)
a ⟨string⟩, e.g., '**complex**$(a[1] + b[1], a[2] + b[2])$'. This ⟨string⟩ happens
to contain an ⟨arithmetic enumerated expression⟩ with ⟨type⟩ **complex.**
We will need to specify in some detail what kinds of ⟨string⟩s we can allow
in ⟨context definition⟩s. They certainly cannot be arbitrary strings; what
they can be will become clearer as we see how they are used.

In the example of **complex** number addition just given, we see a definition of the behavior of an existing ⟨operator⟩, +, on two operands with
the new type **complex.** An interesting possibility may occur to the reader.
Suppose that the ⟨context⟩ were

  real a + **real** b

---

† This is similar to the rule for generic variables in the Markov algorithm rules in
Chapter 1.

Would this allow the $\langle$string$\rangle$ on the right side of the $\langle$context definition$\rangle$ to introduce a nonstandard meaning for **real** addition? It is clear that it could, and in fact, this is quite a handy thing to do sometimes. The exercises will look at this situation in more detail. [Exercise 4.2.1 considers a new rounding operation.]

It is probably true that there aren't enough existing $\langle$operator$\rangle$s for defining a completely new arithmetic. For **complex** arithmetic, for example, we wish to define not only **complex** addition, multiplication, division, and exponentiation, but also conjugation, the computation of the magnitude and the argument, and so on. We must be able to bring in new operators, and first of all, we must be able to name them. As part of the syntax, then, we have $\langle$operator$\rangle$s, which include $\langle$boldface symbol$\rangle$s as well as the standard operators and $\downarrow$ and $\oplus$, with $a \downarrow [i]$ given the interpretation $a[i]$, and $f \oplus (x)$ meaning $f(x)$.

Suppose then that one may write **conj** a, meaning the conjugate $(a[1], -a[2])$ of the **complex** number $(a[1], a[2])$ in our representation using pairs of **real** numbers. Then the question of relative precedence of $\langle$operator$\rangle$s must be settled. For example, do we mean by

$$\text{\textbf{conj}} \ a + b$$

the expression (**conj** a) $+ b$ or the expression **conj**$(a + b)$? We undoubtedly prefer the former interpretation, and we describe this by saying that **conj** has "higher precedence" than $+$. In other words, just as in Section 2.10 we gave the precedence table for ALGOL,

$$
\begin{array}{l}
\uparrow \\
\times \ / \ \div \\
+ \ - \\
< \ \leq \ = \ \neq \ > \ \geq \\
\neg \\
\wedge \\
\vee
\end{array}
$$

so we now must make it possible to establish the position of each $\langle$new operator$\rangle$ in the table. This is accomplished by the $\langle$new operator declaration$\rangle$, such as: **conj** $> +$. This would cause **conj** to be entered (by the processor of the ALGOL language) on a new line of the precedence table *immediately above* the line containing $+$. We require that every $\langle$new operator$\rangle$ have its precedence ranking declared in this way; it follows that we can always supply missing parentheses, even when $\langle$new operator$\rangle$s are involved. [Exercise 4.2.2 asks that missing parentheses be supplied in a few examples.]

EXERCISES 4.2

1. Assume that normal operation for the assignment **integer** $a := $ **real** b is truncation (that is, **integer** $a := $ **real** $b := $ **integer** '$a := [b]$' for $b \geq 0$, and **integer** $a := $ **real** $b := $ **integer** '$a := [b] + 1$' for $b < 0$, where the brackets represent the "greatest integer" function).

a) Give a context definition which will cause **real** values to be "rounded up" to the next highest integer whenever an assignment context is encountered.

b) Give a context definition which will round **real** numbers as follows:
   1) If the fractional part of the **real** number is less than .5, round down (i.e., truncate).
   2) If the fractional part of the **real** number is greater than .5, round up.
   3) If the fractional part is exactly .5, round down if the integer part of the **real** number is even, but round up if the integer part is odd.

2. Using the ALGOL precedence table along with the ⟨new operator declaration⟩s given below, supply the implied missing parentheses.

$$\oplus > \downarrow ; \uparrow < \downarrow ; \supset < \vee ; \equiv < \supset ; , < \equiv$$

a) $a + b \times c \uparrow d \div e - f$

b) $f \oplus a + b \downarrow i + c \downarrow j \uparrow d$

c) $a \wedge b < c + d \times f$

d) $a \supset b \equiv c, d \wedge e \supset f$

4.3 PROCESSING DEFINITIONS

Suppose now that we are confronted with a ⟨program⟩ containing definitions.† Thus there are ⟨set definition⟩s, ⟨new operator declaration⟩s, and ⟨context definition⟩s at the ⟨head⟩ of one or more ⟨block⟩s; and the text in these ⟨block⟩s calls upon these definitions. Since the definitions themselves involve ⟨expression⟩s which must be evaluated, we have stipulated that they are to be processed in the language already in force; the new language takes effect only after all definitions have been handled. The processing of the ⟨new syntax element⟩s is quite straightforward.

1. ⟨Set definition⟩s are retained in a table internal to the processor, ready for use when a set name occurs in a ⟨new operator declaration⟩ or ⟨context definition⟩.

---

† For ease of presentation, we assume that ⟨S-assignment⟩s have been processed to produce various ⟨declaration-context definition⟩s and ⟨context definition⟩s, so we do not need to deal with ⟨S-assignment⟩s at this time. It would not actually be necessary to assume that all of that processing is finished before the processing of definitions begins.

2. ⟨Context definition⟩s are entered into a table called the Context Table.† The table will be searched later from the top down, and we will stop searching whenever we find an entry which satisfies us, so the order of the entries in the table is very important.‡ Each line of the table will be labeled by one or more ⟨operator⟩s, corresponding to the lines of the precedence table. In addition, there will be the following (initially empty, but labeled) lines below the others:

> **(if then else)**:
> (: =):
> (no operator):

If we imagine each ⟨context⟩ (i.e., the left side of each ⟨context definition⟩) represented by a "tree," as shown in Fig. 4.1, we call the

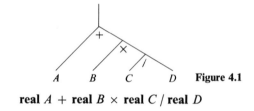

$A \qquad B \qquad C \qquad D$ **Figure 4.1**

real A + **real** B × **real** C / **real** D

highest operator (in this case, +) the "principal operator." A ⟨context definition⟩ is entered into the Context Table on the line labeled by its principal operator. [Exercise 4.3.1 asks for the principal operator of a few examples.] Now it should be clear why the three extra lines have been added to the Context Table, supplementing the lines arising from the precedence table. The lines labeled "**(if then else)**" and "(: =)" accept conditional ⟨context⟩s and ⟨assignment context⟩s, respectively, and the line labeled "(no operator)" accepts ⟨context⟩s which contain no ⟨operator⟩ at all, such as ⟨declaration-context definition⟩s. It should also be clear that a ⟨new operator declaration⟩ may force the creation of a new line in the Context Table, corresponding to its position in the precedence

---

† Because we assume that the language in effect outside the current ⟨block⟩ is to be restored on exit from the ⟨block⟩, we also assume that the Context Table, as well as other pertinent tables, is saved (i.e., pushed down) while a copy of it is modified as described here.

‡ Although we specify that the search is to proceed from top to bottom, any more efficient search technique would of course be better, provided that it successfully encountered first the "upper" of two entries which are identical with respect to the search key.

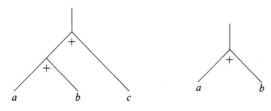

Figure 4.2

table. Should an ⟨operator⟩ already exist when a ⟨new operator declaration⟩ occurs for it, we delete its occurrence as a label on a Context Table line, together with all ⟨context⟩s in which it occurs. Then we treat it as if it were entirely new. In this way it will become possible to redefine existing ⟨operator⟩s, as we indicated earlier. [Exercise 4.3.2 explores some possibilities.]

It is not enough to say that we enter a ⟨context definition⟩ into a line of the Context Table, however. We must indicate its position relative to others already on that line. We will see later that this makes a difference only if one ⟨context⟩ has a tree which is a subtree of another ⟨context⟩'s tree; i.e., one is a subexpression of another. This can occur, for example, with ⟨context⟩s such as

$$(\textbf{integer } a + \textbf{integer } b) + \textbf{integer } c$$

and

$$\textbf{integer } a + \textbf{integer } b$$

which have the trees shown in Fig. 4.2, where one is clearly a subtree of the other. In such situations, the ⟨context⟩ associated with the subtree must be located *after* the larger ⟨context⟩ if they occur on the same line. [Exercise 4.3.3 asks how a few examples would go into the Context Table.]

We have already seen how set names and parameters have allowed us to write one ⟨context definition⟩ which implied many others. There is still another device which is useful for this purpose. In many situations, especially with very regular structures, an arithmetic operation performed on one or more of these structures is actually carried out by traversing the elements of the structures and applying the operation to individual elements only. (We saw this in Chapter 3 when we wished to apply a function f to all the elements of a structure.) As an example, we might have

$$\textbf{matrix} := \sum_m \sum_n \textbf{real}; \ \textbf{matrix } a + \textbf{matrix } b := \textbf{matrix 'matrix begin}$$
$$\textbf{integer } i, j; \ i \rightarrow m \ \textbf{do } j \rightarrow n \ \textbf{do } \textbf{r}(i, j) := a[i, j] + b[i, j] \ \textbf{end'};$$

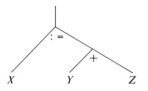

Figure 4.3

which replaces a sum of two matrices by a ⟨program expression⟩ that iterates their elements and adds them. We might also have a ⟨context definition⟩ for the ⟨assignment statement⟩

matrix a := **matrix** b := **matrix** '**begin integer** i, j; $i \to m$ **do** $j \to n$ **do**
    $a[i, j]$:= $b[i, j]$ **end**';

Suppose now that in some program the following occurs.

$$\text{\textbf{matrix} } X, Y, Z; \ldots; \quad X := Y + Z; \ldots$$

Then the ⟨assignment statement⟩ may be represented by the tree shown in Fig. 4.3. When we consider in more detail the order in which ⟨string⟩ replacements are made for ⟨context⟩s involving new ⟨type⟩s or ⟨new operator⟩s, we shall see that the principal operator (in this case, :=) is handled first. Thus, the ⟨context definition⟩ for the ⟨assignment statement⟩ is invoked first, identifying a with X and b with $Y + Z$. We shall assume that due respect is paid to precedence in replacing b by $Y + Z$, so that parentheses are inserted when necessary, as in going from $b[i, j]$ to

$$(Y + Z) \ [i, j].\dagger$$

Thus we obtain

begin integer i, j; $i \to m$ **do** $j \to n$ **do** $X[i, j]$:= $(Y + Z)[i, j]$ **end**;

It would now be unfortunate to have to substitute the entire ⟨program expression⟩ for the sum $Y + Z$, even though the resulting code would be correct:

begin integer i, j; $i \to m$ **do** $j \to n$ **do**
    $X[i, j]$:= **real array** $[1:m, 1:n]$ **begin integer** p, q; ‡
    $p \to m$ **do** $q \to n$ **do** r$[p, q]$:= $Y[p, q] + Z[p, q]$
    end$[i, j]$; **end**;

---

† The actual replacement activity will be described in terms of trees and subtrees, and the work done in the linearized form by parentheses will be implicit in the tree structure.

‡ The **integer** variables i, j of the ⟨context definition⟩ have been renamed to avoid confusion with i, j in the outer ⟨block⟩.

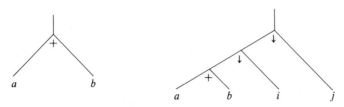

Figure 4.4

While the (i, j)-th element of the array is needed as the right side of the assignment to $X[i, j]$, we would be generating the entire array as the value of **r** before selecting the (i, j)-th element, and this would happen for each value of i and j. We need a separate (larger) ⟨context definition⟩ for the subscription of the sum of two ⟨variable⟩s of ⟨type⟩ **matrix**, as well as the one for **matrix** addition:

$$((\text{\textbf{matrix }} a + \text{\textbf{matrix }} b) \downarrow [\text{\textbf{integer }} i]) \downarrow [\text{\textbf{integer }} j] := \text{\textbf{real }} `a[i, j] + b[i, j]';$$

Then, provided we guarantee by its position in the Context Table that this ⟨context definition⟩ is used and not the earlier one, we obtain the replacement:

$$\text{\textbf{begin integer }} i, j; \ \ i \to m \text{ \textbf{do} } j \to n \text{ \textbf{do} } X[i, j] := Y[i, j] + Z[i, j] \text{ \textbf{end}};$$

which is obviously better. The guarantee comes directly from our insistence that the Context Table be searched from the top. Since the principal ⟨operator⟩s of the trees in Fig. 4.4 are $+$ and $\downarrow$, respectively, and since $\downarrow$ has a higher precedence ranking than $+$, the larger context will be found first. (This will always happen with $\downarrow$, of course.) If the two ⟨operator⟩s had happened to have the same precedence ranking, the larger context would still be selected, because we stipulated earlier that whenever one tree was a subtree of another on the same line of the Context Table, the smaller one would be entered into the table *after* the larger one. [Exercise 4.3.4 gives some ⟨context definition⟩s, and asks which are chosen first.]

We observe now that the ⟨string⟩ in the subscripted ⟨context definition⟩ is almost identical to the innermost part of the earlier one. In one case we have

$$a[i, j] + b[i, j]$$

and in the other

$$\text{\textbf{r}}[i, j] := a[i, j] + b[i, j]$$

We will see later† that the effect would have been the same if the ⟨string⟩ for the subscripted ⟨context definition⟩ had been written with the $\text{\textbf{r}}[i, j]$

---

† When we give the detailed steps involved in replacing a ⟨context⟩ by its definition.

assignment, and thus we introduce the following *notational convention*: If a string in a ⟨context definition⟩ contains boldface parentheses, i.e., **(** and **)**, with a subscripted **r** between them, then we will automatically create an additional ⟨context definition⟩ for the subscripted case. The ⟨type⟩ of the subscripted **r** must precede the boldface left parenthesis, so that the ⟨result type⟩ of the new ⟨context definition⟩ will be known. Thus, if we had written

matrix a + **matrix** b := **matrix** 'matrix begin integer i, j;
    $i \to m$ **do** $j \to n$ **do real(r**$[i, j]$:= $a[i, j] + b[i, j]$**) end**';

then we would automatically replace this one ⟨context definition⟩ by two other ⟨context definition⟩s, where the second one is obtained from the original one by deleting **real(** and **)**:

((**matrix** a + **matrix** b) ↓ [**integer** i]) ↓ [**integer** j] := **real** '**r** := $a[i, j]$
    + $b[i, j]$';
matrix a + **matrix** b := **matrix** 'matrix begin integer i, j;
    $i \to m$ **do** $j \to n$ **do r**$[i, j]$:= $a[i, j] + b[i, j]$ **end**';

[Exercise 4.3.5 asks to have it done.]

One other bit of notation that occurs in some ⟨context definition⟩ ⟨string⟩s needs explanation. We will sometimes precede an occurrence of an ⟨identifier⟩ in the ⟨string⟩ with an asterisk (∗), which has the following interpretation. A ⟨variable⟩ in a ⟨context definition⟩ ⟨string⟩ has a declared ⟨type⟩ because of its appearance as a ⟨context typed identifier⟩ in the left side of a ⟨context⟩. If this ⟨type⟩ is not itself a ⟨fixed type⟩, i.e., one of the original ALGOL ⟨type⟩s, then there is associated with it some ⟨fixed type⟩ as a result of its occurrence in a ⟨declaration-context definition⟩. We use the asterisk to indicate that once the ⟨string⟩ is used to replace a defined ⟨context⟩, that occurrence of the ⟨variable⟩ is labeled with its ⟨fixed type⟩. An example of this is

(**matrix** a ↓ [**integer** i]) ↓ [**integer** j] := **real** '∗$a[i, j]$';

Since $a[i, j]$ is the final form of this text, we indicate here that henceforth a is to have ⟨type⟩ **real array** $[1:m, 1:n]$ instead of **matrix**.

We may now give two examples of definition sets which will illustrate what we have been trying to accomplish. The first defines the built-in standard ⟨expression⟩s of ALGOL, since these must appear in the Context Table also. Note that several sets are first defined, such as **arith**, **N**, and so on. The set **any1** is defined in addition to **any** so that in a ⟨context definition⟩ such as

any a ⊕ **any1** b := **any** ;

the ⟨type⟩s of *a* and *b* do not have to be the same, and yet it is clear that the ⟨result type⟩ agrees with that of *a*. Note also that the operator ↑ is entered into the table just above **if then else,** but that all the other operators are then inserted just below ↑. They thus end up above **if then else.** (Additional notes keyed to specific elements in definitions are grouped at the end of each set.)

arith := (**real, integer**); **arith1** := (**arith**); **any** := (**arith, Boolean**);
     any1 := (**any**); M := (×, ÷); M1 := (×, /); N := (**loc-of, vc-of**);
     A := (+, −); R1 := (>, =, ≥, ≤, ≠); R := (R1, <);
     B := (∧, ∨, ⊃, ≡); ↓ > **if then else**; ⊕ > ↓ ; ↑ < ↓ ; × < ↑ ;
     ÷ = × ; / = × ; + < × ; − = + ; < < + ; R1 = < ;
     ¬ < < ; ∧ < ¬ ; ∨ < ∨ ; ⊃ < ∨ ; ≡ < ⊃ ;
arg < **if then else**; , < **arg**; N = **arg**;   [*see Note 1*]
any *a* ⊕ **any1** *b* := **any**;
any *a* ↓ [**arith** *b*] := **any**;
arith *a* ↑ **arith1** *b* := **real**; **integer** *a* ↑ **integer** *b* := **integer**; [*see Note 2*]
arith *a* **M1 arith1** *b* := **real**;
integer *a* **M integer** *b* := **integer**;   [*see Note 3*]
arith *a* **A arith1** *b* := **real**;
integer *a* **A integer** *b* := **integer**;
A arith *a* := **arith**;
arith *a* **R arith1** *b* := **Boolean**;
¬ **Boolean** *a* := **Boolean**;
Boolean *a* **B Boolean** *b* := **Boolean**;
if Boolean *a* **then Boolean** *b* **else Boolean** *c* := **Boolean**;
if Boolean *a* **then arith** *b* **else arith1** *c* := **real**;
if Boolean *a* **then integer** *b* **else integer** *c* := **integer**;
Boolean *a* := **Boolean** *b* := **Boolean**;
arith1 *a* := **arith** *b* := **arith1**;
any *a*, **any1** *b* := **any**;   [*see Note 4*]
loc-of any *a* := **name**;
any vc-of name *a* := **any**;
arg any *a* := **any**;

Note 1: The operator **arg** may be regarded as inserted automatically by the ALGOL processor after each occurrence of ⊕ and ↓ , after each comma in a list occurring in an ⟨expression⟩, and at the beginning of an ⟨enumerated expression⟩. It may be ignored most of the time, but it can be useful if one wishes to redefine the treatment of arguments.

Note 2: This line replaces one generated by the preceding line. Actually, the official ALGOL specification [8] is

"Writing *i* for a number of **integer** type, *r* for a number of **real** type, and *a* for a number of either **integer** or **real** type, the result is given by the following rules:

$a \uparrow i$ If $i > 0$, $a \times a \times \cdots \times a$ (i times), of the same type as a.
      If $i = 0$, if $a \neq 0$, 1, of the same type as a.
            if $a = 0$, undefined.
      If $i < 0$, if $a \neq 0$, $1/(a \times a \times \cdots \times a)$ (the denominator has $-i$ factors), of type **real**.
            if $a = 0$, undefined.
$a \uparrow r$ If $a > 0$, $exp(r \times ln(a))$, of type **real**.
      If $a = 0$, if $r > 0$, 0.0, of type **real**.
            if $r \leq 0$, undefined.
      If $a < 0$, always undefined."

Note 3: One of the ⟨context definition⟩s generated by this line will replace one of those generated by the line above.

Note 4: This is intended to apply to lists enclosed in parentheses or brackets occurring in ⟨expression⟩s. Commas not within parentheses (sometimes called "zero-level commas") will be recognized by the standard ALGOL processor in the usual way, as in

> **for** $i := 1$ **step** 1 **until** $j - 1$, $j + 1$ **step** 1 **until** n

The second example is that of a definition set for **complex** number arithmetic. Many of the ideas discussed earlier have been used in these definitions.

A := $(+, -)$; **Op** := (**arg, conj, magsq, itimes, isreal**);
arith := (**real, integer**); **complex** a := 'real array $a[1:2]$';   [*see Note 1*]
mag > $\uparrow$;
Op = **mag**;
complex $a \downarrow$ [**integer** i] := **real** '$*a[i]$';
complex a **A complex** b := **complex** 'complex($a[1]$ **A** $b[1]$, $a[2]$ **A** $b[2]$)';
complex a × **complex** b := **complex** 'complex($a[1]$ × $b[1]$ − $a[2]$ × $b[2]$, $a[2]$ × $b[1]$ + $a[1]$ × $b[2]$)';
complex a/**complex** b := **complex** '$(a$ × **conj** b)/**magsq** b';
magsq complex a := **real** '$a[1] \uparrow 2 + a[2] \uparrow 2$';
arg complex a := **real** '$arg(*a)$';   [*see Note 2*]
conj complex a := **complex** 'complex $(a[1], -a[2])$';
itimes complex a := **complex** 'complex $(-a[2], a[1])$';
itimes arith a := **complex** 'complex $(0, a)$';
mag complex a := **real** '$sqrt(\text{magsq } a)$';   [*see Note 2*]
arith a **A complex** b := **complex** 'complex $(a$ **A** $b[1]$, **A** $b[2]$)';

complex b **A arith** a := **complex** 'complex $(b[1]$ **A** $a, b[2])$';
arith a × **complex** b := **complex** 'complex $(a × b[1], a × b[2])$;
complex b × **arith** a := **complex** '$a × b$';
complex b/**arith** a := **complex** 'complex $(b[1]/a, b[2]/a)$';
arith a/**complex** b := **complex** '$(a × $ **conj** $b)/$**magsq** b';
complex a ↑ **integer** b := **complex** '*ciexp*(∗$a, b)$';   [*see Note 2*]
complex a ↑ **real** b := **complex** '*crexp*(∗$a, b)$';
complex a ↑ **complex** b := **complex** '*ccexp*(∗a, ∗$b)$';
integer a ↑ **complex** b := **complex** '*icexp*(a, ∗$b)$';
real a ↑ **complex** b := **complex** '*rcexp*(a, ∗$b)$';
complex a := **complex** b := **complex** 'begin $a[1]$:= $b[1]$;
     $a[2]$:= $b[2]$ **end**';
complex b := **arith** a := **complex** 'begin $b[1]$:= a; $b[2]$:= 0 **end**';
arith a := **complex** b := **arith** 'a := **mag** b';
complex a = **complex** b := **Boolean** '$a[1]$ = $b[1]$ ∧ $a[2]$ = $b[2]$';
isreal complex a := **Boolean** '$a[2]$ = 0';

Note 1: This ⟨declaration-context definition⟩ would probably have come from the structure declaration

$$\mathbf{complex} := \sum_2 \mathbf{real}$$

Note 2: Sometimes the appropriate ⟨string⟩ to use is a ⟨procedure⟩ call. We shall assume that the ⟨procedure⟩s thus invoked are available in a library of some kind.

The Context Table will contain a mixture of these two definition sets after they have been processed. The first part of it would appear as follows:

(⊕):   **real** a ⊕ **real** b := **real**;
                        real a ⊕ **integer** b := **real**;
                        real a ⊕ **Boolean** b := **real**;
                        integer a ⊕ **real** b := **integer**;
                        integer a ⊕ **integer** b := **integer**;
                        integer a ⊕ **Boolean** b := **integer**;
                        Boolean a ⊕ **real** b := **Boolean**;
                        Boolean a ⊕ **integer** b := **Boolean**;
                        Boolean a ⊕ **Boolean** b := **Boolean**;

(↓):   **real** a ↓ **real** b := **real**;
                        real a ↓ **integer** b := **real**;
                        integer a ↓ **real** b := **integer**;
                        integer a ↓ **integer** b := **integer**;
                        Boolean a ↓ **real** b := **Boolean**;
                        Boolean a ↓ **integer** b := **Boolean**;

(mag, arg, conj, magsq, itimes, isreal):

> **mag complex** a := **real** '*sqrt*(**magsq** a)';
> **arg complex** a := **real** '*arg*($*a$)';
> **conj complex** a := **complex** '**complex**($a[1]$, $-a[2]$)';
> **magsq complex** a := **real** '$a[1] \uparrow 2 + a[2] \uparrow 2$';
> **itimes complex** a := **complex** '**complex**($-a[2]$, $a[1]$)';
> **itimes real** a := **complex** '**complex**(0, a)';
> **itimes integer** a := **complex** '**complex**(0, a)';
> **isreal complex** a := **Boolean** '$a[2] = 0$';

(↑):

> **real** $a \uparrow$ **real** b := **real**;
> **real** $a \uparrow$ **integer** b := **real**;
> **integer** $a \uparrow$ **real** b := **real**;
> **integer** $a \uparrow$ **integer** b := **real**;
> **complex** $a \uparrow$ **integer** b := **complex** '*ciexp*($*a$, b)';
> **complex** $a \uparrow$ **real** b := **complex** '*crexp*($*a$, b)';
> **complex** $a \uparrow$ **complex** b := **complex** '*ccexp*($*a$, $*b$)';
> **integer** $a \uparrow$ **complex** b := **complex** '*icexp*(a, $*b$)';
> **real** $a \uparrow$ **complex** b := **complex** '*rcexp*(a, $*b$)';

(×, ÷, /):

> **real** $a \times$ **real** b := **real**;
> **real** $a \times$ **integer** b := **real**;
> **integer** $a \times$ **real** b := **real**;
> **integer** $a \times$ **integer** b := **integer**;

[Exercise 4.3.6 asks for the next few lines.]

EXERCISES 4.3

1. Give the tree and corresponding principal operator for the following:

a) $(A \div B) \times C + D$

b) $A \uparrow B \div C - D \times E$

c) $(A \div B \uparrow C) \times D$

2. a) Suppose that for statistical reasons, one wishes to have a count of the number of times a particular operation is executed in a particular program. Give ⟨context definition⟩s which will do this for **integer** addition, subtraction, multiplication, and division.

b) Suppose that one wishes to simulate a random machine error which is to occur in the low order position of a register of a decimal machine every time **integer** addition is executed. Give a ⟨context definition⟩ which will do this. [Hint: Assume that a procedure *random* exists similar to the one in Chapter 2.]

3. In which order would the following ⟨context⟩s be entered into the Context Table?

a) $a \times (b \div c)$, $a \div (b \times c \div d)$, $a \div b$

b) $a \times b$, $a \times (b \div c)$, $(a \times b) \div c$, $a \div b$

4. In which order would the following ⟨context⟩s be chosen from a Context Table?

a) $a \div (b - c)$, $a \times b$, $a - b$, $a + (b \times c)$

b) $a \times (b - c) \uparrow d$, $a \times b - c \uparrow d$, $(a \times b - c) \uparrow d$

5. Give the two ⟨context definition⟩s associated with each of the following ⟨context definition⟩s.

a) **matrix**(u, v) a + **matrix**(u, v) b := **matrix**(u, v) 'matrix(u, v) **begin integer** i; $i \rightarrow u$ **do** row(v)(r$[i]$:= $a[i]$ + $b[i]$) **end**';

b) **matrix**(u, v) a × **matrix**(v, w) b := **matrix**(u, w) 'matrix(u, w) **begin integer** i; $i \rightarrow u$ **do** row(w)(**begin** row(v) t; t := $a[i]$; r$[i]$:= $t \times b$ **end**) **end**';

6. Give the next fifteen lines of the Context Table for the definition set mixing ALGOL and **complex** arithmetic.

7. Give a set of ⟨context definition⟩s and ⟨declaration-context definition⟩s sufficient to define addition, subtraction, multiplication, and division of rational numbers. In each case, the result of one of these operations should again be a rational number. The ⟨procedure⟩ *diverr* should be invoked for division by zero.

4.4 PARSING THE TEXT

Once we have constructed the Context Table from a set of definitions, we have determined the language to be used in the current block. We shall refer to this language as ALGOL D (i.e., ALGOL with Definitions). How can we tell when text within the block is correctly written in the language ALGOL D? Before that, we might ask how we go about writing text in ALGOL D in the first place. One could give elaborate rules for generating ALGOL D statements from the entries in the Context Table [16], but a good rule of thumb is: Construct ⟨expression⟩s and ⟨assignment statement⟩s as in ALGOL, using the ⟨new operator⟩s in the natural way. If the definitions are not sufficiently complete to cover all the combinations which occur in the subsequent text, then this fact will

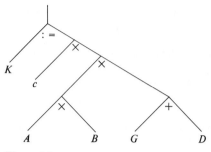

Figure 4.5

be discovered when a search of the Context Table reveals no applicable ⟨context⟩. One can then decide whether the text is illegal, or whether additional definitions are needed to cover these cases.

Suppose then that we have encountered a piece of ALGOL D text, say an ⟨assignment statement⟩ in which c is a scalar, and A, B, D, G, and K are $m \times m$ matrices:

$$K := c \times ((A \times B) \times (G + D))$$

We will find it convenient for the rest of this development to represent this text as a tree (Fig. 4.5), and we will refer to the top node of the tree as the root node. This tree is obtained by means of the precedence table, and it is equivalent to the completely parenthesized text:

$$(K := (c \times ((A \times B) \times (G + D))))$$

Because so much of our work with ⟨context⟩s involves the ⟨type⟩ of operands and subexpressions, we shall label each node of the tree (both terminal and nonterminal) with its ⟨type⟩. Using the tree obtained by means of the precedence relationships, we begin from the bottom of the tree (i.e., from the terminal nodes) and construct for each node in turn a ⟨context⟩ consisting of the operator γ at the node† and the labeled elements immediately below it. Of course, we process a node in this way only when all nodes below it have been so labeled. The entries in the Context Table on the line labeled "(γ):" are then matched against this constructed ⟨context⟩, starting from the left, i.e., larger ⟨context⟩s before any smaller subcontexts. If no match is made, the original text was illegal. Assuming that a match is made, the ⟨result type⟩ of the matching ⟨context definition⟩ is used to label the node containing γ. Let us suppose

---

† Certain obvious departures are made from this description for nodes representing delimiters, such as **begin**.

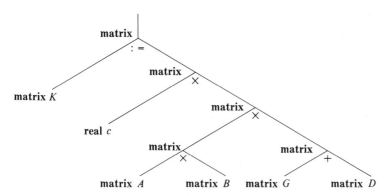

Figure 4.6

for this example that c is **real**, and A, B, D, G, and K are of type **matrix.**
Then the nodes may turn out to be labeled as shown in Fig. 4.6.† Actually,
in the interests of legibility, we shall suppress the printing of some or all
of these ⟨type⟩s whenever they are obvious or irrelevant to the discussion.
[Exercise 4.4.1 asks for the labeling of a few trees.]

　　We observe in passing that the labeling process just described guarantees that even if inconsistent definitions are introduced (as in the following
example), only one of them will be used, consistently. An example of
potentially inconsistent definitions is

$$\begin{aligned}
&\textbf{begin } (\textbf{t1 } a \times \textbf{t2 } b) + \textbf{t6 } c := \textbf{t7 } `\ldots';\\
&\qquad \textbf{t5 } a + (\textbf{t3 } b \times \textbf{t4 } c) := \textbf{t8 } `\ldots';\\
&\qquad \textbf{t1 } a \times \textbf{t2 } b := \textbf{t5 } `\ldots';\\
&\qquad \textbf{t3 } a \times \textbf{t4 } b := \textbf{t6 } `\ldots';\\
&\qquad \textbf{t1 } X;\ \textbf{t2 } Y;\ \textbf{t3 } V;\ \textbf{t4 } W;\\
&\qquad \ldots X \times Y + V \times W \ldots \textbf{ end}
\end{aligned}$$

where the last ⟨expression⟩ can apparently be assigned ⟨type⟩ **t7** or **t8**,
depending on the method of analysis. The procedure outlined above
assigns ⟨type⟩ **t7** to the ⟨expression⟩; there is no ambiguity.

　　The reduction of the text to ALGOL text now consists of the following
steps, to be considered in much greater detail later:

1. Parse the text into a tree T with labeled nodes, as described above.

2. Select a subtree S of T for which a matching ⟨context⟩ Q exists in the
Context Table.

---

† We say "may turn out" here because it depends entirely on the set of definitions
which have been used to define the current ALGOL D.

3. Using the ⟨string⟩ associated with the ⟨context⟩ Q,† construct its tree representation, and replace ⟨context typed identifier⟩s in this tree by their correspondents (via the match) from T.

4. Substitute the new tree for the subtree of T selected in (2).

Since each ⟨context definition⟩ thus invoked is written to provide a ⟨string⟩ which is "closer" to ALGOL, repeated substitutions such as are described in steps (2) through (4) eventually lead to ALGOL text.

Let us follow the progress of the example ⟨assignment statement⟩

$$K := c \times ((A \times B) \times (G + D))$$

through this process. Assume that the following ⟨context definition⟩s, among others, have been entered into the Context Table, where they appear in the order given:

a) $((\textbf{matrix } a \times \textbf{matrix } b) \downarrow [\textbf{integer } i]) \downarrow [\textbf{integer } j] := \textbf{real 'begin integer}$
     $k; \ \textbf{real} \ \ y; \ y := 0; \ k \rightarrow m \ \textbf{do} \ \ y := y + a[i][k] \times b[k][j];$
     $\textbf{r} := y \ \textbf{end'};$

b) $((\textbf{real } a \times \textbf{matrix } b) \downarrow [\textbf{integer } i]) \downarrow [\textbf{integer } j] := \textbf{real } 'a \times b[i][j]';$

c) $((\textbf{matrix } a + \textbf{matrix } b) \downarrow [\textbf{integer } i]) \downarrow [\textbf{integer } j] := \textbf{real } 'a[i][j] +$
     $b[i][j]';$

d) $(\textbf{matrix } a \downarrow [\textbf{integer } i]) \downarrow [\textbf{integer } j] := \textbf{real } '*a[i,j]';$

e) $\textbf{matrix } a := \textbf{matrix } b := \textbf{matrix 'begin integer } i, j;$
     $i \rightarrow m \ \textbf{do} \ j \rightarrow m \ \textbf{do} \ a[i][j] := b[i][j] \ \textbf{end'};$ ‡

The detailed rules for making the replacement will follow shortly; in the rest of this section we discuss their effect on the assignment

$$K := c \times ((A \times B) \times (G + D))$$

---

† We shall see later that the selection process of step (2) always results in a ⟨context⟩ for which a ⟨string⟩ has been provided.

‡ This set of ⟨context definition⟩s does not provide a correct ALGOL program when the same matrix appears on both sides of the $:=$ symbol, if it appears on the right side in a context other than as the leftmost factor in a product. For example, $B := A \times B \times C$ would give incorrect results for B, but $A := A \times B \times C$ would work correctly. This happens because the statements that are generated for the ⟨assignment⟩ $B := A \times B \times C$ cause intermediate values to be stored in B, and then these values are used in subsequent computation as if they were the original values. [Exercise 4.6.2 gives an example of this.] Such a restriction does not imply that these definitions are "wrong." One could of course give alternative definitions to avoid this behavior, but then other undesirable effects might be introduced. As long as the troublesome case mentioned above is avoided in writing ALGOL D ⟨program⟩s, the definitions given above are perfectly acceptable. This precaution only emphasizes the personal nature of the choice of definitions.

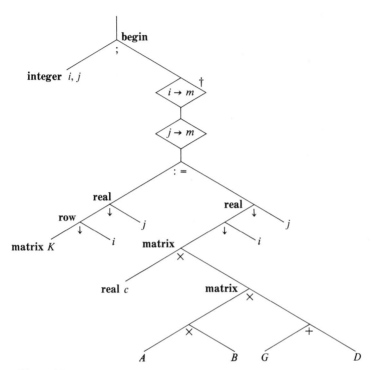

Figure 4.7

Starting from the top of the tree which we constructed above, we find
a matching ⟨context⟩ in (e), with **matrix** *a* corresponding with *K*, and
matrix *b* with the rest of the ⟨expression⟩. Substituting the ⟨string⟩
from the right side of (e), the tree becomes that shown as Fig. 4.7.‡ The
branch involving *K* matches (d), and we now label *K* **real** because of the
asterisk. On the right of the assignment we have an instance of (b), with
real *a* matched with *c*, **matrix** *b* matched with $(A \times B) \times (G + D)$, etc.
Now the assignment part of the tree is as shown in Fig. 4.8. Next we apply
(a), and we obtain Fig. 4.9, which is the tree representation for the text

$K[i, j] := c \times$ **begin integer** k; **real** y; $y := 0$;
    $k \to m$ **do** $y := y + (A \times B)[i][k] \times (G + D)[k][j]$; **r** $:= y$ **end**;

---

† This is the notation for the ⟨for clause⟩. We omit the **do**.
‡ We assume that there is a ⟨context⟩ in the table:

matrix $a \downarrow$ **[integer** i**]** $:=$ **row**;

so that the node just above *K* in the tree can be labeled. Since there is no ⟨string⟩
associated with it, it is not involved in the replacement activity once the tree is labeled.

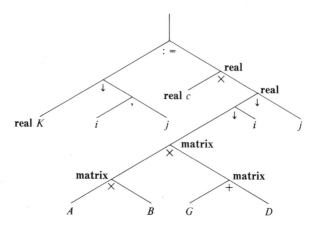

Figure 4.8

We may now observe that the assignment has the form

$$K[i,j] := c \times \langle \text{program expression} \rangle;$$

or, more explicitly,

$$K[i,j] := c \times \textbf{real begin} \ldots; \ \textbf{r} := y \ \textbf{end};$$

Whenever this form occurs, there is a potential waste of storage, since **r** must be assigned storage, but it is needed only long enough for the value to be used in combination with other parts of the ⟨expression⟩, in this case with *c*. While only one storage location is needed for **r** in this example, it is easy to find similar examples in which **r** has the structure **matrix,** or any of the structures **u, v, w, t,** or **z** of the preceding chapter, and the overhead thus incurred is considerable. The remedy is to "move the external context inside the ⟨program expression⟩," so that it becomes the context of that part of the program which computes **r**. Then **r** is no longer needed; in fact, the ⟨program expression⟩ becomes an ordinary ⟨block⟩. For our current example, the effect is

$$\textbf{begin} \ldots; \ K[i,j] := c \times y \ \textbf{end};$$

Since we are leaving the details of the replacement rule until later, let us simply exhibit the tree that results from this transformation (Fig. 4.10), remembering that this is still only the assignment part of the original tree. Another advantage of moving the context inside the ⟨program expression⟩ is that if any additional iterations are introduced by subsequent replacements involving the context, they are inside the resulting ⟨block⟩ and affect only a small part of it. The rest of the ⟨block⟩ is no longer included in these iterations. This advantage is not apparent in the current

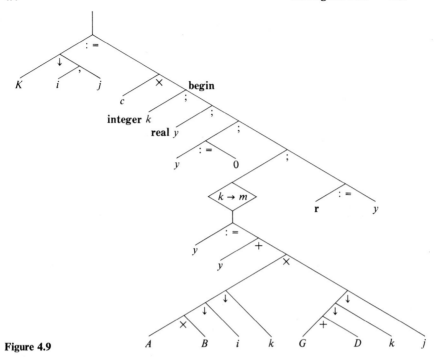

Figure 4.9

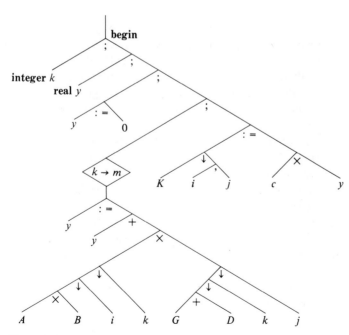

Figure 4.10

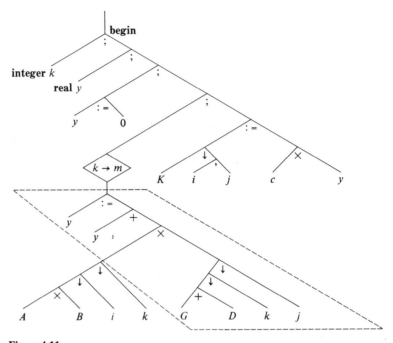

Figure 4.11

example, since the assignment $K[i, j] := c \times y$ already involves only
real numbers. If $K[i, j]$, c, and y were matrices, for example, so that the
assignment to $K[i, j]$ would eventually be replaced by an iteration statement, the difference in the two cases would become clearer. The exercises
will develop this point further. As it is, this assignment needs no further
attention, and we focus our attention on the scope of the ⟨for clause⟩
involving k.

We see from (c) that the tree for $(G + D)[k][j]$ is replaced by the tree
for $G[k][j] + D[k][j]$. To the tree for $(A \times B)[i][k]$ we apply (a), and
again move the context inside. The context involved this time is indicated
by dotted lines in Fig. 4.11. [Exercise 4.4.2 asks for the details of the match
in applying (a).] This part of the tree is shown in Fig. 4.12. By applying
(d) four times (for A, B, G, and D), we can now reduce everything to the
form of ⟨expression⟩s involving **real** numbers, and since the definitions
we use haven't redefined the behavior of the ⟨operators⟩ involved here
with respect to **real** operands, the replacement process terminates. Putting
the pieces together, we obtain the entire tree shown in Fig. 4.13. Thus,
the ⟨assignment statement⟩

$$K := c \times ((A \times B) \times (G + D));$$

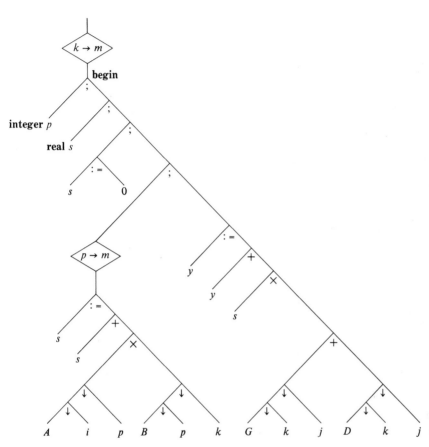

Figure 4.12

has been expanded into

begin integer i, j;
    $i \to m$ **do** $j \to m$ **do begin integer** k;   **real** y; $y := 0$;
        $k \to m$ **do**
            begin integer p;   **real** s; $s := 0$;
               $p \to m$ **do** $s := s + A[i, p] \times B[p, k]$;
                  $y := y + s \times (G[k, j] + D[k, j])$ **end**;
                  $K[i, j] := c \times y$ **end end**;

[Exercise 4.4.3 asks that others be done using (a) through (e).] The
functional parts of the expanded code are easily discerned: (1) The
p-iteration produces as the value of s the $[i, k]$-th element of the product
$A \times B$. (2) The k-iteration produces a value for y by accumulating the

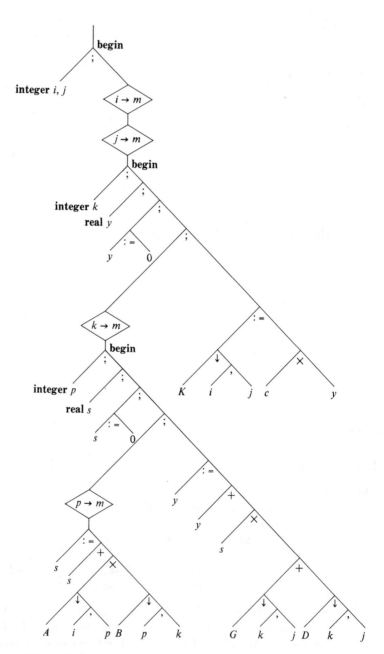

Figure 4.13

product of this $[i, k]$-th element and of the $[k, j]$-th element of $G + D$. (3) The value of y is then multiplied by c to yield the $[i, j]$-th element of K.

EXERCISES 4.4

1. Give the tree (with labeled nodes) for the statement

$$c := (a \times \textbf{conj } b)/\textbf{magsq } b;$$

where

a) a and b are **complex** and c is **real**.

b) a is **real** and b and c are **complex**.

2. Give the tree representation of the example expanded into ALGOL in this section, after the matching of $(A \times B)[i][k]$ to ⟨context definition⟩ (a), but before the context is moved inside.

3. Give the tree expansions for the following:

a) $K := (A + B) \times (C + D)$

b) $K := (A \times B) + (C \times D)$

where A, B, C, and D are $m \times m$ matrices. For the present, do not move contexts inside. [Exercise 4.5.1 asks for this after a more explicit description of the process is given.]

4.5 THE REPLACEMENT RULE

We give here a more detailed description of the replacement rule which we used in the preceding section. This rule includes (1) the matching process by which a ⟨context definition⟩ is selected from the Context Table, (2) substitution after a match is made, (3) moving of the context inside a ⟨program expression⟩, and (4) selection of a particular component of an ⟨enumerated array expression⟩ to eliminate redundant subtrees. The last item, which we have not yet illustrated, refers to the replacement of an expression of the form

$$(x + y, \ldots, \ldots, \ldots) [1] \qquad \text{by} \qquad x + y$$

(It is somewhat more complicated when several subscripts are present, but the treatment described below is quite straightforward.)

We shall define the "natural ordering" among the nodes of a tree as follows: The root node is selected first. In general, after some node of the tree has been selected, the next node to be selected is its leftmost "son"†

---

† The terms "son", "father", "sibling", etc., are commonly used with trees. Their meanings should be obvious.

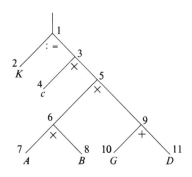

Figure 4.14

or, if it has none, its next right sibling. If it has neither of these, we select the first right sibling of the most recent ancestor that has one. If there is none, the selection process terminates. As an example of this ordering, the first tree exhibited for the previous example (Fig. 4.6) is shown in Fig. 4.14 with its nodes numbered in order of selection.

Continuing with new terminology, suppose that we are given a tree to which we wish to apply the replacement rule. Since one of the activities we shall be doing is "moving the context inside" a ⟨program expression⟩, we must be able to identify this context. To each subtree S representing a ⟨program expression⟩ we associate a unique subtree $max(S)$, determined as follows: From the root node of S, move through the ancestors of S until a node is encountered containing one of the following: ↓, **begin**, a ⟨for clause⟩, **arg**, a comma, ⊕, or a semicolon. Taking the last node not on the above list as root node, the subtree thus determined is $max(S)$. This represents the largest subtree containing S which is still an ⟨expression⟩ or an ⟨assignment statement⟩.

We also define $b(S)$ to be the tree obtained from $max\ (S)$ when S is re-placed by a special terminal character Σ, and we define R to be the subtree representing the ⟨assignment statement⟩ in S that assigns a value to **r**:

$$\mathbf{r} := \Psi$$

Figure 4.15 illustrates this terminology as superimposed on Fig. 4.9. It will be seen that $b(S)$ represents the context that we wish to move inside, and R signals the place to which $b(S)$ is to be moved.

A ⟨context type⟩ α and an ⟨actual type⟩ β are said to "agree" if (1) they are the same ⟨actual type⟩, *or* (2) they have the same ⟨boldface symbol⟩ and the same number of parameters, *and* if the parameters of α which are ⟨basic new type⟩s are identical as ⟨string⟩s to the corresponding parameters in β. Thus the ⟨context type⟩ **matrix(complex,** m, n**)** would

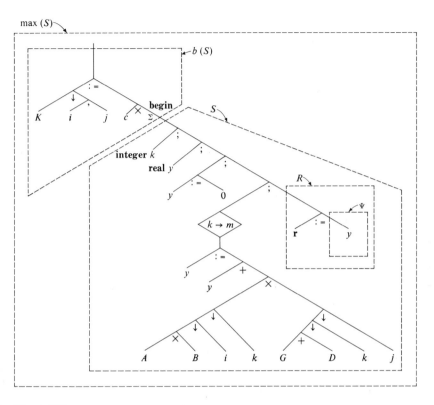

Figure 4.15

match the ⟨actual type⟩ **matrix(complex, 3, 5)**, but **matrix(real,** m, n**)** would not.

A subtree T_1 and context tree T_2 are said to "match" if and only if (1) the ⟨type⟩s of their root nodes agree, *and* (2) *either* the root of T_2 is a terminal, *or* both root nodes are labeled with the same ⟨operator⟩ and have the same number of branches, and corresponding branches represent matching subtrees. Throughout the entire test for a match, all occurrences of a specific ⟨formal type parameter⟩ in T_2 must match the same ⟨actual type parameter⟩ in T_1. It was with this definition in mind that we said, in the example of the preceding section, that the tree for the ⟨assignment statement⟩

$$K := c \times ((A \times B) \times (G + D))$$

matched the tree for the ⟨context⟩

$$\textbf{matrix } a := \textbf{matrix } b$$

We now state *the convention* that in finding a matching ⟨context⟩ for a subtree, the scan of the Context Table is from top to bottom and, within each line, from left to right; the first ⟨context⟩ reached whose context tree matches the subtree is chosen.

We are ready at last to consider the general replacement rule, for which we outlined the steps earlier. In case any ⟨program expression⟩s occurred in the original tree, or now appear as a result of a preceding step,† we first move the context inside, as we did in the example. Our goal here is to eliminate as many occurrences of **r** as possible. The detailed description of this is as follows:

Let S be the first subtree (according to the natural ordering) representing a ⟨program expression⟩ such that $S \neq max(S)$, i.e., for which there is a context to be moved inside. If there is none, we terminate this step. If we have found such a subtree S, let R be the subtree representing the ⟨assignment statement⟩ in S whose left side contains the result **r** of S, and whose right side is an ⟨expression⟩ Ψ, as defined earlier. Then do the following steps in turn:

1. Replace the subtree R by $b(S)$.

2. Replace the Σ introduced as part of $b(S)$ by the subtree Ψ.

Repeat these two steps as many times as possible.‡

The reader should now check that the process just described was that used in the earlier example. [Exercise 4.5.1 asks that the context be moved inside for a few examples.]

After this activity has been accomplished, it may still happen that some redundant occurrences of **r** still remain. For example, from the ⟨context definition⟩

matrix a + **matrix** b := **matrix** '**matrix begin integer** i, j;
   $i \to m$ **do** $j \to n$ **do** **real(r**$[i, j]$:= $a[i, j]$ + $b[i, j]$**) end**';

---

† We are considering here the general step; i.e., we assume that several applications of the rule may already have been made.

‡ A slight bit of extra care is necessary if S occurs as part of a conditional expression: If S is a subtree of either the T (for **then**) or the E (for **else**) branches of a conditional expression (say T), the other branch, E, is converted to a ⟨program expression⟩, if necessary, by replacing it with the tree for the ⟨program expression⟩

begin r := E **end**

Whether this is necessary or not, steps (1) and (2) of this paragraph are carried out on both branches, T and E, simultaneously.

we generated earlier two others, one of which was

((**matrix** a + **matrix** b) $\downarrow$ [**integer** i]) $\downarrow$ [**integer** j] := **real** '$\mathbf{r}$:= $a[i, j]$ +
   $b[i, j]$';

Once this is in the Context Table, it is in fact permissible in ALGOL D to write, for example,

$$(Y + Z)[q + 1][t - q]$$

although it might be improbable. Should it occur, however, we would find in our tree the subtree representing the text

$$\mathbf{r} := Y[q + 1, t - q] + Z[q + 1, t - q]$$

perhaps as part of a larger context

$$W := \mathbf{r} := Y[q + 1, t - q] + Z[q + 1, t - q]$$

and in this case the **r** would be redundant. However rare this situation may be, we add the simple next step: If there is a subtree of the form $\mathbf{r} := \Psi$ not contained in a ⟨program expression⟩, replace this subtree by the tree for Ψ alone. This is to be done as often as possible.

Assuming that these preliminary steps of "moving the context inside" and "getting rid of redundant occurrences of **r**" have been carried out, we must now select some subtree S of the tree T to be replaced by an appropriate definition from the Context Table. The selection of S is carried out in two steps, as described below. (If none can be selected in the manner about to be described, the application of the replacement rule terminates. The resulting tree must then represent an ALGOL ⟨expression⟩ or ⟨assignment statement⟩.) Step I specifies that if there are any "qualified" subscription ⟨context⟩s in the tree, they should be selected first. A "qualified" subscription ⟨context⟩ is one for which a ⟨string⟩ was provided on the right side of the ⟨context definition⟩. This is specified in order to eliminate iterations which are no longer necessary when the $[i, j]$-th element of an array is selected, for example. (We saw this earlier in the

$$(Y + Z) [i, j]$$

example.) Step I also stipulates that if no ⟨string⟩ is provided for the subscription ⟨context⟩, we should next look for a subcontext of that ⟨context⟩ which might qualify. Step II is invoked if the tree (or subtree) under consideration has no subscription ⟨context⟩. Then we select the first available ⟨context⟩ for which a match can be found which gives us a ⟨string⟩ to use. We now give these steps more formally.

Step I: If there is a subtree T_1 whose root node is the subscription operator, we choose the first one (under the natural ordering). Then *either* (a) there is a matching ⟨context⟩ for T_1 which contains a ⟨string⟩, and we choose T_1 to be the S for which we are searching, *or* (b) we regard T_1 itself as the tree and begin again with Step I.

Step II: If no subtree has a subscription operator as root node, then *either* (a) there exists some subtree which can be matched by a ⟨context definition⟩ with a ⟨string⟩, and we choose the first one to be S, *or* (b) there does not exist any subtree for which such a match can be made. If the latter—that is, II(b)—occurred because attention was restricted to a subtree by an application of I(b), we again turn our attention to the entire tree, and we apply Step II again. If II(b) occurs when we are considering the entire tree, we must conclude that no subtree can be selected for replacement, and the application of the rule terminates. [Exercise 4.5.2 asks for a flowchart of this activity!]

The reader should verify that in the earlier example

$$K := c \times ((A \times B) \times (G + D))$$

we selected the subtree to be replaced each time according to the selection rule just stated.

What happens, then, when a match does occur for some subtree S? Let P be the matching ⟨context⟩. Remove the outer ⟨string⟩ delimiters (i.e., quotation marks) from the ⟨string⟩ in P's ⟨context definition⟩. Each occurrence of an identifier with ∗ is now assigned its ALGOL ⟨type⟩, and then all ∗'s are deleted. We now parse the ⟨open string⟩ into a tree $\tilde{S}$ using the current ALGOL D syntax.† To avoid name conflicts, all identifiers declared within $\tilde{S}$ itself must be renamed when necessary in order that no identifier declared in $\tilde{S}$ agrees with an identifier occurring in $max(S)$. Now there is an obvious correspondence between the ⟨context typed identifier⟩s of P and the subtrees of S, which arises directly out of the matching process. Using this correspondence, as well as the formal-actual correspondence between ⟨context type⟩s and ⟨actual type⟩s, we replace the occurrence of any ⟨context typed identifier⟩ in $\tilde{S}$ by its corresponding subtree from S. The resulting tree is then substituted for S in the original tree. [Exercise 4.5.3 asks that this be done for a few.] This step was performed several times in the example above. The reader should verify this procedure in detail.

We have now given the complete replacement rule. One further refinement will be described, however, since it is obviously more efficient

---

† If the text has the form of a ⟨program expression⟩, only the ⟨program⟩ part is parsed; i.e., the ⟨type⟩ and ⟨bound pair list⟩ are dropped.

to use the simpler ⟨expression⟩ $x + y$ than the subscripted ⟨enumerated expression⟩

$$(x + y, \ldots, \ldots, \ldots)[1]$$

in the case where the subscript contains only one or more integer constants. We note that if more than one subscript is used, then an appropriate selector into the ⟨enumerated expression⟩ must be computed, based on the subscript ranges given in the ⟨bound pair list⟩ which specifies the array structure of the ⟨enumerated expression⟩. Thus, if we have

$$[1:2, 1:3](a, b, c, d, e, f)[2, 2]$$

the ⟨bound pair list⟩ $1:2, 1:3$ shows that the ⟨enumerated expression⟩ really represents an array whose first row contains a, b, and c, and whose second row contains d, e, and f. In particular, the desired element is e. Using the ⟨bound pair list⟩ and the formula for the selector function for a **one-level-array** (which we saw in Chapter 3):

$$n(i - 1) + (j - 1)$$

we obtain

$$3(2 - 1) + (2 - 1) = 4$$

and, remembering that we numbered our elements from 0 in Chapter 3,† we select the element e. We now give the formal statement of this simplification. (It is actually stated in a form which peels off one integer subscript at a time, from the front, until any remaining subscripts are not constants.)

If the ⟨open string⟩ for a matching ⟨context⟩ P has the form of an ⟨enumerated expression⟩, let its list of expressions (with ⟨bound pair list⟩) be G. After the ⟨bound pair list⟩ of the ⟨type⟩ of G (as given through a ⟨declaration-context definition⟩) has been appended to the ⟨bound pair list⟩ of G, if the resultant ⟨bound pair list⟩ has only ⟨integer⟩ bounds, say $i_1:j_1, \ldots, i_n:j_n$; and, *furthermore*, if the selected tree S occurs subscripted by an ⟨integer⟩ k, then proceed as follows:

a) Extract the subsequence of ⟨arithmetic expression⟩s or ⟨Boolean expression⟩s in G from position

$$(k - 1) \times \prod_{m=2}^{n} (j_m - i_m + 1) + 1$$

---

† There we wrote
$$S[i, j] \rightarrow (s + n(i - 1) + (j - 1)),$$
implying that $S[1, 1]$ corresponded to $(s + 0)$.

to position

$$k \times \prod_{m=2}^{n} (j_m - i_m + 1), \qquad \text{inclusive.}$$

b) Delete the leading ⟨bound pair⟩ and append the resulting ⟨bound pair list⟩ to the subsequence. Call this G.

c) Replace S and its subscript k by S alone in the tree.

d) Repeat the process, commencing at *furthermore*, until it fails. Then select G as the ⟨open string⟩ to be parsed into the tree $\tilde{S}$. As an example of this last part of the rule, suppose that w and z are declared to be of ⟨type⟩ **complex,** to be represented as **real array** $[1:2]$. Then, since $w + z$ would normally be represented as **complex**$(w[1] + z[1], w[2] + z[2])$, tree (a) in Fig. 4.16 becomes tree (b) in that figure instead of the full tree shown in Fig. 4.17.

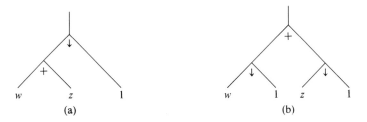

(a)   (b)

Figure 4.16

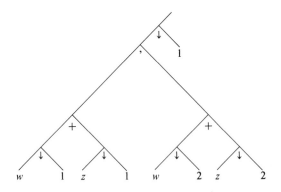

Figure 4.17

EXERCISES 4.5

1. a) Using the tree from Exercise 4.4.3, indicate with dotted boxes, $max(S)$, S, $b(S)$, R, and Ψ. Explain how to move the context inside.

   b) Give the tree expansions for the two examples of Exercise 4.4.3, this time moving contexts inside ⟨program expression⟩s.

2. Give a flowchart for the procedure (Steps I and II in the text) to select a subtree S to be replaced by an appropriate definition from the Context Table.

3. Using the definition set for **complex** numbers given in Section 4.3, give the tree representations for the following, each time indicating P, S and $\tilde{S}$ for each subtree matched.

   a) $e := d/c$
   b) $f := d \times e + mag(c)$
   where c, d, e and f are **complex**.

4.6 EXAMPLES OF DEFINITION SETS

A set of definitions which introduces **complex** number arithmetic was given in the preceding section. We shall give here some additional examples of definition sets. Although some of these examples cover quite general problem areas (such as **complex** and **matrix** arithmetic), we shall see through additional examples that definitions can be used to introduce notation for personal convenience in isolated programming situations as well. [Exercise 4.6.1 carries this point further.]

As an example of the development of a definition set, we consider the definitions necessary to allow ⟨arithmetic expression⟩s and ⟨assignment statement⟩s involving rectangular matrices. The set is developed in stages, as follows:

Stage I: An ⟨S-assignment⟩ is given:

$$\mathbf{matrix}(u, v) := \sum_{u} (\mathbf{row}(v) := \sum_{v} \mathbf{real});$$

This assignment will be replaced by the following set of definitions through an application of the ⟨S-assignment⟩ processor, whose existence we have postulated.

matrix(u, v) $a := $ '**real array** $a[1:u, 1:v]$';
row(v) $a := $ '**real array** $a[1:v]$';
matrix(u, v) $a \downarrow$ [**integer** i] $:= $ **row**(v);

(**matrix**(u, v) $a \downarrow$ [**integer** i]) $\downarrow$ [**integer** j] := **real** '$*a[i, j]$';
row(v) $a \downarrow$ [**integer** i] := **real** '$*a[i]$';
matrix(u, v) $a =$ **matrix**(u, v) $b :=$ **Boolean** 'Boolean begin Boolean t;
    integer i; $i \rightarrow u$ **do begin** $t := a[i] = b[i]$; **if** $\neg\, t$ **then go to** L **end**;
    L: **r** := t **end**';
row(v) $a =$ **row**(v) $b :=$ **Boolean** 'Boolean begin Boolean t; **integer** i;
    $i \rightarrow v$ **do begin** $t := a[i] = b[i]$; **if** $\neg\, t$ **then go to** L **end**; L: **r** := t **end**';
real $f \oplus$ **matrix**(u, v) $a :=$ **matrix**(u, v) 'matrix(u, v) begin integer i;
    $i \rightarrow u$ **do** (**r**$[i]$:= $f \oplus a[i]$) **end**';
real $f \oplus$ **row**(v) $a :=$ **row**(v) 'row(v) begin integer i;
    $i \rightarrow v$ **do** (**r**$[i]$:= $f \oplus a[i]$) **end**';

Note that in the last definitions boldface parentheses were introduced, so that two definitions are actually intended:

    real $f \oplus$ **row**(v) $a :=$ **row**(v) 'row(v) begin integer i;
        $i \rightarrow v$ **do** **r**$[i]$:= $f \oplus a[i]$ **end**';
    (**real** $f \oplus$ **row**(v) a) $\downarrow$ [**integer** i] := **real** '$r := f \oplus a[i]$';

This could not have been suggested in the chapter on data structures, since the general definition facility was not yet available.

Stage II: The ⟨new operator⟩, representing the transpose operator, is declared:

1) **T** $> x$;

Stage III: The desired ⟨context definition⟩s are listed:

2) **matrix**(u, v) $a :=$ **matrix**(u, v) $b :=$ **matrix**(u, v) 'begin integer i;
    $i \rightarrow u$ **do** $a[i] := b[i]$ **end**';

    A := $(+ , -)$;

3) **matrix**(u, v) a **A matrix**(u, v) $b :=$ **matrix**(u, v) 'matrix(u, v) begin
    integer i; $i \rightarrow u$ do row(v)(**r**$[i]$:= $a[i]$ A $b[i]$) **end**';

    arith := (real, integer);

4) **arith** $a \times$ **matrix**(u, v) $b :=$ **matrix**(u, v) 'matrix(u, v) begin integer i;
    $i \rightarrow u$ **do** row(v)(**r**$[i]$:= $a \times b[i]$) **end**';

5) **matrix**(u, v) $a \times$ **matrix** (v, w) $b :=$ **matrix**(u, w) 'matrix(u, w) begin
    integer i; $i \rightarrow u$ do row(w)(begin row(v) t; $t := a[i]$;
    r$[i]$:= $t \times b$ **end**) **end**';
6) **T matrix**(u, v) $a :=$ **matrix**(v, u);

In these ⟨context definition⟩s, parameters u and v are used so that the definitions will be equally applicable to square or rectangular matrices. This is just one choice of several alternative ways of defining **matrix** arithmetic, of course. If (4) were not included, multiplication of a **matrix** by a **real** or **integer** scalar would not be available. Also several alternatives can be considered for (5); this will be discussed later. The ⟨context definition⟩ in (6) was introduced with the matrix transpose operator in mind, but we deliberately chose to provide no ⟨string⟩ in this ⟨context definition⟩. The ⟨result type⟩ in (6) is available for tree labeling, but we do not wish to introduce a ⟨procedure⟩ call at this point to actually form the transpose of the matrix, i.e., to physically move the elements of the matrix. We shall see that in (15), when we have the subscripted form of the transpose, we can accomplish the same effect by transposing the subscripts, thus eliminating the transpose operator **T** altogether from the final ALGOL text.

Stage IV: In order to be able to parse the text resulting from the ⟨string⟩s in stage III, several additional ⟨context definition⟩s are seen to be necessary:

7)   **row**(v) $a :=$ **row**(v) $b :=$ **row**(v) 'begin integer j;
       $j \rightarrow v$ **do** $a[j] := b[j]$ **end**';   [from (2)]

8)   **row**(v) a **A** **row**(v) $b :=$ **row**(v) 'row(v) begin integer j;
       $j \rightarrow v$ **do** **real**(**r**$[j]$) $:= a[j]$ **A** $b[j]$) **end**';   [from (3)]

9)   **arith** $a \times$ **row**(v) $b :=$ **row**(v) 'row(v) begin integer j;
       $j \rightarrow v$ **do** **real**(**r**$[j]$) $:= a \times b[j]$) **end**';   [from (4)]

10) **row**(u) $a \times$ **matrix**(u, v) $b :=$ **row**(v) 'row(v) begin integer j;
       $j \rightarrow v$ **do** **real**(**r**$[j]$) $:= a \times$ (**T**b)$[j]$) **end**';   [from (5)]

Stage V: Additional ⟨context definition⟩s arise from stage IV ⟨string⟩s:

11) **row**(v) $a \times$ **row**(v) $b :=$ **real** 'real begin integer j; real s; $s := 0$;
       $j \rightarrow v$ **do** $s := s + a[j] \times b[j]$; **r** $:= s$ **end**';

Stage VI: Additional ⟨context⟩s arise when one ⟨context⟩ with ⟨result type⟩ γ is substituted for an occurrence of a ⟨context typed identifier⟩ with ⟨context type⟩ γ in another ⟨context⟩; for example, as (3) is substituted in (6). Only those need be listed for which a special ⟨string⟩ is desired, however. In (12) through (15) we take advantage of well-known properties of the matrix transpose operator with respect to addition, multiplication, etc.

12) **T**(**matrix**(u, v) a **A** **matrix**(u, v) b) $:=$ **matrix**(v, u) '**T**a **A** **T**b';
                                             [from (3) into (6)]

13) $\mathbf{T}(\mathbf{matrix}(u, v)\ a\ \times\ \mathbf{matrix}(v, w)\ b) := \mathbf{matrix}(w, u)\ \text{'}\mathbf{T}b\ \times\ \mathbf{T}a\text{'};$
$$\text{[from (5) into (6)]}$$

14) $\mathbf{T}(\mathbf{T}\ \mathbf{matrix}(u, v)\ a) := \mathbf{matrix}(u, v)\ \text{'}a\text{'};$ [from (6) into (6)]

15) $((\mathbf{T}\ \mathbf{matrix}(u, v)\ a)\ \downarrow\ [\mathbf{integer}\ i])\ \downarrow\ [\mathbf{integer}\ j] := \mathbf{real}\ \text{'}a[j][i]\text{'};$
$$\text{[from (6) into an earlier context]}$$

As mentioned above, alternative ⟨context definition⟩s can be used instead of definition (5). For example,

$\mathbf{matrix}(u, v)\ a\ \times\ \mathbf{matrix}(v, w)\ b := \mathbf{matrix}(u, w)\ \text{'}\mathbf{matrix}(u, w)\ \mathbf{begin}$
    $\mathbf{integer}\ i;\ \ i \rightarrow u\ \mathbf{do}\ \mathbf{row}(w)(\mathbf{r}[i] := a[i]\ \times\ b)\ \mathbf{end}\text{'};$

This would eliminate the allocation of temporary storage for t, but some elements would be computed several times in some ⟨expression⟩s. [Exercise 4.6.3 explores this with an example.]

An example of the use of this definition set† is

$\mathbf{real}\ c;\ \mathbf{matrix}(m, n)\ K, G, D;\ \mathbf{matrix}(n, n)A, B;$
    $K := c\ \times\ \mathbf{T}((A\ \times\ \mathbf{T}B)\ \times\ \mathbf{T}(G\ +\ D));$

A straightforward ALGOL program for this computation (not resulting from our definition set) would be that shown as Fig. 4.18 (opposite page). That program requires $n^2 + nm + 1$ locations for temporary storage. The expansion via the original definition set above appears as Fig. 4.19. That program requires only $2n + 2$ locations for temporary storage, but it takes more time. [Exercise 4.6.4 asks for the comparison.] One of the greatest advantages of a definition facility is the freedom to choose among such alternatives easily, and to have the scope of such a decision be as small as a single ⟨block⟩.

Another Example (Information Retrieval)

As another example, we consider the maintenance, updating, and interrogation of a file of information. We envision our file as a vector of names of records, with each record itself a vector of information. The information in each record will consist of **real** numbers, referred to below as "attributes"; more specifically, the creator of the file will declare his own names for elementary structures **attr**(1), **attr**(2), etc., to represent various attributes of the elements in the file. We assume that our maintenance needs to include creating new files as arithmetic or Boolean combinations

---

† See footnote, p. 244.

```
real c; array K, G, D[1:m 1:n], A, B[1:n, 1:n]
  begin integer i, j, k; array P[1:n, 1:n], Q[1:m, 1:n]; real s;
    i → n do j → n do
      begin s := 0; k → n do s := s + A[i, k] × B[j, k];
      P[i, j] := s end;
    i → m do j → n do Q[i, j] := G[i, j] + D[i, j];
    i → m do j → n do
      begin s := 0; k → n do
        s := s + P[j, k] × Q[i, k] end;
      K[i, j] := c × s end end;
```

Figure 4.18

```
real c; array K, G, D[1:m, 1:n]; array A, B[1:n, 1:n];
  begin integer i;
    i → m do begin array t[1:n];
      begin integer j; j → n do t[j] := G[i, j] + D[i, j] end;
      begin integer j; j → n do
        begin array z[1:n];
          begin integer k; k → n do z[k] := A[j, k] end;
          begin integer k; real s; s := 0;
            k → n do begin integer h; real y;
              y := 0;
              h → n do y := y + z[h] × B[k, h];
              s := s + t[k] × y end;
            K[i, j] := c × s end end end end end;
```

Figure 4.19

of old ones, and also computing a count of the number of records in which some ⟨Boolean expression⟩ is **true**. The values **true** and **false** will be stored in "truth vectors" with structure **TV**.

file $:= \sum_m$ **name-of** (**rec** $:= \sum_n$ **real**); **TV** $:= \sum_m$ **Boolean**;

B $:= (\wedge, \vee)$; **A** $:= (+, -, \times, /, \div)$;

R $:= (=, \neq, <, \leq, >, \geq)$;

arith $:=$ (**real, integer**); **rat** $:=$ (**arith, attr**(j)); **rat1** $:=$ (**rat**);

on $= \downarrow$;

countof $<$ **on**;

countof TV $a :=$ **real** 'real begin c; **integer** i; $c := 0$;
   $i \to m$ **do** $c := c + $ **if** $a[i]$ **then** 1 **else** 0; $r := c$ **end**' ;

Boolean a **on file** $y :=$ **TV** 'TV begin **integer** i;
   $i \to m$ **do Boolean**($\mathbf{r}[i] := a$ **on y**$[i]$) **end**' ;

rat a **on file** $y :=$ **file** 'file begin **integer** i;
   $i \to m$ **do rec**($\mathbf{r}[i] := a$ **on** $y[i]$) **end**' ;

(**Boolean** a **B Boolean** b) **on rec** $c :=$ **Boolean** 'a **on** c **B** b **on** c' ;

($\neg$ **Boolean** b) **on rec** $c :=$ **Boolean** '$\neg(b$ **on** $c)$' ;

(**rat** a **R rat1** b) **on rec** $c :=$ **Boolean** 'a **on** c **R** b **on** c' ;

(**rat** a **A rat1** b) **on rec** $c :=$ **rec** 'a **on** c **A** b **on** c' ;

attr(j) a **on rec** $c :=$ **real** '$*c[j]$' ;

arith a **on rec** $c :=$ **arith** 'a' ;

(**if Boolean** a **then rat** b **else rat** c) **on rec** $y :=$ **real** 'if a on y then b on y else
   c on y' ;

rat a **R rat1** $b :=$ **Boolean**;

rat a **A rat1** $b :=$ **real**;

file $a :=$ **file** $b :=$ **file** 'begin **integer** i; $i \to m$ **do** $a[i] := b[i]$ **end**' ;

rec $a :=$ **rec** $b :=$ **rec** 'begin **integer** j; $j \to n$ **do** $a[j] := b[j]$ **end**' ;

TV $a :=$ **TV** $b :=$ **TV** 'begin **integer** i; $i \to m$ **do** $a[i] := b[i]$ **end**' ;

Note that although the ⟨context⟩s represented by

   (**Boolean** a **B Boolean** b) **on rec** c
   ($\neg$ **Boolean** b) **on rec** c

appear above, it was not necessary to provide a ⟨context definition⟩ for

     Boolean a **on rec** c

because the only way in which the latter can occur is as

     (**rat** a **R rat1** b) **on rec** c

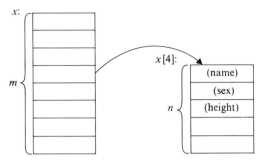

Figure 4.20

which is treated, producing ⟨context⟩s which are handled by the ⟨context definition⟩s

$$\textbf{attr}(j)\ a\ \textbf{on rec}\ c := \textbf{real}\ `{*}c[j]\text{'};$$
$$\textbf{arith}\ a\ \textbf{on rec}\ c := \textbf{arith}\ `a\text{'};$$

[Exercise 4.6.5 asks which definitions come from declarations such as **file** w.]

An example of the use of this definition set is

file x; **attr**(1) *name*; **attr**(2) *sex*; **attr**(3) *height*;
real *count*; *count* := **countof**($sex = 1 \wedge height \geq 6$) **on** x;

This may be assumed to occur within a ⟨program⟩ where $n \geq 3$, and where the file may be pictured as in Fig. 4.20. To reach the *height* entry for $x[4]$, we take the contents of $x[4]$, interpret it as the name of a vector, and then subscript it by 3. The ⟨assignment statement⟩ will therefore be expanded into the ALGOL text

```
begin real c;  integer i;  c := 0;
    i → m do c := c + if (vc-of x[i])[2] = 1 ∧ (vc-of x[i])[3] ≥ 6
        then 1 else 0;
    count := c end;
```

[Exercise 4.6.6 asks for further examples using this definition set. Exercise 4.6.7 asks for ⟨context definition⟩s for **car**, **cdr**, and **cons** for lists, as introduced in Chapter 3.]

Another Example

Suppose now that, since both the **real** and the **complex** arithmetics are available, we wish to develop a definition set for **real** and **complex** matrix arithmetic. We already have access to the **real matrix** definitions given earlier, and it should be possible to extend these definitions to accommodate **complex** matrices as well. One might begin by representing a variable of ⟨type⟩ **complexmatrix** as a pair (i.e., an ⟨enumerated expression⟩), of **real** matrices:

$$\textbf{complexmatrix} := \sum_2 \textbf{matrix}(u, v)$$

Unfortunately, when ⟨expression⟩s are expanded, iterations will be generated which deal with the elements of the first matrix of the pair separately from the elements of the second matrix, and there will be a great deal of duplicated iteration machinery. For example, we would define some of the arithmetic as follows:

complexmatrix a + **complexmatrix** b :=
    complexmatrix 'complexmatrix $(a[1] + b[1], a[2] + b[2])$';

where $a[1] + b[1]$ and $a[2] + b[2]$, being sums of **real** matrices, would be expanded by means of the earlier **matrix** definitions. But these two sums would generate independent iterations, and there would be no advantage to using this system.

An alternative method is to construct a definition set for a field **w**, then let **w** be given by a set definition, for example, **w** := (**real**, **complex**), and provide a ⟨formal type parameter⟩, p, in ⟨declaration⟩s whose ⟨actual type parameter⟩ would be **real** or **complex**. The matrix definition set would now be

w := (**real**, **complex**);

1) $\textbf{matrix}(\textbf{w}, u, v) := \sum_u (\textbf{row}(v) := \sum_v \textbf{w});$

    $\textbf{T} > x;$

2) $\textbf{matrix}(p, u, v)\, a := \textbf{matrix}(p, u, v)\, b :=$
        $\textbf{matrix}(p, u, v)$ 'begin integer i; $i \rightarrow u$ do $a[i] := b[i]$ end';
    $\textbf{A} := (+, -);$

3) $\textbf{matrix}(p, u, v)\, a\ \textbf{A}\ \textbf{matrix}(p, u, v)\, b :=$
        $\textbf{matrix}(p, u, v)$ 'matrix(p, u, v) begin integer i;
        $i \rightarrow u$ do row$(p, v)(\textbf{r}[i] := a[i]\ \textbf{A}\ b[i])$ end';

    arith := (**w**, **integer**);

4) **arith** $a \times \textbf{matrix}(p, u, v)\, b :=$
        $\textbf{matrix}(p, u, v)$ 'matrix(p, u, v) begin integer i;
        $i \rightarrow u$ do row$(p, v)(\textbf{r}[i] := a \times b[i])$ end';

5) $\textbf{matrix}(p, u, v)\, a \times \textbf{matrix}(p, v, w)\, b :=$
        $\textbf{matrix}(p, u, w)$ 'matrix(p, u, w) begin integer i;
        $i \rightarrow u$ do row(p, w) (begin row(p, v) $t; t := a[i]$;
        $\textbf{r}[i] := t \times b$ end) end';

6) **T matrix**(p, u, v) a := **matrix**(p, v, u);

7) **row**(p, v) a := **row**(p, v) b := **row**(p, v) 'begin integer j;
   $j \to v$ **do** $a[j]$:= $b[j]$ **end**';

8) **row**(p, v) a **A row**(p, v) b := **row**(p, v) 'row(p, v) begin integer j;
   $j \to v$ **do** $p(r[j]$:= $a[j]$ **A** $b[j])$ **end**';

9) **arith** $a \times$ **row**(p, v) b := **row**(p, v) 'row(p, v) begin integer j;
   $j \to v$ **do** $p(r[j]$:= $a \times b[j])$ **end**';

10) **row**(p, u) $a \times$ **matrix**(p, u, v) b := **row**(p, v) 'row(p, v) begin integer j;
    $j \to v$ **do** $p(r[j]$:= $a \times (Tb)[j])$ **end**';

11) **row**(p, v) $a \times$ **row**(p, v) b := p 'p begin integer j; p s; s := 0;
    $j \to v$ **do** s := $s + a[j] \times b[j]$; r := s **end**';

12) **T(matrix**(p, u, v) a **A matrix**(p, u, v) $b)$:= **matrix**(p, v, u) 'Ta **A** Tb';

13) **T(matrix**(p, u, v) $a \times$ **matrix**(p, v, w) $b)$:= **matrix**(p, w, u) 'Tb $\times$ Ta';

14) **T(T matrix**(p, u, v) $a)$:= **matrix**(p, u, v) 'a';

15) **((T matrix**(p, u, v) $a)$ $\downarrow$ [integer i]) $\downarrow$ [integer j] := p '$a[j][i]$';

EXERCISES 4.6

1. Exhibit ⟨context definition⟩s for the following:

a) unary operators **sqrt** and **intsqrt** which take as operands **real** and **integer** ⟨expression⟩s, respectively, and which are expanded as calls on library ⟨procedure⟩s *sqrt* and *intsqrt*, respectively.

b) a binary operator **pleq** with two **real** or two **integer** operands, such that in each case "a **pleq** b" is computed as a := $a + b$.

2. Expand the ALGOL D ⟨assignment statement⟩

$$B := A \times B \times C$$

according to the definition set given at the beginning of this section. Show that an incorrect result is obtained even for $u = v = 1$, that is, when the matrices A, B, and C each contain only one element.

3. Using the alternative ⟨context definition⟩ for (5) in Stage III,

a) compute the amount of temporary storage needed for

$$K := c \times (A \times B) \times (G + D)$$

where c is **real** and all the matrices are $n \times n$.

b) state which computations are performed several times in (a).

4. For each of the expansions given in the text for the statement

$$K := c \times T((A \times TB) \times T(G + D))$$

compute a "measure" of the computation time, as follows: Count each operation, such as $:=$, $+$, $-$, etc., as one computation unit, a single subscription as one unit, and a double subscription as two units. If an iteration is performed n times, multiply the number of units in the scope of the iteration by n, and so on.

5. What ⟨context definition⟩s and/or ⟨declaration-context definition⟩s will be generated from each of the following?

a) **file** w;

b) **rec** v;

c) **TV** z;

6. Using the definition set for files as given in the text, how would each of the following expand into ALGOL?

a) **file** s, t, v; $s := t + v$;

b) **file** s, t; **real** c; **attr**(1) *color*;
    $c :=$ **countof** (*color* $= 3$) **on** $s +$ **countof** (*color* $= 2$) **on** t;

7. Using the ⟨declaration-context definition⟩ for lists as given in Chapter 3, give appropriate ⟨context definition⟩s for **car**, **cdr**, and **cons**.

4.7 EXAMPLES INVOLVING SEQUENCING

So far we have considered ways of defining into the ALGOL language new data structures, new operators, and new kinds of arithmetic. The form of ⟨statement⟩s and the order in which they are evaluated has been fixed, so far as our definition facility is concerned. Even within the restriction that we can redefine only ⟨expression⟩s and ⟨assignment statement⟩s, however, important changes can be accomplished. Suppose that we wish to introduce Markov sequencing into ALGOL, for example. We postulate the existence of two ⟨procedure⟩s: *match*(x, y), which yields the value **true** if x is a substring of y and **false** otherwise; and *subst*(w, x, y), which does not produce a value, but leaves as the value of y the ⟨string⟩ obtained by substituting the ⟨string⟩ w for the leftmost occurrence of the ⟨string⟩ x in y. We also assume for the present discussion that there is a ⟨type⟩ **label**, although we have not really provided for it properly in earlier developments.

We now decide what we would like to write, i.e., what the appropriate notation should be if the language is to allow us to express Markov sequencing. Because the LMA is simpler to handle than the MA, we leave it to the exercises [4.7.1], and we shall show here how the MA can be accommodated. We must choose a notation which *appears* to be in the form of an ⟨expression⟩ or ⟨assignment statement⟩, since these are the only parts of the language our definition facility allows us to redefine. This example shows how one can satisfy this restriction while actually accomplishing much more. Whenever restrictions must be circumvented, however, it is time to reexamine the system containing those restrictions; it is probably not general enough in its point of view. We shall return to this point later.

Remembering that the comma has been treated here as an operator, we choose the notation

$$\textbf{string } a, b, c, d, x; \ \textbf{label } L;$$
$$L: L := (a \textbf{ by } b, c \textbf{ by } d) \textbf{ on } x;$$

which is to be interpreted as (and should in fact expand into):

$$L: \textbf{if } match(a, x) \textbf{ then begin } subst(b, a, x); \ \textbf{go to } L \textbf{ end};$$
$$\textbf{if } match(c, x) \textbf{ then begin } subst(d, c, x); \ \textbf{go to } L \textbf{ end};$$

so that it corresponds to Markov sequencing. We must allow any number of "rules" of the form p **by** q, of course, and this is a key point in the construction of this definition set. Another is the need to recognize L at one end of the "expression" and x at the other end, and propagate (or "distribute") both of them throughout, no matter how many rules there are. The following definitions suffice. First we have the ⟨new operator declaration⟩s needed to make it appear as if we were handling an assignment statement:

$$\textbf{m} > , ; \ \textbf{on} > \textbf{m} ; \ \textbf{by} > \textbf{on} ;$$

where **m** is an auxiliary operator which will appear in the ⟨context definition⟩s. Now we must provide the ⟨context⟩s needed to parse the "assignment statement" and generate the desired ALGOL constructions.

string a **by string** $b := $ **s**;
s a, **s** $b := $ **s**;
s a **on string** $x := $ **s3**;
label $L := $ **s3** $b := $ **s2**;
label L **m string** $x := $ **s1**;
s $a := $ **s1** $b := $ **s2**;
label $L := $ **s** a **on string** $x := $ **s2** '$a := (L$ **m** $x)$';
(**s** a, **s** b) $:= $ **s1** $c := $ **s2** '$a := c; b := c$';
string a **by string** $b := $ **label** L **m string** $x := $
    s2 'if $match(a, x)$ **then begin** $subst(b, a, x)$; **go to** L **end**';

[Exercise 4.7.2 asks for an application of this set.]

The double occurrence of L to be used in the text, as

$$L : L := \cdots$$

is not very elegant. It stems from our inability to include a label in an ⟨expression⟩ or ⟨assignment statement⟩ (or to generate one via a ⟨definition string⟩). We could go back into the syntax of ALGOL and change it to include the **label** construction in a different way, but this would be treating symptoms rather than finding out what the disease is. The real problem is that we have limited ourselves to a small part of the syntax of the language, and it is quickly evident that a more general definition facility should allow one to name and manipulate any syntactic unit in the language. We are not really doing justice to the semantics side of it, either. The only action we provide for when a matching of ⟨context⟩s is obtained is a string replacement. To be sure, this is followed by an application of a replacement rule designed to conserve temporary storage, but some additional facilities are missing. For example, there is no way to maintain records about the progress of the definition processing. Moreover, we have not provided for actions beyond the substitution of text. Actions which might prove desirable are: (1) manipulation of variables available to the ALGOL D processor for its own decisions; (2) construction of tables containing various attributes of variables encountered in the process; (3) reference to such attribute tables, both during ALGOL D processing and later, during execution of the program; and (4) signaling for input or output action during ALGOL D processing, e.g., communication with the person responsible for the processing. Such generalizations are being studied by several people (see [17]) and one may expect important developments in these areas in the future.

There is still a great deal we can do with our present facility, however, even in the area of sequencing. Suppose, for example, that we wish to introduce an "iterated expression" in the spirit of the summation sign $\sum$ commonly used in mathematical notation. [18] A notation which does not stretch the ALGOL iteration notation too far is

$$(i := E_1 \textbf{ Step } E_2 \textbf{ Until } E_3 \textbf{ Do } v \textbf{ is } (E_4, \ldots, E_n));$$

where the outer parentheses are required, the inner parentheses are required if $n > 4$, and the ellipsis (...) is not allowed at all. The interpretation (and intended expansion) of this form is the ALGOL ⟨program expression⟩:

(type) **begin for** $i := E_1$ **step** E_2 **until** E_3 **do begin** $v := E_4$; $v := E_5$; ...;
    $v := E_n$ **end**; **r** $:= v$ **end**;

where (type) represents the ⟨type⟩ of v, needed for the form of a ⟨program expression⟩. As an example of the use of such an iterated expression, consider the computation

$$y = a_0 + \sum_{i=1}^{n} a_1 \frac{\sin 3i}{i}$$

This could be written

$v = a[0]; y := (i := 1 \textbf{ Step } 1 \textbf{ Until } n \textbf{ Do } v \text{ is } v + a[i] \times sin(3 \times i)/i);$

Of course, since this iteration notation does not have the operation of addition built into it, we were forced to write $v + \cdots$ explicitly in this example; but on the other hand, we can write iterated products now as well. [Exercise 4.7.3 will explore this further.]

In order to define this notation into the language, we must identify such symbols as **Step, Until, Do** and **is** as ⟨new operator⟩s, give them precedence relative to each other and to existing ⟨operators⟩, and so on. We write

Step $>$:= ; **Until** = **Step**; **Do** = **Step**; **is** = **Step**;
arith := (**real, integer**); **any1** := **any2** := **any3** := (**arith, Boolean**);
any1 u **is any2** v := **any1**;
arith u **Do any2** v := **arith**;
arith u **Until any1** v := **arith**;
arith u **Step any1** v := **arith**;
arith i := **arith** a **Step arith** b **Until arith** c **Do any1** v **is any2** d := **any1**
     '**any1 begin for** i := a **step** b **until** c **do begin** v **is** d **end**; **r** := v **end**';
any1 v **is** (**any2** a, **any3** b) := **any1** '**begin** v := a; v **is** b **end**';
any1 v **is any2** a := **any1** 'v := a';

As Exercise 4.7.4 will show, the expansion of some calls on this defined construction will introduce some redundant **begin–end** pairs, but to avoid this would be more difficult. Exercise 4.7.5 extends the notation to facilitate the use of subexpressions.

EXERCISES 4.7

1. Develop appropriate notation and ⟨context definition⟩s for LMA sequencing, similar to that for the MA developed in the text.

2. Expand the sequence

     string p, r, s; **label** Q; Q: Q := (r **by** s, '$a + b$' **by** '$a - b$',
         '∗' **by** '×' **on** p;

     using the definition set for Markov sequencing.

3. Using the iteration notation of the text, write the ALGOL D statement to compute the polynomial

$$\prod_{n} (x) = (x - x_0)(x - x_1) \cdots (x - x_n)$$

4. Using the iteration definition set, expand the following:

$(j := k \text{ Step } 1 \textbf{ Until } m \textbf{ Do } y \text{ is } (y + cos(j \times t), y \times b(j), y + c(j)));$

5. If we could use several **is** subexpressions in the **Step–Until–Do–is** construction, we could use the first to compute a subexpression whose name is used in the second one, and so on. Modify the definition set exhibited in the text to do this.

4.8 MACROS

So far in this chapter we have considered a particular kind of definition facility. If we look at this as the substitution of text on the occurrence of some signal, such as the appearance of a particular pattern, then we are dealing with a specific kind of "macro-expansion." The word "macro" was introduced into the literature because there is usually a sizable segment of text introduced for a modest amount of original text, the process being called "expansion." Early macro facilities generally allowed patterns of the form

$$\text{name}, \text{arg}_1, \text{arg}_2, \ldots, \text{arg}_n$$

where "name" is a special word triggering the expansion process, and arg_1, arg_2, etc., are arguments indicating positions in the definition string in which replacements are to be made from corresponding positions in the "call." A typical definition would be written in some language very close to a "machine language," such as:

ADD	MACRO	A,B,C
	CLA	A
	ADD	B
	STO	C
	END	ADD

More elaborate macro facilities allowed some decision making with respect to which part of the definition might be used to replace the call. For the example just given, a call might appear as:

	ADD	X+2,Z,Q

In such macro facilities, although parameter substitution was provided, and some decision making was allowed as to the actual text used in the replacement, no rearrangement of the resulting text was provided, and the syntax was restricted to that of the very primitive language which it served.

Only recently have there been attempts to provide macro (or definition) facilities for the "higher-level languages" such as our ALGOL [19, 20, 21]. Cheatham [17] has identified four main types of macro facilities which could be used with such higher-level languages. These are related to the facility proposed in this chapter, but they differ in some ways.

The first form of macro he identifies is called the "pre-lexical macro." Here, on a signal that a macro name has occurred (possibly with parameters), a string of characters is generated to replace it, with the actual parameters in the call substituted into the string. No syntactic analysis is done, and no checking is provided. To use one of his examples, one might give the definition

MACRO   MATRIX (N) MEANS 'ARRAY (1:N,1:N)';

Then, using the percent sign (%) as the signal that a macro call follows, a specific call might be

... %MATRIX (25) ...

which would have the effect (i.e., be replaced by):

... ARRAY (1:25,1:25) ...

Something like the percent sign is needed here because in this macro facility there is no interpretation of the input text, and thus there is no way to recognize the occurrence of a macro name. The advantage of this kind of macro facility is that one is not bound by the need for correct syntax in the original text. The disadvantages are the necessity for writing a special character (%) as a signal, plus the lack of error checking which could be provided if a syntactic analysis were being used.

There are two other important macro-expanders identified by Strachey [22] and Mooers [23], both of which work at the pre-lexical level. For example, in Mooers' TRAC, a typical example might be

#(DS,ED,(#(PS,#(DS,OLD,##(RS))#(IN,OLD, ...

which is the beginning of a call on a macro called "Define String," which is built into TRAC. This macro call defines a string ED for later expansion, whose definition starts:

#(PS,#(DS,OLD,##(RS))#(IN,OLD, ...

A second kind of macro identified by Cheatham, though still a pre-lexical macro, allows some checking. Here one would include information about the parameters, such as syntactic type, and the expansion would include checking for this type. Thus the example given above would now be written

LET N BE INTEGER;
MACRO MATRIX (N) MEANS 'ARRAY (1:N,1:N)';

while the call and the effect of the expansion would be the same as before.

A third type of macro is introduced to allow one to specify the kind of context in which the macro call is to be recognized, thus eliminating the need for the percent sign as a signal. Cheatham calls this kind a "syntactic macro" (or SMACRO). The previous example would then be written

LET N BE INTEGER
SMACRO MATRIX (N) AS ATTRIBUTE MEANS
    'ARRAY (1:N,1:N)';

where "attribute" corresponds to the term ⟨type⟩ used in this book. Now the call becomes

... MATRIX (25) WALDO ...

where WALDO is being declared of ⟨type⟩ MATRIX(25). The expansion is then

... ARRAY (1:25,1:25) WALDO ...

Another example of the use of a SMACRO, which shows that various syntactic types can be included, may be used to introduce the idea of multiple relations, such as

A < B < C

with the intention that this expand as

A < B ∧ B < C

Assuming that the language has syntactic types ⟨expression⟩, ⟨relation operator⟩, and ⟨relation⟩, one might give the definition

LET X BE EXPR; [†]
LET Y BE EXPR;
LET Z BE EXPR;
LET R1 BE RELOP;
LET R2 BE RELOP;
SMACRO X R1 Y R2 Z AS RELATION MEANS
    'X R1 Y AND Y R2 Z';

[†] The notation in this example is that used by Cheatham. Its relationship to the notation of this book should be clear.

Now a typical call would appear as

$$... A+1 < B < C+1 < D ...$$

and this would expand to

$$... A+1 < B \ \text{AND} \ B < C+1 \ \text{AND} \ C+1 < D ...$$

In the fourth kind of macro, the processor of the language is expected to digest the definition into the corresponding "computation tree" and store it away in that form. Whenever a call occurs, the actual parameters (which might be expressions) are dropped into place in the already existing computational tree for the macro definition. Each actual parameter tree is inserted at the appropriate point.

The main differences in these various forms of macro expansion lie in the internal treatment and in the degree of interaction expected between the notation of a call and the surrounding text, and between the expanded text and the context in which that expanded text is found. In none of the forms proposed by Cheatham is there any idea of rearrangement of the resulting tree so as to improve the result. On the other hand, there is a great deal more flexibility in these proposals, with respect to the variety of syntactic types which can be employed, than in the definition facility developed here.

In [24] Leavenworth has proposed another macro-expander, which is very similar to the "computational tree" type of Cheatham, except it goes even further in that it allows conditional macro generation. Here the pattern used for matching a call is allowed to contain alternatives and/or optional constructions. During the match, the call determines which of the various options and alternatives have actually been used, and these determine the final form of the string to be used in the expansion. Since Leavenworth allows for various syntactic types also, it is a very powerful facility.

Yet another macro facility has been proposed by Garwick [15] with which it is also possible to introduce some new data structures, but not in a completely general way. There is no rearrangement of the resulting text here, either.

Interest in definition facilities, or as many refer to them, "extensible languages," has become more popular in recent years. There are still problems of completeness of the languages that can be generated, error detection, processing time, and so on. But the recent jump in activity of this kind leads one to suspect and hope that some significant developments are not too far off.

REFERENCES

1. A. A. Markov, *The Theory of Algorithms* (tr. from the Russian by J. J. Schorr-kon), U.S. Dept. of Commerce, Office of Technical Services, No. OTS 60-51085. [p. 3]*

2. A. M. Turing, "On computable numbers, with an application to the Entscheidungsproblem," *Proc. London Math. Soc.*, ser. 2, vol. 42 (1936–1937), pp. 230–265. "A correction," *ibid.*, vol. 43 (1937), pp. 544–546. [p. 4]

3. S. C. Kleene, *Introduction to Metamathematics*, Van Nostrand, New York, 1952, Chap. 13. [p. 4]

4. E. L. Post, "Finite combinatory processes—formulation I," *J. Symb. Logic*, vol. 1 (1936), pp. 103–105. [p. 4]

5. J. W. Backus, "The syntax and semantics of the proposed international algebraic language of the Zurich ACM-GAMM conference," International Conference on Information Processing (ICIP), Paris, June 1959. [p. 60]

6. R. E. Griswold, J. F. Poage, and I. P. Polonsky, *The SNOBOL4 Programming Language*, Prentice-Hall, Englewood Cliffs, N.J., 1968. [p. 78]

7. R. W. Floyd, "A descriptive language for symbol manipulation," *J. Assoc. for Computing Machinery* (ACM), vol. 8 (1961), pp. 579–584. [p. 111]

8. P. Naur (Ed.), "Report on the algorithmic language ALGOL 60," *Comm. ACM.*, vol. 3, no. 5 (May 1960), pp. 299–314. *See also:* P. Naur (Ed.), "Revised report on the algorithmic language ALGOL 60, *Numer. Math.* vol. 4 (1963), pp. 420–453, and *Comm. ACM*, vol. 6, no. 1 (Jan. 1963), pp. 1–17; A. van Wijngaarden (Ed.), "Report on the algorithmic language ALGOL 68," Report MR 101, Mathematisch Centrum, Amsterdam, Feb. 1969. [pp. 139, 237]

9. B. A. Galler, "Memorandum—MAD/I: preliminary draft," The CONCOMP Project, University of Michigan, Nov. 1966. [p. 162]

10. P. Z. Ingerman, "Thunks," *Comm. ACM*, vol. 4, no. 1 (Jan. 1961), pp. 55–58. [p. 166]

11. J. McCarthy, P. W. Abrahams, D. J. Edwards, T. P. Hart, and M. I. Levin, *LISP 1.5 Programmer's Manual*, MIT Press, 1965. [pp. 183, 210]

12. L. G. Roberts, "Graphical communication and control languages," *Proc. 2nd Cong. on the Information System Sciences* (1964), Spartan Books, Washington, D.C. [p. 197]

* Appended page numbers refer to citations in this book.

13. A. Newell, F. M. Tonge, E. A. Feigenbaum, B. F. Green, Jr., and G. H. Mealy, *Information Processing Language-V Manual*, 2nd ed., Prentice-Hall, Englewood Cliff, N.J., 1964. [p. 200]

14. A. J. Perlis, and C. Thornton, "Symbol manipulation by threaded lists," *Comm. ACM*, vol. 3, no. 4 (April 1960), pp. 195–204. [pp. 201, 202]

15. J. V. Garwick, "GPL, a truly general purpose language," *Comm. ACM*, vol. 11, no. 9 (Sept. 1968), pp. 634–638. [pp. 217, 275]

16. B. A. Galler, and A. J. Perlis, "A proposal for definitions in ALGOL," *Comm. ACM*, vol. 10, no. 4 (April 1967), pp. 204–219. [p. 241]

17. T. E. Cheatham, Jr., "The introduction of definitional facilities into higher level programming languages." *Proc. American Federation of Information Processing Societies* (AFIPS), Fall Joint Comput. Conf., vol. 29, Spartan Books, New York, pp. 623–673. [pp. 270, 273]

18. B. A. Galler, and M. J. Fischer, "The iteration element," *Comm. ACM*, vol. 8, no. 6 (June 1965), p. 349. [p. 270]

19. B. W. Arden, B. A. Galler, and R. M. Graham, "The MAD definition facility," *Comm. ACM*, vol. 12, no. 8 (Aug. 1969), pp. 432–439. [p. 273]

20. *FORTRAN 63/General Information Manual*, Control Data Corp., Publ. no. 514, Minneapolis, Minn., Aug. 1962. [p. 273]

21. C. Christensen, and C. J. Shaw (Eds.), *Proc. Extensible Languages Symposium*, SIGPLAN Notices, vol. 4, no. 8 (Aug. 1969), Special Interest Group on Programming Languages of the ACM. [p. 273]

22. C. Strachey, "A general purpose macrogenerator," *Computer Journal*, vol. 8, no. 3 (Oct. 1965), pp. 225–241. [p. 273]

23. C. N. Mooers, and L. P. Deutsch, "TRAC: a text handling language," *Proc. ACM 20th National Conf.*, Cleveland, Ohio (Aug. 1965). [p. 273]

24. B. Leavenworth, "Syntax macros and extended translation," *Comm. ACM*, vol. 9, no. 11 (Nov. 1966), pp. 790–793. [p. 275]

INDEX